Wind, Waves and Sunburn

The world's record: Egyptian army major Abdel-Latif Abo-Heif walks from the waters of Lake Michigan after swimming for thirty-five hours and sixty miles. Abo-Heif's wife waves the Egyptian flag while swim promoter raises his hand in victory. Courtesy **Chicago Tribune.**

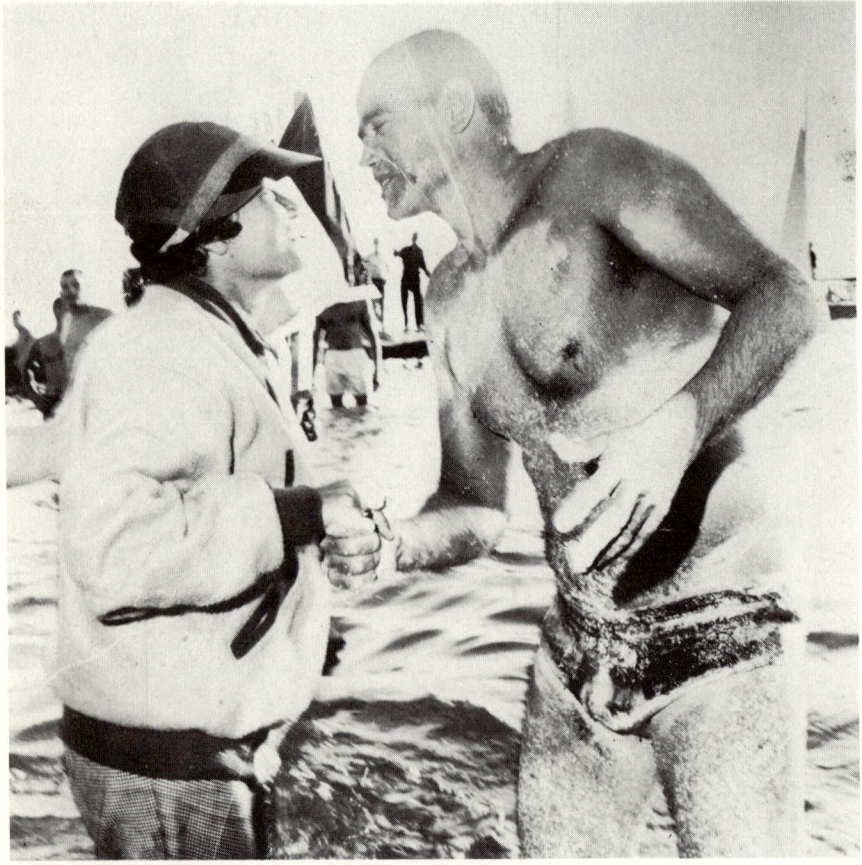

Abo-Heif receives a well-earned kiss from his wife. He also earned $15,000 for his efforts. Notice the lanolin still clinging to his body after thirty-five hours. Courtesy St. Joseph Herald-Press.

Wind, Waves and Sunburn

CONRAD A. WENNERBERG

South Brunswick and New York: *A. S. Barnes and Company*
London: *Thomas Yoseloff Ltd*

© 1974 by A. S. Barnes and Co., Inc.

A. S. Barnes and Co., Inc.
Cranbury, New Jersey 08512

Thomas Yoseloff Ltd
108 New Bond Street
London W1Y OQX, England

Library of Congress Cataloging in Publication Data

Wennerberg, Conrad A   1932–
    Wind, waves, and sunburn.

    1. Swimming—History.   I. Title.
GV837.W45   797.2'1   73-128
ISBN 0-498-01168-2

PRINTED IN THE UNITED STATES OF AMERICA

To the Swimmers. They understand all too well the following:
"... this means an energy expenditure probably averaging 750 calories an hour—i.e., a total expenditure of 9,000–15,000 calories. This makes Channel swimming possibly the greatest feat of endurance in the world of sport."

"The Physiology of Channel Swimming"
Lancet, **October 8, 1955**

"It is horrible, yet fascinating, this struggle between a set purpose and an utterly exhausted frame."

Sir Arthur Conan Doyle,
on seeing Dorando Pietri
collapsing three times in the
last hundred yards of the 26-mile
marathon run: 1908 Olympics.

Contents

	Preface	9
	Acknowledgments	11
	Introduction	13
1	How It All Began: Some Great Animal Swims	17
2	Endurance in General, and What Makes a Great Marathon Swimmer	22
3	The Physiology of Endurance	43
4	The Channel	45
5	Why?	78
6	Catalina Island: The Chewing Gum Swim	83
7	The Canadian National Exhibition and the Thirty-grand Swim	96
8	Abo-Heif Is a Garbage Can	130
9	Atlantic City: Convention Mecca of the World	134
10	They Don't Start Out Slowly: The World's Record Sixty-mile Lake Michigan Swim	145
11	The Incredible Abo-Heif	183
12	Lake St. John: The Paul Bunyan Swim	190
13	Swim, Man, Swim! This One's for Real: Some Great Life-and-death Swims	209
14	Tools of the Trade	223
15	The Twenty-four-hour Swim: La Tuque	228
16	"La Belle Extraordinaire": Greta Andersen	254
17	The Solos	265
18	How to Swim Six Miles or More an Hour: The River Swims	277
19	Two of the Toughest Swims in the World: Juan de Fuca and the Farallons	283
20	The Saguenay River Swim and Ralph Willard	304
21	The Drugs	317
22	Discovery	325
	Appendix I	329

Appendix II	334
Sources	336
Index	339

Preface

Every day millions of fans enter sport palaces all over the world to watch their favorite heros in action. In approximately two hours the event is over and they begin the trek home or to the local bar. About fifty years ago baseball, soccer, and football assumed such importance in the daily lives of many that it soon attracted the promoters. Money was to be made. Later came the advertisers, movie-makers, and television. They soon created the superhero. It wasn't long before the spectators believed that these highly organized creations were the means and ends of life itself. The average city dweller today would be surprised to learn that around the turn of the century every sports-minded individual identified with the endurance or marathon athlete. In those days very few had the time or money to attend any kind of sports event.

England was a site of many an amateur and professional race-walk in the 1700s and 1800s. Thousands of dollars would be bet on walkers racing between cities hundreds of miles apart. The record books are full of names of men who would average some fifty to ninety miles a day for many days. In Mexico there still exists today a tribe that holds a race in which the participants will run continuously for one hundred miles. Participants range in age from seventeen to forty-eight. Himalayan letter carriers have been known to cover one hundred miles in less than twenty-four hours, carrying the messages of their mountain-climbing employers.

As the reader continues he will learn not only about the great marathon swims of history, but also of other endurance feats. He will become aware of how incredibly tough the human body is. As I researched the literature I became fascinated with feats, side issues, and personalities involved. To treat the subject of marathon swimming alone would be to ignore the equally remarkable feats accomplished on land. However, since my experience and familiarity is with marathon swimming, the concentration will remain in that field.

I hope that the reader will enjoy learning about some of the most remarkable events that man has accomplished as much as I have enjoyed writing about them.

Acknowledgments

To Mr. Milton F. Adair, the friendly curmudgeon, whose analytic mind has amazed me for over twenty-three years. His patience is hereby recognized.

The librarians of the Chicago Public Library, The New York Public Library, and the Regenstein Library (University of Chicago) were ever resourceful in locating obscure material. I can still remember vividly one particular occasion when I received the ancient, dusty, and twine-tied octavo volume of *Land and Water* for the year 1875. It contained the original report of Captain Webb's famous swim. It took three days to exhume it from the second basement of the Chicago Public Library.

Charles Moseley and Virginia McKemie, whose collegiate enthusiasm turned my dog-eared typewritten manuscript into clean, presentable pages.

The photographers and publishers who so kindly gave permission to use their photographs. They are identified along with their works.

My swimmers, Ted Erikson and Dennis Matuch (President World Professional Marathon Swimming Federation), not only deserve praise for making some of the history in this book, but for following my advice and making sure that accurate records were kept on those swims I was not able to attend. They also made available to me some of their own files.

Mr. Free Chin converted my sketch maps into a form pleasing to the eye. He will make his mark in commercial art.

International correspondence may be difficult but it was not evident in the speed and generosity with which Mr. Juhl Bentzen of the Copenhagen Swimming Union replied to my request for data on Jenny Kammersgaard. The same can be said for the once venerable Mrs. I. Kellam-Smith (deceased), one time Honorable Secretary of The Channel Swimming Association, whose response was just as gratifying.

Mr. Joe Grossman (deceased), Secretary of The World Professional Marathon Swimming Federation, and I became master traders in our quest for knowledge. His ten-year reign did much to further the cause of accuracy and promotion of professional swimming events.

Mr. John Starett's benevolent action in allowing me access to Mr. Irving Davids' collection, which he inherited, before donating them to the Swimming Hall of Fame was most appreciated.

Mrs. Margaret Park of Toronto gladly sent information about the Park swimming dynasty of Canada of which she is no mean member.

Mr. Robert Noble of Chicago, a descendant of a one-time member of the Royal Society, continued the clarity of thought of his ancestor by clearing up certain of my questions about navigation.

Mr. Mike Paesler's sympathetic running around campus at the University of Chicago was of lasting importance. This extraordinary young man, who is a physicist at the Fermi Institute, spends his summers making long solo swims and entering professional races. Mike's dedication to his hobby earned him the fastest solo swim of the English Channel for 1970 (France to England).

My editor at A. S. Barnes Miss Dena Rogin deserves special mention for her discerning eye.

I have done my best to be as discriminating as possible in seeking out the facts in a much muddled field. Human fallibility being what it is, however, I plead *mea culpa* to any that have escaped me.

Introduction

On Wednesday, August 23, 1961 Chicago's population awoke to a wet, overcast day. As they sat down to their breakfasts they switched on their radios or opened their newspapers. They were in for a pleasant surprise. For once the headlines were not political, nor did they highlight some catastrophe. Even the radio newscasters were beginning their reports with a different slant. The news of the day concerned a world's record swim across Lake Michigan by a local Chicago chemist. It was the first time in history that the lake had been conquered by a swimmer. The *Chicago Tribune's* headlines and leads were especially catching:

SWIMS LAKE, SETS RECORD
Erikson goes 43-miles in 36½ hours;
Wins bout with wind, waves.

The full-length column, giving the facts of the swim, was continued on page two along with photos and map. The photo page, on the last page of the newspaper, contained four more photos of the event. There were many real-life Walter Mittys that identified with the heroic swimmer that August day. Erikson had completed his swim at 8:35 P.M. of the previous day. It marked the end of a swim that had begun thirty-six hours earlier. The swim had started on Monday, August 21, at 8 A.M. at Chicago's lakefront exhibition hall at Twenty-second Street. Six swimmers had lined up along the waterfront wall to await the starting gun. A prize of $3,600 ($100 an hour) would be awarded the first swimmer to arrive at Michigan City, Indiana on the other side of the lake.*

Erikson's swim remains one of the all-time feats of endurance in the sporting world not only because of the distance involved, but also

---

* The longest swim to that date had been the thirty-two-mile swim across Lake Ontario by the Canadian schoolgirl Marilyn Bell in 1953. The sixteen-year-old captured the hearts and imagination of millions. Her swim will be discussed later.

because of the fact that it was accomplished under the most inclement of weather conditions. The first twenty-four hours of the swim was done while the swimmer was heading directly into three-foot waves caused by eighteen-mile-per-hour winds. The next five hours brought diminishing winds and leveling of the water. It was only a temporary reprieve, for the winds again picked up and the final hours of the swim were accomplished against one-and-a-half-foot waves and rain.

When Erikson finished his thirty-six-and-a-half-hour ordeal there were over thirty thousand spectators awaiting him on the pier and beach at Michigan City. Television cameras recorded the memorable event. Radio microphones were crammed by the dozen before him as he was bundled into a stretcher to be taken for a routine checkup at the local hospital. He had a smile and a handshake for anyone near. The scene was made all the more dramatic because many tears were shed along with the thunderous roars acknowledging his finish. The reception awarded him was one of the most remarkable in the annals of folk heros. It was reminiscent of the famous Lindbergh reception in Paris and the Wall Street parade given Gertrude Ederle.

To tell the story of marathon swimming might seem straightforward. You tell of the great swims and elaborate the circumstances under which they were accomplished. However, there are the equally fascinating viewpoints of physiology, anatomy, and promotion. There are also the intriguing facts concerning the prelude to human marathon swimmers. Those are the swimming feats of our animal cousins the mammals. Our time will be well spent in examining some of these little-known facts. So, settle back, light that pipe, and be prepared to enter not only the world of human endurance, but also the world of natural history.

*Wind, Waves
and
Sunburn*

1
How It All Began: Some Great Animal Swims

Man takes great pride in his accomplishments and rightly so. In many respects he is the Lord of Creation. He is an untouchable among the animals as far as intelligence is concerned. In feats of physical endurance man need not take second place either. His accomplishments in this realm are tempered, however, by those of his mammal cousins. The noted American biologist W. J. Schoonmaker,* in his book *The World of the Grizzly Bear,* tells about his experience with animal swims. He once saw a wounded brown bat that had fallen into the waters of Lake Placid in New York attempt to swim toward the shore. He has seen many forest animals in the water including a mother black bear with two cubs that plunged into a river and swam sixty feet to the opposite shore. He has, however, seen the grizzly bear swim only once, but cites other accounts of grizzlies swimming, including that of Enos A. Mills, who saw a grizzly swimming between islands in Alaska that were seven miles apart.

Nature has endowed many of the land mammals with the capacity to adapt to water. In time of flood, swimming of course means survival. But mammals have great curiosity and energy: to explore and

---

* Schoonmaker makes the comment that he knows of no mammal that cannot swim. The author found this an intriguing and fascinating statement which he was about to include in the text when he came across June John's book *The Mating Game: Sex, Love, and Courtship in the Zoo* (St. Martin's Press, 1970). She and other zoo workers say that giraffes, camels, orang-utans, gorillas, and chimpanzees will drown without a struggle should they find themselves in the zoo moats. I don't wish to take sides on this question. There is no doubt, however, about the boa constrictor that once swam two hundred miles from the mainland of South America to the island of St. Vincent. The beast arrived in perfectly good condition. The famed zoologist Dr. Bernhard Grzimek mentions the feat in his book *Animals of Africa* (Stein and Day, 1970).

wander increases the chance of finding food. They do not indulge in competitive swims as man does, naturally. There may be short spurts of competition to reach a prey first, but there is nothing like the long-term pull that characterizes man's efforts.

However, some sea mammals travel great distances. Whales, following their plankton food supply, will migrate thousands of miles, and so will seals. In a study of the common seal of the British Isles, R. M. Lockley found that a swimming speed of 5.5 miles per hour (land miles) was common. This is only a very conservative cruising speed, for others have clocked the seals of the polar regions at 20.4 miles per hour. Such speed is required to catch their food.

Porpoises, those benevolent, intelligent sea animals, have often been reported to swim fifteen knots for distances of five to ten miles. One famous porpoise called "Pelorus Jack," a Risso's dolphin, accompanied a mail steamer between North and South Islands, New Zealand, and traveled along with the ship while it was doing thirty knots. Other similar reports are sometimes questioned by researchers because a porpoise can ride the bow wave of a vessel and obtain a free ride, much like a surfer on his board. But there seems to be no doubt that they can sustain these speeds for at least a short distance.

In countless ways a species can adapt partially or completely to water. The twelve-hundred-pound sea turtle can swim as fast as a man can run, about twenty-two miles per hour. He does it by sculling, a peculiar back-and-forth motion of his flippers. The penguin, in his aquatic search for food, actually flies underwater. His flippers become paddles while his feet act as planes and rudders. Aerial birds are lifted by the downward movement of wing action, but the penguin gains his forward motion on the upstroke.

The penguin can attain a speed of ten miles per hour, and increase that in short bursts to twenty-eight to thirty miles per hour underwater, where drag is tremendously reduced in comparison to surface swimming. Almost all penguins can keep up a steady fifteen miles per hour plunging in and out of the sea. This porpoiselike motion allows them to obtain air, but lose none of their forward momentum. Penguins are no slouches as distance swimmers either: they have been spotted one thousand miles from the nearest land.

The members of the grebe family, when diving for food, reverse the penguin's technique. They close up their wings against the body and swim with their broad, flat toes. The velvet scoter uses half-open wings and feet. Throughout nature there are almost infinite variations of these methods.

A most impressive swimmer is the master of Arctic snows, water, and ice—the polar bear. Hunted so ruthlessly that he is now a threatened species, the polar bear has diminished in numbers to an absurdly small four thousand. Russia has totally banned the hunting of these magnificent creatures. It would be a severe indictment of man if they should be allowed to disappear from the earth.

The polar bear, beautifully insulated from water temperatures and air that can reach seventy degrees below zero, makes his way unperturbedly. Mothers have been observed swimming with one or two cubs alongside or riding on their backs. Many have been spotted fifty miles from the nearest land or ice, with no sign of distress; and at times bears have been seen seventy-five miles from the nearest solid support.

A trained human swimmer can attain the speed of three miles per hour for no more than one or two hundred yards—but the polar bear can steadily cruise along at six-plus miles per hour. Mothers with cubs plod along at four miles per hour. They maintain this speed with only the front legs, as underwater motion pictures of the swimming bear show.

Most bears spotted in water seem unconcerned with their surroundings, but others have been seen in fatal accidents. Some have been swept under the ice by strong currents and drowned, or crushed in storms by pack ice. While all creatures are able to cope with most environmental conditions, no animal in nature is indestructible, and exceptional conditions can destroy the individual mammal, regardless of his strength or intelligence.

Other members of the bear family, while not as proficient as the polar bear, are quite able to make long swims. The black bears of the North American continent routinely cross rivers and ponds in their incessant wanderings. Robert Leslie, a Canadian-Indian biologist, tells of his remarkable experiences in raising, but not training, three black bear cubs. Two of the bears as adults swam across a five-mile lake in British Columbia in the fall and then swam back. The book is a fascinating account of superb natural history and animal psychology.

Perhaps now is the time to introduce the reader to a very select group of professional biologists known as zoo-geographers. They study the distribution of animals over the surface of the globe and how they got there. Most land mammals simply walk to their destinations. But zoo-geographers were at a loss to explain how tigers reached the islands surrounding the Malayan peninsula. Many of these islands were fifteen to twenty-five miles from the mainland or the next island in the chain. Certainly the natives in the area had not caught them in cages and transported them, to make life more difficult. When in the 1800s there were reports of tigers swimming in the straits of Malacca and the South China Sea (also the Java Sea) as far as fourteen miles from the nearest land, they were not believed. Later there was clear evidence that the animals had reached the islands by swimming; it is possible that the tigers can go even farther than fourteen miles.

There are fascinating reports of elephants that were seen twenty-five miles off the east coast of Africa. What they were doing there is anyone's guess. One encounter was most unusual because the animal was being devoured by sharks. The ship's captain who spotted the sensational affair altered his vessel's course to watch the horrible but intriguing sight. When the elephant was devoured the officers duly recorded the event in the ship's log, and it reached newspapers all over the world.

The small aquatic hippopotamus has been sighted twenty miles off the coast of Africa. Brother to the larger river hippo of the interior, this smaller version is semiadapted to an almost permanent water existence.

On a subtropical Japanese island has lived, since prehistoric times, the pink-faced monkey (*Macaca fuscata*), which may reach a weight of forty-four pounds. For years none of these monkeys were observed near the water that surrounded their island, Koshima Island. In recent years tourists began tossing peanuts to them into shallow water. An adventurous member of the tribe tested the water and soon—in a matter of days—there was competition among the hundreds of monkeys for the booty. Now the young are to be seen taking to the water and stroking sixty feet out into the surf whether there is food in the water or not. As soon as they reach the adult stage there is no longer swimming for its own sake. Adults will only enter the water if there is food there—a trait of the *professional* human swimmer, as we shall later see.

The exploits of these Japanese monkeys bring to mind a personal observation of the author that verged on the tragi-comic. It happened on a warm fall day along the shore of Lake Michigan. The owners of a pair of "putty-nosed" monkeys had for several days been exercising and airing them in a lakeside park on Chicago's South Side. The monkeys' antics delighted the passersby. Children laughed and adults smiled as the monkeys scurried along the ground and climbed trees or people.

Suddenly in the midst of glee, one of the monkeys gave a horrible scream as it darted for the water twenty yards away and ten yards down a rocky slope. A scant five inches behind him was an eighty-pound German shepherd hell-bent for murder. For a moment it seemed the monkey was doomed, but he managed to keep a lead of inches to the water's edge. Reaching the last rock, he gave a tremendous leap that ended about fifteen feet from shore. The dog came to an abrupt halt and everyone's eyes turned to the place where the monkey had plunged. Nothing was to be seen but ripples. I began to tick off the seconds and when I reached ten I feared the creature had drowned. A few more seconds went by, and suddenly the animal burst to the surface, doing the monkey version of the dog paddle. He had risen to the surface about ten feet from where he had entered. Luckily he was grabbed by a wader and brought ashore cringing and frightened, but none the worse for wear.

These are remarkable feats of animals we might expect to swim. There are other cases, sometimes very strange, of animals we would never imagine swimming. Don Ornitz, of *True* magazine, took some startling photographs of animals placed purposely in his backyard pool. You may be pleasantly surprised by his photographs. What one learns from such examples is that preconceived notions about behavior, even animal behavior, are not particularly useful.

Men in the Arctic regions are often surprised to see the speed at which the caribou moves through the water. The comment made about caribou crossing the Yukon River is that their "surprising speed" and buoyancy, due to their hollow hairs, makes it appear as if they were running half out of the water.

These are observations of wild animals in a natural habitat: there are also experimental observations of animals swimming. The rat, a very adaptable and successful species, has been timed at swimming fourteen hours steadily in a laboratory tank. Probably only a fraction of this time is needed by those rats who leave sinking ships to colonize land. They do require warm water, as their small size causes rapid heat loss. Water temperatures in the seventies and eighties seem to be optimum; temperatures in the fifties considerably reduce their survival time.

Tests with other small mammals resulted in some interesting occurrences. A female woodchuck swam for about eight hours in water at sixty-six degrees. When the temperature was raised to seventy-seven degrees, the animal swam for forty-one hours. Chipmunks scored a low of eight minutes at seventy degrees due to their small size. Skunks and opossums did better at around the seven-hour mark for water temperatures at about seventy-five degrees. A little further on I will discuss the importance of water temperature. Considering their adaptation to land, the land mammals do quite well in the water, certainly better than sea mammals like the whale and seal can do on land. Of course nature likes to make fun of the classifier and pedant. The sea otter, beautifully adapted to spending its life in the kelp beds of the Pacific Ocean, can play just as well on the mud slicks of the shore.

2
Endurance in General, and What Makes a Great Marathon Swimmer

The word *endurance* in any conversation, whether in a teenage hangout or an old people's home, pricks up ears. Everyone is concerned with the word and the concept. The fascination of great feats of endurance is never ending and human. Enduring means lasting until the job is completed and the check is picked up. It means survival by catching food, or by outlasting the predator. Finally, it means survival through time, against destruction or decay.

To use the word may be wrong to begin with when we apply it to a biological system, for it may then be a subjective, humanly oriented concept. In fact, many scientists think of endurance as nothing more than genetics and change. Animals, including man, may be doing nothing more than living up to their maximum capacity. For example, birds, before they make their long migration flights, are prepared for the event by certain stimuli. The increased length of daylight causes a profound effect on their glandular system. Hypertrophy of the glands and the increase of body fat prepares them for the long energy expenditure ahead. The Arctic tern, which migrates between the North Arctic Circle and the South Antarctic Circle, will fly as much as eleven thousand miles or more one way. Some investigators think this is done nonstop. If true, this is a tremendous feat that would lay to rest the idea of training beyond a certain point. Certainly these birds do not do daily stints of thousands of miles in preparation for the eleven-thousand-mile "race."

Ornithologists have come up with very interesting records of bird flights. In 1952 a flock of blue geese went nonstop from Hudson Bay to Louisiana, a distance of seventeen hundred miles. This was an average of thirty miles per hour for sixty hours.

The lesser yellowlegs goes nineteen hundred miles from New England to the West Indies in six days, averaging 316 miles a day. The golden plover makes a twenty-four-hundred mile nonstop flight from Eastern Canada to South America, losing only two ounces in weight.

These cases are remarkable, but the following staggers the imagination. Some scientists believe that the young sooty tern goes to sea and remains there until ready to breed, which may not be for several years. C. Brooke Worth, in his book *A Naturalist in Trinidad*, elaborates on the evidence in support of the fact that fledged sooty terns leave their natal island and fly *constantly* for a period of three to five years before landing again. He cites the fact that the terns do not return to the islands after breeding and are not seen until the next nesting cycle. During the nonbreeding season the terns are never seen offshore, being observed only in mid-ocean, far beyond a day's flight from a resting place. Floating jetsam is no answer, for the number of perches that it would provide is far too small for the millions of sooty terns. In addition, the birds themselves, unlike gulls, are not naturally buoyant and sink if forced to alight on water. There is no other conclusion—they *do* fly constantly for as much as five years.

Certainly any other bird attempting to duplicate the sooty's feat would no doubt be labeled, in the words of modern-day psychology, an overachiever. Attempting to live up to a standard not your own always leads to illness, neurosis (in animals, too), or death.

In wandering through the curiosities of nature we come to the amazing salmon. The Pacific salmon frequently makes upriver journeys against strong currents of five hundred to one thousand miles, overcoming all kinds of obstacles, such as rapids, waterfalls, dams, and predators. Swimming steadily day and night, they neither rest nor eat. Speeds of about two miles per hour are maintained for twelve or more days to cover the necessary distances. To handle this high energy output the salmon undergoes adrenal hypertrophy. This huge increase in the size of the animal's adrenal glands allows it to utilize body fat. But upon reaching its goal—which is to spawn—the animal dies, its life cycle completed.

Natural history gives numberless examples of animal migrations of impressive distances. Some human feats are rather impressive also. The hunter in quest of game sometimes follows a quarry for days on end to get within dispatching distance. Old hunters of Africa mention being on the trails of their quarries for as long as a week, their only rest being catnaps along the way. Eskimo hunters tell the same story in their quest for meat.

Our present-day sedentary living makes these treks seem awesome, but then they were a natural part of life. Before modern mechanization everyone walked. Charles Dickens was known for his perambulations around London; he, as others, claimed it had salubrious effects. According to Nietzsche, "The sedentary position is a positive hindrance to the holy spirit. One gets his ideas only by walking."

There were many long-distance walkers in England in the 1700s and 1800s. Large sums of money were bet on the outcome of pedestrian races, in which daily distances of fifty to seventy-five miles were covered for many days. Not all of the walks were accomplished by younger men. In 1792 a certain Mr. Eustace, seventy-seven years old, walked from Liverpool to London (over two hundred miles) in four days. A renowned German paleontologist in his late eighties covered one hundred miles in three days to attend a scientific meeting.

As the sport grew popular in England, the distances and times became more impressive. A Mr. Glanville in 1806 walked 142 miles in 29¾ hours. Going back to 1773, Foster Powell walked from London to York and back again (402 miles) in six days.

In 1808 the noted Captain Barclay walked one thousand miles in one thousand successive hours. A thousand guineas was his reward. From these humble beginnings sprang up hundreds of competitors trying for records.

Some records are accomplished for extrinsic reward. Himalayan letter carriers, for example, will carry letters from their mountain-climbing employers to civilization, and run them a hundred miles or so in less than twenty-four hours.

Recently a group of physicians studied the Tarahumara Indians of Mexico, who run a hundred miles or more. It's part of a game played by males of ages eighteen to forty-eight, who kick a ball in a team effort a hundred miles. The complaint at the end of the game is that of leg cramps or urinary problems.

It is most interesting to compare these feats, carried on in the sporting spirit, and those done under threat of death. The motivation or chance involved would certainly be difficult to assess in any case. A well-rested, well-endowed individual will do well in either circumstance, whereas a dissipated one will give a low response.

In the 1800s during the Arab uprisings in Morocco there were constant shifts in power from one tribal leader to another. Eventually there was established one leader and his surrounding advisors who were at one time tribal leaders themselves. To bring back into the fold dissident leaders, political amnesty was offered to the uncaught rebels, plus a position in the new government. When wounds were healed and old times discussed the conversation moved to how these men, in the years past, had out-run the palace guards who had been selected for their fleetness of foot. One old leader answered for all his

Endurance in General

fellows: "Your Majesty, your guards were running for you. We were running for ourselves." Which leads to our next exploit.

During the Mau Mau uprisings in Kenya during the 1950s the police put into effect a system that proved highly effective. Whenever they got onto the trail of a Mau Mau party or leader, they would instigate a round-the-clock chase. As soon as the chase party showed signs of fatigue, a fresh party would be substituted. Thus the criminals being chased found no chance for rest, and in a matter of sixteen hours or so, a party could be run to the ground. However, there remains one exceptional case that offers true insight into human endurance.

Word had been received at the central police headquarters that the camping site of Kimathi Dedan, leader of the whole Mau Mau group, had been located. Immediately a patrol was dispatched to the area and the hunt began. For eight hours Dedan and his party managed to stay ahead of the patrol in the rough terrain that varied from jungle to plains. Seeing that the outcome was inevitable if the party stayed together, they split, each man for himself. One by one each was caught in an exhausted state by the fresh hunting patrols. That is, all except Dedan himself. Spurred on by the certainty of execution if he were caught, he managed to keep going until nightfall. Each time he looked for a place to snatch a few hours of sleep, a fresh search party would be thrown on the trail. Pushing his weary frame on, the famous killer managed to stay ahead of every new party. In daylight hours his lead would be reduced at times to as little as one hundred yards. The third chase party repeatedly came within hailing distance of Dedan, only to lose him in the brush afterward.

At the end of the second day, the fifth fresh party was put into action for the night chase. By this time Dedan had stretched his lead to a few miles, which allowed him to catch a few hours sleep. By the end of the third day, nine fresh parties had been unable to catch the fleeing Mau Mau leader. However, on the beginning of the fourth day, exhaustion took its toll and Dedan was caught by the police. A photo showing him a few minutes after his capture vividly shows the fire and alertness in his eyes. His only nourishment throughout the ordeal had been water and a few pounds of flour. In the three and one half days of the chase Dedan had covered over 350 miles. This distance was not over flat roads but through jungle scrub, over mountain ranges, and across rivers. Only rarely did he have the "comfort" of jungle paths, and then for only short periods. An interesting point was made during the interrogation of his cohorts that will have some bearing on my discussion of physiology later. Dedan's wife and mistresses complained of his incessant sexual demands.

The popular journals and newspapers of the Victorian era were fond of publicizing and sponsoring great endurance and exploration feats. It sold copies. It was newspapers that sponsored the famous "source of the Nile explorations," although the Royal Geographical Society contributed a little. If they didn't sponsor such events beforehand they were sure to hop aboard the wagon after an exploration party returned. Such a case was that of E. S. Grogan, an Englishman who tired of the boredom of a clerk's existence. With money accumulated from his pittance of a salary he set out for Johannesburg, South Africa. There, after buying the necessary knapsack and camping equipment he set out to walk the length of Africa. An account of his trip is admirably set forth in his fine book, *From The Cape To Cairo*. Suffice it to say that his adventures were minimal. His biggest trouble came from the Arabs when he entered the Sudan and Egyptian territories. He overcame these difficulties by staining his skin with walnut stain and assuming a prayerful posture to the East three times a day. Two years later he walked into the city of Cairo and eternal fame.

Before we overpraise man in his endurance efforts it would perhaps be a good time to recount the famous true story of Baldy, a Virginia red fox, and Boston, part bloodhound and part foxhound. This story originally appeared in *Recreation Magazine*, July 1898. It made such an impression on Daniel P. Mannix that he fashioned a prize-winning novel on it entitled *The Fox and the Hound*. What makes this novel so readable is the fact that there is none of the *ad nauseam* anthropomorphism that colors so much nature writing. Mannix's interpretation of the animals involved is based on the most recent scientific evidence. Hunting alone, Boston followed Baldy for a day and a half covering a distance of 150 miles. Both animals dropped dead at the end of the hunt and were buried together. It seems you don't have to be a human to have a long attention span.

Around the turn of the century frontier Alaska offered high pay to professional packers. Men were hired because they were more efficient than any other animal over the rough terrain. Loads up to 120 pounds were carried up and down the steep grades. Feet were taped with adhesive tape, much like a boxer's hands. Iron stoves, flour, clothing, and other fundamentals were carried on a packboard. Today a similar thing is done in the Himalayan Mountains by the Sherpas. They do it at altitudes of ten thousand to twenty thousand feet. Modern-day opium runners cross the Turkish-Syrian border, running eight miles in 90 minutes carrying a thirty-five pound load. They make two trips in six to eight hours. Their ages are from fifteen years to sixty years.

The real work of this kind comes when we learn of the old French voyagers in Canada. These men combined the grueling work of paddling and portaging all day and half the night. When coming to a portage all twenty to fifty paddlers would hop out of the transport canoe, which was larger than the conventional canoe, and begin the portaging. Most packages were conveniently divided into ninety-pound loads. Knapsacks were not used since shoulder straps, with the heavy weights, compressed the lung cage and effectively prevented deep inhalation. Instead, one ninety-pound package was tied onto the end of a long leather strap and another to the other end. The first was swung onto the small of the back followed by the other onto the shoulder blades. The middle of the strap had a widening that conveniently crossed the forehead and served as a tump line. In a half crouch the voyager would literally trot the portage nonstop if it were a mile or less.

There were some exceptional portages, the most famous of which was Grand Portage which led from Lake Superior to the first of the inner lakes of what is now Quetic-Superior National Forest. This portage was nine miles long with a five-hundred foot rise. A round trip, with 180-pound loads both ways, took six hours. A three-mile-per-hour average was standard. Every one third to half mile there was a *pose* where packs were deposited before going back or on. On shorter portages of one quarter mile, bales of fur weighing three hundred to five hundred pounds would be carried. A modern, vivid example of such a feat was given in 1927 when Harry Pitlegans, a Montagnais half-breed, on a bet carried over six hundred pounds of flour in ankle-deep soft sand for one quarter mile.

These men were formidable as rowers and paddlers also, and the remnants of their feats are in the Athabaskan Canoe Race across Lake Winnipeg. They will cross the lake in forty hours keeping up a sixty-stroke-a-minute pace.

Not even the Atlantic Ocean has remained inviolate against man's muscles. Leaving the Vikings for other records, since they combined sails with oars, our attention is called to the 1896 feat of a couple of Norwegians. George Harbo (1865–1945) and Frank Samuelsen (1869–1946) left the Battery, on Manhattan Island, on June 6; fifty-five days and three thousand miles later they landed at St. Mary's in England. Their boat was an eighteen-foot double ender with a five-foot beam; five pairs of oars were used.

Getting back to land, one of the epic feats of endurance and survival took place in 1823. Hugh Glass, a member of a fur-trapping party consisting of two other men, was mauled by a bear. His scalp was torn until it and his left ear hung over his face. Severe gashes covered the rest of his body. A few broken bones completed his agony. His pals stitched the scalp approximately back into place. For two days they attended him before they decided that there was no hope. Taking his rifle they went off to complete their journey. When Hugh awoke and became aware of his situation he was fired with animosity and brimstone hatred of his ex-friends. Thereupon began one of the most agonizing crawls in history, for at no time was he able to stand on his two feet. He crawled over one hundred miles to the banks of the Cheyenne River living on gophers, bugs, berries, roots, and rattlesnakes along the way. When he arrived at the Cheyenne River several months later he constructed a crude boat from a hollow log and floated down the Cheyenne to its fork with the Missouri and then another 150 miles to Fort Kiowa. He recovered. Later he was killed in a brawl on a riverboat.

Back in the world of "sport," the foot race, against the clock, of J. Saunders on February 21 and 22, 1882 is impressive. In twenty-two hours and forty-nine minutes Saunders covered over 125 miles. The longest distance ever run in twenty-four hours was accomplished by a South African named Wally H. Hayward who did 160 miles. His age was forty-five. The event took place in England. He lost seven pounds.

I mentioned earlier the distance covered by Himalayan letter carriers. It was something like one hundred miles in twenty-four hours. This is accomplished over extremely steep grades and high altitudes. Near and at sea level primitive peoples do faster times over similar distances. During the Riff uprising in the 1920s, Arab tribesmen would carry messages to their sheiks over the hot, blistering desert. One of the more remarkable accounts is of one tribesman who covered ninety miles in fifteen hours. This works out to an average of six miles per hour, which is a slow trot. Marathon runners in modern Olympics will cover twenty-six miles—over paved streets—in about two hours ten minutes for an average of almost twelve miles per hour. Six miles per hour is about one mile per hour slower than what a fast-speed walker will do under ideal conditions. I myself, who am by no means a fast walker, have done forty-three miles in nine hours which works out to be an average of 4.5 miles per hour. The "ooing" and "ahhing" of modern man may be out of place. During the 1950s, President Kennedy's Physical Fitness Program advocated a person covering fifty miles in three days. Any normal person would have little difficulty doing the fifteen-plus miles per day. However, there sprang up a crop of youngsters and oldsters who did the distance in one set. Fifty-mile hikes became the fad. When stimulated average people will do remarkable things.

The above feats are somewhat humbled by the accounts of some old-timers. While there were many, the following should give you an idea of what can be done by age. Dan O'Leary, a noted pedestrian, on July 19–20, 1919, at the age of seventy-eight walked one hundred miles in twenty-three hours and forty-two minutes. He did his feat under the watchful eyes of observers in a ballpark in Chicago.

We are now ready to examine the longest professional foot race on record—the 1928 Trans-Continental Race across the United States. The race was the idea of a promoter who planned to make some money out of the event. $48,500 in prize money was offered. The race attracted some of the top men from all over the world. It also attracted freaks and publicity nuts. At any rate, three hundred contestants, after paying a twenty-five-dollar entry fee, started on February 13, 1928. By the halfway mark there were only eighty-four runners left. As the race progressed toward the finish, which was New York City, more and more of the marathoners dropped out. As the two month mark was passed there were only three men in competition for the top prize of $25,000. Fifty others lagged behind. The winner turned out to be Andy Payne, an American Indian, who made the 3,422-mile trip in 525 hours for an average of six miles per hour (a slow trot, remember). The second place man, John Salo, was seventeen hours behind and received $10,000 for his efforts. Forty-five other competitors who finished received only compliments for their efforts.

One could go on and on with other equally impressive examples. The literature is replete with not only individual feats of endurance in the world of running, walking, and swimming, but also of mass or cooperative feats such as armies and families. In the pioneering days for example, marching great distances for days and weeks was common. Marching hundreds of miles unencumbered is one thing but carrying a thirty- or sixty-pound pack is another. By this time the reader may be wondering what it takes to do such things. Do the people represent some special category or are they just ordinary souls reacting to the stress of the moment? Modern-day investigators are just beginning to come up with the answer. Let us turn to the swimming.

For many years physiologist and trainer have been making tests to determine what makes for a nonswimmer, mediocre swimmer, and excellent swimmer. The results of such tests are striking. For example one would expect to find a high degree of buoyancy among marathon swimmers. However, most of the tests show that there seems to be an almost equal percentage of neutral or slightly buoyant individuals and those who are not buoyant. This looked perplexing, but further analysis gave the answer. A high degree of buoyancy is of little value if it is not accompanied by the proper anatomy and muscle power, to say nothing of glucose conversion rates, oxygen uptake, and so-forth. To be exceptionally high in one category and lacking in another leads to naught. Let's take an example.

Ted Erikson, one of the top marathon swimmers in the world, was given a battery of specially designed tests to determine his rating as compared with a large series of top-rated amateur swimmers. When completed, the results were quite surprising. While he scored high and average on all tests he *did not surpass* the scoring of other champions on *any* individual test. His arm pull (measured in pounds) was slightly above average. His leg kick was above average. His roll was average. His oxygen intake was above average, as was his glucose conversion rate. His buoyancy was a little negative. Other specific tests showed the same results until the psychological test measuring persistency was reached. Here he scored very high. When summation came the results showed that while he scored slightly above average on specific tests he was consistent to the extent that he scored the highest on summation. Another way of putting it is that while he scored say ten percent higher on each test while others scored say fifty percent higher on one specific test, but fell ten percent or twenty percent on others, the final summation showed that his superiority came in being just a "little" above average in all categories.

While many of the tests given by investigators can be quite sophisticated others are not. For example take the test for buoyancy. Buoyancy is academically called specific gravity, which means a body's density as compared to water, which is given the arbitrary figure of one. Thus, all objects with a figure greater than one will sink when placed in water and all those less than one will float. Thus, practically all metals sink while substances like cork, wood, and oil float. The test for buoyancy is a simple one. The investigator merely takes his subject to the eight-foot-depth end of the pool and has him jump in, making sure that he is a swimmer of course. With stopwatch in hand he measures the time it takes the subject to come to the surface. The subject has been instructed to maintain a lungfull of air. Most subjects rise to the surface without using any body motions in varying lengths of time. Some just keep on sinking until they rest on the bottom of the pool. When the need for new air is manifested, they have to swim to the surface. These are the nonfloaters, or the individuals who have negative buoyancy. Other individuals rise neither to the surface, nor sink to the bottom. These are the more-or-less neutral densities. Then there are the positive buoyants who pop to the surface in quick time and actually find it extremely difficult to even swim down. The time it takes for an individual to "seek his level" is noted and charted.

The test is then repeated with as much air as possible expelled from the lungs. This test leads to some interesting results. Some of those who previously showed high buoyancy with filled lungs now sink. Their buoyancy was due to the buoyant effect of the trapped air, which offset their body's specific gravity of greater than one. Those who sank even with full lungs earlier now sink even faster with emptied lungs. A small percentage actually remain floating high and "dry" with expelled air and without moving a muscle. These are the real floaters. Now the reader may be tempted to say, "Ah, it's as simple as that. Good swimmers are good floaters." Things are not as simple as that, however, for it takes more than that to make a great swimmer. It now becomes important to determine how the buoyancy is distributed. The human body being an irregular mass, having an uneven distribution of its weight, will not float or sink symmetrically.

Endurance in General

Endurance in General

A sphere of constant density is a regular body since its weight is evenly distributed at all points from its center. In the human body, arms, legs, torso, and head all weigh different amounts. Muscle mass and fat are unevenly distributed. The next test determines approximately this distribution. The individual holding on to the side of the pool extends his legs and body full length. The upper part of the body being supported does not sink. The lower part either floats or begins to sink. The angle at which the body comes to rest is noted plus the length of time it took to attain this angle. The determination of the body's lower buoyancy is thus determined.

Next, the body is reversed. The feet are hooked over the slop channel of the pool and the body extended outward with the arms at full length beyond the head. Some will float, some sink. The proper measurements are noted. When completed the results are interesting, for we find that few individuals are symmetrically buoyant. With some individuals the upper half is buoyant while the lower is not, or vice versa. Thus there may be wide variations as to the center of gravity of individuals who appear to be anatomically similar. The reader can now see that the disposition of buoyancy becomes important in that it determines the angle at which the individual floats when motionless. Some floaters will float in a vertical position while others lie at the surface of the water as if they were in bed. It must be remembered that these tests are given while the body remains "motionless" in the water. As soon as the arms are used to propel the body the situation changes, for now a dynamic situation has been created. The reader may now jump to the conclusion that given a high degree of buoyancy and muscle, we have a swimmer, and, judging from the literature, he would appear to be right. However, he would do well to remember what one wit said, "Never claim to have made a scientific discovery unless you have made due allowance for nature's misplaced sense of humor."

If one had no experience in watching champion swimmers he would accept the conclusion. But once the observer watches scores of top world-rated champions he will come up with altered conclusions. A large percentage of them will be neutrally buoyant, or slightly negative. This appears to be a paradox, but a knowledge of hydrodynamics solves it. Shipbuilders and biologists have long known that vessels and animals that move below the surface of the water expend much less energy than those moving on the surface if both are moving at the same speed. The reason for this is that whirlpools, erratic currents, and waves all serve to add resistance to the object moving on the surface. Below the surface, however, there is a minimum of this formation, and in most cases a smooth laminar water flow is maintained. In fact, in the case of the porpoise this laminar flow is perfected to the utmost because of the constant buckling and bulging of the animal's skin, which immediately neutralizes any beginning eddy. Getting back to our human aquanauts, those who ride a little lower in the water than the highly buoyants may significantly decrease the amount of drag that forms. To be buoyant but not too buoyant may be the next conclusion, but this too will be in error, for muscle power (or shall we say horsepower developed) and arm lengths are important in adapting to the water. For example, the good female marathon swimmers, who are in all cases buoyant, need the buoyancy because of having less muscle power than the men. Their high degree of buoyancy coupled with the lesser muscle power enables them to compete quite favorably with the men who have less buoyancy but more muscle. We have here what is called in the academic circles a complex variable. There is a point at which buoyancy, muscle power, and center of gravity "come together" for an individual, which is his or her optimum position in the water. It is certainly striking to see two of the world's top swimmers stroking together for fifteen to twenty-five miles and each occupying a different position in the water. Greta Andersen's whole upper back, derriere, and thighs are almost constantly visible as she strokes away with only her lower back partially hidden by the water. On the other hand, Abo-Heif's upper back is only free of the water when he gulps for air. As he brings his face down to complete the stroke cycle his whole upper back becomes awash. Yet this seeming anomaly disappears when the observer tenders his observation with the laboratory studies.

In the foregoing I slipped in the phrase, "arm lengths and ratios," which may cause the reader to wonder what it means. It refers to the total length of the arm, and its parts, forearm, and upper-arm. This is also a very important part of swimming, for to have too long an arm means a decreased leverage when the underwater pull is made. Poor swimmers are characterized by a slapping entry into the water and an inefficient underwater pull. If the arm is relatively short and the articulation of the shoulder proper, the arm is lifted from the water with the elbow naturally high and the entry made by the forearm and hand at a definite angle of about forty-five degrees. If the individual is an exceptionally adapted swimmer he may, as in Abo-Heif's case, have a lower elbow and entry of approximately twenty degrees. This is because Abo-Heif pivots off his breast bone, which means that not only are the arm muscles being used but the larger muscles of the chest and the side of the rib cage. They also gain the added leverage of the body since the arm is used more in conjunction with the body than most other swimmers. I believe this type of stroke is natural to the swimmer and not learned.

Trainers and coaches, previous to about 1950, were fond of pushing the classic stroke or style. That is, the pull starts here and ends there. The head turns to the side for inhalation and returns face down in the water—the classic crawl or freestyle.

The legs were kicked from two to six beats per arm cycle. They were supposed to be kicked at the proper depth and conscious efforts were made to integrate it with the arm cycle. With the great success of the Australian crawl in the early Olympics, great stress was put on teaching it all over the world. It turned out to be the most efficient stroke for the short races, that is, races eight hundred meters and under. One would like to think that the evolution of the crawl stroke was an orderly, well-thought-out one in which each step was arrived at logically. However, this is not the case. What happens is that a good or successful swimmer is copied. Whenever a record is set the stroke used by that swimmer is copied and becomes the latest "thing." Over and over the swimming world has seen slight and major changes in the style of the crawl. Its basic structure, overarm recovery with face down and side breathing, remains inviolate, however. The reason for this is that the crawl (another name is the freestyle, but this can confuse because freestyle means any style) is the most efficient for two basic reasons. The recovery is made out of the water. In the breast stroke and side stroke the recovery is made against the forward motion. Thus the arms, and legs (in the trudgeon or scissor kick) are actually pushing against the water as they are brought forward for the power part of the cycle. The other reason is that the large muscles of the arms and chest can "bear" down, gaining greater leverage, when the individual is face down in the water. It might appear that the back stroke would be just as efficient. It isn't because of the anatomy involved. As the back stroker pulls through he actually pushes himself slightly downward into the water. This slows him down. The crawl swimmers actually lift themselves slightly with each stroke thus introducing a slight planing action.

Studies have shown that the calorie expenditure of the different strokes varies considerably. Swimming the crawl stroke and breast stroke at one mile per hour expends a similar 410 calories per hour. The back stroke takes five hundred. When we move up to the higher speeds things begin to change. At 2.2 miles per hour the back stroke takes about twenty-one hundred calories per hour, the breast stroke about nineteen hundred calories. The crawl registers a low sixteen hundred calories per hour. If the legs are not used in the crawl the figure becomes even lower—a significant increase of efficiency since the speed is the same.

When world records of fifteen hundred meters and over began to be set by swimmers who had a minimal or no kick style investigators began to think. Maybe the kick was not as important as they thought. If they had been aware of the marathon swimmers of the 1920s and later they would have arrived at this conclusion much earlier. However the science of swimming did not receive its impetus until the

1950s with the advent of sports-minded physiologists and physicists. They brought to their studies some of the marvels of space-age techniques and instrumentation. The big question asked was, "What happens in the water as a person swims?" First they got the water, then port holes for watching what goes on under the water. Pressure measuring and current sensitive instruments followed. Dyes and fine silts were added to the water to make visible currents and eddies. Breathing apparatus that collected expired air from the swimmers along with the physiologist's laboratory equipment completed the paraphernalia. When the first studies were completed there was a drastic sinking (no pun intended) of coaches' and trainers' concept of the kick. The kick was worthless. Yes, you can hold a float in front of you, as swimmers have been doing for generations, and make slow progress, but it is because the upper part of the body is held in a planing position, and the legs kick much faster because no blood is being delivered to the arms. If you take away the board you get extremely inefficient and slow progress. The reason the kick is nonproductive as far as forward motion is concerned is because the swimmer's legs are moving water up and down, i.e., vertically. A lot of good that does you. You want water moving horizontally. This is why the arms are so efficient. They move the water parallel to the surface. In other words the swimmer in the water is similar to a man pulling himself up a rope. One hand over his head pulls, and then for a short distance pushes as the other hand takes over above his head. Forgetting the complexities of minor variations due to water flow and pressure, the swimmer is essentially doing the same thing as the rope climber, only lying horizontally. There is of course the slight "slide" as the hand goes into the water before the "grab" and catch as the hand and arm make purchase, but the swimmer does pull and push himself through the water. The legs actually can hinder a swimmer since hard thrashing deprives the arm muscles of the blood they need, thus slowing down the arm stroke rate. The heart in this situation is in the unenviable position of having two masters. Being unable to serve one effectively it serves two ineffectively. Blood must be supplied to working muscles. It is sent to the arms and legs, thus both operate at less than the optimum rate.

Proof of the inefficiency of the legs in swimming came with a very intriguing test performed by the United States Navy. They had swimmers swim the length of a hundred-meter pool that graded from a two-foot depth at one end to eight feet at the other. On the bottom of the pool was placed a two-inch layer of very fine siltlike material. With underwater cameras ready, they recorded the following. Every swimmer who kicked disturbed the silt along every inch of the one-hundred-meter pool. By the time they reached the eight foot-deep end of the pool the silt was coruscating and tumbling to a height almost

Endurance in General

to the surface. What it meant was that even moderate kicking disturbed water—meaning it had to move water vertically—through a depth of almost eight feet.

When the surface area of the front and back of the legs is measured, we come up with several hundred square inches. When the leg is moved up and down in the water you are actually "pumping" water up and down. In a long swim a swimmer is lifting, as the leg moves upward in the kick, and pushing, as it moves down, tons of water needlessly.

The legs do, however, perform a useful function through no conscious effort of the swimmer. They will oscillate in opposition to the arms, minimizing the roll inherent in the crawl as the swimmer takes a breath. If we would believe what the coaches and trainers say— that one should kick to keep the legs high thus eliminating the resistance to the water as the swimmer's body moves through it—the kick has some function. Even such a world-renowned coach as James Counsilman of Indiana University maintains that kicking brings the legs higher. Nonsense! Only the speed of the swimmer allows the legs to be lifted by the water pressure of horizontal movement much like the air pressure that gives lift to the wing of an airplane. You might say, "Well, a bird flaps his wings and lifts off the ground." A man's legs are not wings, however, and don't allow seepage of water on the up stroke like a bird's wing does. Counsilman is not meant to be maligned, for he has done much research that has shown the inefficiency of the legs. I only question the "lifting" purpose. Granted the legs do kick in the shorter races, but only because they have to balance the arms. A world record was set a few years ago in the women's fifteen-hundred-meter event by twelve-year-old Patty Caretto who used her arms only. The current world-rated number four professional, who also holds the world record for thirty-six miles, Dennis Matuch, has absolutely no leg kick at all. Let us now examine again some of the seeming paradoxes of the different styles of the crawl.

THE PERFECT STROKE DOESN'T EXIST

I wish that every coach and swimming trainer the world over could have seen the $36\frac{3}{4}$- to 50-mile race that originated in Lake Michigan in 1962. No, the reader did not see a misprint in the above. This was perhaps one of the most unusual races ever held, and the distances mentioned need explaining.

The previous year, 1961, saw the establishment of a new world's record for open-water swimming. Ted Erikson of Chicago established the record of $36\frac{3}{4}$ miles when he swam across Lake Michigan from Chicago to Michigan City, Indiana. He actually swam forty-four miles because three- to four-foot waves pushed him off course during the night. The following year the promoter offered a unique two-part race. He wanted to see if the previous year's record of thirty-five hours for $36\frac{3}{4}$ miles could be broken, and also if the world's record could be extended to fifty miles. If weather conditions were satisfactory there would be a good chance of breaking Erikson's record since he had made the swim under the most adverse of conditions. He thus offered $4,000 to the first swimmer to reach Waukegan, Illinois, a distance of $36\frac{3}{4}$ miles north of Chicago. The swim course this year was along the shore line, rather than across the lake. The first swimmer to go $14\frac{1}{4}$ miles farther North to Kenosha, Wisconsin and thus swimming fifty miles would receive $10,000. A swimmer arriving first at Waukegan could get out of the water and collect his $4,000 if under the previous year's time, or stay in the water and try for Kenosha and the fifty miles with no time limit. If the same swimmer who was first at Waukegan was also first at Kenosha he was only eligible for the $10,000 prize. On the other hand if the swimmer who was first at Waukegan finished second or failed to make Kenosha, his prize money was not jeopardized for the Waukegan leg. Correspondingly any swimmer who was not first to Waukegan could still be in the race by trying to be the first to Kenosha—a very unique race.

The morning of the race day proved to be idyllic. Offshore winds made the water flat along shore. The air temperature at 8 A.M. was seventy-five degrees and water temperature seventy-two degrees. About twenty competitors lined themselves along the lakefront wall waiting for the starting gun. As the gun went off the swimmers dove into the water and began to stroke. All types of the crawl were to be seen. If one had looked at the only three swimmers who were to finish the race he would have seen something interesting.

Ted Erikson was "poetry in motion"—the classic stroke with hardly a millimeter variation between either arm as it entered the water. His legs beat in a steady, even throb that impressed the observer. His powerful arms carried him through the water at a speed close to two miles per hour. Here was the man to watch. His forty-eight strokes per minute would prevent his burning out.

Looking ahead one's eyes would have seen some violent splashing. Moving ahead in the boat to closer observe this "amateur" who appeared to be in trouble staying afloat, one would recognize Dennis Matuch, a Chicago lifeguard. His arms worked in what seemed like frenzied action. Eighty-five strokes per minute was their rate. Extremely short, his high stroke rate prevented any smooth entry of his hands and arms into the water. Consequently there was a splash upon entry into the water and corresponding flurry of water upon recovery. The average spectator would also have been amazed at the total nonuse of his legs. They simply dragged along behind him. This swimmer also wore no goggles or noseclip. Spectators scratched their heads and said, "This man will drown shortly."

The third swimmer that concerns us was Greta Andersen. The world-famous Dane who had beaten every man she had ever swum against at least once, was stroking a steady sixty strokes per minute about one hundred yards behind Dennis. What one would have observed would have been an extremely uneven stroke. As Greta turned her head to the right to breathe, her left arm reached only a little more than half the distance ahead as the right arm. One would have been tempted to say, "What a cock-eyed stroke." It was very uneven and looked quite uncomfortable to the swimmer.

After watching these three swimmers for fifteen minutes the following conclusion would have been arrived at. Ted Erikson would win this race. Greta Andersen, if she were lucky, would go half way. Dennis Matuch would drown in about another ten minutes. Self-satisfied, the general observer would sit back and await the "sure" and inevitable outcome.

If the observer stayed around for another hour there would be a look of mild surprise on his face. Dennis was still leading Greta, and Ted was still behind Greta. Three or four hours later the situation was the same between Dennis and Greta, but Ted had now fallen two miles behind Greta. Now the observer would have been mildly irked. Such things can't be. By the twelve-hour mark he would begin to show amazement, for things were unchanged. Dennis was still stroking an extraordinarily high eighty-two strokes per minute and was now a half mile ahead of Greta. For twenty-five miles he had kept up this seemingly exhausting pace. Ted was now about five miles behind the leaders.

As the lesser swimmers began to drop out with nightfall, the leaders' pace kept up. Throughout the early hours of the evening it was nip and tuck with Greta and Dennis. She would pull to within agonizing feet of Dennis only to have him pull away to a block lead. Again and again this happened in a fascinating battle. A couple of times during the night Greta had her boat turn off their lights so Dennis could not tell where she was. The first time she pulled this gambit it was successful and she pulled up to Dennis. When Greta suddenly appeared next to him in the water all hell broke loose. Cursing his handlers in the boat for allowing her to sneak up on him, Dennis immediately unleashed a powerful surge of energy for the next half hour that again put him a third of a mile in the lead. At this point he told his boatmen to let him go ahead of his boat. Let Greta work to catch the boat, thinking him to be with it, and when she did have it pull ahead immediately to him. By doing this it would be a tremendous psychological blow to Greta. She would think that she had again caught Dennis, only to find empty waters as his boat pulled far ahead to Dennis. Twice this happened and it did much to break Greta's spirit, for awhile anyway.

Twenty-one hours later Dennis crossed the finish line at Waukegan, covering the distance of 36¾ miles in a world's record time that still stands. Five minutes and three hundred yards behind came Greta. About three hours behind Greta came Ted.

The most revealing and astonishing thing about this swim was the fact that the finishers placed in the exact opposite order to the swimming styles used. What appeared a most inefficient stroke turned out to be efficient enough to carry its possessor to the winner's circle. Ted Erikson's classic style was good only for a slow third.

However the second part of the race was now to be swum by those who chose it. Dennis, with $4,000 in hand, elected to leave the water at Waukegan. Greta, after twenty-one-plus hours of swimming, had no choice but to try for the fifty-mile mark and $10,000. There was no second place money for any segment. Upon learning that she had lost the first part of the race she immediately slowed down from the hectic two miles per hour rate to about one and a half miles per hour and set her goal for Kenosha. Since Ted was so far behind she could afford the luxury of the slackened pace. Ten agonizing hours later she had covered the fourteen remaining miles to Kenosha. In doing so she had set a new world's record for open-water swimming—fifty miles in thirty-one hours. Five hours later Ted Erikson arrived in Kenosha to become co-holder of the record for distance.

The moral to be learned from the above is that one should never stress the importance of "evenness" and proportion that characterizes the classic swimming stroke. The individual variations in human anatomy and physiology preclude warping an individual's personal adaptation to the water into the closed channel of "water ballet" perfectionism.

The author with Greta Andersen, fifteen minutes before the start of the Lake Michigan 36¾-50-mile race. That's Ted Erikson lying on the ground. He looked in better shape at the end of the race since all the nervous tension was worked out of him. Ed Kirk, a Chicago lifeguard, standing behind the author, did a respectable twenty-five miles before leaving the water. Courtesy Louis Waitkus.

Ten minutes before the start of the race. Greta points to clarify a point on the course to be taken upon leaving Chicago's Burnham Harbor. Ted Erikson stands to her right putting in an ear plug. Courtesy Louis Waitkus.

Three minutes before the start of the race. Don't let the smiles on Greta's and Ted's faces fool you. They're half grimaces from the mounting tension. Dennis Matuch (in half crouch and wiping hands) intently plots his course. Only twenty years old, he set a world's record in the first part of this race (36¾ miles in twenty-one hours). Notice he wears no goggles or cap. He swam the whole distance without them. Every other swimmer eventually put them on. Courtesy Louis Waitkus.

The race begins (8:00 a.m., Aug. 21, 1962). The promoter fires the starting gun. While everybody else seems to be in a hurry, Dennis Matuch (standing next to the starter) calmly waits for the water to clear before starting his dive. Courtesy Louis Waitkus.

The torrid start. Courtesy Louis Waitkus.

The start of the 36¾-mile swim begins like a hundred-yard sprint. Courtesy Louis Waitkus.

After one-half hour the swimmers appear off Chicago's downtown section. Courtesy Louis Waitkus.

3
The Physiology of Endurance

It is a cherished myth of man that anyone can become anything he wants: that if someone does not reach the goals he has set, it is because his "drive" was not strong enough. Attainment is always possible for one who struggles long and hard, it is said. This is a concept that should have disappeared with the ancient Greeks, but hasn't. Man is always ready to believe that success is just around the corner.

But a person does possess absolute characteristics that are genetically determined, and among these are buoyancy and anatomy. No amount of training will increase or decrease buoyancy or the length of a person's arms or legs, any more than the color of one's eyes can be changed. At birth every individual is dealt a "hand" of genes, which remains inviolate, and the fetus is programmed for specific development. Not only apparent physical characteristics are determined, but also the chemical reactions that govern an individual's metabolic rate.

Researchers have shown that there are wide variations in people, genetically determined, that deeply influence their reaction to environmental stress. And even without stress there are wide differences. For example, everyone is familiar with what is called normal body temperature, pulse rate, and blood pressure: 98.6°, 72 beats per minute at rest, and 122 mm of mercury, plus your age (if you are over thirty). Yet what is "normal" is nothing more than the average. A large segment of the population falls below these figures and an equally large segment is above them.

Thus "normal" when applied to a group refers to statistics. If we examined a population in which eighty percent of the members were fat, fatness would be called the average or norm. In the matter of blood pressure and pulse rates we find that there is a small percentage of the population that deviates from the norm. They are considered abnormal in the statistical sense, but from the standpoint of health and physiology we reach another conclusion. It has been shown that people who have a blood pressure ten or twenty points below the average, and a pulse rate correspondingly low, have other accompanying characteristics, endurance and longevity being two of them. Just as blood pressure too high above the norm carries the consequences of a shorter lifespan, kidney complications, increased heart attack, and stroke possibility, blood pressure below the norm carries the above-mentioned benefits. Great marathon athletes, workers, and "livers"—if they have no overwhelming vices—have been shown to have "magnificently" low readings. Instead of registering the average blood pressure readings of 120/80, they may read something like 90 or 100/60 or 70. Their pulse rates may be as low as forty-five at rest. In fact, the famous track stars of the past, Gunder Hagg and Paavo Nurmi, registered pulse rates of thirty-five at rest.

Of what significance are these low readings? They mean efficiency of the body processes, and efficiency means reserve. If the body has these low readings at rest it means a low metabolism. Less food is needed to keep the body functioning at its resting state. And more efficiency at rest means greater efficiency at work. When this individual steps up his work rate he will not be working as hard as the individual who has the "normal" readings. Under a heavy work load, the average man's blood pressure will rise to as much as 180/100, and his pulse rate to 180 or 200 beats per minute. The man who starts with lower readings will go up only to a high blood pressure reading of 130 or 150/90, and a pulse rate of 140.

However, blood pressure and pulse rates are not the whole story; there are also an infinite number of chemical reactions that characterize an individual's metabolism. What is the man's ability to convert his body fat and sugar into energy? What is his stored adenosine triphosphate level? How much thyroid, pituitary, and adrenal hormone does he have available? We could go on and on listing the other important chemical factors in performance, but it would take a book on biochemistry and physiology. Suffice it to say that there are differences to be found among those who are quick and long-lasting. Marathoners show a greater hormone storage, greater sugar production and utilization rates, and a host of other factors. But what is to be stressed is that they show these traits even in an *untrained* state.

If an average person is trained, his endurance improves because his body learns to handle stress more efficiently. His blood pressure and pulse rate come down, and his hormone output is increased. But the person who already has these qualities to begin with will make even more significant improvements. Starting from a lower level he goes further down in blood pressure and pulse rate, and up higher in his hormone output. In the final analysis, the average becomes better, but the individual who is genetically adapted from the start becomes much better.

4
The Channel

> "Thirty hours and three minutes. The thirty hours weren't bad, but, oh, those last three minutes."
>
> Ted Erikson's answer to a question on the time of his nonstop two-way crossing of the English Channel.

Every swimmer, no matter what his accomplishments are, is eventually asked, "Have you done the Channel?" If he answers, "No," a slight loss of esteem is discerned in the questioner's eyes. If the answer is "Yes," the swimmer has proven his reputation. The Channel is the maker of reputations—if not world or nationwide, certainly locally. A man who has swum the Channel is at least recognized in his own neighborhood.

Rich in history, it was the playground of the Vikings, a fence to be leaped by the Normans, and the burial ground of the Spanish Armada. It has, does, and will serve as a backdrop for historians, poets, and admirals, to say nothing of Lloyd's of London. In fact Lloyd's tells us that more ships have been sunk in the Channel than any other equivalent area in the world. The last fact should give the reader an idea of what kind of weather can be expected. If in doubt just spend ten consecutive days anywhere along its coastline. The odds are fifty-to-one against experiencing three straight days of fair weather. The famed English lifeboat service wasn't organized for show. The Channel is no child's pond.

If the reader at this point is now asking himself why any man in his right mind would want to swim such a forbidding stretch of water, I would suggest he has bought the wrong book. He would probably wonder why anybody does anything. To ask such a question would not only identify the individual as mordant, but in an advanced state of decay.

Man, being the creature that he is, would naturally want to extend his limits. Mid-nineteenth-century England spawned the sportsman.

Swimming the bays, lakes, estuaries, and rivers was no doubt accomplished every time the working man or loafer had a spare day or two. Thus it was only a short psychological step to the Channel. The first recorded attempt was by an anonymous Frenchman claiming to be one of Napoleon's soldiers. We can safely discount his claim to fame since the captain who accompanied him made entries in his log that the swimmer on many occasions took ten-minute rest periods aboard his vessel.

The next would-be claimant to world fame was a pompous, medal-bedecked English bath-house swimmer who in 1873 rode down to the straits in a fancy carriage followed by a twenty-piece band and the local barroom maids. Three hours of fanfare ended with the swimmer plunging into the water and swimming out for one hour. He then decided he had had enough and climbed aboard his boat shivering. His name should be forgotten, but for the record it was J. B. Johnson—not the first, nor the last of the nuts to seek publicity.

On December 20, 1862, English seaman Hoskins got all the way across—at least halfway legitimately. He stroked, kicked, and floated across the Channel on a bundle of straw as if he were playing Huckleberry Finn of the Channel. At least the cases presented give an idea of what strange things aspirations can do to a man.

1875 saw the arrival of two unique men on the scene. One left a footnote in history; the other changed it. First was the American Captain Paul Boyton who brought to England with him his patented rubber life saving suit with built in floats. Boyton felt the Channel offered the perfect advertising medium for him and his suit. On April 10, 1875 at 3:20 A.M. he began swimming from Dover. Twelve hours later he found himself being pounded in the surf six miles off Cape Griz-nez, France. Three more hours of pounding convinced him he had enough. He left the water short of his goal.

Back on shore, while recuperating from the muscular strain, Captain Boyton made plans for a second attempt. By the time he was ready for his second try he had not only made alterations on his rubber suit but alterations in his departing site and time. On May 28, 1875 Boyton began swimming from Cape Griz-Nez. Twenty-three hours and thirty minutes later he landed at Foreland near St. Margaret's Bay. One never hears much about Boyton because of his suit. To many he was just another inventor testing his creation. Only naval and commercial specialists would take interest in Boyton and his invention. I like to remember Boyton as one of those all-important men who marked the route that eventually led to the ever-present scuba diving suits that contribute so much to underwater salvage and research work today. Boyton's two swims in the Channel so early in the year when the water was in the forties caused another man to speed up his plans. This man left a more permanent, if not more sensational, mark in history and it would do well to learn something of the man.

Matthew Webb was born in 1848 in one of those countless hamlets that dot the English countryside. The son of a successful surgeon, Matthew took all the advantages, or disadvantages, that accrued to the son of a professional man. Being of a less cerebral nature than his father, he inclined toward the physical side of life. By the age of nine he had taught himself to swim. Soon thereafter he joined the Conway training ship, an organization similar to our Seascouts, where he quickly earned a reputation as a good swimmer. When he was fourteen he was apprenticed to a Liverpool firm whose main business was in the East Indian trade. Leaving this service at eighteen, he then signed up with various other companies whose business was mainly with India, Africa, and the Faroe Islands. It was while he was in Port Natal working on a wreck that he made the first of his marks in swimming. None of the natives of the area could be persuaded to take the rowboats through the surf to the wreck lying beyond. Webb hooked up a line from the wreck to the shore, entered the water with one hand on the rope, the other on the prow of the boat, and proceeded to guide the rowboat through the surf. Spectators and workmen alike marveled at the man's strength. For his efforts the salvers paid Webb about five dollars a day plus all the floating wreckage of value he could find. Webb never worried about sharks since he believed the water was too shallow for them, a belief since disproven by the studies of shark researchers the world over.

Webb was a man who took immediate physical action whenever the occasion called for it. It was while he was in the Cunard Mail Service that he earned the Royal Humane Society's gold and silver medals. The steamship *Russia* was outward bound from New York in April 22, 1873. Speeding along at fourteen and a half knots in the midst of a gale that churned the sea to waves of eight feet and more, the *Russia* lost one of her men overboard. The unlucky seaman fell from the rigging while performing his official duties. Webb, who witnessed the plunge, immediately dove overboard to aid the man. Anyone who contemplates the act will see its heroic aspects. Mid-ocean, eight-foot waves, water that was no doubt in the mid-forties, and a steamship plowing away at fourteen and a half knots—the likeliness of being lost at sea was tremendous. Luckily observers reported the incident. Word was sent to the bridge, all of which takes time. You don't stop a steamship on a dime. By the time the ship had stopped, made a circle and lowered a boat half an hour had gone by. Slowly backtracking in that vast expanse of ocean, the rescuers tried vainly to spot the men. A tense fifteen minutes passed before one of the seamen spotted a head some one mile away. Again and again it was lost as wave and trough combined to obscure the swimmer. After a considerable length of time, the excellent seamanship of the rowers brought them alongside Webb, who gallantly awaited rescue. As reported later by Webb, the unlucky seaman who fell from his perch never rose to the surface after his initial plunge. Webb had made a few abortive dives and then awaited rescue. Back aboard the *Russia* Webb received an ovation from the passengers and crew. Immediately one hundred pounds was raised and given to Webb for his act. Forty-five minutes to an hour in that kind of water deserved the recognition of the queen herself. The duke of Edinburgh's words upon awarding the Royal Humane Society medals were as follows: ". . . the greatest act of bravery during the year in connection with saving life . . . jumping overboard in a heavy gale in mid-ocean after a man had fallen overboard." This award is jealously guarded and any claim must be thoroughly documented.

Having accumulated enough money to take time off from his rather routine profession, Webb drifted down to Dover in the early months of 1875. Ever since J. B. Johnson's abortive attempt two years earlier, a plan had been forming in Webb's mind. Realizing that an attempt on the Channel took money—money that he didn't have—he proceeded on a well-formulated series of actions that were to lead to eventual success. With the acumen that would do justice to our present day public relations men, he announced that he would undertake an eighteen-mile swim in the Thames River. He would start from Blackwall Pier and finish at Gravesend. Betting ten pounds on himself at two-to-one odds, he entered the water and calmly proceeded by breast stroke down the Thames. Some five hours later he emerged from the water at Blackwall, collected his money, talked with reporters and went to the nearest restaurant for dinner. A wide variety of reports appeared in the newspapers the following day. Most reported the incident as the feat of an oddball; a few as an exhibition of swimming power and skill. There was great discussion of the distance he had actually swum, which may sound like nit-picking today. But we must remember that this was the beginning of an era; the crawl stroke had not yet become popular and many people had neither the interest nor the time to indulge in such "larks." However, one point was made by the newspaper that looked favorably upon the feat. Other men of proven speed in the bath-houses of England had been taken from the waters of the Thames and the Channel almost insensible after only an hour or so immersion. This means that if they found themselves taking to the water from a sinking ship a scant two miles from shore they could not save themselves. Here was a case where a man was in the same water four or five times as long and came out none the less for wear. We can see that Webb did not actually swim the map distance of eighteen miles because in order to do so he would have had to swim over three miles per hour, an obvious impossibility for a breast stroker. We may safely say he did make one mile per hour, which would mean about five miles covered under his own power. The current took care of the rest. Webb's accomplishment would be considered nothing today, but in his time it was. It also served to attract the attention of one of England's most unusual men, Frank Buckland.

Buckland was one of those multifaceted individuals who characterized the era. A writer, naturalist, and world traveler, he had some years before created a most unusual newspaper called *Land and Water*. In it he covered all the week's news pertaining to natural history and sports—such wide and varied items as the latest fossils delivered to the British Museum, the results of the London to Brighton walk, sailing races, new animals discovered and named by the zoologist, and the latest reports of zoological expeditions over the world. Buckland, realizing the value of publicity for his weekly, saw value in Webb's swimming feats. Learning that Webb had set his goals on crossing the Channel, Buckland immediately sponsored him.

With solid financial backing Webb now began long training swims. He made an eighteen-mile swim from Dover to Ramsgate in nine hours. Picking up speed on the way, it was calculated that he swam fourteen miles of the distance. This was by no means a small accomplishment when we consider that the water temperatures were in the high fifties and low sixties. As we shall see only men conforming to a particular body structure can handle such temperatures. Webb conformed perfectly. Two hundred and four pounds spread over a five-foot eight-inch frame gives us a man of superb adaptation to cold water. The fact that he was only twenty-seven years old also weighs in his favor.

In early August Webb felt ready for his attempt. *Land and Water*, outside of training expenses, was prepared to offer him fifty pounds if he succeeded in crossing the Channel. The publicity stirred up by Buckland's weekly stimulated wealthy members of the stock exchange to donate money to Webb if he were successful. Little by little the five and twenty pound notes piled up until the subscription, now known as Captain Webb's Subscription, totaled several hundred pounds. Buckland assigned a special reporter to cover Webb's attempt. In the edition of *Land and Water* published a week before his scheduled attempt, an account of the preparations were given. Porpoise oil would be used as insulant. Brandy, strong beef tea, rich glutinous soup, strong hot coffee, meat, and stale bread would be his nourishment while in the water. Later meat extracts and beaten eggs were added. The question of goggles was discussed, but they were not used for at the time they were not adequately developed.

The next problem was the course to be followed. Everybody had a solution. Some had merit, others were the ramblings of ignorance. Obviously to leave at flood tide or shortly thereafter would aid the swimmer, since he would be moving outward with the water. The course to be taken during and after the tidal change presented a problem. Should one alter his compass heading so that he was aided by the current? To do so would carry the swimmer parallel to the shoreline with little headway made. He would also risk making the swim several miles longer by having to land at a point receding away from the closest point to England, Cape Griz-Nez.

There were also arguments over the strength of the currents. Many held that these tidal currents would preclude any successful swim. As will happen when men are short of facts, they are heavy on theory. When all arguments were in Webb made his decision. It was now that he showed his canniness. He would swim always toward one point of the compass, completely ignoring the tidal stream. By doing so the tidal streams would cancel each other out. The only real problem would be in starting and finishing. Here, close to shore, the stream would offer a problem since the peculiarities of the shore and seabed could cause eddies and outward flowing water at certain points. Webb's decision was later proven right by the professional Channel swimmers of the fifties. Once clear of the shore by two or three miles, the tidal streams are *never* directly *against* you. They are always some angle to the side. Thus a good swimmer should always be able to make headway *across* the direction of flow. An approach or departure near bays or estuaries can be either extremely helpful or disastrous depending upon whether you ride the current in or attempt to go against it.

Thus, while the Channel does have significant currents, they do not present an insurmountable barrier to the swimmer of championship calibre. The celebrated accounts of swimmers "fighting" the tide to get in represents three possible situations, or combinations thereof. A first-rate swimmer has gotten sick or cold and consequently can no longer make headway. A second possibility is a second-rate swimmer at the end of his strength; or thirdly, a swimmer, due to faulty position or bad navigation, might try to come into the mouth of a harbor or estuary when the current is coming against him at a speed equal to or greater than his swimming speed. The reader should not confuse tide and current. The tide itself along the French and English coastline will ebb and flow at speeds that can be measured in tenths of a mile per hour. It is only where you have exceptional shoreline formations that you will find accelerated speeds. When a large body of rising water is forced through a relatively narrow inlet, the limited exposed seabed can be inundated at terrifying speed at flood tide. Such is the sand bar connecting Mount St. Michel and Tombelaine Rock with the northern coast of France. It was here that five tourists drowned many years ago when they tarried too long on Tombelaine Rock and the swiftly moving tide and current inundated the previously exposed seabed.

After the question of tides and currents had been settled, Webb

The Channel

decided on a departure date sometime during the second week of August, 1875. He and his crew would wait for favorable weather and then leave from Admiralty Pier, Dover. As it turned out, threatening weather delayed a planned morning start on August 11th. Webb made the best of the enforced delay and rescheduled the departure for the late afternoon of the following day. That day was a repeat of the previous one's inclement weather. However, later on in the afternoon the weather cleared and at 5 P.M. Webb began his swim, entering the water from the Admiralty Pier at Dover.

Considering the stroke that he used Webb made excellent time for the first hour, but then just about any good swimmer can look good for an hour. Webb could hardly have picked a more inopportune time to start, for he was swept immediately in a northeasterly direction up the Channel. The current, if one is to believe the plot of the boat captain, moved him more or less parallel to the shore. By 8 P.M. it had moved him some four and a half miles in a lateral direction from his position at 6:15 P.M. He had, however, managed to cover some four miles of the necessary twenty-one. By 9:00 P.M. he had progressed only one-fourth mile from his position at 8:00 P.M., but the currents had pushed him another four and a fourth miles northeasterly up the Channel, paralleling the cliffs of Dover.

One wonders at this point about the navigation. Either the tug captain was neglecting his compass or he misread the shore and buoy lights. An hour later it was the same story. Ten P.M. found him another two and a half miles up the Channel and no further across. At 8 P.M. Webb had had his first feeding of solid food. The tug captain and newsmen had felt optimistic. The sea had calmed down and the moon had made its appearance in a cloudless sky. Webb had been in high spirits; his repartee with the people on the boat had been a good sign. At 10 P.M. an ominous bank of dark clouds made its appearance in the southwest, moving swiftly over the area with accompanying winds. The sea rapidly picked up until three and four foot waves rolled and pitched the tug. By 11:30 P.M. the combined sea and current had moved Webb another five miles up the coast with an insignificant gain toward his goal. Fifteen minutes later Webb recognized the futility of continuing. Listening to the pleas of his attendants he hauled himself aboard the tug still fresh and hearty. The tug made for the safety of the harbor at Calais.

The next edition of *Land and Water* made a great story of Webb's attempt with the claim that he had gone "more than half-way across the Channel in six hours and forty-nine minutes." There is a great discrepancy between the words printed and the map of the course plotted by the tug captain. According to the map Webb had drifted eighteen miles "up" the Channel, but had made only five miles progress across it. Considering the circumstances and the usual literary license of most reporters, one would be disposed to accept the tug captain's version of Webb's swim. However one would do well to keep in mind that this attempt could have been a contrived failure, considering the shrewd publicity heads of Webb and Buckland. A failure at that point would solidify and increase public interest in a later attempt. One is persuaded to this view in light of the follow-up article in *Land and Water* and the large amounts of money received for a second attempt. When six London newspapers had been forced to send reporters to cover the event, you can be assured that wide public interest had been stirred up by Buckland's original blurbs. Thus the stage was set for Webb's coming world fame.

THE HISTORIC CONQUEST

On Monday, August 23, 1875, eleven days later, Webb was ready for his second attempt. The scheduled 1 A.M. start was cancelled when a falling barometer boded inclement weather. Plans were hurriedly changed and a 1 P.M. start was scheduled for the following day. The start would be two hours after high water at Dover.

Tuesday morning Webb awoke to a beautiful sunlit day. Looking out over the Channel from his Dover hotel window he sensed that his lucky day had arrived. No wind and no waves made the Channel look like a pond. The excitement was felt by all concerned with the endeavor. All morning the tug captain and crew leisurely checked last minute preparations. Food and drink for the crew and newsmen were secured. The small rowboats that would stay close to Webb made their way from inner harbor berths to Admiralty Pier. By noon Webb was aboard the tug talking over last-minute preparations. Tension made him curt and fidgety as he awaited departure time. The tug captain and newsmen found it necessary to calm him with pleasant demeanor. At 12:30 P.M. Webb took off his clothes and liberally applied the porpoise grease supplied him. Present-day readers will no doubt cringe at this, considering the facts that have been learned since Webb's day about these highly endearing and intelligent mammals.

At 12:56 P.M. Webb dove from the steps of Admiralty Pier. He stroked strongly for the first few hours. It was a perfect start. The decision to leave two hours after high water at Dover was an excellent one, for by 4 P.M. Webb had covered almost five and one-half miles. The ebb tide flow had managed to aid him by some one-half mile per hour during this time. If one refers to the map one can see how favorable his position was. By drawing a series of parallel lines from each recorded position to the line joining his departure and intended arrival points (constant compass heading) one can see just how much progress has been made. The southwesterly current almost immediately began to move him toward Folkestone and by 3 P.M. had moved him

The Channel 53

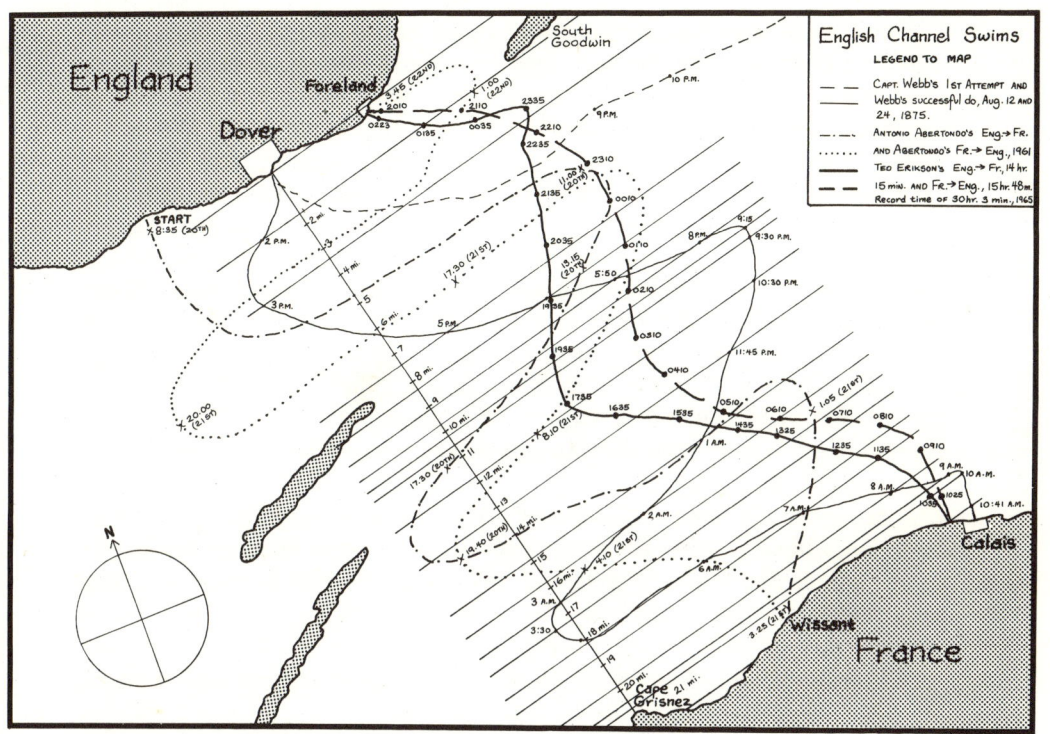

When a Channel swimmer keeps a constant compass heading, he will end up swimming not much more than the twenty-one miles separating England and France at their closest points. The tidal currents give him a free lateral ride. Most swimmers aim for Cape Griz-nez. The straight line joining Dover and Cape Griz-nez is the shortest distance separating the two countries. The author has dropped perpendiculars from Webb's course to this line, which gives a good idea of Webb's progress throughout the swim.

about three miles west of a straight-line course. One's appreciation of Captain Toms, who was setting the course, increases in light of subsequent developments.

At 3:30 P.M. the flood tide began. Now the boat and swimmer began to be "swept up" the Channel in an easterly direction. There were a few moments of soul-searching by Captain Toms when he expressed to reporters that he may not have succeeded in getting his swimmer far enough to the west, toward Folkestone. If Webb was not sufficiently clear of the Goodwins by the time the currents had swept him "up" the Channel, there would be a repeat of his earlier venture. But there was no need to worry, for Webb was now far enough out into the Channel to make good use of what we may call the second stage of the swim.

The last of the small sight-seeing boats had now left. Webb's stroke rate had dropped from twenty-three to twenty per minute. Haze began to dim the already weakening rays of the sun. At 4 P.M. Webb took his first feeding, beef tea warmed aboard the mother boat. When one reads in the later accounts of would-be Channel conquerors that they consumed sandwiches and other solids and subsequently had stomach troubles, one's appreciation of Webb's sound thinking is further enhanced.

Five P.M. found Dover gradually disappearing in the haze. Seven miles out and the water was still flat. It was an almost idyllic scene. Porpoises made their appearance leaping after schools of fish. At 6:15 the *Land and Water* reporter stripped down and joined Webb for ten minutes. Webb had expressed a desire that whenever possible a swimmer should join him to stimulate and relieve him from the monotony. The anonymous reporter thoroughly enjoyed the affair and it's sad that his name wasn't recorded. His conversational writing takes on added charm when he tells of a colleague leaving for Dover in one of the rowboats to give the latest report on how the swim was progressing. It seems that the colleague had hired one of the rowers at a certain rate per hour. Dover was an expected two hours row away. The rower and reporter spent five hours of tedious rowing before reaching Dover with aching muscles.

Progress was excellent for the next few hours as Webb maintained a steady one mile per hour average gain even though the current continued to carry him easterly. Another boat left the park at 7 P.M. with the latest news. Seven-thirty found the last rays of the sun disappearing. Now the plankton began to rise to the surface. These luminescent microscopic creatures added an eerie effect to Webb's efforts. With each stroke a luminescent trail was left giving the swimmer a halo of light. Weather conditions, to everyone's satisfaction, remained perfect.

At 9 P.M., just as the tidal current was reversing itself, Webb gave a yell as he was painfully stung by a jellyfish. Nausea swept over him and he immediately backtracked. Webb asked for brandy and immediately received it. He took several hefty swallows before continuing and gave the immediate area a wide berth. People have been killed from receiving hundreds of stings from a large man o' war jellyfish. Almost one hundred years later, Ted Erikson would give a vivid description of his fright from receiving such stings on his two-way Channel crossing. Like Webb he carried the marks of stings for two weeks after the swim. It would take more than this to stop a man of Webb's character.

It was now that Webb made the best time of his swim. With the shift in direction of current he would have a considerable vector behind him. From 9:30 P.M. to 10:30 P.M. he made one and a half

The Channel

more miles to give him a total of eleven miles covered since the start. From 10:30 P.M. to 1 A.M. he made his best progress: three miles. At this time a paddle steamer carrying passengers between England and France came to within one hundred yards of the swimmer to give everyone aboard a look at the affair. Passengers and crew alike gave hearty cheers to the swimmer and his crew, picking up their morale considerably. The moon in a cloudless sky gave good feelings to all concerned.

According to observers, the first signs of fatigue appeared at 2 A.M., but Webb doggedly continued to make progress. Baker, the young diver hired for emergency, put on his belt with a life line attached and entered the rowboat attending Webb.

Three A.M. found Webb a tantalizing four miles off Cape Griz-nez. He had now been in the water fourteen hours. At this point he rolled over onto his back and floated for five minutes, resting his aching muscles. He asked for some beef tea which he received. Anxiety was evident in Webb's face. He knew the tide would again shortly change. If caught too far from land he would have an extremely difficult, if not impossible, time making shore since the current at this point takes a slight vector away from land. It would make the job of completion difficult even for a good crawl swimmer. For a man like Webb, swimming the breast stroke and averaging one mile per hour, it would be close to impossible. Webb asked, and was told, his stroke rate. It was now down to sixteen strokes per minute.

It was now that Captain Toms wished that he had persuaded Webb to start two hours earlier. If this had been done Webb would now have been west of Cape Griz-Nez and thus in a favorable position to be swept into the Cape with the change in tide. However in retrospect it seems inconceivable that Webb could have done any better considering his speed and style.

Webb clearly showed his disappointment at being so far out at this time. After his short rest he continued stroking with a determination to accomplish his goal regardless of conditions. If he succeeded in getting through these early morning hours of darkness until sunlight his spirits would pick up. Early morning hours are the most difficult of all for swimmers. Fatigue and darkness are very depressing indeed, and they have combined to make many good men give up.

From 3 A.M. to 4 A.M. Webb made another mile of progress as the tide made its third shift of the swim. It now ran in an east by northeast direction paralleling the coast of France. In the next hour he made no further progress whatsoever but continued to be carried along the coast.

Up to now Webb had taken only liquids: hot coffee, beef tea, brandy, and some cod-liver oil. He stopped for a moment and now chewed some raw meat. With the coming of dawn around 6:30 A.M. the wind picked up. Everyone recognized the seriousness of the situation. There were now short, choppy waves which seemed to distress Webb. His stroke rate dropped to fifteen as the tide continued to carry him away from Cape Griz-Nez toward Calais.

Eight A.M. found Webb drinking some beef tea and brandy. Between 7 and 8 A.M. he had succeeded in making about one-half mile further progress. Captain Toms told him that if he managed to hold out there was a possibility of making Calais Pier. The wind again picked up and by 9 A.M. the waves were washing over the rowboats. There was talk of imminent failure. However, Webb, exhausted as he was, continued to make incremental progress. By 10 A.M. the current had carried him to a point directly off Calais. It had moved him almost thirteen miles along the shore from Cape Griz-Nez in six hours. He was now some one and a half miles from land. The observers noticed that his fingers were beginning to open as fatigue and cold made further attacks upon his frame.

Observers at Calais at this time sent out a boat which served a useful purpose in taking up a station to the windward of Webb. It served to break the force of waves which were periodically sweeping him under. Webb's legs could hardly come together to finish their stroke. The tide now turned slack. Webb appeared to have difficulty staying afloat. He had succeeded now in coming to within a scant one-half mile of the shore. Exhausted as he was it could be seen by observers that Webb was making progress. Again his stroke rate dropped. It was now twelve strokes per minute. Young Baker now dove into the water and began swimming alongside Webb in an effort to stimulate him. By 10:20 A.M. only three or four hundred yards separated Webb from his goal. Excitement among the observers and spectators, both on shore and in the boats, became intense as it became evident that he would succeed. Cheering and hand clapping stirred him on. The last few yards found Webb stumbling as he sounded. When he attempted to walk ashore from waist deep water he fell forward for lack of balance and fatigue. He rose, walked a few more feet until he was knee deep then pitched forward again. Two spectators quickly went to his side to lift him up and help him maintain his balance. There was hardly a dry eye in the crowd of several hundred spectators as they cheered the man who had single-handedly conquered the historic straits. Captain Toms's face was covered with tears. Webb gave him a wave, then a salute as his weary frame was hastily bundled in a rug and placed aboard a rig for transport to a hotel. The salt-encrusted face of Webb managed a smile from an exhausted, creased, fatigued countenance. Webb had landed on the shores of France after twenty-one hours and forty-five minutes of swimming in water that averaged sixty degrees. His conquest remained the sole one for thirty-six years. It took that long for any other swimmer to be successful.

Webb, wrapped in his rug, was taken by rig to the Paris Hotel, Calais. A Dr. Smith was called and he made an examination of Webb. His stethoscope showed a strong heart and clear lungs. His pulse rate was seventy-two and temperature was 98°. Three hours later Webb's temperature was 101°, a sign of Webb's excellent recuperative powers. Webb, after greetings from well-wishers, slept for three hours in the luxuriousness of a hotel bed. Upon awaking he ate some fish and then went back to sleep for another six hours.

With the word of Webb's success flashed around the world by telegraph, he became a hero. Subscription funds poured in and by the year's end he had received some $20,000. The Prince of Wales gave him another $25,000 for his feat. With recognition he was in demand for exhibitions. He received $2,000 for swimming seventy-four hours in a pool at Scarborough. When he had fulfilled the requests for appearances in England, he moved to America, married, and settled down in Boston where his wife had two children. For awhile he received $1,000 a week for exhibitions. By 1883 he had $15,000 left and decided to make another "money" swim. This one would be across the Niagara River above the falls. That story is succinctly told in the newspaper captions in the *Buffalo Express* of July 25, 1883:

WEBB LOST IN THE RAPIDS . . . THE GALLANT SWIMMER REACHES THE WHIRLPOOL AND IS SEEN NO MORE . . . A FOOLHARDY UNDERTAKING . . . SKETCH OF THE CAPTAIN . . . A FRUITLESS SEARCH . . . BODY LOST IN WHIRLPOOL AT FOOT OF THE FALLS . . . LAST SEEN 15 MINUTES AFTER ENTERING THE RIVER . . . BODY BURIED AT LEWISTON WHERE RECOVERED.

Webb was thirty-five years old when he died with his trunks on.

GERTRUDE EDERLE

In the years that followed Webb's success there were many other attempts. Time after time swimmers entered the water only to be defeated. An aura began to surround Webb's feat. Then serious questions were posed as to the authenticity of the feat. Was he a superman or had the public been swindled by an impostor? Errors could be found in the captain's plot of the course. One of the big questions posed by modern-day coaches is his surprisingly good time for a breast stroker. After fourteen hours of swimming he was only three miles or so off Cape Griz-Nez, a time that compares very favorably with what an excellent crawl swimmer would do today. The one fact that remains in Webb's favor is the large number of people in attendance throughout his swim. There were at least seven on the mother boat. It would have been very difficult to carry out a conspiracy with such a large number, a number that would be increased if the number of spectators were taken into account that visited the swimmer during the course of the swim at all hours. To quiet the skeptics a series of affidavits were signed in the first decade of the twentieth century by those still living who had witnessed the swim some twenty-five years earlier. These affidavits remain to this day as permanent records of the Channel Swimming Association.

The onslaughts by swimmers attempting to duplicate the feat continued, but it wasn't until 1911 that another Englishman, Thomas Burgess, succeeded. His time of twenty-two hours and thirty-five minutes was almost an hour longer than Webb's. One gets an idea of the man's tenacity by the fact that it was his fourteenth attempt. Ever since 1904 he had averaged two attempts a year. Like Webb, he made his crossing from England to France. A few more years were to elapse before it was discovered that the France to England crossing was a little easier.

After Burgess's success the Channel was to remain inviolate for another eleven years. The year 1923 broke the long chain of unsuccessful tries. That year was marked by three successes, two of which were from the opposite direction of Webb's. The first that year was by an American named Henry Sullivan. His conquest set somewhat of a standard because he took so long—twenty-six hours and fifty minutes. However his swim seemed to be a pivot point for all who followed. A few short weeks later, an Argentinian, Enrico Tiraboshi, decided that individuality was the cornerstone of personality. He would leave from the shores of France. When he walked out onto English soil he created quite a stir, for he had accomplished the Channel in the phenomenal time of sixteen hours and thirty-three minutes. The dam had burst. Channel swimming was never the same afterward. The era of oddball wildcat attempts, while not ended, was surely taking a back seat to the more serious approach of dedicated men. A few days later an American named Charles Toth duplicated Tiraboshi's feat with a time of sixteen hours and fifty-eight minutes, only twenty-five minutes longer.

These successes were no doubt a reflection of the establishment of large numbers of pools to handle the sportsmen interested in the Olympic Games that were then becoming important in world affairs. Coaches and trainers had begun to approach swimming in a scientific manner. 1926 brought the world to its feet when a young American girl of eighteen not only became the first woman to conquer the Channel, but the holder of the fastest time in which it had ever been done. Supporters of male dominancy were, to say the least, taken aback. Gertrude Ederle captured the hearts of millions.

Trudy, as she was affectionately called, was one of those "beautiful people." Her youthful, innocent charm was a delightful contrast to the wickedness of the world. With the publicity that attended her success she became a folk hero. Born in 1908 to a German immigrant who ran a delicatessen in New York, she learned to swim at an early age. As thousands have learned since, it is a perfect way to combat the frustrations of living in a large city. At thirteen she joined the Women's Swimming Association. Her natural talents soon came out when a year later the club supervisors entered her in an international three-mile race in New York Bay. At the tender age of fourteen she beat fifty other world-recognized swimmers, including Britain's foremost swimmer. A year later she won a similar event. Naturally, talk turned to the Channel, which offered a double incentive of being unconquered by a woman. The first serious attempt by a woman was in 1900 when a Madame Isacescue tried and failed. Five years later a Miss Kellerman also failed.

The meager funds of the club were tapped and, in 1925, accompanied by the club president, Trudy sailed for England. The infamous Channel weather frustrated a success and she was forced to leave the water broken hearted as only the young can be. Her girlish enthusiasm, however did not go unnoticed and during the winter that followed she was contacted by two giants in the publishing world. The *Chicago Tribune* and the New York News Syndicate offered to sponsor her the following year.

Her boat, with a surprisingly large entourage, sailed early in 1926. It had been decided that a month or so of training in the Channel off Cape Griz-Nez would give her the necessary experience and hardening. Her crew included a *Chicago Tribune* columnist later to attain worldwide fame, Westbrook Pegler, a New York News reporter, her coach, Thomas Burgess (the same Burgess who had conquered the Channel in 1911), and her older sister. They set up headquarters in Cape Griz-Nez and the long training began. Well-oiled publicity and news releases accompanied her training. The releases told of intrigue by the English and French. Difficulty in obtaining boats, bad food, the disappearance of personal belongings, and a whole list of petty annoyances were described in reports. However, it seems hard to believe that people would try to prevent an eighteen-year-old girl from swimming just because she was American. When one learns of the difficulties encountered by the entourage, they seem no more, or less, than those encountered by any tourist. However, readers must be won and the yellow journalism continued. The professional writers felt that the "dull" sport must be given drama.

There was no need for drama to be created once the swim began on the morning of August 6, 1926. Trudy entered the water from the coast of France under favorable weather conditions. Newsmen and photographers from competing newspapers hired their own vessels from fishermen and sportsmen. As in the future, beer became the solace of those who looked upon the venture as a lark. Unless you have a direct interest in the swimmer the monotony becomes depressing after the first few hours.

For twelve hours Trudy made excellent progress. A new era of training and style had begun and during the twenties the crawl stroke was used almost exclusively. The beginning of the thirteenth hour brought a change in the weather. A squall moved over the boats and swimmer. The wind whipped up the waves and another story began that was to be repeated time after time with other swimmers in coming years. She was only a couple of miles off the English coast. Every time Trudy sank and rose with the waves the crew thought it was hopeless. Conditions always look much more dire to observers than to the swimmer. The swimmer is nestled, cradled, and supported by the water. He, or she, does not rock nearly as much as the boats alongside. The boats and their occupants suffer more from the turmoil because of riding on the surface where every angle is accentuated.

It was a tribute to Trudy's pluck that she ignored her trainer's plea to leave the water. Two and a half hours later she stalked out onto the sands of Dover with a smile. She became not only the first woman to swim the Channel, but the holder of the fastest time recorded to date. With the impetuosity of youth and utter disdain for the world of publicity clamoring for her soul, she left immediately for Germany to visit her grandmother. During her stay of several weeks in Germany, a Mrs. Mille Carde Corson, mother of two children, became the second woman to conquer the straits. It took her an hour longer, but being a mother made her popular with the press and its readers. However Mrs. Corson's feat in no way detracted from the tremendous ticker-tape parade held for Trudy when she returned to New York. Hundreds of thousands lined the sidewalks of Broadway Avenue to welcome the young heroine. Another drama was about to unfold some five months later in the waters of the Pacific Ocean. The chewing gum magnate, William Wrigley Jr., was dangling $25,000 on the shores of California to the first person to swim the Catalina Island Straits. But that is another story. The years 1926 and 1927 were to offer the largest purses ever offered in professional swimming; prizes of such size were never again to be offered.

Oh, yes, there was one other man who snuck under the wire as the final conqueror of the Channel in 1926—a German named Ernst Vierkotter whose remarkable time of twelve hours and forty minutes was two hours faster than Gertrude Ederle's. His time went relatively unnoticed since he was the third conqueror that year. Vierkotter's name would go down in history a year later when he would win the largest prize ever offered in the history of the game—$30,000. He won this in the first professional swim of the Canadian National Exhibition at Toronto. William Wrigley Jr.'s $30,000 in 1927 was truly an offering worthy of the sport. That kind of money is equivalent to $75,000 to $100,000 today. It would last a frugal man a lifetime and a dissipator thirty minutes. The record doesn't tell us to which category Vierkotter belonged.

The years between 1927 and 1950 were the "slow years" in the Channel. Whenever an afficionado accumulated enough money he would book a trip to Folkestone on his vacation and set across. In those years, according to the records of the Channel Swimming Association, there were ten crossings from France to England and none from England to France. The Association was formed to authenticate claims of success since several phoney swimmers claimed to have succeeded. In later years the Association would place an observer aboard the swimmer's vessel free of charge. The swimmer, however, had to pay for the vessel and navigation. Swimmer's times hung around the fifteen-hour mark.

It wasn't until 1950 that Channel swimming received the tremendous worldwide publicity that has characterized it ever since. That year marked the advent of the professionals. The *London Daily Mail*, a newspaper of wide circulation, decided to sponsor a cross-Channel race from France to England. The coming race was widely publicized and it wasn't long before entries were received from all over the world. Prizes offered were: £1,000 (about $2,800) for first place and £250 (about $700) for second through fifth place. The first woman to finish, regardless of position, would receive £1,000. The field would be limited to twenty competitors, a number the *Daily Mail* felt it could safely accommodate. The swimmers had to pay their own fares to England, but the sponsors would pay living and hotel expenses for the week preceding the event. That week was full of the bally-hoo that became a standard of all such enterprises since Webb. Daily articles were run in the newspaper giving the background of the swimmers and where the readers could watch them train. The most impressive group, and only team, that arrived was an Egyptian one. Swimming has never been the same since. For sheer noise, excitement, and practical joking the Egyptians were never to be exceeded. But let no one be fooled by the gaiety. Ten of the country's most select swimmers had been carefully primed for the coming event. A trainer and doctor were provided and all expenses were being paid by the Egyptian government. The staid English countryside was never the same after their arrival. Horseplay, laughter, and fun-loving activity characterized them. Beneath the surface, however, they were deadly serious. They were always the first down to the beach for the morning workout and the last to leave in the evening. In most cases they would patronize the local grocery stores for the fresh fruits and vegetables that were all too lacking in the restaurant menus. The eight miles of swimming a day they had done in training while in Egypt would not be wasted as subsequent events proved.

Halfway through that first race an Egyptian army lieutenant was in the lead. Close behind a Frenchman named Morvan was coming up. From then on the pair changed leads periodically. Toward the end of the race the forty-one-year-old, fat-padded Egyptian father of five, with the superb inheritance and training, beat the twenty-six-year-old Frenchman ashore by twelve minutes. El-Rheim fell six times as he stumbled ashore attempting to regain his land legs, but was still strong and smiling. Shouting, "Allah be praised. A record, a record," he shook the hands of spectators. A record it was, for the indomitable Egyptian had set a new record of ten hours and fifty minutes. The six-foot, 217-pound Egyptian's hearty personality captured the newsmen's attention and he was feted by businessmen for weeks following his feat.

That first year marked the beginning of an annual pilgrimage by the Egyptians. Indeed, an Egyptian swimmer, if offered the chance, would rather make a once-in-a-lifetime pilgrimage to compete in a Channel race than one to the holy city of Mecca. The second year the race was held established the myth, which has lasted until this day, of the invincibility of Egyptian swimmers. The winner was a bodyguard to King Farouk, thirty-four year old Hamad. One can imagine the drama of the 1951 race by just looking at the times of the finishers. Only one minute separated first and second place. The frustration of the Frenchman, Morvan, can only be surmised. To be beaten by only twelve minutes the year before and by one minute this year after twelve hours of exhaustive effort would have left lesser men seeking the purchase of a stout rope for hanging. Whether to use on his competitor or himself would be of interest to those seeking an explanation of human personality. Further examination of the record shows that minutes separated each swimmer finishing down to sixteenth place. Either it was a tight race or the swimmers themselves decided to make the spectacle a water ballet endeavor.

The enormous publicity and public interest proved this second year's race satisfying to the promoters. However all was not well. The Egyptians created a *cause célèbre* at the award ceremonies. When their names were called before the large gathering of businessmen, politicians, sports representatives, and general public to receive their checks and trophies, the Egyptians stood up and left the ceremonies in mass. There were horrified looks of despair and embarrassment of all concerned. The reason given by the Egyptians was that the sponsors of the race, the *Daily Mail,* had published the day before an article extremely critical of the Egyptian king. Regardless of the failings of Farouk the actions of the Egyptians becomes understandable when one learns that the previous year's winner, El-Rheim, had been given a home and a lifetime pension for his success. The same awaited the

1951 winner. Nobody can blame the Egyptians; for what is a $2,800 purse compared to what awaited him at home? The repercussions were quick. The *Mail* immediately dropped sponsorship of the Channel Race. When 1952 rolled around no one had picked up the tab; thus no race. Lovers of the sport got to work and by the spring of 1953 fast talking and enthusiasm, plus the aura of publicity, had convinced one of England's wealthy businessmen to take over the expense of a race. Mr. Billy Butlin, of Butlin's Holiday Camps and other sundry businesses, proved his merit and discernment over the next seven years he sponsored the races. Those years were marked by thrilling races characterized by worldwide publicity. The 1956 race saw no finishers because of inclement weather after eleven hours. Prizes were awarded according to position in the water at that time.

Some say the most remarkable years were the 1957 and 1958 races which saw the indomitable Greta Andersen winning both races. She became not only a winner, but established a new record for women. She also became the only person, male or female, to ever win two Channel races. Greta was on her way to becoming the greatest female swimmer in the history of the game. 1959 was the last year the races were held. For whatever reason, be it increasing costs or diminishing publicity, Billy Butlin had done well.

As in any endeavor there are those who never enter the winner's circle. Swimmers are no exception. There are some who, though never fast, will always finish. Consequently, for whatever reason one may wish to assign, they will attempt the longer swims. Now that the Channel had been conquered many times there was a minimum of reward left for them. To ring up a time of sixteen, eighteen, or twenty hours would lay them open to jests. "See you took the slow train." "How come so slow?" "You're wasting your time." Such a swimmer was Antonio Abertondo. A short, stocky brute who packed 225 pounds on a five-foot-four-inch frame, he was never known for grace either in or out of the water. But Tony had lasting power. Twice he had swum across the River Plata from Uruguay to Argentina. Each swim was over fifty miles and he had been in the water over thirty hours each time. Also on his list of accomplishments were a number of swims down the Parana River, each one taking over sixty hours. This is testament enough to his staying power. Before the reader becomes too enamoured of Tony, he should remember the "other" Argentine, Pedro Candiotti, who has at various times been labeled the "greatest distance swimmer of all time." (The label was attached before the age of Abo-Heif.) The "Shark of Quilla Creek" made his reputation in the 1930s and early 40s. Candiotti's main ambition was to swim 204 miles down the River Plate, from Rosario to Buenos Aires. He made over seventeen attempts but each time the river conquered him. His last try was in 1943 when the tide and fatigue forced him to quit after being in the water seventy-four hours and thirty minutes. Candiotti's longest swim was in 1935 when he accomplished 281 miles down the Parana River from Santa Fe to Zarate, which entailed being in the water some eighty-four hours. As can be seen, Antonio Abertondo had quite a heritage to follow.

After his two poor placings in Channel races Tony drifted back and forth between England and South America. The biblical "Time and chance . . ." now entered into Tony's life. An English newspaperman named Sam Rockett recognized the public's need and demand for novelty. What would be more natural than a Channel "double cross?" A double crossing attempt would rekindle the public's interest in Channel swimming. Rockett, with his worldwide connections, soon got a hold of Tony, who showed himself amenable to such an attempt. Rockett, being the typical brazen newspaperman, however, was no slouch. He had swum in the first Channel race in 1950 and had placed a respectable fourth. As so often in history two admirably suited personalities found themselves brought together to seek their respectful goals. All of 1960 and early into 1961 Tony would methodically train. Eight hours a day kept him in the peak of condition. Anyone looking at this pudgy man would hardly believe that he was a man in such condition that few in the world attain. At the end of a training session Tony would down three or four pounds of meat, two quarts of milk, a loaf of bread, plus the accompanying tidbits.

As fate would have it, one month before Tony's swim a world record open-water swim was established in Lake Michigan when a Chicago chemist, Ted Erikson, swam forty-four miles across the lake. Another psychological goal was tabulated on Tony's psyche. There were some who said that Tony and Rockett's plan for a Channel double cross crystallized only after Erikson's feat. In any case it should be remembered that Tony's first attempt came two weeks after Erikson's feat and that it takes longer than that to get in condition. It is possible that Rockett and Abertondo were opportunists and capitalized on the knowledge that a man could stay in the water for over thirty-five hours. The reader should keep in mind that thirty-five hours in seventy-two-degree water is a far cry from thirty-five hours in sixty-degree water. However the mold was set.

About two weeks after Erikson's new world record that served as a new goal for Tony, he took to the water. The oft-repeated story again took place. After fifteen hours in the water the Channel weather stopped Tony while only two miles from Cape Griz-Nez. He left the water to await another day. It came two weeks later when on September 20, 1961 at 8:35 in the morning Tony began his swim that was to encompass three calendar dates and *seven* changes in the tide. That first leg of the swim—from England to France—took Tony eighteen hours and fifty minutes. Tony was no speedball. Landing at

Wessant, France he was greeted by a large surging crowd of two: a French newspaperman and a photographer. Within ten minutes Tony had regreased, taken the proverbial hot drink, spoken a few words and was back in the water stroking toward the unseen cliffs of Dover. Sam Rockett proceeded to go below deck to catch some sleep after telling the crewmen to wake him when Tony had decided to give up the swim. Rockett felt that the cool overcast weather and Tony's more than erratic stroking were too much for success. Rockett awoke three hours later to find the weather had turned beautiful. The clouds had disappeared and the sun was bathing the scene with its delightful, warm rays. When he looked at Tony it seemed that all the erratic stroking had disappeared and that he was now stroking stronger than at any other time. By 5:30 P.M. of September 21, some thirty-two hours into the swim, Tony was three-quarters of the way through the swim. The cliffs of Dover were now visible and lured him on even though fatigue had now made great inroads. This point in the swim marked his ordeal by fire. What had gone before was limbo. What lay before was hell. The saltwater had swollen Tony's lips and tongue until his face seemed like some grotesque humanoid mushroom hardly distinguishable as human. His arms hardly cleared the water, and indeed at times did not. Hallucinations began. Posts, dogs, and other strange objects appeared in the water. Paranoia crept in. Why were the handlers turning back toward France? Why were they holding back his food? He was beginning to experience short periods when he lost consciousness. A physiologist was not necessary to recognize that the end of the swim was near. Tony was now only a couple of miles off the cliffs. He could not have arrived at a more inopportune time. It was one o'clock in the morning. All was dark. A member of the Channel Swimming Association had made her way along the top of the cliffs and had placed a guide light there since the swimmer and boat were coming in at a spot that offered no beach. Those last few hundred yards were sheer agony. Inch by inch they fell away as the indomitable Argentine stroked away. At last Tony sounded at the base of a three-hundred-foot cliff. The beaten, exhausted shell of a man who dragged himself the last few feet over the rocks was a sight never to be forgotten by those who witnessed it. The spotlight from the boat shone on him as he sagged over a rock. For ten minutes Tony lay there. Blankets were placed over him. At 3:45 A.M. on September 22, 1961 after forty-three hours and ten minutes of swimming Tony Abertondo had landed. Tony was put back into the boat and it made for harbor. "Tony was no speedball, but he could last," was the understatement of the year. He was the first man to swim the Channel both ways nonstop.

"Time and tide wait for no man."
Folk saying

"Time and tide will wait for no man, saith the adage.
But all men have to wait for time and tide."
                    Charles Dickens
                    Martin Chuzzlewit (1843)

In the Age of Aquarius Abertondo's record was to last only four years. Ted Erikson, Chicago chemist, who created world sensations in 1961, 1962, and 1963 with his crossings of Lake Michigan, established a new record for a double crossing of the English Channel in 1965. He had tried and failed to make a double crossing the year before. In 1965 he came back armed with a carefully plotted, computerized course, worked out by him and his colleagues at the Illinois Institute of Technology Research Center in Chicago. As worked out in theory, Ted would take advantage of the tide throughout the swim. His compass heading would change hourly, placing him always perpendicular to the tidal stream. When the time came to merge theory and plot with application things began to go astray. The boat captain was unable to put into practice the fairly technical plot during Ted's first two attempts that year. Ted, on the third attempt that September, dispensed with the computer program and made the swim in the conventional manner. There was nothing conventional in the remarkable time that he made for the swim, however. The first leg of the double crossing, from England to France, was accomplished in fourteen hours and fifteen minutes. The return trip from France to England was made in the remarkably consistent time of fifteen hours and forty-eight minutes. His total time was thirty hours and three minutes, knocking thirteen hours and seven minutes off of Abertondo's record. Ted had ideal weather throughout his swim. At times the Channel, he said, "was like glass." For pure drama one has only to read the official Channel Swimming Association Report by the official observer on the swim, Dick Powell. It is an example of how all swims should be documented. Water temperatures, sea conditions, and feeding times are all there. The complete report follows.

    Ted Erikson, the world's fastest two-way conqueror of the English Channel, told how he won the battle of the jelly fish and of the roses that grow in the sea.
    The 37 year old swimmer from Chicago had to cleave his way through a shoal of jelly fish on his way to France.
    The roses were an illusion, as he struggled over the last few miles of the return trip to England.
    Ted completed the two-way swim in 30 hours, 3 minutes.
    "I had about two miles to go and everything started to go black," Erikson said.
    "My pilot boat faded into a black smear. Then it turned into a rose bush. Suddenly there were roses growing all around me.
    "I just closed my eyes and swam on. I guess that was the moment of crisis."

Erikson, a research chemist who started long distance swimming only five years ago, plotted to lower Abertondo's time with the help of a computer, operated by his Chicago scientist colleague Tony Dundzilla.

Dundzilla fed the computer Erikson's swimming speed and the complicated tidal current which make the channel a nightmare for swimmers.

Ted attempted the swim in 1964 but gave up after 23 hours, defeated by the cold weather conditions on the second leg. Twice in the last two weeks he attempted the crossing but was swept off course and gave up. These two attempts were planned by computer.

"This time I decided not to stick rigidly to the computer, although the point of start was a computer working and formed the basis of my plan," Erikson said.

"I relied on my pilot Peter Winter, to amend our course as we went along. I had perfect weather and it worked out fine."

After the swim Ted took four hours sleep and then got up to read the messages of congratulations.

Facts: Point of Start. 1 mile West of St. Margarets Bay
Point of Finish. Within ¼ mile of Starting Point.
Ted Erikson   America

Report of Swims 1965

PILOT	PETER WINTERS & ARTHUR LIDDEN
BOAT	VEGA

12th SEPTEMBER 1965

POINT OF COMMENCEMENT	20 yds. EAST OF THE EASTERN ARM DOVER
POINT OF FINISH	APPROX. 10 MILES FROM ENGLISH COAST
TOTAL TIME	5 HOURS 20 MINUTES

14th SEPTEMBER 1965

POINT OF COMMENCEMENT	20 yds. EAST OF THE EASTERN ARM DOVER
POINT OF FINISH	3 MILES OFF WISSANT
TOTAL TIME	10 HOURS 2 MINUTES

19th SEPTEMBER 1965

TWO-WAY NON STOP

POINT OF START	1 MILE WEST OF ST. MARGARETS BAY
POINT OF FINISH	¼ MILE EAST OF STARTING POINT (¼ mile off St. Margarets Bay, England)
ENGLAND TO FRANCE TIME	14 HOURS 15 MINUTES
FRANCE TO ENGLAND TIME (return)	15 HOURS 48 MINUTES
TOTAL TIME	30 HOURS 3 MINUTES

RECORD

OLD RECORD: ANTONIO ABERTONDO 1961—
43 HOURS 10 MINUTES
13 HOURS 7 MINUTES OFF

TED ERIKSON   AMERICA
RECORD BREAKING ENGLISH CHANNEL DOUBLE SWIM—
30 HOURS 3 MINUTES

The motor yacht 'Vega' left the inner harbour at Dover on 19th September 1965 at 7.15 p.m. and proceeded to St. Margarets Bay some 3 miles to the East, on board were the Capt. P. Winter, the pilot A. Lydden, the engineer Miss C. Sharp, and the Channel Swimming Association Officials Miss N. Martin and myself. The Vega cruised some ½ mile off shore, it was very dark. Capt. Winter, Miss Martin and myself went ashore in the dingy clad in swim-suites to verify the time of starting, and to see that the rules of the C.S.A. were carried out.

The pilot gave me instructions as to the time of starting and to take the swimmer about one mile from the bay Westwards and to start from the rocks, the starting time, 8.15 p.m.

At about 7.50 p.m. we struck the beach with our punt in an awkward swell to give us our first "ducking", there we found Reg Barrett our Assistant Secretary of the C.S.A. busy greasing up the swimmer; the swimmer entered the punt after another ducking, and the Capt started the outboard. It was not long before we reached our starting point; we got Ted into the water some 20 yards off the rocky shore, in a few minutes he was standing on the rocks; I shouted him in at 8.10 p.m. There was no sense in making him wait another 5 minutes in the cold. Ted then followed us to the Vega where the pilot took over, and we dried off and put on our warm clothing.

9.10 p.m. We now have St. Margarets about 1 mile astern with a starlight sky, but very dark; the water temperature is 59°F., lights on sea fronts of Deal and Ramsgate very clear, as all those at Dover, the South Goodwin lightship is on our port bow some 2 miles away, as the remainder of the flood tide takes us to the East, we are steering 135°.

10.15 p.m. Passing South Goodwin lightship 300 yards on starboard beam, land side. Ostende ferry passed ½ mile ahead, sea calm, air temperature 54°F., sea 59°F., stroking 60.

11.30 p.m. Steering 140°, water slack, very dark but clear for all light houses and vessels.

12.18 a.m. South Goodwin lightship dead astern and Calais dead ahead.

12.30 a.m. First feed, coffee and glucose warm.

1.30 a.m. Second feed, yoke of egg, milk and glucose, hot, he requests bigger feed next time.

2.40 a.m. Ran through shoal of jelly fish, Ted flew across to the starboard side for 10 mins. no complaints about being stung, but rotten feeling against his body, we could see the white patches quite plainly, Ted now back on port side.

3.15 a.m. Ted has another feed of corn syrup and mashed peaches. I estimate the South Goodwin lightship some 6 miles astern. Cap Gris Nez some 8 miles to the South, the ebb tide is taking us away to the West now, steering 135°.

The Channel

4.45 a.m. Another feed as before, we appear to be about 5 miles from France.

5.45 a.m. Our position is not too good, we are not far enough to the West, now the flood starts to set.

6.30 a.m. Ted has good feed, peaches mashed, corn syrup and carton brown sugar. We are about 3 miles off Sangatte, the pilot has asked Ted for a spurt for an hour, to get inside of the next flood tide, & now probably make Calais.

7.30 a.m. We are now closing with the memorial of the French Dover patrol on top of the cliffs looking at us.

7.45 a.m. The pilot and I have just had breakfast; cereal, 2 eggs, 2 rashers bacon, 2 sausages, 2 tomatoes, 2 slices of toast, marmalade and coffee. Thanks to our engineer.

8.00 a.m. Now only 2 miles from Sandgatte, steering 165°. Ted takes coffee and glucose.

8.05 a.m. Enterprise II slows down and passes 300 yards on port beam.

8.10 a.m. No complaints from Ted after 12 hours, his stroke has dropped to 58, and I tell him I want the other two.

9.10 a.m. Ted full of beans now, 1 mile from Calais Harbour with any luck, we should start back with about 7 hours ebb, could not be better, hope the weather holds out.

10.10 a.m. After 14 hours we are now running in on West side of Calais Harbour some ¼ mile in slack water steering 160°.

10.17 a.m. Enterprise I entering Calais Harbour on our port side.

10.17 a.m. Peter Winters, Miss Martin and myself leave in the punt for another ducking and to receive Ted on the sands, before leaving I instructed all not to touch him (Ted) during his stay of 10 minutes, if he wanted grease on his back, I would put it on.

10.20 a.m. We are welcomed ashore by a dozen ladies and men and a shrimper, Peter's French tells them to keep clear and we are swimming back.

10.25 a.m. Ted leaves the water, falling once only, then coming straight in, he was very cold, he asked for grease on his stomach and back. I put on about 3 lbs. lanolin, Ted takes hot coffee, I then escorted him back in the water.

10.35 a.m. Ted restarts his swim back to England, the sea away from the shore is dead calm but we take the usual ducking before getting into the punt to return to the Vega laying off shore some ¼ mile, I took a whole sea in my lap. We reach Vega all aboard except 'one.' and we set course 310° for home.

10.45 a.m. Compagne leaving Calais.

11.40 a.m. Enterprise II. car ferry passing ¼ mile port beam going to Calais.

11.50 a.m. Enterprise I car ferry passing ¼ mile port beam going to Dover.

12.25 p.m. Air temp. now 78°F. in the sun, sea dead calm 60°F. steering 310°, leaving war memorial in France 4 miles on port beam.

1.00 p.m. Wind increasing to force 3 with swell and chop, we all pray this will not increase.

1.15 p.m. Wind now force ¾ W.N.W., nasty chop boat rolling unable to write, only between rolls, steering 310°. Ted feeding every 75 minutes, tomato soup, corn syrup, coffee and glucose, mashed peaches.

1.40 p.m. Normania passes 2 miles to starboard to Calais.

2.00 p.m. Just received Shipping Forecast over the air. S.W. force 3 or less, this is good news which we quickly pass on to Ted as at the moment it is quite rough, and we ask him to come round on the lee side.

2.20 p.m. Enterprise II. passing on starboard beam 2 miles; heading to Dover.

3.30 p.m. We have the French Patrol Memorial dead astern 6 miles, the ebb is not very strong, and we want to go West. Ted has another feed of tomato soup, corn syrup, He is now feeling the cold, and showing signs of fatigue.

4.35 p.m. Ted stiff, feeling the cold and asks for hot coffee often, we are about halfway back, and he wants to know how long it will take.

5.00 p.m. We estimate he will require another 8 hours, which will mean some 15 hours or more, this added to the 14 hours 15 minutes in water at 59°F. is pretty terrible. Now white lies start, we cannot tell him the truth.

5.45 p.m. We can now see Dover Castle and the Harbour, our fix gives us about 10 miles out from Dover, the flood tide starts shortly, this should, we hope bring us inside the South Goodwin Lightship, we gave Ted the news, told him if he kept going we should be home by Midnight, that is another 6 hours, what a hope! but we must keep him going, he says he is so cold, All lies told on Channel swims are not entered in the big "Book" above, there is no book big enough.

6.35 p.m. More food, steering 310°, we grumble at him every time he stops, our position is 9 miles S.E. of Dover.

8.30 p.m. We are rolling so badly I cannot write and take the temperature.

8.35 p.m. Another shoal of jelly fish, Ted shouts, he wonders in the dark what are hitting his body. Ted has been swimming 10 hours back to England and so very tired and cold. We have to start going for him, we cannot show pity, he has now been swimming for 24 hours 15 minutes, it is very dark, and out come the torches again, partly for company, and partly so that we do not lose him, we will have got some fifteen hours holding torches, cold job! but we know he is watching us 25 feet away.

12.35 p.m. We are now about ½ mile from St. Margarets Bay, he is very tired, we have told him a thousand lies, this ½ mile is getting to be murder, it is a good job we are in slack water, we try very hard to get him on the land side of the South Goodwin Lightship earlier, but he was stopping so often, we passed the Lightship on the East side, then the Lightship buoy, after which we knew, we had only to keep him in the water to WIN.

Between 1 a.m. and 2.20 a.m. we had to fight all the way, Peter, Nioma and I got into the Punt and tried to get him along, what we called him, is nobody's business. The Vega left us to continue with the swimmer for the last 400 yards, it was very dark and required two torches to keep him in view, we dare not get too close for he would have grabbed the boat, we shouted him all the way in, we lied so often he rumbled us, we could see our friends and their lights on the beach at St Margarets Bay, now only 200 yards away.

We were unable to make it into St Margarets Bay, and took him in to the rocks straight ahead, we heard a woman's voice shouting from the cliff 200 feet above, it was Mrs. Martin. We finally made the rocks, not more than 300 yards from the spot where he started some 30 hours before. Ted soon recovered lying on a hung rock attached to the base of the cliffs with about a foot deep in seaweed as a cushion. After a few minutes rest we got Ted into the boat which was bumping into the rocks, we were about to leave for the Vega when two photographers who had been clambering over the rocks somehow, called us back 20 yards and took many flashlight photos. We then started back to the Vega getting Ted aboard to warm him up, The Vega then made off for Dover where we arrived about 3 a.m. to be met by all our friends and many photographers and press representatives. By now Ted was full of beans, and was taken home for a nice bath to remove the grease, and so ended a swim of 30 hours 3 minutes that will probably last for many years, having beaten the record by 13 hours 7 minutes.

Signed: Dick Powell
CSA Observer

On August 15, 1970 Kevin Murphy, a twenty-one-year-old reporter, became the first Englishman and third person to make the double cross. His time of thirty-five hours ten minutes is about half way between that of Abertondo and Erikson. Kevin added to his laurels the following year. On September 24, 1971 he completed the first circumnavigation of the island of Wight in the English Channel. The swim took him twenty-seven hours. He swam at least fifty-six miles.

The passing years have seen younger and younger swimmers making the swim. With the advent of scientific training the world records at each Olympics are being set by swimmers in their early or middle teens. The same holds true for some of the marathon events. In 1964 a young American schoolgirl by the name of Lenore Modell swam from France to Dover in fifteen hours and forty minutes. The young lass was only fourteen years old. The year before she had at the tender age swum the length of Lake Tahoe—a distance of twenty-five miles. The water was seventy-eight degrees. Her coach attributes her striking performance to scientific training, raw liver, and iron pills. The physiologists may query, "Because of or in spite of?" Lenore's performance set in motion a surge of attempts by the younger generation. In 1965, Philip Gollop, sixteen, of England established the youth record for boys when he made the route in fourteen hours and thirty-one minutes. One thing leads to another naturally, so Ted Erikson, famed record holder of the Channel double cross, put his talented son to work in 1968. The results were striking. On August 11, 1969, Jon became the youngest boy (he was only two months older than Lenore) to accom-

Tidal Information

Place	Height above datum of soundings			
	High Water		Low Water	
	Mean Springs	Mean Neaps	Mean Springs	Mean Neaps
Dungeness	23.6 feet	18.6 feet	1.3 feet	5.7 feet
Folkestone	20.6 "	16.4 "	0.3 "	4.5 "
Dover	19.1 "	15.1 "	0.3 "	4.5 "
Deal	17.3 "	14.2 "		
Ramsgate	16.2 "	13.0 "	0.7 "	4.1 "
Margate	14.1 "	11.6 "	0.1 "	2.7 "
Herne Bay	15.6 "	12.6 "	0.0 "	2.1 "
Dunkerque	19.0 "	15.7 "	2.3 "	4.6 "
Gravelines	19.5 "	15.9 "	1.8 "	4.2 "
Calais	22.6 "	18.6 "	2.3 "	6.0 "
Wissant	24.6 "	20.6 "	2.0 "	6.9 "
Boulogne	29.2 "	24.0 "	3.1 "	8.5 "

BRITISH UNITS — METRES

Feet	6	12	18	24	30	36	42	48	54	60
Fathoms	1	2	3	4	5	6	7	8	9	10
Feet										
	1.8	3.6	5.5	7.3	9.1	10.9	12.8	14.6	16.4	18.3
1	0.3	2.1	3.9	5.8	7.6	9.4	11.3	13.1	14.9	16.7	18.6
2	0.6	2.4	4.2	6.1	7.9	9.7	11.6	13.4	15.2	17.0	18.9
3	0.9	2.7	4.5	6.4	8.2	10.0	11.9	13.7	15.5	17.3	19.2
4	1.2	3.0	4.9	6.7	8.5	10.3	12.2	14.0	15.8	17.7	19.5
5	1.5	3.3	5.2	7.0	8.8	10.6	12.5	14.3	16.1	18.0	19.8

TIDAL STREAMS REFERRED TO H.W. AT DOVER

[Detailed tidal stream tables with directions and rates (knots) at Springs and Neaps for multiple positions, referenced at hourly intervals before and after H.W. Dover]

One of the most important tables to a Channel swimmer. It tells the speed and direction of tidal streams at hourly intervals. Used with a nautical chart of the Straits of Dover, its value is inestimable (or so thought by many). Some swimmers, however, have ignored the chart and just kept a constant compass heading. Its greatest value probably lies in leaving and arriving at the shoreline.

plish the trick. Jon's time became the fourth fastest ever recorded for the France to England route, eleven hours twenty-three minutes. The record of nine hours thirty-five minutes is currently held by Barry Watson of England who clocked it in 1964.

Jon is one of the best built boys ever for his age. His weight of 178 pounds is spread over a muscular five-foot-nine-inch frame. He lost about twelve pounds during the swim—one half of which was fat, the rest water.

Like any other endeavor undertaken by man, the Channel offers innumerable possibilities. Legless, spastic, and blind persons have made the attempt all with poor results. At least a goal is offered. A

Young Jon Erikson three weeks before he became the youngest man to ever swim the English Channel. Jon was fourteen when he swam from France to England in the fourth-fastest time ever recorded, eleven hours and twenty-three minutes in 1969. The photo shows a powerful 178-pound frame spread over five feet nine inches. Jon is the son of the current record holder of a Channel double cross, **Ted Erikson.** Courtesy Verne Petro Photo.

few times the goal is misappropriated by unstable individuals. The result is death. The first recorded death of a swimmer trying to make the swim unescorted was in 1926. On September 29th of that year the body of a young Spaniard, who was a member of a prominent Madrid family, was washed ashore at Boulogne. Young Luis Rodriguez Delara entered the water secretly from the shores of France and struck out for England hoping to be the first man to make the swim without the benefits of guide boats and food. Nature just as secretly took care of the deluded young man.

Around September 20, 1954 an Englishman by the name of Ted May met the same fate. May, forty-four and weighing 240 pounds, had been refused entry into the Butlin Channel Race a few weeks before for medical reasons. He went home and concocted a plan for a solo swim. Sometime during the day on September 19th, May walked down to a secluded spot on the beach at Cape Griz-Nez carrying a bundle. Taking off his clothes and unwrapping the bundle, which contained an innertube with liquid food, he greased up. After setting his watch, attaching a rope around his waist to which the innertube was fastened, he entered the water and struck out for France. The weather turned sour after about twelve hours. About fifteen hours after entering the water he was spotted by a merchant ship wildly waving his arms amidst the huge seas that had built up. By the time the ship had turned back they had lost sight of him. Radio reports brought out a full-scale sea and air search. It was abandoned after thirty-two hours. No trace of Ted May was ever found.

The latest fad for those who do not have the speed or stamina to complete a channel swim nonstop is the relay pitch. Four or more swimmers will team up to swim segments of the distance. When one gets tired or cold he is relieved by another swimmer from the boat. The lure of a channel accomplishment is endless.

> There was a young man from Ostend
> Who said he'd vow to the end.
>   But when half way over
>   From Calais to Dover
> He did what he didn't intend.

CHANNEL RACE RESULTS

1950 RACE

			Prize
1. Hassan Abd-el-Rheim (Egypt)	10 Hrs.	50 Min.	£1,000
2. Rober de Morvan (France)	11	02	250
3. M. H. Hamad (Egypt)	12	10	250
4. Sam Rockett (England)	14	20	250
5. Ned Barnie (England)	14	50	250
6. Eileen Fenton (England)	15	31	£1,000 (first woman)

The Channel 75

7. Jason Zirganos (Greece)	16	19
8. Antonio Abertondo (Argentina)	16	25
9. Jenny Kammersgurd (Denmark)	16	30

1951 RACE

1. M. H. Hamad (Egypt)	12 Hrs.	12 Min.	£1,000
2. Roger de Morvan (France)	12	13	500
3. Hassan Abd-el-Rheim (Egypt)	12	25	250
4. Said el Arabi (Egypt)	12	42	250
5. Brenda Fisher (England)	12	42	£1,000 (first woman)
6. G. Chapman (England)	12	56	
7. Winnie Roach (Canada)	13	25	
8. Enriquetta Duarte (Argentina)	13	26	
9. Lars B. Warle (Sweden)	13	28	
10. Raphael Morand (France)	13	45	
11. Daniel Carpio (Peru)	13	50	
12. Jenny James (England)	13	55	
13. Jazon Zirganos (Greece)	14	10	
14. Antonio Abertondo (Argentina)	14	14	
15. J. van Hemsburgen (Holland)	14	20	
16. Sally Bauer (Sweden)	14	40	
17. Ned Barnie (England)	15	01	
18. Jenny Kammersgurd (Denmark)	15	38	

1952

No Race Because of lack of sponsor

1953 RACE

This is the first year in which a new sponsor took over the race. There were no finishers. Looking at the names of the competitors leads one to believe that the race was organized too late to inform the top swimmers spread out over the world. Inclement weather and/or no top-notch swimmers led to no one completing the swim. Those who lasted the longest are listed. No times given.
1. W. E. Barnie (Scotland)
2. Margaret Feather (England)
3. Kenneth Wray (England)
4. Elna Andersen (Denmark)
5. Victor Birkett (England)
6. Fred Gill (England)

1954 RACE

1. B. Periera (Portugal)	12 Hrs.	25 Min.
2. M. H. Hamad (Egypt)	12	49
3. Brenda Fisher (England)	14	36
4. Jason Zirganos (Greece)	16	23
5. Margaret Feather (England)	16	52
6. Antonio Abertondo (Argentina)	16	53
7. M. El Soussi (Syria)	17	55

1955 RACE

1. Abdel-Latif Abo-Heif (Egypt)	11	44
2. Tom Park (U.S.A.)	12	02
3. Syder Guiscardo (Argentina)	14	33
4. Damien Beltran (Mexico)	15	08

1956 RACE

Inclement weather from the start. No finishers. The swimmers listed below lasted for about eleven hours. Prize money was still awarded.

1. Tom Park (U.S.A.)
   Jack McClelland (Ireland)
shared 1st place prize

1. Diane Cleverly (New Zealand)
   Maria Meesters (Holland)
shared 1st place women's prize

1957 RACE

Inclement weather. Twenty-four started, two finished.

1. Greta Andersen (U.S.A.)   13 Hrs. 53 Min.   WOMAN. All round winner.
   Picks up men & women's prizes.
2. Ken Wray (England)   16   00

1958 RACE

1. Greta Andersen (U.S.A.)   11 Hrs. 01 Min.   WOMAN. All round winner.

This year the sponsors divided the race into two. Men and women. Even though they started at the same time they would be competing for different prizes. Such an announcement doesn't stop the competition by any means though once in the water.

1. Brojan Das (Pakistan)   14   52   A purist calls it 2nd
2. Ronald Tarr (England)   15   12
3. Raphael Morand (France)   16   22
4. Ramon Ocana (Mexico)   17   05

1959 RACE

1. Alfredo Camerero (Argentina)   11 Hrs. 43 Min.
2. Herman Willemse (Holland)   12   49
3. Baptista Periera (Portugal)   13   12
4. Helge Jensen (Denmark)   13   17

   Helge went on to set a Channel record in a solo swim in 1960. His time for that swim was 10 hours 23 minutes—England to France.

5. Brojen Das (Pakistan)   13   53
6. El Nawab (Iraq)   15   12
7. William Bristowe (England)   18   01

Women

1. Greta Andersen (USA)   15   25
2. Myra Thompson (USA)   15   35

1960 RACE

This race was cancelled and no professional race has been held since.

Sponsoring of professional swimming events is loaded with pitfalls. The amount of money that can be spent reaches almost astronomical heights. Boats must be provided for each swimmer, professional course setters must be hired, room and board provided and paid for by sponsors. Press meetings, medical examinations, insurance are just a few more of the insidious expenses that creep in. I was told by the sponsor (and I believe it) of the 1963 Lake Michigan Swim (sixty miles) that the swim cost him $35,000 exclusive of $15,000 prize money. Everything is relative however for he probably got $100,000 free advertising for his auto sales shop, which at that time was the largest Ford dealership in the world.

The Channel Swimming Association records list the successful English Channel swims made by solo swimmers. To date only about seventy persons have made the England-to-France course, about 150 have made the France-to-England course. Since the solo swimmer can select his day, whereas the professional usually leaves on the official race day (regardless of weather and conditions), his time can compare quite favorably with the professional. It should be kept in mind that the solo swimmer in most cases (unless he is also a professional) is not of the same calibre as the professional.

5
Why?

"Why do they do it?" is a question asked by many. At times that question irks me. Other times one can be more compassionate. The only answer that can be given to the person who asks that question is, "Because they are different." The same question may be asked on one practicing any profession. What keeps the research scientist in the laboratory for sixteen hours a day month after month? What keeps the professional boxer or football player periodically exposing himself to possible serious injury? What keeps the executive constantly driving to surpass his competitors? The answer to these questions may have been partially answered in the opening chapters. It is man's heritage that keeps him going. A possible reason may lie in the answer given by the recreated Neanderthal man being questioned by a modern-day newsman in a comedy skit. The questioner puts to the Neanderthal man the following: "Sir, people living in today's modern world are overwhelmed with the stresses and tensions forced upon them: paying the rent, commuting to and from work in traffic snarls, crime, and loss of individuality. Many of them out there in the audience would like to know primitive man's secret in coping with the stresses and tensions of his time. How did Neanderthal man cope with savage beasts ready to eat him, floods, disease, and starvation? What kept you going in that era without tranquilizers?" Neanderthal man answered with: "It was very simple. I can answer that question with one word: FEAR." That answer comes closer than we would like to admit. It is true of many today that it is fear that keeps them going. There is nothing in that to be ashamed of for it is nature's way of assuring survival. There are too many elements that can take advantage of prolonged indifference or acceptance of one's present state.

However, fear is not the only answer, though it may certainly be a major one. In my twenty years of observing the world-champion swimmers I have discovered an interesting common denominator. It became evident while discussing their personal lives with them. Hours of conversation with fourteen swimmers who were crowned world champions, or number two, for one or more years brought to light the fact that twelve of them were under severe emotional tension during the time they were champions. Only two were not under such tension and seemed to have planned a course of action that led to their achievement without emotional involvement. The others were reacting to the tensions incurred by: 1) the breakup of a marriage and divorce 2) loss of a job 3) sexual maladjustments. Physiologists tell us that such serious threats to one's personal life are manifested by bodily response. The pituitary gland lying at the base of the brain secretes more of the substances that monitor brain and bodily functions. One of the responses is extreme nervousness and tension. Luckily, those professional swimmers reacted normally to the stimulus by working it off in training. They were tranquilizing themselves in the most sensible fashion: action. Of course, this is not the whole answer, but I believe it is an important one. Certainly the need to earn one's living and the human drive for recognition by his fellows are also important. One must give weight to all these possibilities and their combinations.

In summary we must also return to the inevitable differences in those who undertake these gargantuan feats. Certainly the neurasthenic does not undertake a twenty-five-mile swim. Nor do the depressed attempt to seek action. We must also remember that man's heritage as a hunter kept him on the move, sometimes for days. The marathon swimmer's ten-, twenty-, and thirty-hour endeavors pall behind the feats of our primitive brethren. This in no way denigrates the feats described in our history. It only places them in the proper perspective. One can lose oneself in the philosophy of "why." In the final analysis all one can do is describe the laws of nature and man's accomplishments and let each individual arrive at his own interpretation. We are all the products and the victims of our heredity and our experiences. The spindly limbed bookkeeper may read of such feats with admiration, or say, "What a stupid thing to do." The pursuit of easy-chair activities like cards and chess are truth to him. The marathoner may consider such stale air pursuits the height of degeneration. They are both right and both wrong. One always brings himself to whatever challenge he undertakes.

It may be of interest to the reader to learn that the Greeks, in their Olympic games, never ran the marathon. Some historians say that the longest event was the mile, and they are not even sure it was that long. The basic Greek view of athletics was that a sense of well-being was the goal. They recognized the importance of *ponos*, or the feeling of well-being, not only in games, but in all phases of their life. They practiced their basic principle of "nothing in excess." This view of life, admirable though it may be, could only be practiced by the wealthy and the political class. The tribulations of environment and nature precluded the farmer and manufacturer from practicing such an ideal. The Greeks were great slave owners and you can rest assured that the slaves didn't work only when they felt like it.

The rewards, we must deduce, are meaningful to those who compete. I can only recount and describe some of the turmoils that the swimmers undergo and let the reader form his own conclusions. A fact all too evident to doctors, psychologists, and discerning laymen is that no two individuals react to a situation in the same manner. This is no more evident than in what takes place in each swimmer the night before a swim. Some pace the floor. Others go to bed at their accustomed hour and fall asleep, although this is uncommon. The explanation is mainly physical. Since all of the swimmers have stopped their heavy training about a week before the event the rest has allowed the body to recharge its batteries. Soon, if planning and chance are right, nervousness and tension build up. Whereas the energy had been previously expended it is now bottled up. Instead of rest the body is demanding expenditure of energy. Consequently rest and sleep become almost impossible the night before. One way this is handled is by prolonged social contact among the swimmers. Hour after hour is spent in joking, talking, movie going, and parties. When the long day is done they hope that the tired brain will allow them repose. A few swimmers will actually go in the opposite direction the day before. They become more sullen, withdrawing from all social contact. They hole themselves up in their rooms unable to relate to anyone or anything. They are the unfortunates.

Others will take sleeping pills, the lesser of two evils: a sleepless night or a hazy start the next day. Perhaps I make too much of "why." Perhaps the answer is lost in the recesses of man's psychology. Perhaps in the final diagnosis it is a foolish question. The police officer facing the armed criminal, the climber of Mount Everest, the sea captain taking his vessel through a typhoon, as well as the swimmer facing the cold waters of the English Channel or the Straits of Juan de Fuca all are doing nothing more than what they or society asks. Whenever man enters the water to swim he is taking a risk, and perhaps that is all he asks; otherwise life would be dreary indeed.

The risk may be other than cold and waves, for other living creatures inhabit the water also. Man is entering an element that is not solely his own and when he does interesting things happen. Sharks may be a very serious threat to life and limb. In the world's oceans, the area between the forty-two degrees north and forty-two degrees south latitudes offer solicitude to those famous predators of which man is but one delicacy. Greta Andersen and Keo Nakama used wire cages in their Molokai Straits swims. Linda McGill used them in her

Australian swims. Shark authorities over the world have sent documented cases of shark attacks to a central clearing house for years. The coasts of the United States, Mexico, South Africa, and Australia are notorious for the "feeding" of human flesh to sharks for years. Man calmly proceeds on his accustomed ways after a fatality. You don't stop driving your car after a traffic death. Dr. Verne Coppleson for years visited the site of every shark attack in Australia and gathered as many facts as possible. After a lifetime of study he published a book called *Shark Attack* that will chill your bones. Case histories are vividly and factually presented. In those cases in which they were available, photos are given. Corpses with missing arms or legs leave the viewer queasy whether he is a swimmer or not. Coppleson even describes a few cases, with photos, in which the whole lower body was severed in one bite. It is very easy to elicit a hatred for the shark, but one should remember that it is man who is imposing on the wild creature's ground. The shark, when he bites man, is only living up to his natural instincts that have evolved over millions of years. Nature has made him one of the most efficient predators of the sea. He cannot be blamed for being attracted to such an easy meal as man presents. After all, sharks venturing or being washed up on land would be considered food by the land predators and carrion eaters.

Porpoises, even though harmless and highly intelligent, have caused their share of fright to men in the water because of their superficial resemblance to sharks. Few swimmers remain in the water after they spot them because they are not about to get out an identification manual. Discretion then becomes the better part of valor.

When a swimmer runs into a jellyfish there is no doubt about the fact. Jellyfish and the renowned Portuguese man 'o war are beautiful examples of nature in action. Below the gelatinous "sail" that floats on the surface there dangle many fine threads that contain specialized organs known to marine biologists as nematocysts. They contain a finely coiled living spring. Whenever this organ is touched, excepting a few rare species of fish, it immediately releases this coiled barb that pricks and pierces the skin of the animal body touching it. A few are harmless. A solid contact means hundreds, if not thousands, of these nematocysts are triggered into the body. Along with this prick goes the release of a poison that numbs and kills the animal. Small fish so benumbed are brought slowly up to the main body to be eventually dissolved and absorbed by the jellyfish. When man runs into a man 'o war the results vary from minor irritation, serious skin eruption, and sometimes death if the victim is allergic to the poison. When Ted Erikson made his world-record round trip of the English Channel he ran into a colony of jellyfish at about the twenty-five hour mark. His skin was severely lacerated, but luckily he was through the colony in a short time. He carried the lacerations for a week after the swim.

While the "big" things can bring havoc, the little things cannot be discounted. The fungus, bacteria, and viruses can make serious inroads in the well being of swimmers just as they do to the rest of us. Anyone who has ever had an ear infection knows that it is a very serious matter. Life, no matter what form it takes, is always ready to take advantage of a good thing. Eyes, ears, sinuses, and skin are all fair game to these living forms. The little things, like coral, can grow into big things. The number of swimmers and bathers that have cut themselves on coral reefs is legion.

One of the most unhappy things that can happen to a marathoner is to swim into an oil slick. While the experienced swimmer can ignore it, and he better be wearing goggles if he chooses to ignore it, it can make the tender quit. The problem becomes even more serious when there is gasoline on the water. Evaporation at the surface causes the swimmer to inhale the vapors. A short time of this is enough to put the most stalwart of marathoners out of the game. Ships releasing dirty bilge water have been known to stop some swimmers because of nausea.

There can be the lighter moments, like the time a seal popped up alongside Abo-Heif in the Saguenay River during a swim. Abo-Heif and Matuch had been swimming alongside for hours in first place with the nearest competitor two miles behind. Abo-Heif at this moment went for the lead and slowly pulled ahead of Matuch. Suddenly fifteen yards to the side of Abo-Heif an "object" popped out of the water. It confused me for I couldn't see how a swimmer could have gotten so near us so soon. Then I thought of sharks. When, after a few moments study, I saw that it was a curious seal, I broke out in laughter. The seal swam toward Abo-Heif with his head held high in curiosity. When he came within five yards of him he dove and was never seen again.

In any case the attractions of marathon swimming are great enough to lure the men whom it must lure. If one would understand the irresistible attraction he would do well to read two famous fiction pieces that describe with literary beauty the attraction that exists between man and water. Two of these stories deal with death by drowning. Pierre Loti's *Icelandic Fisherman* tells of a sea captain's final drowning as his wife accompanies him to the edge of the sea. The other, *The Women* by Ray Bradbury, is much the same only in a modern setting. All that can be said is that man is attracted to water in the same fashion as he is attracted to a beautiful woman or a tasty meal. Would we say it was a matter of chemistry? Such things are the mysteries of life.

6
Catalina Island: The Chewing Gum Swim

William Wrigley, Jr. laid down his newspaper and stared off into space. The banner headlines carried the story of Gertrude Ederle's great swim across the Channel. In the weeks that followed, Wrigley found himself again and again thinking about Trudy's ticker-tape reception in New York and the hundreds of thousands who lined the sidewalks awaiting their chance to glimpse the heroine. He read of the movie contracts and speaking engagements she was offered. Like most wealthy men, William Wrigley, Jr.'s mind worked on many tangents at the same time. The multimillionaire chewing gum king found it hard to separate business and pleasure. Indeed they were inseparable to him. Ever since that first headline describing Trudy's successful swim, he had begun to form an idea. The later articles only solidified it. If successful his idea would result in millions of dollars of free publicity and a like number of new chewers for his snappy product.

In 1919 Wrigley, in the course of finding things to do with his millions, had bought a large island off the coast of Southern California. The island, Santa Catalina, is among a group known as the Santa Barbara Channel Islands. Discovered in 1542 by Portuguese explorers they had an interesting history as an Indian habitat, pirate station, seal hunting area, and finally as the locale of silver and gold exploitation. The last touched off a migration of cut-throats that lasted for twenty years before peace was once again restored to the island. From the middle of the 1800s to when Wrigley took over in 1918 the island had served as a focal point for land speculators, tourists seeking respite from Los Angeles summer heat, and deep sea fishers. When Wrigley took over the island he had several prospects in mind. One was to build a private estate on it. The castlelike estate, which was soon built, was reminiscent of the feudal era. His estate, and the island's only harbor, Avalon, would also serve as a jumping off place to one of the world's finest deep-sea fishing areas. When Wrigley bought the island he knew that it was being used during the summer months by many thousands of mainlanders. His first idea was to put up no trespassing signs like other owners did on the other Santa Barbara Islands. But when he was told that the summer tourist trade amounted to thirty thousand people he had second thoughts. These thirty thousand people bought tickets on the ferry boats taking them to the island. They also bought tents to pitch while on the island, picnic equipment, deep-sea fishing gear, and a host of other accoutrements necessary to the vacationer. The dollar sign wheels began to turn in Wrigley's mind. As mentioned before Wrigley was a man to mix pleasure with profit. He suddenly waxed keen over a profitable island home. Wrigley immediately decided to keep the island open to tourists. He also began to drop millions in investing in the island's future. He bought stock in the ferry service, which was getting five dollars a head to bring the tourists across twenty-five miles of water. New docking facilities were built at Avalon. Three hotels, a gambling casino, bird sanctuaries, and golf courses were built. Low dams were erected to catch the very limited rainfall. Yes, he saw it grow and it was good. In a very short time Wrigley had converted the island from a fly- and goatridden stew to a romantic island tourist trap. With each passing year the profits increased. The only catch, and a catch that bothers all businessmen, was that the profits from Catalina were irregular. The reason was simple. From a high of thirty thousand tourists in the summer months, the island's population dwindled to a paltry fifteen hundred in winter. The majority of these were employees of the various concessions. Along with the diminishing numbers of people visiting the island went the corresponding depressing financial return. Yes, the winter months from November through March were financially depressing ones to a man of Wrigley's bent. The reason for Wrigley's master plan of publicity—gum chewers and tourists—now becomes clear. If Gertrude Ederle's Channel swim demanded such publicity, why shouldn't a Catalina Channel, or to be more exact, a San Pedro Channel swim receive a like amount, especially if a large amount of money, say $25,000 or $50,000 was offered as an inducement to the swimmers.

Wrigley got his promotion rolling in late fall of 1926. Within days the news traveled over the world. The swim became known as the Wrigley Catalina Island Swim. Total prize money offered for the race, which was to be held January 15, 1927, was $40,000. $25,000 would go to the first person, man or woman, to reach the breakwater at Point Vincente, one of the suburbs lying on the outskirts of Los Angeles. The Point was marked by a lighthouse and surrounded by golf courses, private yacht clubs, and parks. $15,000 would go to the first woman to finish. There was no stipulation concerning what would happen if the first person happened to be a woman. Theoretically she would, according to the contract, be eligible to collect both prizes, a total of $40,000. On second thought, it is possible that the promoters felt that such an offer added further incentive and would make for an exciting event. It would be of interest to turn a possibly exciting race into a thrilling and compelling extra by turning it into a battle of the sexes. Perhaps they assumed that the winner would automatically be a man, an assumption that had to wait until the 1950s to be proven wrong.

The race would be open to all comers. There would be no entry limit. Wrigley, not to be outdone, touted his swim as a greater challenge than the English Channel. While the English Channel was only twenty-one miles, his Catalina Channel swim would be a twenty-two-mile race. In fact it was likely to be longer because of the tidal streams. This distance became erroneously entered into the record because of the following circumstance. The advertised distance of the swim was from the island's only city, Avalon, to Point Vincente on the mainland. The straight line distance was twenty-two miles. However, the point from which the swimmers left on that fateful day was not Avalon but the Isthmus of Catalina, a point some ten miles to the northwest, toward the other end of the island. The straight line distance from this point to the mainland was only 18.5 miles when measured on a United States Coast and Geodetic Survey Nautical Chart. The reason for this last minute change is lost in time but conjectures can be made. Perhaps the harbor at Avalon was not suited to handle the two hundred boats that would be accompanying the swimmers. There would be badly needed space for the expected sightseers coming to view the event. The holiday atmosphere would fill up the island hotels and restaurants. Another, and more likely reason, was that Wrigley had become impressed with the gambling odds as quoted by the newspapers. All odds were against anyone making the swim. Wrigley, after learning this, probably shifted the starting point to another part of the island that would make the swim some $2\frac{1}{2}$ miles shorter. Above all he wanted a successful swim. An unsuccessful swim would lead to adverse publicity.

Wrigley received some four hundred entries to his swim. As they were received, his agents culled the big names and issued carefully worded accounts of their accomplishments. Among the entries were ex-Channel conquerors and amateur world-record holders. Henry Sullivan and Charles Toth had swum the Channel. Leo Purcell and Mark Wheeler were renowned Californian swimmers. Charlotte Schoemmel, who became the first woman to swim around Manhattan Island in New York, was entered. Others of like fame, for one reason or other, did not enter. Gertrude Ederle was one who didn't. Whether the swimmer's fame was worldwide, national, local, or nonexistent, they all grasped at the chance to win the coveted $25,000. That amount of money would be equal to $100,000 in today's market. A man could make lifetime plans with a bank roll of that size.

The man who got the biggest play of all however was "Big Moose." Two-hundred-and-fifty-pound Norman Ross was recognized the world over. A product of the Illinois Athletic Club in Chicago, Ross held many national and world swimming records. From four hundred yards to two miles he was considered untouchable. In fact Ross was the idol of Johnny Weismuller who would later be named the "Swimmer of the Century." After winning many Chicago and national records Ross earned a berth on the 1920 and 1924 American Olympic swimming teams. He went on to win the four-hundred- and fifteen-hundred-meter events in the 1924 Olympics. Now, three years later and forty pounds heavier he was to test his prowess in the professional ranks. Ross got to California early and began training in the San Pedro Channel. He would leave nothing to chance. Along with his handlers, he studied tide tables and currents. $25,000 would go to the man not only physically best equipped, but also with the plan tactically perfect. Ross, because of his past record and glib tongue (he went on to later laurels as a famed Chicago radio announcer), became the favorite among the newsmen and bettors. If anyone would win the race it would be Ross. His powerful frame was adequately covered with an insulating layer of fat, which would be highly important in the cold water. Combined with the superb body and excellent condition went a first-rate mind that made good copy for publicity. In conversation with the newsmen Ross castigated the swimmers who planned to use grease. "What's the use," he said. "The friction of the water would wear it all off within an hour." Urbane, friendly, and always talkative he made many friends. Ross also planned to swim nude to eliminate any possible drag and to make the elimination of any body waste uncomplicated. Followers of the printed word went down to the beaches off which the swimmers were training. They timed the swimmers in their workouts. All were in agreement that Ross was at least one minute faster per mile than his nearest rival.

The two weeks before the event saw the arrival of most competitors. About fifty of those packed up and went home after their first dip in the cold waters of San Pedro. The average for that time of year was sixty degrees. The readings at various points along the course ranged from a low of fifty-four degrees to a high of sixty-five degrees. The slender swimmers went home. The less intelligent and self-deluded who stayed around for the race left the water after a half hour or so.

Among the 145 entries that actually showed up on the race day, forty-three were scratched for various reasons. There was one name received that got no publicity of note. A seventeen-year-old Canadian amateur champion named George Young. Young, a member of the Toronto West End YMCA, had, during his middle teens, accumulated many trophies and medals for swimming. Included were several Canadian records from two hundred yards to one mile. When Young heard of the race in late September he became immediately enthralled. Living a borderline economic existence with his partly crippled mother in Toronto he felt he had experienced enough of poverty. Besides, the age of seventeen is conducive to adventure.

Young was in his prime. At the peak of condition from swimming four to five miles a day in the "Y" pool he felt he could make a good showing in Wrigley's race. Besides, the rewards of medals and trophies had somehow lost their glitter. It was a tribute to Young's maturity that he decided to lay everything on the line and make plans for the "big race." That decision, he knew, would forever remove him from amateur competition. Away went his entry form.

While keeping to a rigorous training schedule during those fall weeks, Young took up part-time jobs to finance his forthcoming trip to California. As the departure date approached, Young had talked a buddy into making the journey with him. Between them they decided that railway fare was too expensive. They would have to find the cheapest possible transportation. The decision came when serendipity and a second-hand motorcycle with side car attached was offered for sale by a neighborhood cycle shop. Together the two pooled their resources and bought the machine. Young's "Y" coach told him that he was undertaking a foolish venture. He said the prolonged journey would rapidly dissipate any condition he was in. Young replied with the resiliency of youth that he would find many a swimming hole en route to swim in. With only his mother's kind words and a few extra dollars given him from her meagre savings, Young, his buddy, and the second-hand motorcycle embarked on the twenty-five-hundred-mile journey to California sometime during the last week in November 1926. If everything went well they would arrive in Los Angeles sometime around December 25, which would allow about three weeks for him to familiarize himself with the swimming conditions.

The tale of the boy's trip to California would be one of horror to the old and infirm but to youth it was adventure. Time after time the cycle broke down. Young and his buddy were forced to find odd jobs to pay for repairs and their own sustenance. Time began to work against them. Sometimes it was three days before Young could find a pond, lake, or river to train in. The end seemed to come when they reached Little Rock, Arkansas. There the cycle broke down beyond repair. For two days they made abortive attempts at repair only to be frustrated by lack of funds. What Young's coach had said in Toronto seemed to be coming true. The four- to six-week journey would remove his fine physical condition. On their third day in Little Rock they met a young honeymooning couple. With natural boyhood ebullience they told of their plans to reach California and enter the Wrigley swim. The aspirations of youth and the love of humanity that characterize newlyweds resulted in Young and his companion being given a lift all the way to Los Angeles. There they and their new-found friends parted, little realizing the fortunes of fate to be played. Their arrival was perfectly timed. Young bedded down for three weeks of planning and conditioning.

It was a very short time before Young made his first trip out to the Los Angeles beaches to swim. There he would plunge into the water without giving thought to some of the world's greatest swimmers who surrounded him! He delighted in coming down to the beach daily and swimming his three, four, or five miles and then lolling on the sands to absorb the sun's rays. When the winter winds were too cool, for Southern California in January while not cold was neither very warm, he sought out an indoor pool. It was in one of these pools that an unscrupulous operator took advantage of Young's youth and naïveté. Being away from home for the first time in his life and without funds Young was a perfect set-up for a confidence man. Gaining the confidence of Young, the man offered to pay his expenses for the three weeks until the swim date. He would accompany Young in a boat and feed him. In return for these services he would receive forty percent of the prize money if George should win. He would also get forty percent of any sums coming to George for one year following. George readily agreed, being hungry for a father figure. His new found "coach" and manager, realizing that George was under the legal age for the signing of a contract, shrewdly mailed one off to his mother for signing. Within a week, by return mail, an iron bound contract signed by George's mother was in the manager's hands. Never was $10,400 more easily earned for three weeks of friendship. That would be about $40,000 today. More would come later in the year.

As the swim date approached the fanfare and preparations increased. The Catalina Company that Wrigley had shrewdly incorporated a few years earlier, issued daily blurbs. Boats by the hundreds were solicited to offer their services to the swimmers for free. In fact Wrigley had to hire only about fifteen official boats. They would set the course, observe the swimmers, and issue progress reports during the race. Ferry boats to Catalina were expected to be carrying full loads of spectators and tourists to watch the start of the swim. Two days before the swim the hotels on the island were overflowing with tourists. Employees of the concessions who had been let go with the decrease in business at the end of the summer season were all recalled to handle the winter crowds. One can easily imagine the gala holiday season. 1927 was the heyday of American financial splurging. Money was evident all over the continent. The stock market kept exceeding the previous day's high. The world was still two years away from the financial crash of 1929. America was riding the crest of a financial boom that was making millionaires overnight. Nowhere was this more evident than in the tourist paradise of Southern California. The yachts and sailboats that daily sailed the offshore islands had more than their share of financial pashas. The Wrigley $40,000 Catalina Marathon Swim was but a reflection of the times. There would be no swim in the future that would create this kind of publicity.

January 14 saw the swimmers and their coaches being brought to the island. There they were bedded down for the night and last minute preparations made for the swim which would begin at 11 A.M. the following day. Most of the swimmers would be asleep by 8 P.M. Others would spend a restless night attempting to lure the god Morpheus. Coaches attempted to locate their assigned boats. Many could not because they were still on the mainland and would not make their run to the island until early the following morning. Little did the swimmers realize when they went to sleep at Avalon that night that in the morning they would all be put aboard boats and taken to the other end of the island. A last-minute decision had been made by Wrigley and his men to shorten the course by having the swimmers leave from the Isthmus of Catalina. The isthmus was some ten miles to the northwest toward the other end of the island. The straight-line course would thus be shortened to 18.5 instead of twenty-two miles. Wrigley's advisors had decided that the predominant southerly current would make the arrival at Point Vincente too difficult. This bonus to the swimmers would hardly make a note in the publicity to follow. All that the readers would remember would be that the swimmers left from Catalina Island.

At dawn Saturday preparations were hectic. Most swimmers were still sleeping, trying to take advantage of every last moment of rest. By 8 A.M. the last slug-a-bed was aboard the boats that began to ferry the swimmers to the other end of the island. Pennants, loudspeakers, and festivities abounded. Newsmen, radio announcers, and tourists all clamored for attention. For the swimmers there was only tension. Many became queasy and incontinent. Others decided that this was not their day. During the few hours before the swim forty-three withdrew from the race. At 10 A.M., one hour before the start, the total withdrawals had numbered forty-three. The survivors awaiting the gun on the beach numbered 102.

During the last minute ceremonies the mix-ups and general disorientations increased. A few coaches with thermometers waded in the waters of the cove and dipped their instruments into the water. There were gasps at the reported fifty-five-degree temperature. Surely conditions would prevent anyone from finishing even though temperatures farther out were reported to be running sixty-four degrees. It was at this point that many swimmers decided not to try the swim. As delay followed delay tempers began to flare. The Wrigley Swim set a standard that became characteristic of many professional swims that were to follow. The carnival atmosphere offered a titillating subject for those reporters who were humourously inclined. Almost any incident can be viewed from different angles. Those who looked upon the event as a carnival wrote it up as such. Those who looked upon it as a serious sporting event reported that. To a few it was similar to the Roman arena, where instead of the Christians being tossed to the lions, it was the swimmers being sacrificed to the icy waters of San Pedro Channel for the great god Publicity. One reporter commented that he would not have been surprised to see the beefy competitors swinging from trees, such was their similarity to cavemen. Yes indeed, the Wrigley swim to them was no more than a circus. The reader is left to his choice as to how to view the swim. Only one point was clear to the swimmers. While the bally-hoo was ephemeral the $25,000 was cold, hard, and real. So was the water.

As the official starting time approached, a touch of black humor was added as a legless teenage San Francisco newsboy, riding in a cart with rollers, pushed his torso along the planking to the sands. There he was lifted from the cart by two retainers who placed him on the sands near the water's edge. At the starting gun he would be bodily lifted and swung by his arms into the water. He lasted some four hours and for six miles. He went farther and longer than thirty per cent of the other swimmers.

The planned starting time of 11 A.M. came and went. The final ceremonies had still not been completed. Photos and more photos were made. Unassigned boats had to be assigned. Forgotten swim suits and goggles were searched out. A myriad of details gradually diminished. The final humorous (to some) incident before the start occurred was when one swimmer donned a full-length suit of underwear and proceeded to heavily coat it with grease. While his appearance brought laughter to some, to others it brought dismay. It only served to remind them that the water was cold.

Slowly the clock ticked on. Ten after eleven. Fifteen after. At last all 102 swimmers were standing on the beach just inches from the water. At 11:21 A.M. the starter's gun boomed and was followed almost instantaneously by the roar of the massed crowd and blasting boat horns. Immediately the 102 swimmers leaped for the water and the legless boy was thrown in. It took some four or five leaps before they were in thigh deep water where they could then start stroking. The whole spectrum of swimming ability was evident in that first minute after the gun. The excellent ones immediately flailed their way to the lead like it was a hundred yard race. The cautious took up a slow, deliberate pace. Others would stand waist-deep in the water to adjust goggles or hats and to await swimming space. The incompetents took to treading water.

It took some three minutes for the lead swimmers to clear themselves from the mass. At the end of that time two swimmers had significantly pulled ahead. It was soon evident that these two were set on getting the lead from each other. Only twenty yards separated them. The man in front was not the world champion swimmer Norman Ross, but the seventeen-year-old Canadian amateur champion George Young. The 240-pound giant Norman Ross was desperately churning the water in an attempt to catch George even at this early stage. Spectators and observers commented that George might as well enjoy his lead while he could since it would only be a matter of time before the giant would catch him.

In order to clear the harbor and its outlying rocks it was necessary to swim directly out from shore for about a mile. Then each swimmer could adjust his or her course according to what he thought best. When George cleared the harbor in about twenty-three minutes he still held a tenacious twenty-yard lead over Ross. At this point George's coach changed the boat's heading so that instead of making a rum-line toward Point Vincente he made for a point a mile or so to the north. His course was more or less to be "up" the Channel. This was a tactical move thought up by George's coach to take advantage of his swimmer's early strength in combating the southeasterly direction of the current. Then, if all went well, during the latter part of the race George could take advantage of the current in "riding" down-Channel toward Point Vincente. The reasoning is fallacious and the reader is advised to read the chapter on the English Channel. Years later Greta Anderson, who made a roundtrip Catalina crossing, and Florence Chadwick would make their records on constant headings.

George's coach was surprised when minutes later Norman Ross's boat made the same move. Norman was going to stay right on George's heels until he weakened.

Most of the other swimmers took a direct line route to Point Vincente. The first hour saw thirty swimmers quit. Steadily George and Ross widened their lead over the others. It was suddenly evident that George was now improving his lead over Ross. At the end of two hours, George had widened his lead to about 150 yards. The young Canadian looked like a scared rabbit being pursued by a predator. All through the afternoon hours Ross again and again tried to pull up with George. It seemed that every time he would burst into a sprinting pace for two or three hundred yards George would do the same. Only George would keep his sprint up for five or six hundred yards. Thus Ross would find that he had lost ground instead of gaining it.

Around 3 P.M., when seven miles out from Catalina, George ran into a heavy oil slick which gave him some trouble. For two hundred yards he plowed through the thick oil. When he finally cleared it he took his first substantial feeding of the swim—two cups of hot chocolate. The feeding was quick and efficient and was an auger of his trouble-free eating for the rest of the swim. When the final tally was made he had consumed three quarts of hot chocolate, three chocolate cakes, and a pint of beef tea.

The afternoon hours took their toll as more and more swimmers left the water. By 5 P.M. there were only thirty swimmers still in the water. At 5:30 P.M. Charlotte Schoemmel, who had set a record swimming around Manhattan Island in September, left the water totally incapacitated. Her left knee was swollen. She spent three days in a local hospital before she could leave on crutches. Wrigley & Co. paid the bill.

By 7 P.M. further inroads had been made on competitors. Channel conqueror Charles Tooth was out followed two hours later by another Channel conqueror, Henry Sullivan. The 8 P.M. radio reports said that twenty of the original 102 swimmers were still in the water. Eight and one half hours of swimming in fifty-seven- to sixty-four-degree water had done its work. The Catalina Island Swim was living up to its name as being tougher than the English Channel.

The early evening hours saw George still increasing his lead over Ross. At 9 P.M. he was leading Ross by about 1½ miles. After 9½ hours of swimming George had logged about seventeen miles, which was very close to the 2 miles per hour he expected to average. Conditions remained ideal. A full moon rose to complement the gentle waves which never exceeded a foot in height. Those who had lasted this long were a determined and select coterie drawn together by only one overwhelming desire—to beat every other swimmer to Point Vincente. The longer they lasted the more real the $25,000 became. Those trailing the leaders hoped they would burn themselves out. George Young, playing the rabbit to Norman Ross, doggedly, doggedly, or should one say "rabbitedly," stayed in the lead.

Toward midnight spectators began to gather by the thousands at Point Vincente. Those who had cars pointed them seaward and flicked on the headlights. Loudspeakers set up by Wrigley gave information to the ever-increasing crowd. Out in the Channel George and Ross could see the hundreds of auto headlights added to the winking Point Vincente lighthouse. Although neither they nor their coaches knew what the lights were they headed the boats for them. News came that Norman Ross was having periodical arguments with his boat crew. Time after time he would curse them for letting George get away. Ross was now having serious doubts about being first in.

Around 1:30 A.M. Clarabelle Barrett of New York gave up. She was nine miles from the finish. The women were in summation to make a good showing.

At 2 A.M. George was riding the height of the southward running current. He was in an ideal position about a half mile north of Point Vincente. By 2:30 A.M. his goal became clear. The lights, horns, and loudspeakers all emanated from one spot. It was now that George ran into a bed of kelp. Much was made of it in the press, but George, not to be bothered now by anything less than an earthquake, stroked through it with the minimum of difficulty. News flashed back to Ross that George would land within a half hour. Ross took the news with despair. There was no sense in continuing. He had lived long enough to realize that there is no room for second place. The "winner take all" stipulation of Wrigley and the humiliation of being beaten by a seventeen-year-old boy were enough to force Ross to heave himself aboard his boat and ask to be taken immediately to his hotel.

The searchlights from hundreds of boats played on George as he stroked through the kelp beds toward the beach. Judges waded out to shake the boy's hand as he stood up in hip-deep water. Their handshake was worth $25,000 with another $1,000 coming from the owners of the private property on which George had landed. The crowd cheered its approval. George, with blanket thrown over him, waved and stepped into a waiting dory to be taken to the California Yacht Club. There he shook the hands of the rich and famous for an hour whereupon he was taken to the Sea Side Hospital at Long Beach for a good night's rest. George had swum an estimated twenty-seven miles in fifteen hours and forty-five minutes. He had swum at least seven miles more than necessary due to the amateur navigation on the part of the boat captain. Most of the other swimmers suffered the same bad navigation. All the more remarkable was the crowd of fifteen thousand people who had deemed it worthy to stay up and see him finish at 3:06 in the morning.

As always there was nothing left but loneliness for those still in the water when George finished. Most of the spectator boats left to see George finish. Peter Meyer quit at 4:20 A.M. about two miles from Point Vincente. He had lasted seventeen hours. However it was two women that gained secondary fame for their efforts. Mrs. Margaret Hauser and Miss Martha Stager were in the water for nineteen hours twenty-six minutes and nineteen hours six minutes respectively. They both got out about 6 A.M. with only a mile to go. As special recognition for their efforts they each received $2,500 from Wrigley.

When Young arrived at the hospital the doctors attested to his fine condition. All tests were normal. George had lost only five pounds during his jaunt. He was to lose more than that in the coming weeks for different reasons. His worldwide fame would lead him into the byways of showmanship, sensationalism, and newsmongering. While a master of his element—water—he was no match for what followed. When news of his venture reached his mother in Toronto, friends and well-wishers flooded into the little frame house to congratulate the frail, sickly woman who was temporarily lifted from her lonely anguish. Her spirits would be short lived considering what would happen later.

On Monday with his ever-present new-found manager, now calling himself "George's business agent," standing close by, George received his check from Wrigley personally. After the ceremonies he escorted George to the nearest bank. There George endorsed the check over to him. His manager cashed it and "benevolently" gave George his share after deducting the forty percent his iron-bound contract called for.

By the end of the week George was hit by every promotor and con artist in California. He, or should I say his manager, accepted a contract for five nights at a Hollywood theatre for $1,000. At the end of the week screen tests were given at the studio of a Hollywood movie company. The all equivocal "promises" were given. Subtle manipulation had the young man believing he would be sitting on top of the world soon, if he wasn't already. The sordid story of manipulation of an innocent boy is best left for another telling.

George became known subsequently as "father of the marathon swim." Whenever the history of the sport is discussed among the old-timers his name is sure to be mentioned. He not only became the first man to swim the San Pedro Channel, but the winner of the largest prize to date ever offered in the sport.

That the Catalina swim was a publicity and financial success for William Wrigley, Jr. and the Wrigley Chewing Gum Co. was evident in the tremendous increase in sales for the company. So successful was the promotion that Wrigley decided to inaugurate a professional swim later that year at the famous Canadian National Exhibition at Toronto, Canada. This was a twenty-one-mile swim. The first place prize would be an astounding $30,000. That swim marked the beginning of the longest annual series of professional swims in the history of the sport. George entered that swim and became yesterday's hero when he left the forty-eight-degree water after four hours. Nobody finished the 1928 race because of water temperature. George recaptured the confidence of his fellow Canadians when he won the 1931 event. It was in 1931 that he also married the woman winner of the race Margaret Raviour. Evidently marriage and swimming didn't mix for they were eventually divorced. In 1947, at the age of thirty-six, George decided to make a comeback. He failed miserably. Today, remarried, George lives and works for the Department of Parks and Recreation at Niagara Falls. Whenever George reminisces he can glance on the photos and medals that adorn his modest home. He can take pride in the fact that he is considered one of the greatest professional swimmers that ever stroked the waters of this earth.*

* Young died in 1972.

When William Wrigley, Jr. died he laid claim to being buried on one of the largest, if not the largest, plot in existence—Catalina Island. There he rests in a specially built mausoleum on his estate at the southern tip of the island. The dream factory, Hollywood, could hardly have come up with a better story than the Catalina swim. What better ending could there have been than that of a penniless seventeen-year-old boy winning fame and fortune by beating a twenty-six-year-old world champion swimmer? One would think that William Wrigley, Jr. would turn over in his marble mausoleum.

Other famous swimmers were to conquer the San Pedro Channel in coming years, but none received the fame and fortune that George did. While George received headlines, Florence Chadwick, Tom Park, and Greta Andersen (even with her double crossing) received only a few short paragraphs on the sporting page. They made their swims only with sponsorship. For some reason public interest was no longer there. Such is the fate of man and his accomplishments.

7

The Canadian National Exhibition and the Thirty-grand Swim

William Wrigley, Jr. and his chewing gum company obtained great publicity from the Catalina Island Swim and the consequent profits were gratifying. Naturally the board of directors began to think ahead. When the Canadian George Young won the Catalina swim the newspapers played it up big. Here was a chance to enlarge the Canadian market for Wrigley's product. More Canadians should chew gum. It took only a short time to realize that the famous Canadian institution, the Canadian National Exhibition, was being held during the last and first weeks of August and September 1927. Furthermore, this famous exhibition was without a Wrigley exhibit or extravaganza. Held for many years in Toronto, the exhibition was a venerable Canadian institution. Toward the end of the summer each year, the large manufacturers would set up publicity displays. Intermixed with the displays were athletic events and entertainments of various sorts for the visitors. People by the thousands would flock to the exhibition to enjoy the carnivallike atmosphere and spend their money. What better way to advertise chewing gum than to incorporate a Wrigley swim during the exhibition?

It didn't take long for the officials of the exhibition to be converted to Wrigley's way of thinking, especially when the oil of $50,000 in cash prizes, plus expenses, was offered for the swim. Two months after the Catalina swim, in March of 1927, the newspapers announced the first professional Canadian National Exhibition Swim. This was the beginning of an annual event that was to crown the world's champion professional swimmer. The date set for the swim that year was August 30th.

When the prize money was announced, the cortical cells of thousands of swimmers the world over were stimulated. Savings were tapped and money was borrowed to obtain transportation to Toronto. Rigorous training schedules were set up by those who were set on obtaining a lifetime retirement fund in this era before social security. The prizes offered were: 1st place, $30,000; 2nd place, $7,500; 3rd place $2,500; 4th place $1,000; 5th and 6th places, $500 each. The first woman to finish would receive an additional bonus of $5,000 plus the original place money. There was $2,500 extra for the second woman and $500 extra for the third woman to finish. If one were to equate the 1927 dollar with today's dollar that $30,000 would sound something like $100,000 today. The first C. N. E. swim represents the largest single prize offered for a marathon swim to date.

The sponsors and promoters, taking their cue from the English Channel and the Catalina Island swims, decided on keeping the twenty-one-mile length. Over the months a straight line course proposal was dropped in favor of a triangular one adjacent to the exhibition grounds in Lake Ontario. Each leg of the course would be about 2.3 miles long. Adjustments were made so that the last mile would be along the waterfront area so as to allow maximum view to the thousands of spectators expected to watch the finish.

They were all there including Norman Ross from Chicago, George Young, George Michel from France, Lottie Schoemmel, record holder for the Manhattan Island Swim, Edward Keating, winner of the Lake George Marathon, Mark Burdett and Byron Summers, aces from California. Among these giants of the swimming world appeared Ernst Vierkoetter from Germany who had just come from establishing a record time across the English Channel. His time of twelve hours forty minutes for the France to England Crossing the year before was to stand for twenty-four years until in 1950 El Rehim of Egypt sprinted across in the first Channel race in ten hours fifty minutes.

On the swim day the Lake Ontario water showed the dark side of its personality, one that has smashed the hopes of many and at the same time smiled on a few. For six consecutive days the wind blew offshore around Toronto. This simple fact was meaningless to the majority of the city's population. To a select group of beach and waterfront swimmers, it was the reason the water registered a bone-chilling fifty-one degrees. The surface waters of any body of water are subject to being moved by the wind. The surface is much like a sail. It is in a horizontal plane rather than a vertical one. Since air and water have weight they are subject to friction at their point of contact. Since the surface area of Lake Ontario is many thousands of square miles there is the equivalent contact with the air. When the wind is blowing a few miles an hour and is steady, its effect will be to move the surface water along in the direction it is going. Every schoolboy knows that hot air rises and it rises because it is less dense. The same holds for water. The warmer water usually lies on the surface. Since wind conditions can be, and usually are, local, there are to be found patches of water that vary in temperature over a large lake. (I am kindly thinking of the reader as I eliminate thermoclines, currents, etc., which play a minimal effect in Lake Ontario.) As the warm water moves out from the shore, it is replaced by the upwelling deeper and much colder water. Lake Michigan and others of the Great Lakes experience the same phenomenon. Many a swimmer has forsaken the pleasure of going to Lake Michigan for a swim on a cool summer day because of the supposedly chill waters. They equate the cool weather with cold water whereas in fact, if the wind has been blowing long enough, the warmer surface water has been pushed to the southern part of the lake around Chicago. On the other hand a warm or hot breeze from the southwest or west (offshore breezes in Chicago) brings cold upwelling water. The opposite holds true for Toronto, for it lies along the northern boundary of the lake. Cool north winds mean cold water because they are offshore. Warm and hot winds from the south and southwest bring in the warm water. So dramatic an effect can the wind direction and speed have on water temperature that cities on the north and south boundaries of the lake have experienced a twelve-degree drop in as little as two hours. Usually it takes overnight. Such were the conditions that brought about the fifty-one-degree water temperature.

With the bull-horn blaring out directions to the swimmers, the pennants flying, and the Ferris wheel turning, the stage was set. Moments later the gun went off, marking the beginning of the richest swimming race (*official* cash purse) in history.

It looked like a repeat of the Catalina swim. The winner of that race, George Young, took off like he did there. A few yards behind him were the determined world-famed swimmers bent on holding down his lead. It remained similar to the Catalina swim in only one aspect. George was in the lead, but instead of just Norman Ross being behind him, it was a pack of five men and one woman. These swimmers learned one thing from the Catalina Swim. You don't start out slow. Whether George knew it or not this was a determined rat pack he was in front of. Every few moments he would put on an extra burst for a few hundred yards, attempting to increase his lead like he did at Catalina. When he finished his "super-sprint" his eyes bugged wide, for the pack was still the same distance behind him. It is entirely possible that the cold water prevented him from increasing his speed significantly, but it is also possible that he had competitors who knew what they were doing. After the first two hours George managed to have two hundred yards on the second-place pack, but from here on things began to deteriorate fast. When George reached the four-mile mark he began to falter ever so slightly. It was then that the iron man from Germany, Ernst Vierkoetter, made his move. Slowly the big German pulled out ahead of the pack and began to go for George. Inch by inch he crept up on the young Canadian. Twenty-eight minutes later at the five-mile mark the "Black Shark," as Vierkoetter was called, pulled even with George. George attempted to stay with Vierkoetter, but try as he might it was not his day. By the time Vierkoetter had pulled one hundred yards ahead of George, George had collapsed. He waved to his boat. Despondently he climbed aboard saddened by the fact that he had failed his home town of Toronto.

Vierkoetter was never headed from that point on. Hour after hour he stroked evenly and strongly. He found himself lapping fewer and fewer swimmers as he made his rounds of the triangular course. Edward Keating, winner of the Lake George Marathon, had dropped out after seven miles. The Californian swimmers had left even before that. At the end of eight hours (the swim had started at 8:30 A.M.) there were only twelve swimmers still in the water and two of them were women—Ethel Hertle and Lottie Schoemmel of New York.

During the warm, sunlit daylight hours the water temperature moved up to fifty-five degrees but by 7 P.M. it began to drop again. At that time Vierkoetter had increased his lead to over two miles ahead of his second-place competitor. Eating regularly and giving signs of confidence to his handlers, Vierkoetter kept up his grinding pace. By 6 P.M. 35,000 spectators, in response to the radio coverage of the event, made their way down to the shores of Lake Ontario to watch the German phenomenon come in. By 7:30 P.M. he had only one mile to go and it was here that the spectators began singing "Show Me the Way to Go Home" and clapping their hands for the powerful swimmer. At 8:15 P.M. Vierkoetter touched the end of the dock that marked the finish line. He climbed from the water appearing fresh and in good shape for such a grueling swim. He had accomplished the twenty-one-mile swim under the duress of cold water in eleven hours forty-five minutes. It wasn't until five hours later that the second-place man came in, covering the course in sixteen hours forty-five minutes. The Frenchman, George Michel, was on the verge of collapse. The third-place finisher, William Erickson of New York, took eighteen hours forty-five minutes. He arrived at the finishing dock at 3:30 A.M. The heartbreaks of the swim were the two women Ethel Hertle and Lottie Schoemmel. Miss Hertle left the water at 6 P.M. while in third place and after 9½ hours of swimming. Miss Schoemmel was within three miles of finishing before she gave up.

Vierkoetter collected his $30,000 and made for the nearest bank to send his money home, after deducting expenses. One financial wit came up with the following calculations. Vierkoetter made 33,840 strokes throughout his swim. That came to ninety cents a stroke. Michel took 32,000 strokes for an earned twenty-five cents a stroke.

Be that as it may, Vierkoetter also earned the fame of winning the largest cash prize ever offered in the sport of marathon swimming. That first C. N. E. swim also set the pattern for some of the most famous moments in sports when other thrilling races were held every year until 1937 when, for one reason or another, they ceased. In 1947 they were started again and held, except for a few more intermittent years, until the 1964 "catastrophe."

That first swim held at the C. N. E. was so successful that there was no question as to whether there would be another one in 1928. The turnstiles clicked a merry tune to the promoters of the exhibition, for each spectator was charged admission. Among all the events held throughout the years at the C. N. E., the marathon swim was the most popular. It was held on the last day of the exhibition and crowned its closing hours. When 1928 rolled around there were a few significant changes made. First the event was shortened. Instead of twenty-one miles it would be fifteen miles. With the longer event, as in the previous year, the second and third place finishers arrived in the wee hours of the morning. That reduced the paid admissions significantly. It was hoped that the shortened distance would allow all finishers to arrive at the finish while the exhibition gates were open. A second major change would be that there would be two events according to sex—one for the men and one for the women. While the men's event would be fifteen miles the women's would be only ten miles. The total prize money was the same as the previous year, $50,000.

The exhibition promoters had thought of everything by the time the swim date came. New boats, trained rowers, grandstands, new loudspeakers, and personnel to control the crowds. Little did they realize that nature would have the final say in these all too superficial events of man.

The extraordinary windfall of 1927 had dropped $80,000 in prize money in the laps of the "starving" professional swimmers. When news of the 1928 swim got around jobs were given up to go to Toronto. In a few cases the quick parting from a disgruntled wife led to subsequent divorces. They came from all over the world—England, Germany, South Africa, and France. By far, however, the majority came from Canada and the United States. The only three finishers in the 1927 race were back plus the inimitable Norman Ross. He would try for the third time to finish a professional race. Winners of the famed ten-mile Mississippi River Marathon, held since the 1890s, were there. Channel conquerors, lake crossers, and crack college pool swimmers arrived by the dozen. The day before the swim tallied over 250 entrants.

The romance of being a sports hero was rapidly washed away when dawn broke on the day of the swim. As the year before Lake Ontario was playing its ace card. If the fifty-one- to fifty-five-degree water of

1927 was cold the waters of 1928 were "ice." The lake at Toronto measured forty-four to forty-six degrees. The comment that the water was so cold "it was like fire" was an apt and descriptive statement. Eventually 199 starters massed at the starting line to await the starting gun. Only a matter of minutes after the gun went off, the first swimmer left the water shaking his head. By the end of the first fifteen minutes twenty-five others sought refuge in the warm air. The famed Norman Ross left the water after two hours and twenty-seven minutes, distraught, not only with the cold water, but by the fact that he could not keep pace with the leaders. When Ross left the water there were only thirteen swimmers left of the original field. The water had taken a "mortality" of eighty-five percent in $2\frac{1}{2}$ hours. At the end of three hours fifty minutes Toronto's son, George Young, gave up. He had managed to cover only seven miles in almost four hours, which was quite a bit slower than his normal two-mile-per-hour average. After that first hour the winner of the previous year's race, Ernst Vierkoetter, had taken the lead and now appeared to be on his way to another victory. Gradually a wider and wider gap separated him from the others. The fourth hour of swimming saw four of the remaining thirteen swimmers give up. "A prize of $100,000 wouldn't have kept me in that water," was the comment of one. Three of these four gave up close to the half-way mark of the swim.

The German phenomenon at the halfway mark had an unheard of two-mile lead over the Frenchman George Michel, who shared an unenvious second place with another swimmer from America. It looked like Vierkoetter was on his way to another victory. At the end of seven hours there were only three swimmers to be seen still in the water. The event now became a classic. The spectators, newscasters, and reporters were watching a battle that not only pitted man against man, but man against the environment. It was more than evident that simply to survive the cold water was of greater importance than beating your opponent. Five minutes later the American, Louis I. Mathias, numb and incoherent, was pulled from the water by his handlers. In seven hours and five minutes of swimming he had managed to cover only a little more than eight miles. The one plus mile per hour average he had maintained is testimony enough to the effect of the cold water, for in seventy-five-degree water a top swimmer could average two-plus miles per hour. At 4:00 P.M. the spectators saw Vierkoetter stop and wave to his boat. The boat with handlers moved alongside. Vierkoetter appeared to be carrying on a conversation with his handlers. The minutes dragged by. There was only one other swimmer in the water and Vierkoetter was over three miles ahead of him. Michel was not to be feared. The minutes dragged on as the swimmer and handlers conversed. Almost ten minutes went by as Vierkoetter carried on the conversation. Then suddenly the big German moved closer to the rowboat, laid his hands on the gunwales, and heaved himself aboard. This startling development caused one of the biggest surprises in any C. N. E. race. After eleven hours thirteen minutes of swimming, which had put him less than three miles from his goal, one of the world's great swimmers left the water. When his boat came ashore newsmen flocked around him for his story. Sheathed in blankets and in a stuporous state Vierkoetter waved off comment. He was taken to the nearest building to warm up further.

Heads turned to the only swimmer now left in the water. What was being watched now was a mockery. George Michel, now only four miles behind Vierkoetter's leaving point, struggled in the water. He alternated between crawl, back, and breast stroking as he inched along. When news came of Vierkoetter's departure from the race he picked up his stroke rate, but only temporarily. He soon slipped back into his agonizing, inefficient battle. Everyone commented that it would only be a matter of minutes before the Frenchman would follow the others. The surprise came when he lasted a phenomenal three hours thirty-two minutes more. He was taken from the water semiconscious. After eleven hours thirteen minutes of swimming Michel had managed to come up to Vierkoetter's twelve-mile mark and then go another block. That $1/6$ mile more was enough to get him half of the winner's purse.

After all the hoopla had quieted down the swim made great conversation. The promoters were forced to distribute half the prize money to the fourteen swimmers who had covered the greatest distance. While the swim was a failure to the swimmers, the publicity gained by the promoters was not. It wasn't until thirty-six years later that a like situation would happen when the C. N. E. would hold the thirty-two-mile cross-lake swim in 1964. At that time Lake Ontario, in collaboration with the god of the winds, would slip a Mickey Finn to the swimmers and the C. N. E. Only this time there would be more drastic consequences. But that is another story.

The swims held in the years to follow became the focal point of the exhibition's closing days. The distance of fifteen miles was kept because of its inherent suitability for exhibition purposes. In 1929 Vierkoetter made Canada his home. The profits to be earned in his new homeland were vast compared to what he had been earning in Germany. The least he could do, he felt, was to spend some of the cash where he earned it. Vierkoetter must have had second thoughts after a few years for he was never again in the winner's circle. By 1932 he had moved back to the land of bratwurst and schnitzels.

The reader, by perusing the summary of the C. N. E. swims, can see that the time for the fifteen-mile swims dropped sharply when the water was warm. When Herman Willemse, the "Flying Dutchman," won the 1962 event he established a remarkable record of six hours thirty-eight minutes. The water temperature that day was seventy-three degrees. Behind each swim there "was a story," to use the platitude hummed by every newspaper editor to his reporters. Ross came back again and again in an attempt to recover his flagging reputation, only to fail. Never again was Ross to bathe in the splendor of his earlier years as an amateur when he was toasted the world over. The one-time holder of every amateur world record in the short distances was never in his career to win a professional swimming event. Each time he returned to the hallowed walls of the famed Illinois Athletic Club in Chicago his head hung lower. He learned what every amateur, then and now, eventually learns. The professional swimmer is not daunted by reputations. While the amateur has been conditioned to compete for trophies and words, the professional has been conditioned to know that he is swimming for "survival." Meat on the table and a rent receipt are his "trophies." He has been forced early to accept a more realistic view of life. In the years to come the C. N. E. race became famous as a destroyer of reputations.

In the thirty-six-year history of the C. N. E. swims (there was a nine-year lapse from 1938 to 1946 because of World War II) there were experiments with the distance. There were a few five- and ten-mile events with thirty- and thirty-two-mile ones also. The fifteen-mile distance always proved the most popular. The postwar years saw the appearance of a man who was to become the biggest money winner in the history of the sport. That man was Cliff Lumsden, a native Torontonian, whose fame was gained not only by his phenomenal swimming ability but also by his extraordinary ability to make friends.

Cliff's swimming potential was recognized early by the director of the Lake Shore Swimming Club in Toronto. Gus Ryder took the young man under his tutorship and spent countless hours polishing and correcting the teen-ager's stroke. Every spare moment he could spare Ryder devoted to Cliff. The difficulties of such devotion became evident when one learns that Ryder had the responsibility for the safety of hundreds of other swimmers at the club. By the time Cliff was sixteen Ryder felt he was ready to enter his first professional swim. In 1947 Cliff was entered in the C. N. E. When that race was over, Cliff Lumsden, a sixteen-year-old, had come in a respectable sixth, and in doing so had beaten some of the world's most accomplished professional swimmers. A year later Cliff finished fifth. Each swim was worth about $800. His third C. N. E. race in 1949 saw the now-eighteen-year-old win his first C. N. E. race. Over the next few years Cliff was to win more C. N. E. races than any other swimmer. Each first-place finish was worth about $6,000. His biggest win was in 1955 when he won the thirty-two-mile race in front of the exhibition. This race was originally to be across Lake Ontario from Niagara on the lake to Toronto. The huge publicity gained the year before, 1954, by a sixteen-year-old Ryder swimmer, Marilyn Bell, the first person to conquer the lake, was enough for the C. N. E. to hold another across-the-lake swim in 1955. The across-the-lake route was changed to a triangular thirty-two-mile course when inclement weather stepped in. Cliff completed the course in nineteen hours forty-eight minutes and collected the $15,000 first prize. But that represented only a fraction of what he realized. When the gifts by advertisers, which included a home, consumer endorsements, and $1 for every stroke taken in the last five miles, was added up, Cliff was $84,000 to the good. The fact that Cliff was able to capitalize to such an extent was due to the lucky circumstances of the year before when Marilyn Bell marked the beginning of an era that has not stopped to date.

The Marilyn Bell story is a mini-saga. It has all the ingredients of a teen-age soap opera. A rather plain and ordinary girl works hard to swim as fast as her age companions. She never quite makes it. She is befriended by the male hero of the swim club, she is coached, and her final triumphal success leads to fame, money, and marriage. In 1948, when only nine years old, Marilyn joined Ryder's swim club in Toronto. There she was lost, as is natural for children of her age, in child's play. The club offered many different age-group programs from beginner's lessons in swimming to the highly organized races and games like water polo and ballet. Children love to be massed together. The tightly woven mass of humanity that characterizes children at play may not appeal to the adult, but the children thrive on it. For six years Marilyn made trips to the pool in winter and to Lake Ontario in summer. As she became older she became aware of the serious swimmers that bid for money in the C. N. E. races held every year. Children love, and in fact need, heroes. Marilyn found two at the club—its director, Gus Ryder, and five-time winner of the C. N. E., Cliff Lumsden. With her own ebullience, and their direction, she became lost in swimming. Fate, however, had not endowed Marilyn with the speed so necessary for the standard short races. No matter how she trained she just never was able to place in the first ranks. It was at this time that she was taken over, more as a placation, by the above two giants. She would tag along with Cliff when he would go on one of his five-, ten-, or fifteen-mile training swims. He would give her a half hour lead and then proceed to catch her. She would then get into the rowboat which would pull ahead and drop her off. This would go on day after day. She was happy. After years of this kind of thing Marilyn, Ryder and the first Atlantic City Marathon of 1954 came together. At the age of sixteen Marilyn was packed off with Lumsden, Ryder, and Tom Park to the swim.

Atlantic City, that famous resort and convention city, was always ready to try something new in order to keep, or increase, its lure to those ready to spend money. Over the years the city's merchants, promoters, and politicians had successfully increased its business with conventions. From all over the United States doctors, lawyers, salesmen, and scientists had gathered to hold their annual meetings. Lying toward the North end of Absecon Island, upon which it is located, Atlantic City offers some of the finest beaches in the world to its visitors. The distance around the irregularly shaped island is some twenty-five miles. The eastern coast lies along the Atlantic Ocean, and its western side is separated by a narrow channel that varies from one to two blocks wide. When the trio from Canada arrived they were immediately swept up in the fanfare of the city's first marathon swim. There was just the tides that presented an unknown. Since the island had been swum the previous year by two veteran Atlantic City lifeguards, there was no doubt it could be done. This year would be the inauguration swim for professionals. The reader will find a detailed account of the Atlantic City Marathon in Chapter 9. When the event was over the sixteen-year-old Canadian girl had finished seventh. She was the first woman to finish and thus eligible for the extra purse accorded women. Her fellow Canadians also made excellent showings—in fact excellent enough to take first and second places. Tom Park succeeded in coming in some three minutes ahead of Cliff Lumsden to make the event an all Canadian one.

Flush with their success the Canadians stayed an extra three days in Atlantic City to enjoy the carnival festivities before they booked their way back to Toronto to prepare themselves for the upcoming C. N. E. race. The promoters of the C. N. E., like their Atlantic City counterparts, were trying something new this year. The previous three years, 1951, 1952, and 1953, had all seen ten-mile events. In 1954 they decided on a team swim. Each team would consist of four swimmers. Each member could swim any number of laps as long as he swam at least one lap. He could then, if he chose, be relieved by one of his other three partners. The first team to finish thirty miles was the winner and would be awarded $10,000. Second, third, and fourth place would receive $5,000, $3,000, and $2,000 respectively. Marilyn was picked as alternate to the Canadian team.

Relay, or team races, were not new in the history of sports. For years track and field events, as well as cycling, had made use of this highly exciting exhibition. Athletes, as well as spectators, are highly stimulated by the added incentive that accompanies group action. Individuals brought together as a team are induced to constantly put forth their best efforts. In fact one might say that man's normal state is to function as a member of a group. His hunting and subsequent agricultural heritage are testimony to this fact. The culmination of the marathon swimming relay race was the inauguration of the twenty-four-hour La Tuque Race in 1966. This famous race will be discussed in the proper chapter.

That first C. N. E. relay race in 1954 had its problems. When all was said and done the Canadian team of Ben Gazel, who was forty-three years old, Cliff Lumsden, George Bevan, and Tom Park finished first by completing the thirty miles in thirteen hours. The $10,000 the team pocketed was well earned when one considers that each swimmer got only $2,500. Three other teams finished and their names appear in the listing. Belatedly, it should be mentioned that the C. N. E. relay race had been scheduled as a thirty-two-mile across-the-lake affair that would be a foil (in case things went wrong) for a spectacular solo crossing by the famed English Channel swimmer Florence Chadwick. Chadwick had been solicited by the C. N. E. promoters to try a cross-the-lake swim for $10,000. When inclement weather, that bugaboo of all outdoor endeavors, delayed her start from Youngstown, New York, it also delayed the relay team. The pressure of time because of C. N. E. scheduling forced the promoters to bring back the teams to Toronto for a harbor event. Chadwick was left at Youngstown to await proper weather. Marilyn Bell also waited, for she was to become the pivot point of one of the most famous marathon swims ever held. Let us back-track to see how these unusual circumstances came about.

As mentioned above, the team relay race was scheduled for across Lake Ontario. Florence Chadwick was offered $10,000 for a successful solo crossing. The offer was to her and her alone. Marilyn was an alternate team member of the Canadian team and would swim only if one of its members became sick. Realizing that marathon swimmers are invariably healthy, she knew that there would be little opportunity for her swimming in the relay. Further insult was added by the fact that only Florence Chadwick was being guaranteed money for a successful swim. Marilyn besieged her coach to let her make a wildcat start with Florence. Ryder quickly agreed if Marilyn's parents would agree. Permission was granted and Marilyn found herself bedded down in a Youngstown hotel on September 4, 1954 awaiting the September 6th official start. Newsmen, with their natural inclinations, soon discovered that Marilyn was unhappy that a Canadian was not eligible for the solo prize offered only to Florence Chadwick. A few published stories of the affair quickly materialized into several thousand dollars being offered by Toronto merchants if their beloved Canadian schoolgirl successfully made the swim. Chadwick's contract with the C. N. E. called for a September 6th, 11 P.M. start from Youngstown. If conditions prevented this start she would still be eligible if a start was made within the following five days. The weather had the final word. It wasn't until Wednesday, September 8, that the rain stopped. In the meantime C. N. E. officials had called the relay segment of the event back to Toronto for a harbor swim. Around 11 P.M. of that fateful Wednesday the great Florence Chadwick slipped into the water at Youngstown dock and began her contract. Several hundred feet away, Marilyn made her entry into the water.

Winnie Roach Leuszler, a friend of Marilyn, followed her seventeen minutes later. The days and hours of tense waiting for Chadwick to make her move had ended. Thus began one of the most famous marathon swims ever made.

The spotlights followed the great Chadwick out from the Niagara River. She made her way to the open waters of Lake Ontario. A few photographers had moved over to Winnie and Marilyn to take a few shots before they too entered the water. What should be a simple matter was complicated by newsmen, boats, and the darkness. Locating her boat from which emanated both physical and psychological security Marilyn settled down to a strong and steady pace. It took only a few minutes for her to become adjusted to the sixty-five-degree water. No matter how warm the water, swimmers invariably comment on the shock of immersion. It was lucky for Marilyn that the water was not colder, for if it had been, the outcome would have no doubt been different. After five minutes of swimming she looked up at her coach and asked where Florence was. Ryder quickly responded with, "Don't worry about Florence, we are swimming our race." From that time on Marilyn would not ask again.

In the meantime Winnie Roach Leuszler was having difficulty. Unable to locate her guide boat she had been forced to swim around looking for it with the unhappy result that after one hour of swimming she was forced to return to the dock and start anew.

In her first hour of swimming Marilyn had discarded her goggles. It was shortly after, that the first lamprey eel attached itself to her bathing suit. Luckily she was used to having these creatures plunking on to her during her training swims. She remembered what Cliff Lumsden had showed her. She slipped her thumb-nail under its suckers to break the suction and threw the creature from her. The indomitable Cliff, during a training swim, had three times plucked an eel from his body only to have it return each time. On its third return, Cliff removed the eel, crushed its head between his teeth and threw it away for good. Such knowledge would do the young girl good when she would be bothered several more times by these parasites.

During that first hour and a half Marilyn had surprisingly enough passed Florence in the dark. Neither the swimmer nor the tenders of either crew were aware of this startling development. It wouldn't be until a bit later in the morning that the revelation would come.

Three miles out from Youngstown, Marilyn and Florence hit the open, rolling waters of Lake Ontario. It is always a moment of adaptation for the swimmers to shift from the calm waters of a river to the shifting, rhythmic rollers of a large lake. But adapt they did as they continued stroking.

The early morning hours saw things settled into a routine pattern. Every hour or so Gus Ryder would give Marilyn a mixture of pablum and corn syrup. It was one of the many important factors practiced that would help the girl throughout the swim. Around four in the morning after Marilyn had been swimming some five hours, she complained of being tired. The eighteen hours Marilyn had been awake before the start of the swim was now taking effect. It must have been doubly hard on her psychologically since humans are all too aware of how loss of sleep can affect their strength. However, in many instances, professional athletes learn that this is not necessarily so since it may mean that inability to fall asleep before an event is a sign of a "peak" or "up" cycle. However, Marilyn was too young to be aware of such subtleties.

Her coach, with his vast experience, soon overrode the complaint with sympathetic but firm dominancy. When Marilyn then complained of stomach pains, he skipped a few feedings and also lessened the quantity of food given her. Then came arm and leg pains which took a little time for Gus to explain. That was "normal" because of the effort. "Just slow down a little," he replied. It was half an hour before Marilyn settled down again into a sustained effort free of stops.

In the meantime the great Florence Chadwick was having a vicious time. Beginning at 1 A.M. she had begun to vomit and by 4 A.M. she was deathly sick. The rolling waves only served to increase her already miserable state. By 5 A.M. she was treading water, prolonging the inevitable decision. The minutes rolled by as again and again she'd try to get a stroke going. At 5:45 A.M. her trainers grabbed the thirty-five-year-old famed swimmer and hauled her into the boat. The lure of $10,000 had turned to pelf. Only the peace of immobility seemed important to her now. The sky was now lightening with the approaching sunrise, but for Florence it was a setting sun. Within minutes the airwaves announced her dropping out. Radio newscasters told of her plight to the early morning risers around the lake. As listeners heard the news each one now asked, "What about sixteen-year-old Marilyn?" What about Marilyn?

With the coming of dawn and after seven hours of swimming, Marilyn was now about 14 miles out into the lake, a little less than half the distance. There was still at least sixteen miles to go. Liniment was handed her to rub on her aching legs which now had ceased to function effectively. If Gus had been familiar with current swimming theory he would not have worried too much. But he was of the old school, who believed the legs were important. The coterie aboard the mother boat and rowboat now began to scribble notes of encouragement to Marilyn. All the comments regarding her friends, parents, and lifeguard companions were "fed" to her in an attempt to pick up her spirits. Now reporters on other boats began to appear on the scene since Florence was no longer news. They were surprised to see the sixteen year old still stroking a strong fifty-five strokes per minute.

Suddenly they realized they had a "natural." Here was a story with all the ingredients that would whip up the hearts of thousands of Canadians. The large treacherous lake, a teenager, a famous professional giving up, no promise of reward.

As mile after mile went by things on shore began to happen. Phone calls were being received by newspapers and radio stations asking about Marilyn. Quickly the situation was sized up and reporters on the scene were asked to make more frequent reports to satisfy the increasing demands of followers of the race on shore.

Exhaustion came and went for Marilyn in cycles. By three in the afternoon a particularly depressing exhaustion cycle came on and for twenty minutes Marilyn accomplished only a few strokes. Tears could now be seen welling up in her eyes. Every word of encouragement was given and all tricks played to keep the gallant teen-ager going. Nothing seemed to work. One of her long-time friends, Joan Cooke, who was later to become the wife of Cliff Lumsden, realizing how desparate the situation was, peeled off her clothes and dove into the water to swim alongside Marilyn. The last minute trick worked, and soon Marilyn was back into a sustained rhythm. In twenty minutes Joan was back on the boat and Marilyn was going strong. With the news that Florence had given up and her goal in sight things went a little easier. By 6 P.M. the lights of the exhibition could be seen from her point four miles out. That last mile to the exhibition dock saw the firing of rockets and the cheers of thousands of spectators. When Marilyn finally hit the shoreline pandemonium broke loose. It made no impression upon the dead-tired girl. She was quickly bundled up by her coach and parents and sped to the nearest hotel for the long-desired sleep. Her rewards would come later.

The last eight hours of her swim had seen the tens of thousands of listeners in the Toronto area grow to millions in North America. Radio, television, newspapers, and teletypes had grabbed the story for its intrinsic worth. When the public learned that she was not eligible for the $10,000 offered to Chadwick a clamor arose. As this knowledge sunk in the days following her exploit, businessmen and individuals corrected it. Gifts were sent to her until a warehouse had to be set aside for them. A grocery chain supplied one free of charge, Three automobiles, a year's supply of vitamins, breakfast foods, vacuum cleaners, two fur coats, typewriters, radios, cameras, kitchenware, clothes, silverware, pets, television sets, and thousands of other valuable items were received. Public demand made the C. N. E. come across with the $10,000 offered only to Chadwick. There were legal taboos since a contract had been signed by the C. N. E. with Chadwick, but these were circumvented by legal manipulations. Cash was sent by donors throughout the continent. At the end of the week it totaled over $20,000 and was still going up. The ticker-tape parade held in Toronto a few days later surpassed any like event ever held in that famous city. A legal trust fund was set up with four lawyers and her parents as members. A marathon swimmer was at last reaping the benefits due. The fate of George Young was a thing of the past.

Oh, Yes. Winnie Roach Lueszler, after returning to the dock at Youngstown after an aimless hour of swimming while looking for her guide boat, went ⅔ of the way across Lake Ontario before throwing in the towel. That in itself was a remarkable swim, but like many of life's side stories it was doomed to history's book of forgotten accomplishments.

Marilyn's swim marked the beginning of an already rising era in professional swimming. The hardened businessmen that ran the C. N. E. themselves were amazed at the huge nationwide publicity gained by the swim. This is what they wanted. Instead of tens of thousands of people, millions were being reached. Almost before the great swim ended, plans were being formulated for another across-the-lake swim. The office of George Duthie, the swim master and chief organizer of the C. N. E. swims, was kept busy at a frenzied pace the winter of 1954–55. Advertising consultants were called in, broad sheets announcing and describing the swim printed, boats and security arrangements made, and, most importantly of all, prize money solicited. When spring arrived most of the preparations had been made. As famous swimmers around the world received their entry blanks, they were titillated by the increase in the prize money offered. Increases had been made all down the line with first place increasing from the $10,000 of the previous year to $15,000 in 1955.

When the swim date arrived everything was in its place except the weather. Rain and high winds precluded any across-the-lake try. While the swimmers themselves would not have any difficulty, hundreds of boats, handlers, and spectators had to be considered. Prudence caused the swim master, on competent advice from weather forecasters and security boats, to make a last minute change in the course. Quickly a triangular course was set up inside the breakwater in front of the exhibition. Some swimmers complained, but most agreed to the necessity of the change.

About thirty-five swimmers started the race in 1955 and it was hectic from the start. There was no chance of losing sight of your competitor because of distance, waves, or fog. You always knew where he was. It turned into a rat-race with hardly a chance for the glucose to be swallowed before a trainer or the sight of an approaching swimmer stimulated the competitor back to work. By the end of twelve hours there were only three swimmers left in the water and the one in the lead was none other than Toronto's famous and well-loved personality, Cliff Lumsden. It looked like Gus Ryder and the Lake Shore Club had a monopoly on marathon swims.

Hour after hour bull-necked Cliff stroked away, urged on by the rewards that would be his if he succeeded. No longer worried by a chasing swimmer, he could afford to settle down in a "semi-relaxed" pace. When he reached the twenty-sixth mile things no longer looked so good. He had perceptibly slowed down and doubts began to be raised as to whether there would be any finisher at all this year. During this time the news media was not sleeping. Learning of the public's demand for news of the swim the previous year, they had been careful to make every attempt to satisfy it. Every half hour bulletins were sent out over the airwaves giving the latest report. When Cliff faltered every agonizing detail was described. When the news was not particularly exciting it was dressed up and added to. Muscle fatigue became cramps; burping became stomach cramps. If Cliff did not hear his handlers, which is especially hard when your head is down and ears under water, they said the swimmer was in a daze and not responding. And so it went as the swim was promoted and advertised to the utmost. The last eight miles were hell for Cliff as they had been for Marilyn. The campaign was eminently successful, for one merchant called a radio station and said, "I'll give $1 for every stroke he makes in the last five miles." When this news was transmitted to Cliff he bore down with renewed effort. Shortly after this message another one was received in which the benefactor would give Cliff a hunting lodge if he finished. And so it went throughout the remaining hours of Cliff's swim. When he finally reached the last lap the crowd went wild as only the swim-crazy Canadians can do. With Cliff's completion of the thirty-two-mile course, big time swimming had returned. The strokes taken in that last five miles were good enough for another $15,000 which, when added to the official prize money, swelled his immediate cash earnings for the swim to $30,000. The weeks following saw the deed to the hunting lodge pass into his hands and the signing of consumer endorsement policies. When all was finished Cliff had amassed the biggest cache ever immediately realized by a postwar swimmer. All told, cash and goods added up to $84,000. What made Cliff even happier was the fact that swimmers, spectators, and newsmen all agreed, "It couldn't have happened to a nicer guy." They were right, for Cliff was a rare personality. A surly, self-centered ego-maniac would never have earned a place in the hearts of those who surrounded him as Cliff Lumsden did. Back into Cliff's mind there also came a third satisfaction. He had done the distance in an hour and fifteen minutes less than Marilyn. But Cliff was not the kind to verbalize it. That came from Marilyn herself. "You know, Cliff, you broke my record." "No kiddin'," Cliff replied. "That's a surprise to me." And it was.

The across-the-lake swim was held also in 1956 and 1957, both with and without C. N. E. sanction. In 1956 Brenda Fisher of England registered a remarkable time of eighteen hours and fifty minutes. Later that same year John Jaremy of Toronto did it in twenty-one hours and 13 minutes. But 1957 saw two remarkable crossings. A venerable New York father who was fifty-seven years old succeeded in not only crossing the lake but in reviving hopes in millions that there *is* life after forty. Sadlo's crossing took him twenty-five hours and ten minutes. A few weeks later, another "old man," Jim Woods of Orlando, Florida came out of hiding and startled everybody by setting a new record for the crossing. Landing at Cherry Beach, thirty-eight-year-old Jim Woods did it in eighteen hours thirty-five minutes. Yes, that year was the Geritol year.

Whether it was expense, lagging public interest or what have you, the C. N. E. dropped the event for three years. In 1961 they picked it up again with the distance being fifteen miles. The early 1960s marked the era of Herman Willemse, the "Flying Dutchman," whose story is told elsewhere.

The 1963 race was a thriller that helped make the name of Abo-Heif renowned the world over. That year the water was fifty-five degrees. It separated the gazelles from the bears. For fourteen miles the slender Dutch school teacher led the field until the Egyptian army major and the beautiful Michigan State coed Marty Sinn caught him. Abo Heif stayed with the gorgeous, buxom girl for a couple of hundred yards and then said, "Goodbye." Abo-Heif won the most thrilling race in years with Marty finishing second and Willemse third. This was a remarkably close race considering how cold the water was, and the reader can get an idea by looking at the list. Thrilling as that race was, it was only a tune up for what was to come the following year. It would be called "the greatest nonrace" ever held. That race would cause reverberations that to this day have not ceased.

1964: THE LAKE ONTARIO SWIM COMES BACK

In 1963 C. N. E. officials were jolted out of their complacency by an event that took place in Lake Michigan. In August of that year a new world's record had been set when Ted Erikson and Abdel-Latif Abo-Heif had swum sixty miles across Lake Michigan from Chicago to Benton Harbor. Abo-Heif had completed his feat in thirty-five hours, and Erikson in some 2½ hours longer. This stupendous accomplishment quieted the rumble of critics, and some swimmers, that the Lake Ontario swim was too long and arduous. Public interest in Toronto was revived. The swim-oriented in Toronto resented their thunder being stolen by Chicago. It took a short time for the C. N. E. to announce the return of a lake crossing swim in 1964. It would be a little while longer before it became evident that Lake Ontario waters were not the same as Lake Michigan. While Lake Michigan waters

The Canadian National Exhibition 113

could, and did, change temperature according to wind direction, its change was never as drastic and quick as schizophrenic Ontario. This fact was to be learned the hard way in 1964.

The date of the swim was moved up to August 20th so as to join with the opening day of the C. N. E. In previous years the C. N. E. swim had always been held the last day of the exhibition.

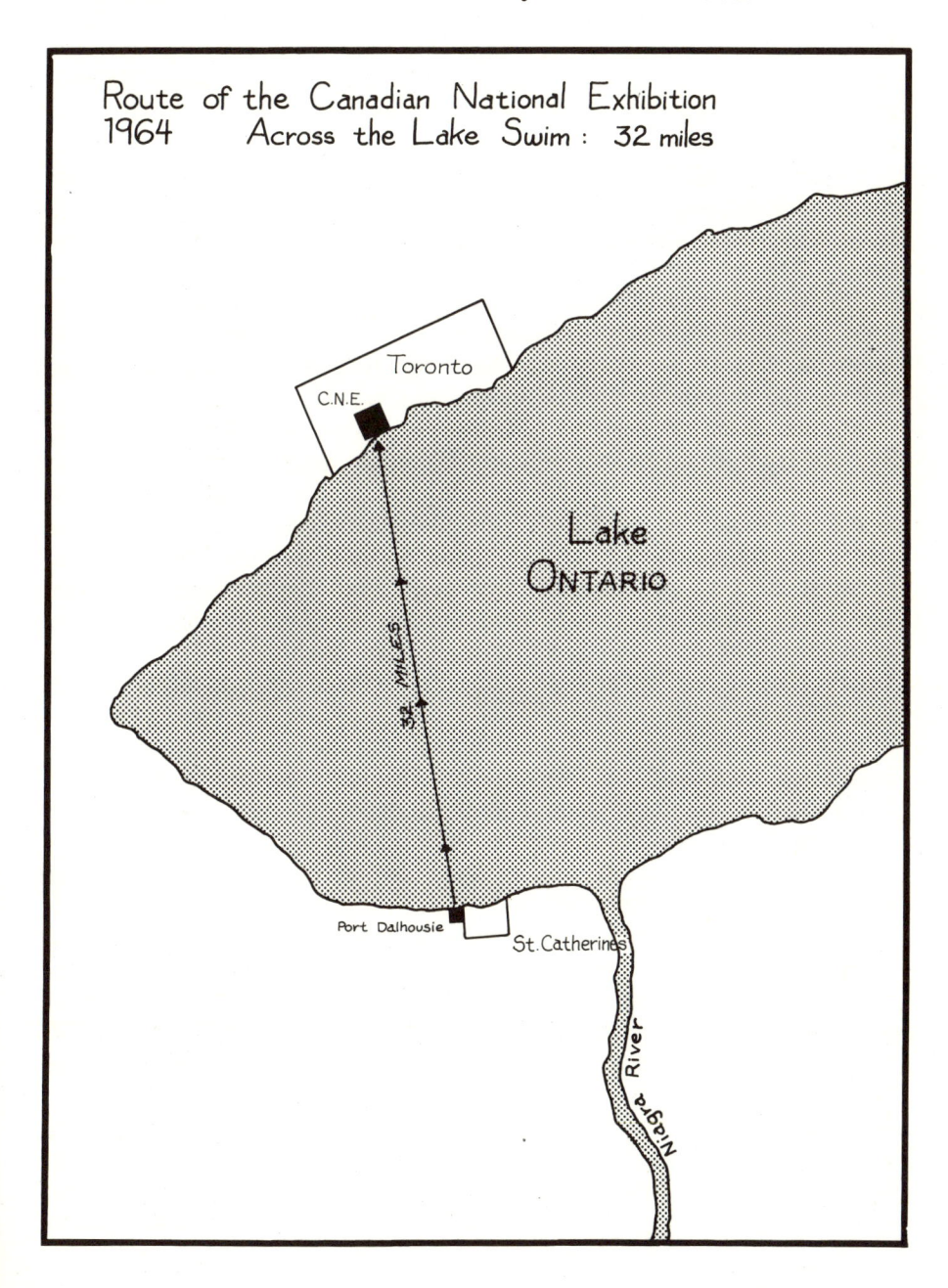

Route of the Canadian National Exhibition 1964 Across the Lake Swim: 32 miles

If ever a swimmer were to be intimidated by big-name competitors in the arrival week, now was the time. They were all there. At least ten of the entrants had won a professional race somewhere in the world. Abo-Heif was there with his Egyptian friends. Everywhere he went he was held in awe because of Lake Michigan and his other records. This would be the man to beat. John La Cousiere of Quebec was there, 1500-meter amateur champion of Canada at one time, winner of the twenty-four-mile Lake St. John, and always among the first three finishers in every race held in the last few years. He was certainly a formidable swimmer who made fellow competitors wince at his appearance on the scene.

The famous Cliff Lumsden walked into the hotel where the swimmers were put up, and while greeted by all for his friendly charm, he was at the same time covertly wished away by fellow swimmers because of his ability.

Jim Woods, who had set the record for a Lake Ontario crossing in 1957, further brought on queasiness when he ambled into the hotel lobby. Although now forty-six years old, he was still capable of upsetting the swimmers by his appearance on the scene.

Bojadzi from Yugoslavia, Mezzadra from Buenos Aires, George Park of Hamilton, Ontario, one time Canadian amateur champion, Reta from Argentina, the "Flying Dutchman" Willemse, and the famed Greta Andersen, whose title of the "World's Greatest Female Swimmer" was duly earned, were all there. Without a doubt this was the greatest field of professional swimmers ever amassed for a swim. Greta had beaten every male swimmer she had ever swum against at least once. She had won the fifty-mile Lake Michigan Swim in 1961, which allowed her to hold the world's distance record, although for one short year. She would no doubt give her best for the swim. Another "unknown" swimmer, unknown only to the public, for the coterie were well aware of her, was twenty-two-year-old Judith DeNys of Holland. The amateur champion of Holland, she was now entering her second professional race. The other swimmers were well aware of her capacities, which only compounded their worries considering the other big names entered.

The week preceding any professional swim is fraught with many happenings. For most swimmers and their coaches it is full of arguments, bickerings, and outright disruption as they hammer out rules and regulations with swim officials. Medical examinations must be taken. Official badges are given to coaches, rowers, and operators of the mother boats. Boats are assigned and given an official number. Possibilities of cheating are discussed. It has been known that some swimmers, especially in Egypt and South America, will let themselves be towed along by rope or wire when they get out of sight of official observers. Swim master George Duthie gave explicit directions to his officials to periodically run their oars behind each swimmer's boat to make sure that no swimmer used a tow. He also stated that a swimmer would be disqualified if he swam for a prolonged time behind his rowboat.

For other swimmers the week before was a holiday. Fortunate souls that they were, they could relax and enjoy the sights. These tranquil ones avoided all the unpleasantries of organization. Some made the forty-five-mile trip to Niagara Falls; others window shopped the streets of Toronto and Hamilton. Not being of an argumentative or "detailing" nature they enjoyed their trip to Toronto. Herman Willemse was one of these. By profession a school teacher in his native Holland, Herman would seek out the sights to be seen. His nature was retiring and academic, but not pedantic. His mind was always planning. While he did sight see while in Toronto his mind was still with the swim. In fact Herman was making auto trips with some of his Toronto friends around the lake. Accompanying him was his trusted and calibrated thermometer. One day he took a trip over to the south end of the lake where the swim would start. At Port Dalhousie he plunked his thermometer into the water and read a satisfying seventy-two degrees. This was followed up with a five-mile boat ride out into the lake where he again took a reading. This time it registered sixty-seven degrees—still comfortable for a swimmer. Then the long ride back to Toronto and the waterfront where the swim would end. As his hand reached down to place the thermometer in the water he only needed its confirmation to tell him what his hand told him. It was cold; a decision-making cold—it registered fifty-two degrees. Herman put the thermometer back into his pocket and murmured a few words to his friends. In the back of his mind he knew that if conditions didn't change he would scratch himself from the race. He knew he couldn't do it—and no one else would either. But Herman was taciturn. The others, not being of a scientific bent, would find out for themselves—the hard way.

Thursday, August 20th, came around fast for some and tediously slow for others. The broad sheet announcing the twenty-four starters and prize money offered was made public. $17,500 in total prize money with $7,000 to the winner brought speculation among the public. Handicappers shifted their attention from horses and boxing to offer the odds to that segment of the public which make any event a betting one. The famed Abo-Heif emerged the favorite for this race, with Greta Andersen a strong second. When three of the top swimmers scratched hours before the race the bookies' hearts skipped a beat. When such things happen they quickly have second thoughts about the odds and there is a flurry to adjust them according to the latest information.

That Thursday most of the swimmers awoke refreshed by noon at the hotel in Port Dalhousie and began last-minute preparations for the 6 P.M. start. Abo-Heif ordered two whole roast chickens and calmly proceeded to finish off his meal before ordering a dozen-egg omelette. His gargantuan appetite was as much a topic of conversation as his swimming ability. Where, oh where, did he find room for this repast in his not-overly-large five-foot ten-inch, 205 pound frame. When he had finished the omelette he then proceded to nibble on a mound of spaghetti and wedges of cheddar cheese.

By contrast, 145 pound, twenty-two-year-old Judith DeNys had tomato sandwiches and tea. Such was the variation all down the line as each swimmer was observed. The experienced swimmers made sure they had plenty of solids for it would be a long time before they could be eaten again.

By 5 P.M. the majority of swimmers were brought by bus down to the waterfront. Rejean La Cousiere arrived by Cadillac. Other swimmers upset his nerves. The news that Willemse, Bojadzi, and Suleimen had dropped out of the race was received and most of the other swimmers began questioning their wisdom in not doing the same. Willemse's decision was something to take heed of.

A long floating dock had been set up in the water from which the swimmers would leave. At intervals along the dock flew the flags of each swimmer's country. Overhead was a huge 2½-foot-diameter clock with a sweep-second hand that ticked away the remaining minutes. Some swimmers were quiet in their thoughts. Others, especially Abo-Heif, were indulging in horseplay to help relieve the tension. Periodically Abo-Heif would dive into the water and stroke around ostensibly to loosen up. "God! Can't he wait," were the thoughts of many. "He'll get all the water he wants, shortly." Suddenly the loudspeaker blared the official water temperature: seventy-two degrees. That was some consolation.

Some of the swimmers now began to apply the grease they held so much faith in. Judith and Abo-Heif applied a heavy coat of yellowish lanolin. Others used the more easily applied vaseline. Special bathing caps, equipped with fluorescent lights that would be activated upon contact with water, were issued to each swimmer. Wiping their hands free of grease the swimmers put them on, followed by goggles. Abo-Heif, forever an instinct swimmer, chose not to use them at the start. He would ask for them when he needed them.

At 5:30 P.M. the swim master began announcing the name of each swimmer, who walked amid cheers to the floating dock and took his position. Eighteen names were called and by 5:55 P.M. all were in place. At 5:59 P.M. the announcer called off the last seconds by tens. Finally with ten seconds to go each individual second . . . 9, 8, 7, 6, 5, 4, 3, 2, 1—then the gun. One of history's most talked about races began. Among the eyes that watched the battle for position were those of the intent Dutchman, Herman Willemse. Behind those observant eyes was an equally observant and working brain. Herman patted the thermometer clipped to his shirt pocket. Now it would only be a matter of time before he and his decision would be vindicated.

The eighteen swimmers thrashed their way out into the lake. Almost immediately a pack of five formed in the lead. Periodically one of its members would sprint ahead a few yards and then have second thoughts as he eased off when the other four shortly pulled even again. The person who started the sprint seemed to have second thoughts about sprinting so early in the race. Better to use the pack as a pacer and company. If one were familiar with the swimmers and their strokes they would recognize Abo-Heif, Judith DeNys, Greta Andersen, Rejean La Coursiere, and Cliff Lumsden. Abo-Heif, Andersen, and Lumsden were stroking just inches away from each other and indeed from time to time an arm of one would actually make an arc over the body of the other swimmer in order to clear him. This is the way these particular swimmers liked it. The closer they could be to their competitor the more they thrived. On the other hand, La Coursiere and DeNys swam some ten or fifteen yards off to the side. Such close swimming was an anathema to them and they considered it interference. It was enough to just be able to see the swimmer off to the side. Even a block would have been adequate. By 8 P.M., after two hours of swimming, the pack had covered some 3.6 miles. Herman, aboard one of the observation boats, leaned over the gunnel and held his thermometer in the water. When he pulled it out of the water his eyes quickly read the scale. It read sixty-nine degrees. The water temperature had dropped three degrees a little less than four miles out into the lake.

At 8:45 P.M. the boat of Argentine swimmer Roberto Reta sent out a distress call saying that they had run out of fuel. Quickly five gallon tanks were sped to the boat and its occupants ordered to start using the oars since the wind had now died down. At 9:15 P.M. the first word of a swimmer in trouble went out. Another Argentine, Romero Florencio, was treading water with stomach cramps due to his overconsumption of food. Pride prevented the Argentine from getting out of the water then because he was told that no other swimmer had yet left the water. He made up his mind to tread water until someone did. He had only twenty minutes to wait.

At 9:30 P.M., forty-two-year-old Charles Grover, way back in about twelfth place, was having difficulty with his fluorescent swimming hat. It had gone out and he wanted a replacement. The replacement never came and Charlie had to make the best of his dark hours swimming a few feet from his escort boat for fear that if he got too far away he would be lost. Charlie would earn his fame, although of a different sort, during the last hours of the race.

The swim master's boat at 9:41 finally received confirmation that at 9:05 P.M. the famed Claudia McPherson had quit the swim due to pulled leg muscles. Claudia at the age of sixteen had been the youngest person to have ever swum the English Channel at that time. When news of Claudia's quitting reached the Argentine Florencio he shortly followed. Ego does strange things to people.

By 9 P.M. the lead pack of five swimmers had dwindled to three. La Cousiere and Lumsden had faltered from the stiff pace being kept up by Judith De Nys, Abo-Heif, and Greta Andersen. La Coursiere was having trouble with his legs and by 9:25 P.M., after heated arguments with his handlers, had pulled himself aboard his escort to make him the third swimmer out of the race. Cliff, although slipping from the lead swimmers, doggedly kept up what he felt was a more realistic pace. He commented to his wife at a feeding that it's hell to have a novice swimmer like Judith in a race. Being "inexperienced" she was going out like a scared rabbit. This made it all the harder for the "pros" for they had to swim all the harder in order not to lose sight of her. He'd be damned before he would keep up her pace. He would keep his own and hope she and Abo-Heif would fade. It was small consolation, but it was better than admitting that the pace was too stiff for him. Back aboard the observation boat Herman pocketed his thermometer for the fourth time. His latest reading, taken at 10 P.M., had registered sixty-five degrees. From this point on the number of dropouts would sharply increase.

At 10:15 P.M. another Argentine, Jorge Mezzadra, was taken from the water. Fifteen minutes later the third Argentine, Roberto Reta, waved his hand and all was over for him. Around 11:15 P.M. Abo-Heif was getting fed up with Judith DeNys's erratic swimming. It seemed that every fifteen minutes or so she would sprint out ahead of him in order to lose his company. Abo-Heif decided to teach her a lesson and put on one of his sustained sprints that lasted for half an hour. In this time he pulled some quarter mile ahead of her. By the time she caught up with him over an hour had elapsed. The lesson had been learned, for the master psychologist, Abo-Heif, had taught her it was better to swim together than alone. As Cliff Lumsden had commented, "Losing Heif was harder than losing a lamprey."

At 12:35 A.M. Canadian Kurt Plunke decided his boat looked more comfortable than the void stretching out ahead of him. He became the sixth swimmer to leave the water. At 1 A.M. Herman took his seventh reading. The thermometer registered sixty-one degrees. Nobody had to tell Cliff Lumsden the water was getting colder. Within minutes of Herman's reading Cliff was clambering into his boat where his wife immediately threw several woolen blankets over him. The veteran champion's lips were blue and he trembled. When such a man as Cliff quits a race, conditions have to be at their worst. In eighteen years of competition Cliff had quit only once before. Perhaps it was conditions, perhaps age, but in any case Cliff was entitled to his rest.

At 2 A.M. the water temperature had dropped to fifty-nine degrees. The position of those swimmers still in the race stood as follows. Fifteen miles out from Port Dalhousie and battling shoulder to shoulder in first place were Abo-Heif and Judith DeNys. Judith would be fed glucose and tea every hour or so by her mother leaning over the side of the rowboat. Whenever Judith did stop to eat, Abo-Heif would stop also, but not necessarily to eat. He wanted Judy for company. Being a master psychologist Abo-Heif knew that the work grew harder and the time longer when you swam alone. Over the years Abo-Heif had gained the reputation of "the leech," for, whenever he could, he would "leech" on to the nearest competitor. If there was a swimmer ahead of him he would immediately make all efforts to pull up to him and "use" him as long as convenient. While Abo-Heif was a champion swimmer he knew how easy it was to be lulled into a comfortable pace that could in the end prove disastrous. Thus he was always ready to strain to put himself in a better position. However, being the master he was, he also knew that conservation of energy was important. If he was already in, or shared first place, there was no need to "improve" the situation because of the many miles ahead. When the showdown came a couple of miles from the finish that would be the time to make his famous move and "kiss" his unwilling pacer goodbye. As many times as he stopped to wait for Judy to finish feeding the "favor" was never returned. This never seemed to bother Abo-Heif, however, for his quick reflexes would have his tea and glucose, or fruit juices down his gullet in ten seconds and the fifteen feet Judy gained was quickly recovered.

About one half mile behind Abo-Heif and Judy was Greta Andersen, holding a strong second place. Greta knew the value of staying within hailing distance of the leaders. Being in an opportunistic position she knew that if anything went wrong with the leaders she could take quick advantage of it.

Two to three miles separated second and third positions. Ken Jensen from the United States was still bearing down, determined to hold his position secure from George Park and Mohomed Zaitoon, who were swimming in "tandem" although separated laterally by some one half mile.

Five miles behind the leaders, but swimming strong, was the amazing forty-two year-old Charles Grover. Of all the swimmers he was having the least trouble. Neither interested in staying with the leaders, for age precluded that, nor concerning himself with anyone else, he doggedly plodded on. He was swimming to finish. Bill Sadlo of New York at the age of fifty-seven had swum the route in 1957 and that was all he needed to know.

At 3 A.M. the official positions given above were corrected when an official reported that Mary Lou Whitwell was "discovered" in fourth place ahead of Grover. She had been missed because her boat was far off course.

At 4 A.M. Herman found the water temperature still holding at fifty-nine degrees. It was a favorable sign; no drop in two hours. Little did he know that race officials at Toronto were reading fifty degrees. Disaster was in the making. Now, after ten hours of swimming, the signs could be read. Those swimmers still in the water began to be more curt and argumentative with their handlers. Swearing could be heard from men and women as they demanded quicker service with their food. "Why wasn't their boat staying with them?" The cold and fatigue were beginning to take their toll. It was now only a matter of time before the next swimmer quit.

At 4:55 A.M. Mary Lou Whitwell gave the sign that she had "had it." It took three handlers to pull her aboard her rowboat where she immediately lapsed in unconsciousness. She would remember her efforts for years to come.

At 5:40 A.M. the famed Greta Andersen, her face paradoxically wreathed in smiles, perhaps knowing the pain and effort was over, hauled herself out of the water. She muttered to herself that from now on she would teach swimming. Thirty-four years old was too old to be doing what she was doing. Hustled off to a cabin-cruiser she was wrapped in blankets and sped to the waiting ambulance in Toronto where she would have her photo taken. It would later appear on the front page of the *Toronto Daily Star*. By that time her smile was gone and the viewer sees a thoroughly beaten and fatigued Greta on a stretcher surrounded by two attendants.

With the quitting of Greta only five swimmers were left: Abo-Heif, Judy, George Park, Jensen, and Grover. It was a welcome sunrise that greeted those weary and determined humans. They were being battered by a 1½ foot chop now but the sun's rays made them forget. The water temperature for the lead swimmers now registered fifty-five degrees. After thirteen hours of swimming the swimmers dared not take too long for their stops. Nor must they put any more effort than necessary to keep moving and warm. At 7:15 A.M. Judy faltered. Abo-Heif, treading water, encouraged her to keep going. After realizing that she had broken, Abo-Heif started out alone. Suddenly Judy snapped out of it and swam back up to Abo-Heif. By 8:30 A.M. Judy could no longer stay with the famous Abo-Heif, who realized that she was no longer of any value to him. Abo-Heif put his remaining strength into picking up his stroke rate to sixty-six per minute. It wasn't long before he had opened up a four-hundred-yard lead on Judith. Cheers broke out among the Egyptian crew and Abo-Heif's wife, Menard, lost her weariness. Menard had been in her husband's boat since the start of the race. After twenty-seven miles of swimming and approximately 14½ hours Abo-Heif found himself the sole possessor of first place. Only five miles separated him from success.

Now it was a horror for Judy. Progress became almost infinitesimal. She had run out. By 9 A.M. she was in tears and her boat found it almost impossible to prevent her swimming in a great arc. A blue tinge had come over her body which signified "stagnant" blood—blood that wasn't circulating. It became evident that Judy was just making the motions. At 10 A.M. the end came quickly when her mother reached over and touched her, thus disqualifying Judy. Quickly wrapped in blankets and placed in the warm cabin cruiser she was rushed to Montreal and the inevitable hospital. She took two days to recover.

With Judy out of the water only four remained. Jensen was the next one out at about the twenty-mile mark. Then the tough George Park decided to call it quits. Abo-Heif had now hit water that registered fifty-three degrees, which, along with the fatigue of sixteen hours of swimming, had dropped his speed down to less than one mile per hour. By noon he had inched his way to the 29½-mile mark and then the bottom dropped out. Now even he was not making progress. He seemed to be swimming laterally away from the boat instead of forward. Shouts seemed to make no impression on him as his wife and handlers attempted to communicate with him. He was beyond communication. He would raise his head and ask where the finish line was. Replies of "2½ miles" made no sense to him, for he immediately asked the question again. His boat would move toward him and he would move away. The great champion was like a punch-drunk boxer. He knew or felt nothing. His handlers, recognizing the seriousness of the situation, decided that Abo-Heif would have to come out soon. The man would die in the water before quitting. A subterfuge was quickly worked out. A rope was wrapped in paper and thrown in front of him. When he reached and felt it everybody cheered as if he had reached the finish line. Momentarily fooled, Abo-Heif stopped his weakened stroke. The rope was quickly swirled around him and he was yanked from the water. It was 12:46 P.M. when Abo-Heif was taken from the water. He had swum almost thirty miles in water that averaged colder than any other for such a long swim. It was a heartbreaking swim for the internationally famous swimmer who had never before quit a race in his entire swimming career. Two miles! As one wit said, "It might as well have been twenty miles considering the water temperature of fifty-three degrees."

Grandpa Charlie Grover had the satisfaction of being the last one left in the race. Charlie came out two hours after Abo-Heif, but he had only reached the twenty mile mark and the fifty-nine-degree water. Well, forty-two-year-old men need some claim to fame.

THE AFTERMATH

That swim doomed the C. N. E. swimming races to this day. Newspaper publicity was so bad that the C. N. E., ever sensitive to such, decided to cancel all future races. The general tone of the articles, with swimmers in stretchers after being taken from the water appearing in photos, was "There's a law to protect animals but what about marathon swimmers?" Conflicting articles by doctors on the physiological effect of such things were presented. Some were of the opinion that the after effects would be none; others felt repercussions would be permanent. Anxious to avoid further bad publicity, the C. N. E. promoters decided to award seventy percent of the prize money according to distance swum rather than adhere strictly to the contract signed by all swimmers that stated essentially, "No show, no money." Abo-Heif pocketed $4,400. Judy $2,850, George Park $1,250, and Charlie Grover $950. Greta Andersen got $775; Ken Jensen $650; and Mohomed Zaitoon $450. Did someone hear William Wrigley, Jr. turning over in his grave? Every other sport, trade, and profession had made financial progress. It would appear that marathon swimming was going backward.

1st Canadian National Exhibition Swim
August 31, 1927
Prize Breakdown (Sponsored by P. K. Wrigley)
From entry blank as seen in records
of Irving Davids per John Starrett

21 miles
1st $30,000   Largest purse ever offered in swimming.
2nd   7,500
3rd   2,500
4th   1,000
5th   500.00
6th   500.00

$5,000 to 1st woman
2,500 to 2nd woman
500 to 3rd woman

2nd Canadian National Exhibition Swim   1928
Two events. One for men and one for women.
Total purse $50,000
15 miles for men.
10 miles for women.

Canadian National Exhibition
Record of World's Championship Professional Swimming Races
Men
1927   Distance—21 miles ("cold" water) Wrigley Co. offers largest prize
money to date—$30,000
$50,000 total purse

1964 Lake Ontario swim: Twenty-two-year-old Judith DeNys a few minutes before her second professional race. She and Abo-Heif were in the lead together for over twelve hours before she broke. Courtesy Toronto Daily Star.

1964 Lake Ontario swim: The famed Egyptian swimmer Abdel-Latif Abo-Heif walking to the starting dock. He set a world's record the year before when he swam sixty miles across Lake Michigan. Courtesy Toronto Daily Star.

The Canadian National Exhibition

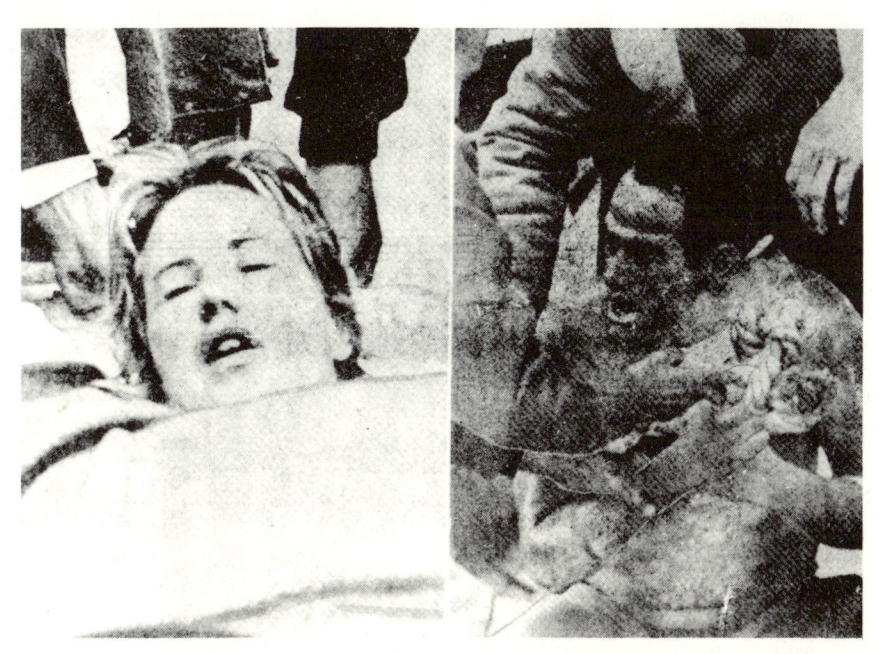

1964 Lake Ontario swim: Judith DeNys and Abo-Heif shortly after being taken from the water. Abo-Heif had gotten to within 2½ miles of finishing before the fifty-one-degree water got to him. Courtesy **Toronto Telegram**.

1 Ernest Vierkoetter, (The Black Shark), Germany   11 hrs. 45 min.
2 Georges Michel, France ($7,500)   16 hrs. 45 min.
3 William Erickson, New York ($2,500)   18 hrs. 45 min.
   (Only three men and no women finished this open event over a distance of approximately twenty-one miles.)

1928 Distance—15 miles
   Not one entrant of the 199 starters in this event succeeded in finishing on account of the extremely cold water. The purse was distributed to those unsuccessful contestants making the best showing.

George Michel, France	11 hrs. 12 min. 57 sec.	12⅛ miles
Ernest Vierkoetter, Germany	7 hrs. 39 min. 37 sec.	12 miles
Louis I. Mathias, Long Island	7 hrs. 5 min. 0 sec.	8⅜ miles
William Erickson, New York	4 hrs. 58 min. 42 sec.	7½ miles
Mendel Burditt, Toronto	4 hrs. 7 min. 10 sec.	7½ miles
Myron Cox, Los Angeles	4 hrs. 49 min. 0 sec.	7⅛ miles
Roland Tegtmier, Seattle	6 hrs. 11 min. 30 sec.	7⅛ miles
Seward D. Holley, Venice, Cal.	7 hrs. 5 min. 28 sec.	7 miles
George Young, Toronto	3 hrs. 50 min. 30 sec.	7 miles
O. C. Humel, Mauvoo, Ill.	5 hrs. 18 min. 40 sec.	6½ miles
Herr Von Papenfus, S. Africa	4 hrs. 0 min. 0 sec.	6 miles
Garnett Cochrane, Cobourg	5 hrs. 25 min. 30 sec.	6 miles
Norman Ross, Chicago, Ill.	2 hrs. 27 min. 27 sec.	5 miles
Harold L. Preston, Toronto	3 hrs. 34 min. 35 sec.	5 miles

1929 Distance—15 miles
1 Ed. Keating, New York   8 hrs. 18 min. 13.1 sec.
2 Ernest Vierkoetter, Toronto   8 hrs. 31 min. 39.3 sec.
3 Norman Ross, Chicago, Ill.   8 hrs. 49 min. 41.1 sec.
4 Isadore Sponder, Port Colborne   9 hrs. 0 min. 0 sec.
5 Mendel Burditt, Toronto   9 hrs. 15 min. 49.3 sec.
6 Myron Cox, Los Angeles   10 hrs. 2 min. 26.1 sec.

1930 Distance—15 miles
1 Marvin Nelson, Fort Dodge, Iowa   7 hrs. 43 min. 36.2 sec.
2 Isadore Sponder, Port Colborne   7 hrs. 56 min. 53.6 sec.
3 William F. Goll, New York   8 hrs. 23 min. 33.6 sec.
4 George Blagden, Memphis, Tenn.   8 hrs. 25 min. 37.4 sec.
5 Ernest Vierkoetter, Toronto   8 hrs. 30 min. 10.4 sec.
6 Norman Ross, Chicago, Ill.   8 hrs. 58 min. 40.2 sec.

1931 Distance—15 miles
1 George Young, Toronto   8 hrs. 8 min. 36.2 sec.
2 William Goll, New York   9 hrs. 25 min. 36.6 sec.
3 Warren Anderson, Sydney, N.S.   12 hrs. 9 min. 36 sec.
   (Only three swimmers finished.)

1932 Distance—15 miles
1 George Blagden, Memphis, Tenn.   7 hrs. 19 min. 25 sec.
2 Ginni Gambi, Ravenna, Italy   7 hrs. 24 min. 27 sec.
3 Isadore Sponder, Port Colborne   7 hrs. 30 min. 7 sec.
4 Marvin Nelson, Fort Dodge, Iowa   7 hrs. 38 min. 27 sec.
5 William Goll, New York   7 hrs. 41 min. 21 sec.
6 Harry Glancy, Cincinnati, Ohio   8 hrs. 11 min. 10 sec.

1933 Distance—15 miles
1 Marvin Nelson, Fort Dodge, Iowa   7 hrs. 0 min. 37 sec.
2 William Goll, New York   7 hrs. 18 min. 33 sec.
3 Frank Pritchard, Buffalo, N.Y.   7 hrs. 20 min. 45 sec.
4 Harry Glancy, Cincinnati, Ohio   7 hrs. 36 min. 29 sec.
5 Stanley Pritchard, Buffalo, N.Y.   7 hrs. 44 min. 56 sec.
6 Eli Radakovitch, Duquesne, Pa.   8 hrs. 1 min. 59 sec.

1934 Distance—15 miles
1 Marvin Nelson, Fort Dodge, Iowa   7 hrs. 47 min. 43 sec.
2 William Goll, New York   8 hrs. 14 min. 47 sec.
3 John Cairo, Toronto   8 hrs. 47 min. 28 sec.
4 Dan Dembicki, Windsor   9 hrs. 26 min. 27 sec.
5 William Sadlo, Jr., Corona, L.I.   9 hrs. 58 min. 6 sec.

1935 Distance—5 miles
1 Ginni Gambi, Ravenna, Italy   2 hrs. 8 min. 55 sec.
2 Frank Pritchard, Buffalo, N.Y.   2 hrs. 11 min. 40 sec.
3 William Nolan, Chelsea, Mass.   2 hrs. 13 min. 30 sec.
4 Sam Shields, Louisville, Ky.   2 hrs. 14 min. 20 sec.
5 Clarence Ross, New York   2 hrs. 17 min. 35 sec.
6 Wilson Padgett, Marion, Ark.   2 hrs. 20 min. 0 sec.
7 William Goll, New York   2 hrs. 21 min. 45 sec.

1936 Distance—5 miles
1 Frank Pritchard, Buffalo, N.Y.   2 hrs. 7 min. 9 sec.
   (2.36 MPH)
2 Warren Priddy, St. Catharines, Ont.   2 hrs. 23 min. 41 sec.
3 Connie Gareau, Sudbury   2 hrs. 28 min. 40 sec.
4 Nicholas Ostapyk, Ottawa   2 hrs. 31 min. 1 sec.
5 John Cairo, Toronto   2 hrs. 32 min. 10 sec.
6 William Nolan, Chelsea, Mass.   2 hrs. 35 min. 58 sec.
7 Richard Brown, Laureldale, Pa.   2 hrs. 37 min. 35 sec.

1937 Distance—10 miles
1 Frank Pritchard, Buffalo, N.Y.   4 hrs. 19 min. 28 sec.
   (2.31 MPH)
2 William Nolan, Chelsea, Mass.   4 hrs. 25 min. 45 sec.
3 Ginni Gambi, Ravenna, Italy   4 hrs. 38 min. 16 sec.
4 Ben Gazel, Toronto   4 hrs. 41 min. 59 sec.
5 Stanley Pritchard, Buffalo, N.Y.   4 hrs. 50 min. 33 sec.
6 Renato Bacigalupo, Rapallo, Italy   4 hrs. 54 min. 45 sec.
7 Ed Faulkner, Kansas City, Mo.   4 hrs. 55 min. 36 sec.
8 Bill Sadlo, Jr., Corona, N.Y.   4 hrs. 57 min. 8 sec.
9 Haward Norton, Dundas, Ont.   5 hrs. 8 min. 35 sec.
10 Nicholas Ostapyk, Ottawa, Ont.   5 hrs. 11 min. 50 sec.

1947 Distance—10 miles
1 Ben Gazel, Toronto   4 hrs. 44 min. 27 sec.
2 Jerry Kerschner, Columbus, Ohio   4 hrs. 50 min. 10 sec.
3 Stephen Wozniak, Buffalo, N.Y.   5 hrs. 5 min. 40 sec.
4 Egbert Courage, Sampson, N.Y.   5 hrs. 26 min. 11 sec.
5 Tom Park, Hamilton   5 hrs. 36 min. 51 sec.
6 Clifford Lumsden, New Toronto   5 hrs. 48 min. 0 sec.

1948 Distance—10 miles
1 Stephen Wozniak, Buffalo, N.Y.   4 hrs. 29 min. 16 sec.
2 Ben Gazel, Toronto   4 hrs. 34 min. 29 sec.
3 Jerry Kerschner, Columbus, Ohio   4 hrs. 36 min. 7 sec.
4 Bob Pirie, Toronto   4 hrs. 41 min. 35 sec.
5 Clifford Lumsden, New Toronto   4 hrs. 47 min. 16 sec.
6 Jacques Amyot, Quebec, P.Q.   5 hrs. 16 min. 55 sec.

1949 Distance—15 miles
1 Clifford Lumsden, New Toronto (18 years old)   7 hrs. 54 min. 55 sec.
   ($5,500 prize + $50 for each of 15 laps + $50 for fastest mile)
2 Ben Gazel, Toronto   8 hrs. 21 min. 24 sec.
3 Bill Sadlo, Jr., Corona, N.Y.   9 hrs. 44 min. 10 sec.
   (Due to the 51° water temperature only three swimmers out of the 82 who started finished the race.)

1950 Distance—15 miles
1 Clifford Lumsden, New Toronto   7 hrs. 18 min. 5 sec.
   (Amer. Jerry Kerschner leads for 8 miles, Lumsden overtakes him.)
2 Tom Park, Hamilton   7 hrs. 29 min. 21 sec.
3 Ben Gazel, Toronto   7 hrs. 36 min. 40 sec.
4 William Goll, Hillsdale, Mich.   8 hrs. 4 min. 43 sec.

5	Jacques Amyot, Quebec, P.Q.	9 hrs. 12 min. 41 sec.
6	Charles F. Grover, Dorchester, Mass.	9 hrs. 32 min. 2 sec.
7	Henry C. Pferr, Brooklyn, N.Y.	9 hrs. 42 min. 19 sec.
8	John Jeremy, Toronto	10 hrs. 5 min. 15 sec.
9	Michael Sadlo, Jr., Whitestone, N.Y.	10 hrs. 19 min. 57 sec.
10	M. Chrostowski, Providence, R.I.	10 hrs. 35 min. 46 sec.

1951 Distance—10 miles
1 Jerry Kerschner, Columbus, Ohio — 4 hrs. 26 min. 32 sec.
2 George Bevan, Winnipeg, Man. — 4 hrs. 31 min. 25 sec.
3 Cliff Lumsden, New Toronto — 4 hrs. 32 min. 28 sec.
4 Stephen Wozniak, Buffalo, N.Y. — 4 hrs. 36 min. 52 sec.
5 Forbes Norris, Winchester, Mass. — 4 hrs. 37 min. 23 sec.
6 Paul Malloney, Buffalo, N.Y. — 4 hrs. 38 min. 59 sec.
(Tom Park out because of cramps.)

1952 Distance—10 miles
1 Cliff Lumsden, New Toronto — 4 hrs. 24 min. 6 sec.
 ($5,000 + $150 in lap money)
2 Forbes Norris, Winchester, Mass. — 4 hrs. 27 min. 56 sec.
3 Stephen Wozniak, Buffalo, N.Y. — 4 hrs. 40 min. 45 sec.
4 Tom Park, Hamilton — 4 hrs. 48 min. 22 sec.
5 Hassan Abov Bakr, Cairo, Egypt — 5 hrs. 5 min. 59 sec.
6 Saied El Araby, Cairo, Egypt — 5 hrs. 8 min. 43 sec.

1953 Distance—10 miles
1 Cliff Lumsden, New Toronto — 4 hrs. 26 min. 46 sec.
 ($5,150) He overtakes Bevan at 8 mile mark.
2 Forbes Norris, Winchester, Mass. — 4 hrs. 29 min. 40 sec.
3 George Bevan, Etobicoke — 4 hrs. 40 min. 5 sec.
4 Charles Grover, Dorchester, Mass. — 5 hrs. 26 min. 25 sec.
5 William Goll, Landing, N.J. — 5 hrs. 30 min. 0 sec.
6 Jack Rosen, Toronto — 5 hrs. 36 min. 21 sec.

1954 30-mile Relay Swim (13 hours)
1 Canadian Team, $10,000 — Ben Gazel (43 years old), Cliff Lumsden, George Bevan, and Tom Park.
2 "Big Ten" (US), $5,000 — Wm. W. Heusner, Jr., Urbana, Ill.; F. Wallace Jeffries, Hinsdale, Ill.; David Anderson, Minneapolis, Minn.; and Matt Mann III, Lansing, Mich.
3 "Buffalo" Team, $3,000 — Chas. F. Grover, Dorchester, Mass.; Paul Malone, Ottawa, Ont.; Paul J. Maloney, Buffalo, N.Y.; and Steve Wozniak, Buffalo.
4 "Mimco" Team, $2,000 — Bill Goll, Landing, N.J.; Bill Sadlo, Jr., Whitestone, N.Y.; Jack Rosen, Toronto; and Jacques Amyot, Quebec, P.Q.

1955 "Across Lake Ontario"
1 Cliff Lumsden, New Toronto — 19 hrs. 48 min. 9 sec.
 $15,000 1st prize to Cliff Lumsden + gifts (Hunting Lodge, House, consumer endorsements, and $1 for every stroke taken in last 5 miles) for a total purse of $84,000
 (Changed on account of weather to 32 mile triangle course in front of Exhibition.)

Successful Lake Ontario Swimmers

1954	Marilyn Bell, Toronto (16)	20 hrs. 57 min.
(1955	Tom Park tried but burned out with 2 miles to go)	
1956	Brenda Fisher, England	18 hrs. 50 min.
1956	John Jaremy, Toronto	21 hrs. 13 min.
1957	Bill Sadlo, N.Y. (57)	25 hrs. 10 min.
1957	Jim Woods, Orlando, Fla.	18 hrs. 35 min. (Cherry Beach)

Men's and Women's Races

1961 Distance—15 miles

1	Herman Willemse, Utrecht, Holland	6 hrs. 54 min. 01 sec.
2	Tom Park, Lakewood, Cal.	7 hrs. 30 min. 40 sec.
3	Mrs. Greta Andersen, Los Alamitos, Cal.	7 hrs. 33 min. 25 sec.
4	Cliff Lumsden, New Toronto	7 hrs. 36 min. 20 sec.
5	Rejean Lacoursiere, Montreal, P.Q.	7 hrs. 39 min. 35 sec.
6	Helge Jensen, Toronto	8 hrs. 01 min. 10 sec.
7	Mary Kok, Hilversum, Holland	8 hrs. 10 min. 15 sec.

1962 Distance—15 miles (Warm water—73°)

1	Herman Willemse, Utrecht, Holland	6 hrs. 38 min. 00 sec.

RECORD (2.25+MPH)

2	Cliff Lumsden, New Toronto	7 hrs. 26 min. 30 sec.
3	Alfredo Camarero, Buenos Aires, Argentina	7 hrs. 31 min. 10 sec.
4	John Lacoursiere, Montreal	7 hrs. 31 min. 11 sec.
5	Mary Martha Sinn, Ann Arbour, Mich.	7 hrs. 31 min. 45 sec.

.55 MPH difference

6	Mary Kok, Hiversum, Holland	7 hrs. 34 min. 45 sec.
7	Thomas Park, Lakewood, Cal.	7 hrs. 53 min. 20 sec.

1963 Distance—15 miles (Water temp.—55°)

1	Abdel Abo-Heif, Alexandria, Egypt (1.7+ MPH)	7 hrs. 37 min. 26 sec.
2	Mary Martha Sinn, Ann Arbour, Mich.	7 hrs. 39 min. 11 sec.
3*	Herman Willemse, Utrecht, Holland	7 hrs. 44 min. 14 sec.
4	George Park, Toronto	7 hrs. 52 min. 50 sec.
5	Alfred Camarero, Buenos Aires	7 hrs. 55 min. 10 sec.
6	Clifford Lumsden, Toronto	7 hrs. 58 min. 45 sec.
7	Syder Guiscaedo, Buenos Aires	8 hrs. 29 min. 05 sec.

* Led for 14 miles.

1964 Across Lake Ontario Swim—32 miles

The weather turned inclement for the final quarter of the swim. No swimmer completed the course. Water temp.—72° at start; 53° at night. Official places and awards for longest distance swum.

1	Abo-Heif 30 miles	19 hrs.	$4,400	(age 34)
2	Judith DeNys 26 miles	17+ hrs.	$2,850	(age 22)
3	George Park 26 miles		$1,250	(age 30)
4	Charles Grover 25 miles		$950	(age 44)
5	Greta Andersen		$775	
6	Ken Jensen		$650	
7	Mohomed Zaiton		$450	

8
Abo-Heif Is a Garbage Can

Food, both in and out of the water, is a great topic of conversation among the swimmers. It offers almost limitless possibilities for gambits by the experienced professional to mislead the unwary new arrival. Young swimmers and mediocre swimmers are always ready to swallow any suggestion offered by the pro. Instead of attributing the speed and endurance of a champion to genetics and hard work, they are quick to assume that it may be due to diet, drugs, or techniques in training. It is the endless search for the magic touch that, once discovered, will allow them to attain perfection. It just isn't so. Scientific studies over decades on athletes and nonathletes have shown that there is no magic food. The ambrosia or nectar of the gods just doesn't exist. All the wheat germ, honey, protein, and vitamins consumed over the basic minimum requirements had no effect on performance. What is swallowed while in the water is important only from the standpoint that it must be a high sugar content liquid with a minimum of solid particles. The fact that doctors can keep patients alive for weeks on glucose administered intravenously is testimony enough to the fact that under stress conditions the primary need is sugar. An athlete expending a large amount of energy in competition doesn't need anything else. If you throw the rest of the stuff in, the body just has to work harder digesting it. The overload can mean the difference between success or failure.

Explorers, both ancient and modern, have marveled at the ability of primitive peoples to carry on prolonged feats of endurance while eating very little. Sherpas living in the Himalayan Mountains carry loads eighty to 125 pounds for twenty-five miles while at heights of ten thousand to twenty thousand feet. At the end of a day's march their employers invariably find them laughing and joking. Throughout their hike their food intake was just a couple of handfuls of curdled milk, cheese, and powdered flour. The examples can be extended to peoples of other areas but varied foods. The modern nutritionist would blanch at the seeming inadequacies. The reader must not be misled into believing that this is the steady diet. Whenever the stress condition is over they do return to a more varied menu. Before I became a trainer of marathon swimmers I used to have a lot of "absolute" knowledge concerning what foods were best for training and swimming. All of it was gleaned from scientific journals and books and from what the U.S. Department of Health recommends its citizens to eat. It is built around the basic seven: meat, milk, eggs, fruits, vegetables, cheese, and bread. Well, after coming in contact with some of the world champions in marathon swimming, a serious revision had to be made in my ideas. Nothing was ever done according to the textbook. True, some of the swimmers consciously tried to select a diet that was "rounded" and varied. It gave them a feeling of security because it was advocated by men who were supposed to know. The men who followed the "sane" diet were never any more prevalent in the winner's circle than those who ate according to their taste; which brings us to the heart of this chapter.

Abo-Heif, who has dominated the sport for fifteen years, presents a fascinating example of instinct in eating. Abo-Heif has no rules. Before a race Abo-Heif is consistently the first one in the dining room. He comes in about four hours before the race is scheduled to start. He makes it a purpose to have a huge meal of basically protein. Two whole roast chickens and a quart of orange juice and milk is typical. Three out of four times he will finish the meal. The fourth time he is not hungry at the time and after two forkfuls he ceases eating. Other swimmers will force themselves to fill up, even though they are not hungry and in some cases end up vomiting in the race because they ate too much too soon before the race. By the time Abo-Heif enters the water his huge meal has had three hours to digest. Let us continue to watch Abo-Heif during the race. If he has had a big meal beforehand his first feeding in the water will come three hours or more after the beginning of the race. If he hasn't eaten big before the event, his first feeding in the water may come as soon as twenty minutes after the start. On the other hand, champion swimmers like Iglesias and Willemse were light pre-race eaters. If the race was early in the morning, as most are, their meal was simply toast and marmalade washed down with coffee. A nutritionist would say it would be inadvisable to begin a hard workday on such a skimpy meal. Iglesias and Willemse were two of the biggest money winners in the sport. They didn't practice what was advocated.

Getting back to Abo-Heif, it must be mentioned that he has a tremendous digestive capacity even while swimming. One of the most humorous incidents I've ever witnessed was during the La Tuque 24-

Hour Swim in 1968. Most of the swimmers were on their own or their trainer's conception of the proven liquids laced with sugar, Abo-Heif included. Sometime around the fifteen-hour mark Abo-Heif felt that he needed some solid food. I went to the nearest restaurant and got two hamburgers and three fried eggs. When Abo-Heif got out of the water after being relieved by his partner, he promptly slurped, and I mean slurped, the eggs and hamburgers down. He then drank five or six glasses of orange pop confiscated from a bystander. Ten minutes later he was back swimming his laps at the same speed as the winners. Abo-Heif and his partner placed fourth. It is typical of Abo-Heif. Anything that smells good at the time is eaten. It is delightful to watch a naturally programmed eater like Abo-Heif in action. Unperturbed with schedules, vitamins, balances and so forth he goes swimming on. It would kill another swimmer. In all fairness Abo-Heif is the only swimmer who can do such a thing. He is an exception. The old saw with which most of us are familiar, "Don't eat sweets before a meal, it will ruin your appetite," has been proven untrue by Abo-Heif and a few others. I've seen swimmers down a banana split or a can of peaches minutes before consuming a huge steak dinner without being in the least bit bothered.

The gambits and ploys that take place in the restaurants are humorous to listen to. Food will be used to "psyche out" the unwary. If asked what they recommend in the water, some will see the chance to put a swimmer out of commission. "There is nothing like raw carrots or apples." Many a swimmer has been tricked by seeing Abo-Heif cart down to the dock for all to see an open box of apples. He doesn't touch them, of course. Some of the beginners may. Scratch one competitor.

One of the best psyche-out artists in the game was George Park. He was a great "con man," not only in food suggestions, but also in "secret" techniques. George, like all con men, has great intelligence and charm. Like all practitioners of the art he had the facts well in hand. He would tell you ten truths in a row and then slip in the one lie. If the listener was not aware, naïve, or not concentrating, the lie was swallowed. George was at his best, as usual, in the 1968 La Tuque 24-Hour Swim. A group of swimmers were sitting around a table discussing swimming that year in one of the local restaurants. Before long George began to pontificate on his "secret" technique for taking advantage of other swimmers during the race to be held the following day. He began by telling how the porpoises ride the bow wave of a ship. They ride the wave effortlessly. He then discussed the physics behind the phenomenon. This was followed by his discovery that he found that by swimming just the right distance ahead of another swimmer he himself could take advantage of that swimmer's bow wave. Also, if he happened to be behind a swimmer, he could take advantage of the bow wave as it spreads outward in a V. In this case he could be "pulled" along behind the swimmer. Then, lowering his voice, as if he did not want to be heard, he would "confide" in one swimmer that the only way for a swimmer to avoid helping George was to swim around him in a wide sweep. This was said in such a confidential manner that the unwary were taken in. It was all hogwash as far as the swimming human was concerned. But George had slipped across the point he wanted. Any swimmer gullible enough to believe the story would now make a wide sweep around George, thus swimming further to pass him, or if being overtaken, would swing out and make room for him to pass. This is exactly what George wanted. It made things easier for him. One could not but admire George's devious and marvelous presentation. It would have no effect on men like Abo-Heif, Matuch, Iglesias, and so forth, but on others. . . .

If an emblem were to be made that represents Abo-Heif and his feats I am sure it would be represented by the following: a big set of beautiful teeth, amidst a friendly grin and a picture of a huge stomach. Abo-Heif swallows just about anything out of the water and he produces results.

When one remembers that a professional or Olympic champion will have swum between fifteen and forty thousand miles in training during his career it is little wonder to learn that he has little time to be overly concerned about what is on the dinner table. After swimming ten miles during the day the exigencies of hunger leave him little time to be dainty.

9
Atlantic City: Convention Mecca of the World

In 1954 Atlantic City, New Jersey began to show a different kind of flesh than that of its famed annual Miss America Pageant. Since 1921 beautiful young ladies from all over the United States made their pilgrimage to "Fun City" to parade their bodies before a coterie of judges in hopes of being selected "Miss America" and thus securing their fame and fortune. In 1954 the well-padded frames of professional marathon swimmers in nylon swimming suits were lured to the sandy beaches of Absecon Island by the promise of dollars. Thus began a decade of swims that was to offer more to the spectator than any other annual swimming event held to date.

Atlantic City lies at the end of Absecon Island, a longish, irregularly shaped island off the eastern coast of the United States. It is a low, sandy place separated from the mainland by a narrow strait that is only some 125 yards wide at its narrowest, and three hundred yards at its widest. At high tide the meadows are partly covered with water. The island was first settled by whalers and oystermen who were soon followed by pirates and privateers. By 1850 industry had moved into the area. Iron plants, shipyards, textile and glass industries soon became important in its economy. Commercial fishing continued to keep pace with other industries in the area. Soon it was followed by sports fishermen casting their lines for the exciting bluefish, bonita, tuna, marlin, and striped bass. Today all these industries play second fiddle to Atlantic City's most remunerative industry—tourism. Hotels, amusement parks, and convention halls are its life blood. It was in 1870 that the first boardwalk was built in response to complaints by the railroads and hotels. Visitors were tracking sand by the ton into trains and hotels. The present famous boardwalk is the fifth and is made of steel and concrete with a wooden floor. Completed in 1939 it is sixty feet wide and four miles long. The boardwalk is a delight to visitors to the resort city because it offers a delightful plaisance on which to stroll while at the same time they can enjoy the ocean view and breezes.

With the growth of the tourist trade the city fathers were always ready to incorporate new attractions for the entertainment of the holiday crowds. In 1876 the first annual Easter Parade was held. A few years later the carnival touch was added when amusement piers were built. In 1921 the first Miss America Pageant was held. Soon large and small conventions were holding their annual meetings at Atlantic City because of the pleasures to be offered when the meetings were over. Today the island has 160,000 visitors per year. There are sixty hotels within a block of the boardwalk on one short two-mile stretch. The income from the hotels alone runs into millions of dollars a year.

It was in 1953 that Jim Toomey conceived the idea of an around-the-island swim. Toomey had no trouble in finding a couple of Atlantic City lifeguards willing to make an attempt. Ed Solitaire and Ed Stetser, perhaps tired of watching sea gulls and bathing beauties, were all for the idea. Toomey, a thinking man, told the men to contain their enthusiasm while he drummed up publicity in a city that was all too aware of its importance. With visiting restaurateurs and radio station owners, as well as amusement park owners, it wasn't long before he had interested backers. Radio station WOND made the first contribution of $100. The owner of the Steel Pier Amusement Center soon matched it. Then a restaurateur came through with $400 and the financial requirements were attained. The beach patrol buddies of the lifeguards quickly offered their services as rowers. In an amazingly short time radio station WOND had spread the word that the two men were to attempt the "twenty-six-mile" round-the-island swim. The swimmers would leave together from Steel Pier on the morning of August 5, 1953.

Knowing of the "weakness" of publicity men, I got out my copy of the U.S. Department of Commerce Nautical Chart 826-SC and checked the mileage of the course around Absecon Island. After all, the Catalina Island Swim had been billed as twenty-two miles, but turned out to be 18.5 miles. In another case, the Lake St. John promoters had their across-the-lake swim billed at twenty-six miles, but in reality it was only nineteen miles. After several checks with dividers, I could get no more than twenty-two miles out of the Absecon Island circumnavigation. I shall discuss the matter in a little more detail shortly, but now back to Ed Solitaire and Ed Stetser.

When they walked onto Steel Pier early that August morning they were certain of one thing. The water would be warm: seventy-six

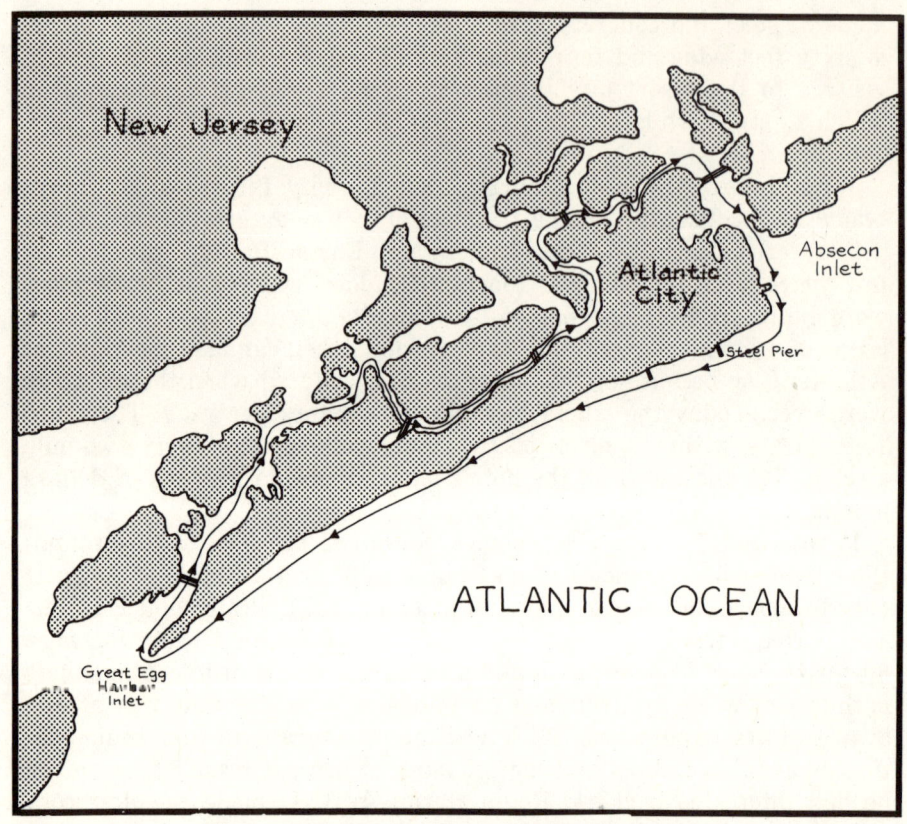

The twenty-two-mile Atlantic City race.

degrees or better. They wouldn't have to worry about chills. Gathered around them were a group of about two hundred interested spectators and newsmen. The bugaboo of tides worried only the inexperienced. They had done enough swimming in the narrow inland waterway to know that it didn't drain a large enough area to cause currents of any major concern. While it was true there could be a considerable current at either end of the island—Absecon Inlet and Great Egg Harbor Inlet—they could be outwitted, as future swimmers learned, by inshore swimming. The average velocity at these points could be two knots. The maximum distance (and only at the Absecon Inlet—see map) a swimmer had to go in this area was little over one mile. The twenty or so piers in this area effectively served to protect the swimmer if it so happened he was in the area at flood tide, which was unlikely. Newsmen, being what they were, however, made the most of such things in order to dramatize a tedious swim.

The swimmers dove into the water from Steel Pier and headed in a southwesterly direction paralleling the more or less straight ocean side of the island. The surf was breaking lightly and all that was necessary was to stay about one half mile out from the sandy beaches for about eight miles before they made the turn into Great Egg Harbor for the narrow channel swim. Early morning strollers on the boardwalk commented on the enthusiasm of youth as the swimmers plowed along. Throughout the morning the pair swam together and by early afternoon they had reached the end of the island and began their turn into Great Egg Harbor Inlet. As planned they reached the inlet at slack tide and no extra effort was needed in doubling back into the inland waterway. By mid-afternoon sightseers began to accumulate in ever-increasing numbers at street ends and bridges to cheer the intrepid men on. Three miles into the waterway Stetser began to falter. While not weakening he decided to step down the pace somewhat. Bidding farewell to his buddy Solitaire, he called, "See you at Steel Pier."

After ten hours of swimming the lifeguards had slacked off considerably from their early pace. Considering that they had no idea of what constitutes training for a marathon swim they were doing quite well. None of their training swims had been over $2\frac{1}{2}$ hours, which is just about half of what a seasoned marathoner does daily. After twelve hours of swimming Ed Solitaire had reached Absecon Inlet and had only three more miles to go before reaching Steel Pier, from which he had started early that morning. He was now doing the breast stroke quite often in order to ease his aching, tired body.

Again things worked out perfectly timewise. He had hit the inlet shortly after high tide. There would be no current to worry about. In fact in another hour or so he might have the gentle help of a beginning ebb tide. It took Solitaire some $2\frac{1}{2}$ hours to make the last three miles, but it was a jubilant Solitaire that smacked his hand on Steel Pier fourteen hours after leaving it. Newsmen and promoters wanted to hustle him off for interviews but Solitaire insisted on waiting for his beach companion Stetser. Stetser came in an hour later and the two friends had the double satisfaction of a shared accomplishment. The groundwork had been laid for a decade of the United State's contribution to the sport of marathon swimming.

1954 was Atlantic City's centennial year. It didn't take long for the owner of Steel Pier to offer his attraction to the city fathers for making it a big year. George Hamid, Sr. put up $5,000 to any swimmer who could duplicate the Solitaire-Stetser feat. Hamid soon received inquiries as to whether there would be any other prizes for those who finished other than first. Realizing that other place money was necessary in order to have a field he quickly offered a piece of the action to other contributors. Soon other businessmen and suburban villages offered prizes down to tenth place, and the scramble was on.

Many swimmers arrived several weeks before the race to enjoy the resort atmosphere. It was a great convenience to have a room in a decent hotel a few short blocks from the ocean beach. The general inactivity soon began to pall for the professionals as the race date approached. They found their minds always returning to the serious business soon to be at hand. Among those who showed up for this first Atlantic City Race were: Cliff Lumsden, four-time winner of C. N. E. races; Tom Park, winner and placer in professional races; and Marilyn Bell, the unknown who was to become known a few weeks later when she set a world-record swimming across Lake Ontario. Interest was high among the local people because of their curiosity as to how the pros would do compared with the home-town boys' swim the previous year.

On race day the conditions were ideal. The ocean was undulating with gentle swells that posed no threat to any swimmer. The inner waterway was flat as usual for its narrow width offered no "bite" to the wind. Only if the wind shifted parallel to this waterway and reached gale proportion would a slight chop build up. This was an extremely unlikely event and would pose more of a hazard to the rowboats than to the swimmers. In other words the inner waterway was a well-protected haven that gave protection to moored boats in some of its larger extensions. There was an added delight when the swimmers learned of the water temperature. There would be no cold water threat. The ocean registered an ideal seventy degrees while the inner waterway registered a somewhat too warm eighty-two degrees. For most of the swimmers these conditions were much preferable to water in the fifties. Added psychological comfort was given the swimmers when swim director James Toomey announced that the time selected for the start of the race had been chosen so there would be no conflict with the tides.

When the gun went off twenty-five swimmers began the circuit. It proved to be a most fascinating race to watch, for no less than eight swimmers were bunched in the lead for the first two hours. Not a single one gave so much as an inch. After two hours of this hectic pace two Canadians began to slowly pull away from their tormentors. Tom Park and Cliff Lumsden were now putting the pressure on, or to be more correct, kept the pressure up while the others slacked off. In just two hours they had covered almost five miles. Like all professional races a livelihood was at stake. After months of spending their own money in training this was the moment to recoup the expenses and make the gain.

Everywhere along the boardwalk and beaches crowds gathered to watch the highly touted event, while vendors hawked their refreshments. After five hours of swimming, race officials looked in disbelief at the lead swimmers. If they kept up the pace they would circumnavigate Absecon Island in ten hours. Park and Lumsden were now well into the inner waterway and had already passed the first bridge that was loaded with over a thousand spectators cheering their efforts. The number three swimmer, Steve Wozniak of the United States, was still a threat, for he was only one block behind and rapidly being overtaken by another American. Experienced swimmers that they were, Lumsden and Park knew there would be no security until one of them touched the finishing platform. Spurred and goaded by each other's presence they continued to keep up an almost 2½-mile-per-hour pace.

It was at the twenty-mile mark with 2½ miles to go that each swimmer realized that each other's company could now be dispensed with. The concept of waiting for the last several hundred yards was what the amateurs did. To wait that long posed too many variables that could go wrong. No pro wants company in that last two miles. He wants the comfort of any lead to be consolidated long before the finish. In fact, a precarious compromise had been reached between Park and Lumsden long hours before when each knew that they were swimming their maximum. As long as they shared the lead, any "over-maximum" effort would be a foolish jeopardizing of their bodies. Being pros they knew where they stood. However, now the time came for the showdown. Each swimmer would burst into a sprint, which at this point took great effort. First Park, then Lumsden would pull ahead for a few feet, but neither was about to let $5,000 slip from his grasp at that point. Each refused to "break." For twenty-five minutes this agonizing process went on and then finally Lumsden failed to regain a ten-foot lead that Park took. Try as he may, Cliff stayed that ten feet behind Park. There was now only 1½ miles to the finish line. Soon it was twelve feet that Lumsden lacked as Park continued to tenaciously "up" his effort. Over the next half mile Park extended his lead to one hundred yards while all the time praying that his lungs and muscles would hold out. Park, with ¾ of a mile to go, flipped over on to his back for a couple of strokes to see where Cliff was. It was a very insecure 150 yards. Bearing down with all the effort and will that resided in him, Park made for the finish line, which he spotted ahead of him. A crowd of 15,000 stood on the pier and the beaches around it. Park had opened up another 250 yards between himself and Cliff by the time he slapped the finish board. At this point there was a close similarity between Park's slumped frame and the sagging pennants hanging in the dead calm. Three minutes later Cliff hauled in and was greeted by a now-smiling Tom who had not yet left the water.

Tom's time of nine hours twenty-one minutes forty-two seconds became a record for the course that in the next ten years was never broken. If the reader looks at the summary of the Atlantic City swims he can see how well his time has stood up. In fact the officials became rather chagrined that in the first three years of the race it looked so easy. They decided to dispense with tide considerations and even began the races *against* the tide. The pros were equal to it however, for they found ways to surmount that by swimming close in toward shore and pulling themselves along the shallow bottom and underwater portions of the piers.

All the following races held at Atlantic City were exciting, that is up to the time of Herman Willemse, who brought ability and science to the sport. His careful analysis of tide tables and use of trusted rowers and navigators gave him a tremendous advantage over the swimmers of previous years.

In 1955 Park again won the race, this time coming in some six minutes ahead of his nemesis Lumsden. However it was in 1957 that Cliff gained revenge, if $\frac{1}{20}$ of a second can be considered revenge, when he came in a single stroke ahead of Park. There were arguments galore over the decision by many swimmers and spectators because of the inherent "unfairness" of judging a marathon event by a single stroke. In horse racing (a much shorter distance is involved, of course) they judge by the nose. In fact, many subsequent races took the hint (when aware of the problem) and watched the heads of the swimmers coming into the finish. Other connoisseurs of the sport suggested that any marathon event be judged a tie if two swimmers finished one half body length or less apart. Promoters and sponsors being notorious for relinquishing any control over their event have nicely avoided the issue to this date. As a consequence such things still happen occasionally, and the arguments begin anew.

Park and Lumsden continued their rivalry for many years at the C. N. E. Even when placing they continued to battle each other for third, fourth, or fifth place. By 1960 an unknown slender Dutchman showed up in Atlantic City. A quiet and reserved grammar school teacher, Herman Willemse brought along his father, brains, and bicycle. While others were sitting around hotel lobbies talking, Herman was reading, talking to boatmen, making friends with lifeguards, and buying nautical charts and tide-tables. Yes, it was a wonderful way to see the island also, on a bike; it was a good way to meet people also, and Herman had no trouble speaking to Americans either for English was his second tongue. When the 1960 race was over Herman had won it, coming in ten minutes before the terrible duo of Park and Lumsden, who tied for second place. For the next four years Herman was never to lose an Atlantic City race. In fact, each subsequent year he lowered the winning time that he set the previous year. He learned, as the others also learned, that when the sponsors made the race harder (Atlantic City itself took over the sponsorship from the Steel Pier owner in 1957) by starting the race against, or shortly before, the beginning of flood tide, advantage could be gained against the tides by grabbing hold of solid objects under the water. Of course this must be accomplished without anyone of an official capacity being around. I can vouch for the fact that this can be done very adroitly.

Atlantic City: Convention Mecca of the World

With the new hardships made by the swim organizers, the Atlantic City Swim was made an obstacle course. In one swim Greta Andersen and Herman Willemse were left high and dry on the top of a pier when a wave dropped beneath them. Willemse convinced the officials that he was driven into the pier in order to avoid the oars of his boat as they were about to chop him in maintaining position in the breaking surf to avoid being swamped. Barnacles and clams presented hazards to the fingers and bodies of swimmers, when they made use of the piers along the inlets and ocean portion of the swim. In the inner waterways clams, wire, broken bottles, and tin cans became hazards of the first order. In the years the Atlantic City Swim was held practically every swimmer, whether he completed the swim or not, had to receive first aid for the cuts and bruises his body bore. In fact Dennis Matuch of Chicago swam the last six miles of the 1964 race with a gash on one of his fingers which he received from a broken bottle while swimming close inshore in the inner waterway. He received six stitches in the bloody wound at the end of the race. Yes, the Atlantic City races became known as an obstacle course race to many of the swimmers.

After Herman Willemse won the race for the fifth consecutive time in 1964 the public lost interest in the race. In fact the swim organizer wrote Herman a letter asking what should be done. Herman, being a businessman, suggested that if Toomey came up with $5,000 in 1965 for Herman before the race, he would gladly finish second. Toomey thought this a fine idea, but that Herman was perhaps asking a little too much. Would $3,000 be enough? Herman thought it over and finally wrote back that considering $2,000 was second place prize, $3,000 was no incentive. As a result the Atlantic City Swims were dropped and no races have been held since 1964. Yes, Herman would miss those kisses from the bathing beauties that awaited the winner of each race. In fact, the kiss from the internationally famous movie star Jayne Mansfield remained as indelibly imprinted in Herman's memory as the $5,000 checks—almost. But those sensuous lips and full-bodied breasts *are* remembered, for one must remember that "man" is also a part of the word "businessman." Should it be any other way?

Past Performances Atlantic City Championship Swim
1954

	Name	Nationality	Time
1	Tom Park	(USA)	9:21:42.2
2	Cliff Lumsden	(Canada)	9:25:10
3	Steve Wozniak	(USA)	9:51:35
4	Roland Aronovitz	(USA)	9:52
5	Herbert J. Simon	(USA)	10:05:30
6	Charles F. Grover	(USA)	10:06:15

7	Marilyn Bell (Canada)	10:07:02
8	Don Sabath (USA)	10:15
9	Baptista Pereira (Portugal)	10:16:10
10	William Goll (USA)	10:23:04
11	Bill Sadlo (USA)	10:35:40
12	Donald M. DeForrest (USA)	10:37:30

1955

1	Tom Park (USA)	9:49:30
2	Cliff Lumsden (Canada)	9:56:25
3	Steve Wozniak (USA)	10:21:30
4	Hamed Mustafa (Egypt)	10:23:25
5	John Lacoursiere (Canada)	10:36:15
6	Don Sabath (USA)	10:44:16
7	Herb Simon (USA)	10:46:50
8	William Goll (USA)	11:10:45
9	Nelson Quiroz (Argentina)	11:26:10
10	Raymond Boraiko (USA)	11:34:05
11	Lies Put Jamnicky (Canada)	11:42:45
12	Heldga Weiss (Germany)	11:44:30

1956

1	Cliff Lumsden (Canada)	9:51
2	Tom Park (USA)	9:51:00.2
3	Steve Wozniak (USA)	10:06:30
4	Greta Andersen (Denmark)	10:17
5	Don Sabath (USA)	10:26
6	William Goll (USA)	10:31:45
7	Muriel Ferguson (Canada)	11:06:30
8	Lies Jamnicky (Canada)	11:18:30
9	Vivian Thompson (Canada)	11:49
10	Willie Tremblay (Canada)	11:52
11	Greta Patterson (USA)	12:15

1957

1	Alfredo Camarero (Argentina)	12:17
2	Tom Park (USA)	12:25
3	Greta Andersen (Denmark)	12:36
4	Don Sabath (USA)	12:40
5	Helge Jensen (Denmark)	12:56
6	Gene Perle (USA)	13:02
7	Paul Herron (USA)	13:06
8	William Goll (USA)	13:09
9	Muriel Ferguson (Canada)	13:32

1958

1	Tom Park (USA)	11:52:45
2	Cliff Lumsden (Canada)	12:09
3	Greta Andersen (USA)	12:15:30
4	Tonatiuh Gutierrez (Mexico)	12:41:15
5	Helge Jensen (Denmark)	12:47:05
6	Don Sabath (USA)	13:05:25
7	Joan Florentin (USA)	13:14
8	Gene Perle (USA)	13:16:30
9	Aloma Keen (Canada)	13:59:45

1959

1	Cliff Lumsden (Canada)	10:54:05
2	Tom Park (USA)	11:00:15
3	Greta Andersen (USA)	11:07:25
4	Helge Jensen (Denmark)	11:31:15
5	John Lacoursiere (Canada)	11:41:37
6	James Lavell (USA)	11:51:25
7	Don Sabath (USA)	12:13:25
8	Myra Thompson (USA)	12:25:20
9	Bill Goll (USA)	12:36:32
10	Dr. Wilfred Slater (USA)	12:58:57
11	Joan Florentin (USA)	13:11:30

1960

1	Herman Willemse (Holland)	10:30:5
*2	Cliff Lumsden (Canada)	10:40:7
*3	Tom Park (USA)	10:40:7
4	John Lacoursiere (Canada)	10:57:19
5	Jorge Mezzadra (Argentina)	10:59:30
6	Carlos Larriera (Argentina)	11:08:25
7	Syder Guiscardo (Argentina)	11:26:30
8	Mary Kok (Holland)	11:31:24
9	Niko Nestor (Yugoslavia)	11:40:27
10	Don Sabath (USA)	11:52:21
11	Myra Thompson (USA)	13:18:12
12	Carol Ann Chaplin (USA)	14:11:10

* Tie

1961

1	Herman Willemse (Holland)	11:14:45
2	Greta Andersen (USA)	11:35:50
3	Cliff Lumsden (Canada)	11:36:35
4	John Lacoursiere (Canada)	11:39:20
5	Tom Park (USA)	11:49:10
6	Mary Kok (Holland)	12:13:5
7	Syder Guiscardo (Argentina)	12:15:45
8	Don Sabath (USA)	12:49:30
9	Benson Huggard (USA)	13:16:55
10	Aloma Keen (Canada)	13:17:45
11	Carol Chaplin (USA)	13:49:45

1962

1	Herman Willemse (Holland)	11:35:45
2	Cliff Lumsden (Canada)	12:01:10
3	Tom Park (USA)	12:11:00
4	John Lacoursiere (Canada)	12:12:15
5	Greta Andersen (USA)	12:57:16
6	Carlos Larriera (Argentina)	13:11:39
7	Helge Jensen (Denmark)	14:00:00
8	Jacques Amyot (Canada)	14:30:00

1963

1	Herman Willemse (Holland)	10:31:15
2	Abdel-Latif Abo-Heif (Egypt)	12:07:31
3	John Lacoursiere (Canada)	12:13:15

4	Cliff Lumsden (Canada)	12:13:16	
5	Greta Andersen (USA)	12:14:5	
6	Marty Sinn (USA)	12:21:32	
7	Alfredo Camerero (Argentina)	13:26:8	

1964

1	Herman Willemse (Holland)	10:08:15 (record)	$5,000
2	Abdel-Latif Abo-Heif (Egypt)	10:31:23	$2,000
3	John Lacoursiere (Canada)	10:31:23.2	$1,000
4	Cliff Lumsden (Canada)	10:32:50	$ 800
5	Jorge Mezzadra (Argentina)	10:34:1	$ 500
6	Dicki Bojadzi (Yugoslavia)	10:35:45	$ 300
7	Marty Sinn (USA)	(record) 10:37:15	$ 200
		Bonus	$ 800
8	Roberto Reta (Argentina)	10:44:38	
9	Sayed El Gelil (Egypt)	10:53:9	
10	Kurt Pluntke (Canada)	10:04:2	
11	George Park (Canada)	11:24:15	
12	Hedy Schmidt (Canada)	12:25:00	$ 400

Taken from water at finish: Wendy Birch, USA; Fausto Ramirez, Mexico; Bill Stevens, USA

Dropouts: Greta Andersen, USA; Mohammed Zaitoon, Egypt; Don Sabath, USA; Carlos Larriera, Argentina.

10
They Don't Start Out Slowly: The World's Record Sixty-mile Lake Michigan Swim

We weren't going to make the same mistake in 1963 we made the year before. We found out the big guns don't pace, especially at the start. Although this was to be a sixty-mile race it would look like a hundred-yard sprint for the first couple of hours. The pros know that when a swimmer lags at any time in the race he rarely makes up the ground. Ted Erikson had "sat back" in the 36/50-mile Lake Michigan swim in 1962 believing that the leaders would burn themselves out. They didn't. As a result Ted came in five hours behind the winners. This year we (I as coach) would be prepared. We would be fighting from the start to stay with the leaders.

How did the Lake Michigan swims originate? These swims, which were the longest open water swims ever held, were due to the foresight of a remarkable Chicago businessman named Jim Moran. He was responsible for the group of world-ranking professional swimmers now standing along the shoreline of downtown Chicago. It was five years before that the story began.

Jim Moran owned the world's largest Ford automobile dealership. His magnetism and charm were known not only to his partners and friends, but to millions of television listeners throughout the Chicago area. Moran sold cars, both new and used, by the thousands. While the heads of most successful businesses sit back and leave the selling to the salesmen, Moran did not. It didn't take long for Moran and his executives to realize that no one could compare with Jim in sales. That was why on his twice-weekly movie presented by Courtesy

Motors it was Moran himself who gave the sales pitch. It was like listening to a relative instead of a salesman. In the age of high pressure babbling it was a relief to listen to warm, genial, and folksy talk.

The secret of Moran's success was his sincere approach to all people. He was also a happily married man with a family, played golf, and swam. His swimming was done mainly at the famed Illinois Athletic Club of which he was a member. Once in a while he would wander out to the North Avenue Beach near Chicago's Loop. It was while he was on one of his beach jaunts that he spotted the man who was indirectly to change the history of marathon swimming.

When Moran swam he wouldn't try to set any records, for record setting was not for people in their late forties. He'd just get in and plod for a mile. It took him about an hour to do the mile. Sometimes it took less, sometimes more, but he always felt pleasantly relaxed afterward. He could then return with renewed energy to the long conferences at the desks and twice-weekly television presentations. Over the weeks he had been coming to the North Avenue Beach he had noticed one other swimmer who was in the water when he came and still there when he left. He learned from the lifeguards on the beach that it was their captain working out. He would swim from five miles to ten miles every day. On this particular day the young man was on his sixth mile. Surely, Moran felt, he could keep up with the youngster. When Moran tried to stay with him he was rapidly left behind. The boy's stamina and determination impressed the wealthy businessman. When Moran left the water he asked the lifeguards why their captain did so much swimming. "He wants to swim across Lake Michigan," they replied. "It's never been done you know."

"How long of a swim would it be?" asked Moran, his interest piqued.

"Chicago to Michigan City, Indiana? $36\frac{3}{4}$ miles," was the reply. "Why don't you talk to Joe when he comes out?"

Business matters prevented Moran from waiting, but what the lifeguards said intrigued him. He knew he wanted to meet Joe. Anyone devoted to a cause, whether the making of money or the fulfillment of a personal goal, intrigued Moran.

A few days later when Moran met the young man he was impressed with his enthusiasm. They talked for hours about a cross-the-lake swim. He asked questions on how such a swim would be done. Joe Griffith told him that a marathon swimmer had to eat in the water. He needed rowers—people to give him feedings. He also needed a motor-launch to set the course. Moran also learned that the young man had been hoping that he could find someone who would be willing to go along with him "gratis." He had been unable to find anybody. Moran said, "That shouldn't be hard. You've already found somebody."

It was about six weeks later in August of 1959 that Joe Griffith began his lake swim. Moran had footed the bill for several boats to aid the swimmer. In fact Moran made sure that he was included in the crew. He loved swimming also. Griffith went about twenty-three miles that year before fatigue forced him out of the water. Moran told him not to worry. He would sponsor him the next year. Just let him know when he was ready.

There was one interesting result of Joe's attempt. It was picked up by all the local newspapers. They told of the young man's gallant attempt. Soon Moran was receiving phone calls at his place of business. The callers wanted to know how the swimmer was and whether he would try again. Somehow, the $100 a mile Moran had offered Joe had also gotten into the papers. As a result others were wondering if the $3,600 would be given to any swimmer who made the swim? In response to public interest Moran introduced Joe Griffith on his television advertising interim. The results were overwhelming. Letters and calls were referring to the Jim Moran Swim. Such was the topsy turvey world of publicity.

In 1959 Moran kept his sponsorship of Joe Griffith restricted to Joe Griffith alone. This year, however, Joe was presented on television to tell of his training and expectations. The public loved it. It was something different. When the August departure date rolled around there were newspapermen along. The big swim had turned into a human interest story. It was almost as if Peary was trying for the North Pole again. Results were sent out every hour on Joe's progress. Public interest grew.

It was shortly after Joe had gone about twenty-seven miles that a tremendous thunderstorm blew up. Huge four-foot waves battered the small armada like match sticks and the lightning seemed to be striking everywhere. The rain reduced visibility to practically zero. The four boats involved found it extremely difficult to keep track of Joe, for it was now around one in the morning and he had been swimming for over seventeen hours. It was a heartbreaking decision, but they told him he would have to come out, for the lives of everyone were being threatened. It took Joe several minutes to be persuaded, but it was a disheartened Joe that strongly lifted himself over the gunwale of the rowboat. The rowboats were tied on the end of a long rope and the flotilla began its run for closest harbor.

Joe Griffith was never again to make a try across the lake. He, at the insistence of his wife, quit. From now on his family would take precedence. But to Joe Griffith goes the title of "originator" of the famous Lake Michigan swims: swims that were to make history.

The winter of 1960–61 continued to bring mail asking about the Lake Michigan challenge. Phone calls increased to the extent that Moran's secretary found herself spending an inordinate amount of time answering them. It was during one of those bleak winter days that Moran suddenly realized what lay in his lap. Here was another advertising approach that waited for exploitation. For the $3,600 reward he had offered Joe Griffith he had received $50,000 in publicity if one were to judge by the space the newspapers devoted to the two previous swims, to say nothing of the number of letters and phone calls to the company. He was not avaricious, but he knew the potential that had built up around the swim. He would make the swim an official one, open to all qualified swimmers. Soon the orders for broad sheets and application sheets were out. He detailed one of his secretaries to find out about previous marathon swims. That secretary's job became a fulltime one to which she had to devote her whole working day. In order that the proper use of publicity was to be made, an advertising-public relations firm was hired. Later on when Moran found out that rowboats, rowers, navigation boats were all needed he winced at the cost. What had started out as a few hundred dollar sponsorship was now running into the tens of thousands. Moran was now at the point of no return. He was committed.

By the time the spring of 1961 rolled around the Lake Michigan Challenge, as it was now called, had received hundreds of applicants. Surprisingly enough none of that year's applicants were professional swimmers. Evidently if they ever heard about it, they felt that the money offered for such a long swim was not large enough. Many of the applications received were from sensation seekers who could barely swim the length of a pool. Others were from competent high school and college swimmers seeking a bigger challenge. Moran decided to limit the number of competitors to a field of twenty. This was a manageable field and it placed a limit on expenses. He therefore announced that there would be a ten-mile qualification race sometime in July. Any swimmer finishing this swim in ten hours or less would be eligible to enter the big swim.

About twenty-five swimmers showed up for this swim, which was begun on Chicago's North Side and ended in the vicinity of the downtown area. Only six swimmers qualified for the big swim. The two swimmers that finished first and second in this ten-mile race were two Chicagoans named Dennis Matuch and Ted Erikson. Dennis was an eighteen-year-old Chicago lifeguard. Ted was a chemist at the Illinois Institute of Technology Research Center. They both were to make history. Little did they realize that the friendship they formed at this first race would evolve into a competition that would push one to the limits of man's endurance.

It was four weeks later on August 21, 1961 at 6:30 A.M. when the swimmers began to arrive at the lakefront just north of Chicago's famed exhibition center—McCormick Place. The organization committee and Park District lifeguards that greeted them had been there since 4 A.M.

From the start there was doubt as to whether the race would even start, for there was a ten-mile-an-hour wind coming off the lake. In fact, once the swimmers cleared the harbor, they would be swimming directly into two-foot waves. Weather reports were being constantly monitored. Moran and his company knew that too much money had been spent on publicity already and that a postponement of the swim would skyrocket the cost. While they realized conditions were not favorable they hoped things would change shortly after the start. Therefore the official word went out to all concerned that the race would start as planned at 8 A.M. It was a momentous decision.

Moran fired the starting gun on schedule and six swimmers dove from the sea-wall on Chicago's lakefront. Of those six, three were Mary Margaret Revel and the two Simecek sisters, Cynthia, 21, and Kathryn, 18. The men included Elmer Korbai, thirty-one, a Hungarian refugee, Ted Erikson, and Dennis Matuch. They flailed their way to the mouth of the harbor where reality in the form of two-foot waves awaited them.

It was Dennis, the eighteen-year-old-lifeguard, who held the lead when the swimmers reached the lake. As the first wave hit him the spray flew over his head, but he bore down more determined than ever. Just twenty-five yards behind him were the Simecek sisters, swimming in tandem. Then came Korbai, the other girl, Revel, and last Ted Erikson. It was just two hours later that the lake took its first toll. Revel left the water. Throughout the morning the swimmers stayed in the same position. Around noon, instead of slacking off as predicted, the wind picked up to fifteen miles an hour and the huge white anchored balloons that were being dropped every half mile by swim officials as guides were being whipped in every direction by the combined force of wind and waves. At 2 P.M. with the waves now cresting at three or more feet, Dennis Matuch left the race saying that no one would make the swim under those conditions. All afternoon the wind steadily increased in velocity until the top of the waves were actually being whipped from the wave crest. Conditions were so bad that two of the cabin cruisers making up the flotilla attending the swimmers were forced to seek shelter. At 5 P.M. the younger of the Simecek sisters, Kathryn, left the water. It was not her day even though she had gone almost twenty miles.

The early evening hours were a horror. Though the water registered seventy-two degrees the waves began to seriously hamper three of the remaining swimmers. Twenty-one-year-old Cynthia Simecek, who held a commanding lead of over a mile on second-place swimmer Ted Erikson, was now beginning to weaken. Erikson, a bull of a man whose powerful muscles were well padded with fat, was indifferent to the waves. His methodical fifty-two strokes per minute carried him effortlessly through the water. Korbai, whom Erikson had been trying to shake all day, was also maintaining a steady pace. Ted had passed him sometime in the afternoon but he maintained his position some ¾ mile behind.

With the approaching darkness it became increasingly harder to keep track of the swimmers even from the rowboat. They would be lost in the intervening troughs and rising crests. Little did the swimmers, tenders, and officials realize that the wind had now shifted to the northeast and was slowly and surely pushing flotilla and swimmers towards the southern end of Lake Michigan. It was an error on the part of the boat captains. They were not compensating for drift. Running and maintaining a heading while a boat is traveling ten or twenty miles per hour presents no problem. It becomes one hell of a problem when you are forced to idle along at less than two miles per hour in order to stay with a swimmer. It would only be at dawn that the serious consequences of their error would be realized.

It was at 9 P.M. that Cynthia Simecek's attempt ended in defeat. The waves had been too much for her. It was now that the swim, where other marathon swims would be approaching their end, was beginning. The thirty-one-year-old Chicago chemist now found himself in first place with only the elements to worry about—that is, if only the Hungarian Korbai would quit. But Korbai hung on for another four hours and was still causing concern among the members of Erikson's crew, even though he had now slipped to two miles behind Ted. It wasn't until 12:30 A.M. that he finally broke. When word was passed up to Erikson it was accepted with little joy for it was still six hours until dawn and anything could happen when you are bouncing around in the middle of Lake Michigan in darkness and five foot waves. But there was one irrefutable fact. Of the original six swimmers to start the race there was only one left. It was now that the press headquarters of the major Chicago newspapers began to stir. Local reporters were being dispatched to hire cabin cruisers. A few television stations were booking airplanes to fly over the lake at dawn. Old-time newsmen knew that the beginning of a major news story was possibly in the making.

Throughout the early morning hours the wind maintained a steady fifteen- twenty-mile-per-hour speed from the northeast. Inexorably the swimmer and flotilla were being pushed farther and farther south. At dawn the wind dropped and a gradual diminishing of the waves began. It wasn't until around 7 A.M. that the light intensity was enough to break through the haze. As visibility grew, so did the shock of Ted's coach. Off to the south and southeast at a distance of about six miles appeared the horizon. The horizon was sand dunes. The only dunes they could be were the Indiana State Dune Park that extended east and north of Gary, Indiana all the way to Michigan City. The worst expectations were confirmed. The dead reckoning of the navigation boat had not been enough during the night. They were way off course. In the twenty-four hours that Ted had been swimming he had covered about thirty miles. Now, instead of having only $6\frac{3}{4}$ miles to go, he had to make a long diagonal alongshore to reach Michigan City, which lay another thirteen or fourteen miles up the east coast of Lake Michigan. The forboding news was kept from Ted. It would be a disheartening blow to inform him of the situation.

With the coming of dawn the wind died down until there was hardly a breeze. Along with it the waves dropped to almost nothing. As the morning wore on the clouds increased until the gradual pall of an overcast day settled in. The flattening of the water picked up the spirits of Ted as he kept his stroke going. Around 9 A.M. press boats began to appear filled with photographers anxious to capture the drama taking place. By the dozens they leaned over the side of the motorcraft to get shots. One group piled into a rowboat that made circles around Ted as he kept swimming. Then a single-engine plane with a cinematographer leaning out of its window circled for several minutes while movies were made. They were rushed back to Chicago to be shown on the afternoon and evening TV news programs.

By 1 P.M. the two smokestacks of the electric plant at Michigan City appeared on the horizon. Ted was now stopping more often as he asked over and over, "HOW far?" His speed had now dropped to less than one mile per hour since he was now breast stroking much of the time. After a feeding of Sustagen and corn syrup he would breast stroke for as long as forty-five minutes. When he felt the food would not come up on him he would then start the crawl. He would keep the stroke up for an hour or so and then the whole procedure would begin again. Feed, breast-stroke, crawl, feed.

Late in the afternoon it began to rain and the wind picked up enough to cause a $1\frac{1}{2}$ foot chop. It couldn't have come at a worse time. Dante's Hell could not have come up with a more diabolical trick to play on the weakening swimmer. The only heartening sign was that Ted was now only five miles from Michigan City. Almost as if by magic spectator boats by the dozen began to appear to cheer the iron man. Every boat was loaded with women, children, and men who began an almost incessant clapping and cries of encouragement. Several young teen-agers dove into the water and swam alongside Ted for fifteen or twenty minutes. Ted would stop and smile every once in a while to wave and to acknowledge the crowd. Little did they suspect that there were serious doubts among Ted's crew that he would finish. He was moving ever so slowly and his back appeared purple from the long battering he had taken. Inch by inch the swimmer wearily stroked on in a "race" to finish before dark. It was felt that if Ted had to face a second night it would be catastrophic. By 6:30 P.M. the last remaining light was rapidly disappearing and with it the landmarks of the finish. Boats were asked how far to the beach and when the replies of two to four miles were given, Ted's crew felt like strangling the informers. Didn't anybody know exactly how far? By 7 P.M. the pitch blackness of the second night began. Spotlights from several boats focused on the swimmer and his rowboat. Suddenly in the distance at an estimated 1½ miles could be seen the lights of Michigan City Pier and the thousands of cheering spectators on it. When this was pointed out to Ted he agonizingly picked up his stroke. It seemed to take an eternity to cover this last 1½ miles, but by 8:30 P.M. Ted had come even with the tip of the pier. The thousands of spectators went wild as they cheered the exhausted swimmer. Two-foot waves battered Ted as he rounded the pier by inches. It was here that he stopped, waved and asked, "Is this it?" Someone from an official boat said, "No, into the beach." Ted's coach asked, "How far is that?" Ted heard the reply of "About ½ mile." It was then that Ted yelled out his famous answer, "What do these ——— people want of me?" Ted's coach decided that he had had enough. "You've made it. Climb out here." The rowboat was docked alongside of the pier as many hands reached out to pull the exhausted swimmer from the waters of Lake Michigan. With Ted's emergence a tremendous roar went up. The swimmer had made it. At 8:37 P.M. after swimming for thirty-six hours thirty-seven minutes Ted Erikson had become the first person to swim Lake Michigan. He had made the swim under the most adverse conditions of waves, rain, and a course that extended the original of 36¾ miles to forty-three or forty-four miles. This swim was to go down in history as one of the toughest and most famous swims ever made.

Ted walked the length of the ⅓ mile pier before he was met by ambulance men with a stretcher. He was quickly wrapped in blankets and tucked in while being carried to the beach where the television cameras and newsmen awaited him. It was pandemonium as wellwishers and interviewers vied to shake the hand of the modern day Prometheus. When all was over Ted was taken to the hospital for a rub-down and bath. For another two hours at the hospital the wellwishers paraded in to congratulate him. By midnight Ted dropped off to sleep. He awoke a couple hours later as spasms and pain began. He was given muscle relaxants by the doctors. He dropped off to sleep for another five hours. When he awoke the next morning it was a tired but happy man that greeted more of the public. A limosine was sent later that day for Ted and his wife for the ride back to Chicago. Ted had set a world's record and the next few months would be hectic as he fulfilled award ceremonies and speaking engagements. He was now famous. The headlines that appeared in the *Chicago Tribune* the day after the swim told the story in capsule form: SWIMS LAKE, SETS RECORD. Only those who had been with him knew the conditions

They Don't Start Out Slowly 153

under which he had conquered the lake. Most men would have settled back with this great accomplishment, but not Ted. He was to go on for the next five years to set world records.

The pundits were shocked out of their complacency by Erikson's swim. The Lake Ontario swims were relegated to second place. Erikson had gone twice the distance of the renowned Catalina and English Channel swims. The long river swims were never really considered swims at all since they were carried out in tepid waters approaching eighty degrees while the swimmer intermittently stroked and rested within a current. Every inch gained in open and currentless water must be earned. Naturally the promoter and sponsor was pleased. Being a sportsman at heart it was a triumph for his faith that such a swim could be done. He was also doubly pleased with the publicity he received. Here was publicity that would have cost him hundreds of thousands of dollars if he had attempted to buy it. Headlines do not come cheap. There would be no question that there would be a swim every year if this kind of publicity kept up. Moran, seeing that the

Ted Erikson about one hour before the start of the 1961 Lake Michigan swim. He set a world's record of forty-four miles. He is flanked by his wife and coach. Courtesy Louis Waitkus.

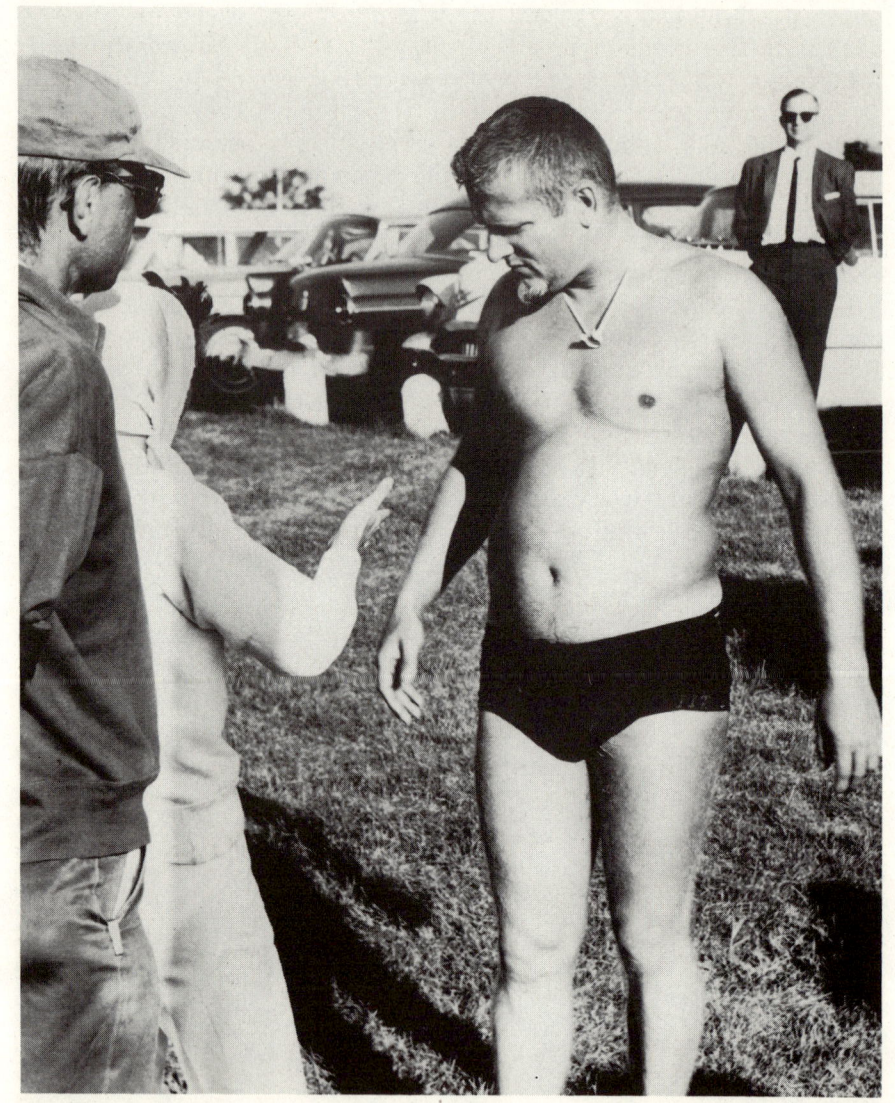

The final greasing. Since the water was warm, Ted only greased the friction points (armpits, crotch, chin, and neck) on his body. Courtesy Louis Waitkus.

swim had been accomplished under the most adverse of conditions, wondered what could be done under conditions approaching the ideal. It was only natural for a businessman to figure that if sales could be increased yearly, swim-length could too.

When the Lake Michigan Swim for 1962 was announced both swimmers and public were startled. Moran was offering $4,000 to anybody

They Don't Start Out Slowly

who broke Ted's record for 36¾ miles (an unfair thing considering the fact that Ted had really swum 44 miles) and $10,000 to the first person to go fifty miles. The course was changed so that it ran along the western side of Lake Michigan and north of Chicago. Waukegan, Illinois would be the 36¾-mile mark and Kenosha, Wisconsin the fifty-mile mark. The swim attracted the famous professional Greta Andersen, who smelled the $10,000 from halfway across the continent.

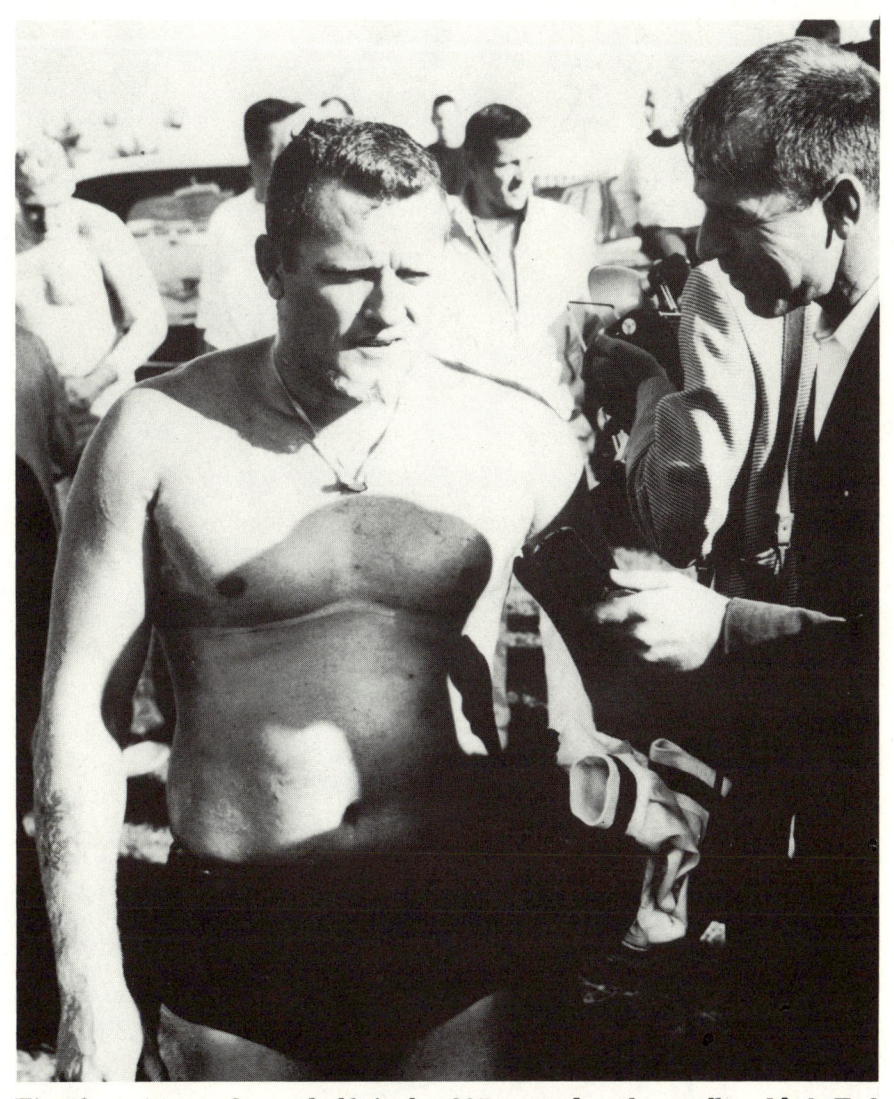

Five-foot ten and one-half inch, 205 pounds, the well-padded Ted Erikson gives an interview fifteen minutes before the start of the swim. Courtesy Louis Waitkus.

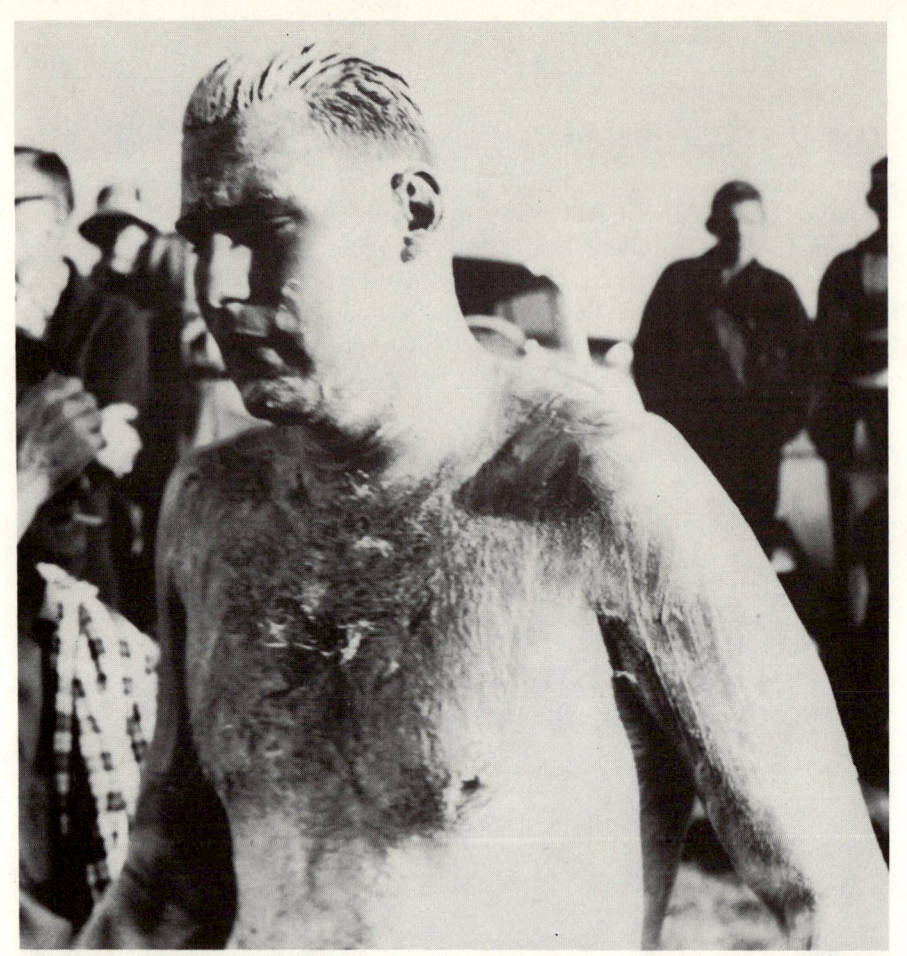

Nineteen-year-old Dennis Matuch decided to use lanolin over his whole body. Dennis left the water after six hours of swimming. Courtesy Louis Waitkus.

The female entrants get their final greasing. Courtesy Louis Waitkus.

The start of the race. From the left: Revel, Matuch, Cynthia Simecek, Kathy Simecke, Korbai, and Erikson. Outside the harbor were waiting two-foot waves. Courtesy Jim Moran.

The next morning, after twenty-four hours of swimming, Ted finds the lake still rough. Courtesy Jim Moran.

Twenty-seven hours later, conditions are still bad. The shoreline off to the right of the photo is the Indiana State Dunes Park. Ted at this point had covered about thirty-two miles. He still had twelve miles to go. Courtesy Jim Moran.

At 2:00 p.m. the crowds began to arrive at the Michigan City beach. They had a long wait. It would be another eight and a half hours before Ted would arrive. Courtesy Jim Moran.

Ted's coach tells him he has about three miles to go. The conditions of the lake had improved somewhat. Shortly there were to be two-foot waves that were to hamper Ted's finish. Courtesy Jim Moran.

Among those awaiting Ted Erikson at Michigan City was his six-year-old son Jon. Today Jon is a successful marathon swimmer himself. Courtesy Jim Moran.

Ted's wife is helped ashore by the sponsor of the Lake Michigan swims, Jim Moran. Courtesy Jim Moran.

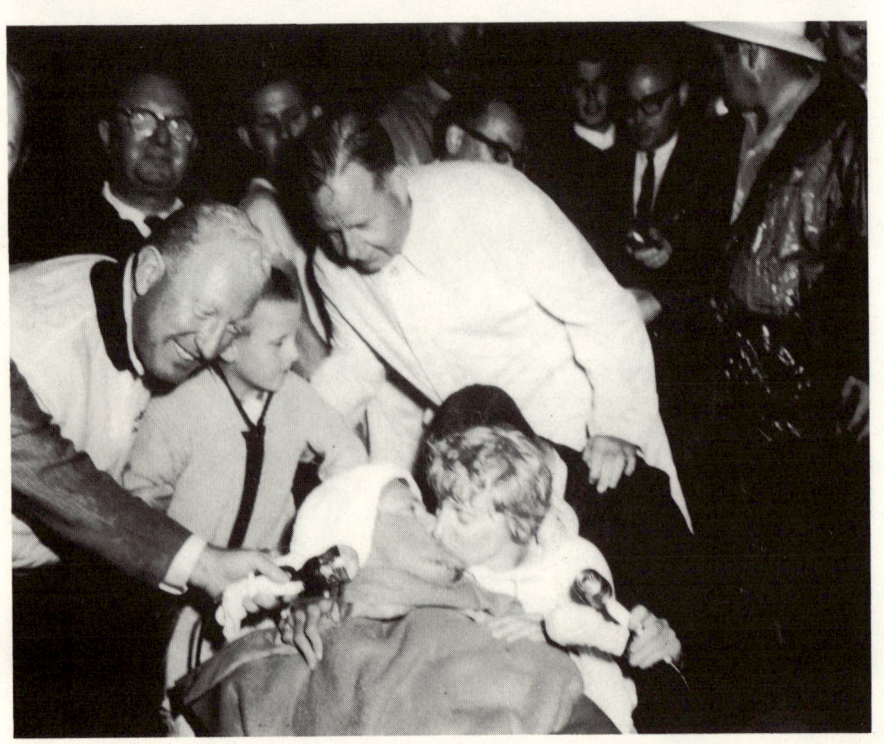

The $4,000 kiss that Ted received from his wife Loretta. Courtesy Jim Moran.

Peace at last. Courtesy Jim Moran.

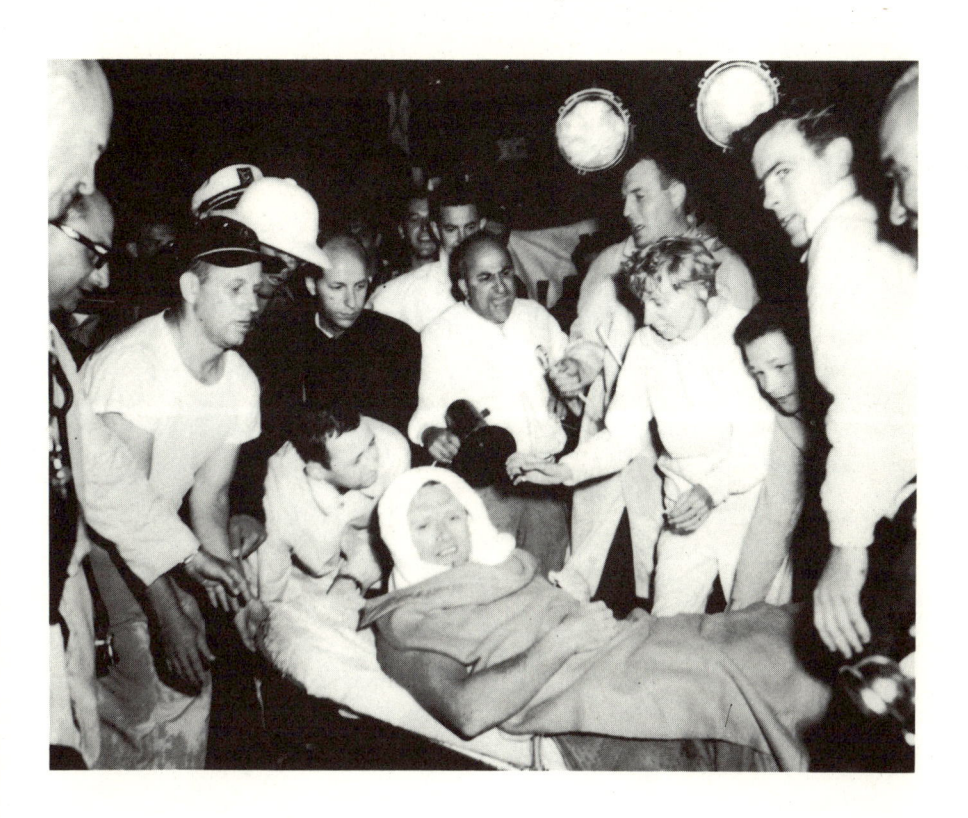

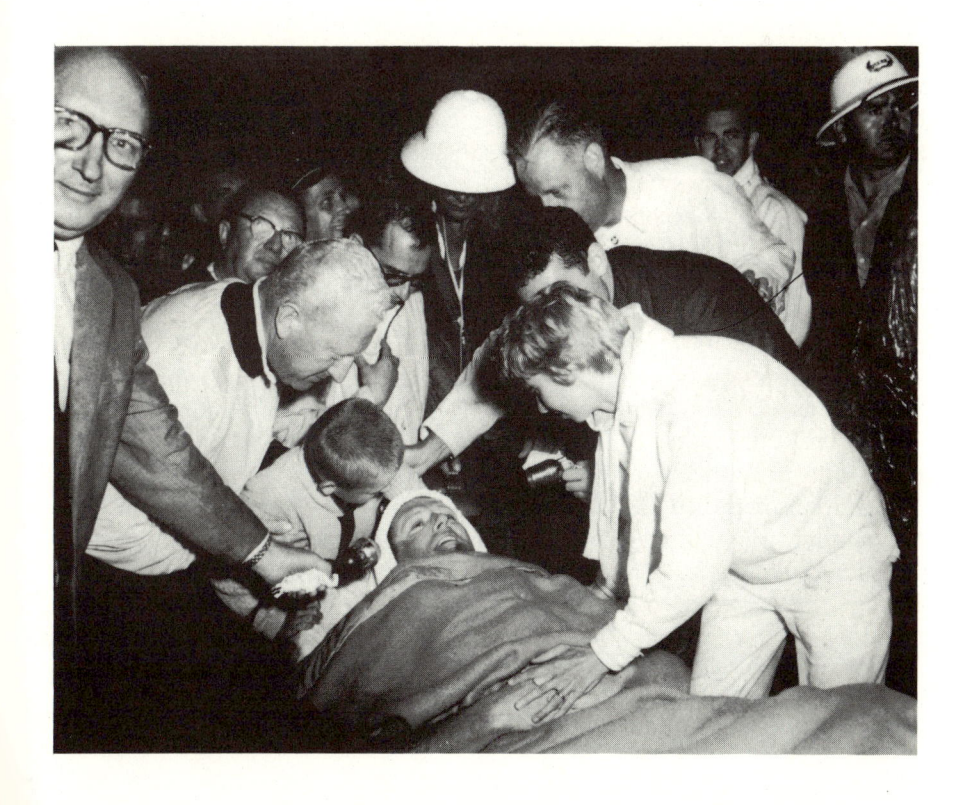

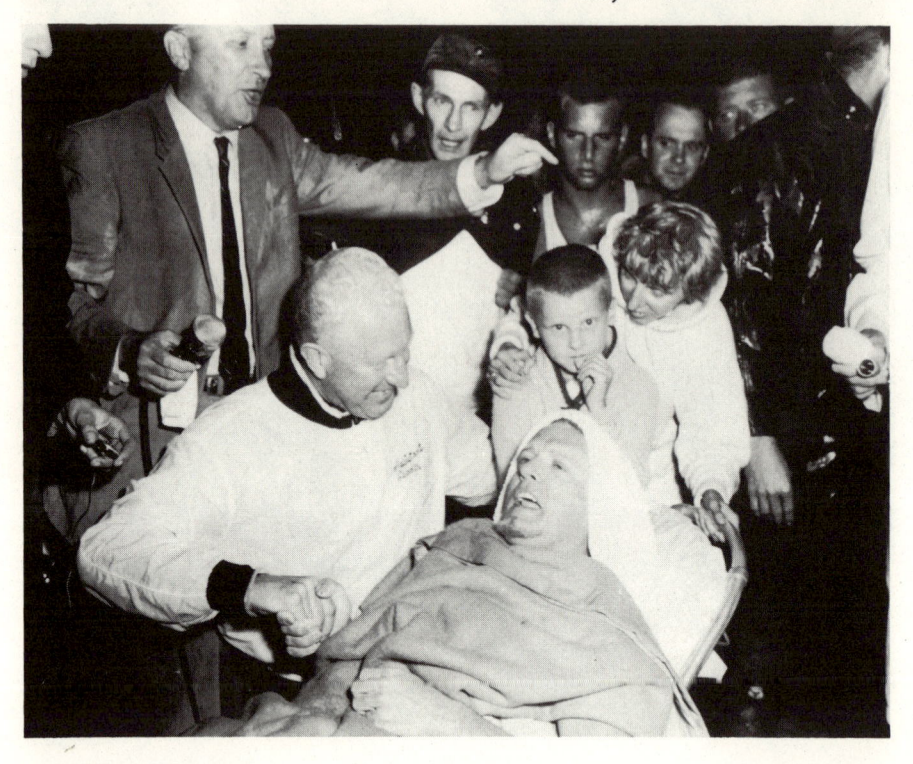

This swim is discussed in detail in chapter 2. When it was over there were two new world champions in marathon swimming: Dennis Matuch and Greta Andersen. Fame and congratulations rolled in for the swimmers and sponsor. All awaited the announcement of what the details of the 1963 swim would be.

The impressive accomplishments of Matuch and Andersen showed that almost anything could be asked of a swimmer. The limit of man had not yet been reached. Matuch had been chased to Waukegan by Greta in twenty-one hours and had averaged 1.75 miles per hour for the 36¾-mile course. Greta, with no choice, had proceeded on until she had successfully swum fifty miles. It took her thirty-one hours. She averaged 1.6 miles per hour. Ted came in hours later behind Greta at Kenosha after swimming fifty miles for a time of 35¾ hours and a 1.4-mile-per-hour average.

The sponsor pulled all stops for 1963. The swim that year would be a sixty miler. It would be from Chicago to Benton Harbor-St. Joseph, Michigan. The course the swimmers would take would be across Lake Michigan at a wider point than that to Michigan City. It would be a swim of such challenge that the eyes of the world would anxiously await the news. It was now that the promoter put to use what all promoters eventually learn—the reward. It took several years, but Moran learned with the arrival of Greta Andersen that his swims were not attracting the big name professional swimmers because of the low purses offered. If he wanted the best he had to pay. Moran, with this information, offered a prize of $15,000 for his 1963 Lake Michigan Swim. It would be the third largest prize ever offered in the history of the sport. When the applications began to be received he knew that he was on the right track.

It was at the swim briefing two days before the swim that I first saw him. He was quiet then. It was just the day before that he had won the fifteen-mile C. N. E. swim. He had been trailing the leader for thirteen miles before catching him in the fifty-five-degree water. Abo-Heif had reason to be quiet. It had taken a lot out of him. He walked into the room just before the meeting got under way. He took a seat at the table and slumped down, his eyes flicking from individual to individual. I didn't know if he knew English or not so I nodded and smiled at him. It was then that he broke into his broad and famous grin that is legend. He is a handsome man. He didn't look like an army major, but then what does an army major look like? When Abo-Heif entered the room Greta leaned over to Ted and said, "This is the man to watch." It was, to say the least, a prophetic statement.

Forty-four-year-old Jim Woods from Orlando, Florida was his genial self. He had reason to be. He held the record for a Lake Ontario crossing and owned a successful business in Orlando. A sixty-mile swim was a strange way to seek recreation for a man of his age. Cynthia Simecek, her beautiful features enhanced by marriage over the winter, added charm to the serious meeting in which rules, discussion of the course, and boat assignment would be the main topics. There were the famous Mexican swimmers Hernandez and Gonzalez, but they are now a blur in my memory. Syder Guiscardo, the famed Argentine swimmer, would not appear until early the next morning.

It was well into the briefing when a unique question was proposed by Ted Erikson to the swim committee. He had severely injured his leg in a home accident some five weeks before. He did not want to jeopardize his long months of arduous training by stopping. He sought medical treatment. His doctor, after hearing Ted describe his commitment to making the upcoming swim, regardless of the injury, prescribed cortisone in an attempt to prevent further injury to the leg. Ted wanted to know if he would be disqualified if he took the medication during the swim. After fifteen minutes discussion by the committee and its medical representative permission to use the cortisone was given if it were medically prescribed. The committee no doubt felt that Ted's great contributions in the earlier swims entitled him to the current swim.

After the meeting the banter of the swimmers took over. All except

Abo-Heif were nervous, for the training was over and they were now approaching the tension point. One by one they gradually left the meeting. The next time they would see each other would be the following morning. It would be a short seventeen hours for some.

Tuesday, August 20, 1963 was a beautiful day. Ted, his wife, and I drove into the parking lot at the harbor around 6:30 A.M. We unloaded our supplies. The bottles, cans of fruit juices, syrups, sandwiches, hats, and other paraphernalia would come in handy. Policemen were directing the new arrivals to parking locations. We got a spot as close to the water as possible. Park District officials were giving commands and directions to the forty or so lifeguards that would be assigned to the swimmers. Each swimmer would have two lifeguards. As swimmers dropped out of the race there would be extras. I walked away from the crowd to a relatively clear area, climbed into one of the rowboats and placed the thermometer in the water; it read sixty-six degrees. Now the air. It registered seventy-six degrees. Next the wind. A gentle breeze was coming out of the southwest. The sky was clear and even at 6:30 A.M. the warmth of the sun could be felt. It would be hell later on as it heated up.

We found our assigned boat. Mrs. Erikson, since she didn't know how to swim, would ride in the motor launch. I would stay in the rowboat for the start. As the clock moved toward the 8 A.M. starting time more and more swimmers arrived. When Abo-Heif showed up the general quietness was ended. It was not the same Abo-Heif who had been at the briefing. Instead it was an outgoing, talkative, and clowning man. He had only 2½ days rest since his C. N. E. race, but it was enough. He seemed to be overboiling with energy. He talked and clowned with everybody. Greta was nervous. Ted was quiet and brooding. He wanted this one. He had "crossed" the lake twice. He would do it again. He was prepared for the hectic start, or so he thought.

At 7:40 A.M. Abo-Heif began to apply a heavy coat of yellowish lanolin. Extra heavy layers were put on his neck, back, and chest. When all was on he would walk up to anybody near and threaten to embrace them in his greasy arms. Abo-Heif was a showman. There was none of the serious brooding demeanor that characterizes some athletes. Perhaps he was attempting to overcome basic deficiencies, but I don't think so. He was friendly by nature.

The final attentions being paid to Ted, I told him I would be in the rowboat awaiting him at the harbor entrance. It would take half a mile for most of the swimmers to clear each other. Then I could work myself up to him. If he were on course and swimming with a pack I would stay twenty yards off to the side so they would have freedom of action. A final handshake and I left. In fifteen minutes the start of the sixty-mile swim would begin. It would hold thrills for those who understood what would be happening. Hell would be breaking as the experienced swimmers fought for that all important lead.

I walked over to where the rowboat assigned to us was moored. It was one of those flat-bottomed Park District jobs. They are heavy, but stable in waves. For rowing long distances round-bottomed ones would be easier, but who knows what may kick up. I was thankful for the flat-bottoms in 1961. I say hello to Ray. It gives me comfort to see him. He's everything that one thinks of when "lifeguard" is mentioned—young, only nineteen, and powerfully muscled. He holds the Chicago Park District rowing championship. Ray is not new to me. Four years earlier when he was only fifteen, I got him a job as a lifeguard. He was a top swimmer even then, and it didn't take much doing on my part when they saw him—only some baptismal certificate manipulation stating he was seventeen. He rowed for Ted in 1962 on the fifty miler. Damn near did the whole stint himself. Dependable rowers are a must. When you have to change rowers every hour you jeopardize your swimmer. His only point of reference in those wide open expanses is the boat. He needs it. Many a swimmer goes extra distance because an untrained rower and coach will inadvertently start following a swimmer when he starts to drift away from the boat. The properly trained and informed crew will maintain the course and let the swimmer drift, knowing that he'll come back. It can be a lonely place out there. He wants company. Yes, it's a good feeling to have Ray. They should give out awards to the rowers on this swim also.

Taking a seat at the rear of the boat I tell Ray to pull out to the harbor entrance about a third mile away. It's always tough to miss a close-up of the start, but there'll be too many other boats jostling for position. It pays to stay clear of that. I'll watch them with my binoculars.

In no time Ray has us out beyond the hassle. Shortly there comes the *Asteria,* our mother boat. I give a wave to its captain, Chuck Bross —phlegmatic, amiable, and a man with brains. He's an engineer, built the *Asteria* himself, and piloted us on the other two swims. Got less sleep than anybody. Never left the helm in 1961. Was awake over forty-eight hours on that swim. Mrs. Erikson is aboard; she smiles and gives a thumbs-up sign.

There must be a crowd now of over four hundred people around the starting point. It's normal. Through the binoculars I see that all the swimmers except one are standing quiet. Abo-Heif, covered with the yellowish lanolin, is gesticulating and walking back and forth among the swimmers. It looks like he is the one who is going to start the race instead of Moran. I wonder if it is bluff, camaraderie, or nervousness. Suddenly there is the muffled report of the starting gun and the harbor wall where the swimmers were standing is empty. I look at my watch. 8 A.M. It has begun.

The water surrounding the start now looks like the playground of porpoises. There is white water everywhere as all effort is put into the start. It looks strange through the binoculars, somewhat like a slow motion movie. The swimmers are a third of a mile away and swimming toward us. It's what's called depth-of-field, I guess. The perspective is very short. They'll be up to us shortly. Maybe seven minutes. In five minutes I begin to distinguish the swimmers as they approach us at two hundred yards. It's hectic. Only someone who has been in a race can really know how they suffer that first third of a mile. Their bodies are in the process of shifting gears from a resting state to one of maximum effort. It is a painful state until equilibrium between the demands of the body for more air, sugar, and hormones are satisfied. When it is met things become easier. But now they are hurting.

Dennis is pumping his fantastic ninety strokes per minute. He's fighting to hold a slim twenty yard lead over Greta, Abo-Heif and Guiscardo. Trailing the three big names comes beautiful Cynthia Simecek Julian. Something appears not quite right to me about Cynthia. She's stroking faster than she did last year, but strangely enough she's fifty yards behind Dennis. It's much too early to tell but she may be having an off day. Then there is Ted. His stroke is beautiful to watch. He is stroking at a much slower rate than the leaders—only fifty-two, but he moves fast. I whisper to myself, "Stay with them, stay with them." I know he doesn't hear me, and I know he is desperately trying to stay with them. Hundreds of hours have gone into the planning of this race. Behind Ted come the others. There are seven of them, but I have no interest. I am concerned only with those who are in front of Ted.

The guide boat setting the course rounds the harbor entrance as the swimmers begin their journey into the open waters of the lake. Ted is lifting his head every tenth cycle or so as he keeps himself aware of the pack, now some one hundred yards ahead of him. I tell Ray there is no need to work up to Ted. We stay thirty yards off to the side. I swing the binoculars up to Greta, Abo-Heif, and Guiscardo and begin a count. Five minutes later the entry in the notebook is made. Both Greta and Abo-Heif are stroking seventy-five, Guiscardo seventy. They are all even and only inches separate them. Slowly the distance between them and Ted increases. Damn! Only twenty minutes have gone by but there is still tension in the pack. Sporadically one of the three will burst into a flurry and come within feet of Dennis. Almost instantaneously, as if attached by a spring, the other two come up immediately and all three are just about to engulf Dennis before he seems to put a "sprint on a sprint" and again pulls twenty yards ahead of his harassers. It's a desperate battle that only serves to put Ted farther behind. One of the "nice" things about being in a pack is that you are stimulated beyond what you think you can do. Ted,

They Don't Start Out Slowly 167

realizing he is losing ground redoubles his efforts. Surprisingly we gain some on Cynthia. The minutes tick by as the swimmers behind Ted begin to lose ground and identity.

Ray stops rowing for an instant as he puts on a pair of leather gloves. Last year, after rowing about twenty five hours, he had blisters that leaked blood. This year he is prepared. I take off my shirt and let the sun add a couple of shades to an already tanned body. A sip from the canteen and a dip of snuff puts me in a frame of mind ready to act should action be needed. The thermometer is plunged and comes out reading sixty-six degrees—same as the harbor.

8:45 A.M. Ted is moving up on Cynthia. She is only twenty yards ahead.

9:00 A.M. Ted has caught Cynthia. She is now about twenty yards off to the side. I tell Ray to drop the boat back a few feet so Ted can see her. I scribble Cynthia on the board and give him thumbs up and a smile. It's hard to tell whether she has weakened from the pace or whether Ted is gaining. I look through the binoculars. They've caught Dennis and are passing him. Cynthia is now falling behind. It's a paradoxical scene of contrast. She is stroking seventy-six and losing ground to Ted who is doing only fifty-two. I decide to take a close look at the lead swimmers. I write on the board to tell Ted that I will have the mother boat take me up to the navigation boat. I wave the *Asteria* over and climb aboard leaving Ray with Ted. At the last moment Loretta jumps into the rowboat to take over. The *Asteria* idles away from Ted and when far enough away guns up to the navigation boat.

The *Northland* is a twenty-two-foot sailboat. Its master is "Fats." The sail is never used on the swims and she idles along on her accessory motor. She was chosen for two reasons. Her master has had long experience on the lake. The other was a brilliant spur of the moment decision. With so many craft likely to be around at various times it would be difficult to identify the navigation boat if she were similar. Her high mast is easily picked out among the motor launches. She's the only sailboat around. As we pull alongside the *Northland* I wave to "Fats" and ask permission to come aboard. He quickly acquiesces. We're old friends. He's been captain of the lifeguards for many years in Chicago. He's never told me how he got his nickname, for he is all muscle and a winner with the women.

"Fats" continues to scrub the deck as I come aboard. It's his nature to be constantly at something. One of his lieutenants maintains the tiller. "Fats" knows it's going to be a long trip. His only concern is to set the course. I'm somewhat startled at his seeming unconcern with the struggle taking place just thirty yards off our stern. There, Greta, Abo-Heif, and Guiscardo swim together. They are "pumping." That means they are still pushing and have not settled down to a comfortable pace. None of the three will allow it. The stop watch comes out. A few minutes later I have it. Greta is hitting sixty-eight strokes a minute. Abo-Heif the same. Guiscardo, sixty-four. Watching through the binoculars is fascinating. Guiscardo is the smoothest, but his effort to maintain the pace is seen as his head turns for air. One can now see one of the reasons why Greta is so great. She floats well. At times it looks like the entire top part of her body is out of the water. Only the small of her back remains constantly under. Otherwise her shoulders, buttocks, and at times the back of her thighs and calves are almost always visible.

The entries are made in the notebook along with the time: 9:30 A.M. The binoculars are swept back to the other swimmers. Dennis has lost considerable ground to the lead swimmers. He is now almost two blocks behind them and I can see that Ted is gradually moving up to him. There are only fifty yards separating them. There is a big gap between Ted and the swimmers behind him. One half mile or more. Too far to tell who is next. So early in the race and already two surprises. Cynthia and Dennis. Our strategy seems to be paying off. Ted is not laying back. Dennis is doing seventy-two strokes a minute. I can see Loretta pointing out Dennis to Ted. Ted now goes after Dennis just fifty yards ahead of him. It is good that these two battle each other at this stage for, hopefully, it will prevent the leaders from pulling any farther ahead. Fifteen minutes later I notice that Dennis and Ted have lost more ground to the leaders. It is a bad sign. At 9:55 A.M. Ted is given his goggles by Loretta. It takes him about thirty seconds to adjust them before he resumes his stroking. Cynthia swims over to her boat and receives the first feeding of the race. My attention is drawn back to the lead.

One cannot help notice the erratic stroking of Abo-Heif. He seems to be working the hardest of the three. He pumps, that is, it appears that with every stroke he "lifts" himself a little out of the water. It can't be very efficient. I also notice that each is kicking hard, a fact that means they are sprinting. When and if they settle down the kick will almost disappear. It will only be used as a balancer to the arm rhythm. It becomes evident that something else is going on. Every ten minutes or so either Greta or Abo-Heif will sprint out on the other two. They will get a five-yard lead. The lead will disappear quickly as the other two come up. Yes, they are testing each other. It is a constant pressure they are keeping up.

By 10:15 A.M. Greta, Abo-Heif, and Guiscardo have increased their lead over Dennis and Ted by ½ mile. I can see through the binoculars that Dennis still leads Ted. It is difficult to tell by how much.

At 10:28 A.M. Abo-Heif goes into a sprint and pulls ahead of Greta and Guiscardo. Greta pulls even quickly enough but Guiscardo lags. He stays five yards behind. What has happened absorbs my attention.

They Don't Start Out Slowly

Abo-Heif's stroke rate is taken. It is seventy-four. Greta stays alongside him with sixty-four. Abo-Heif twists his head every once in a while to watch Guiscardo before he returns to renew his now prolonged sprint. Guiscardo drops back another ten yards. It has taken Greta and Abo-Heif seven minutes to get this lead. They have "broken" Guiscardo. I'm sure. By 10:45 A.M. Guiscardo is slipping badly. He is now fifty yards behind the lead. Greta and Abo-Heif do not relax an iota. Both of their stroke rates are up—Greta to sixty-eight; Abo-Heif to seventy-eight. I say to myself that he can't last. He's had only two days rest since the C. N. E. He should burn out soon. I haven't learned from Dennis's swim the year before. I will be wrong.

Through the binoculars Ted's stroke rate is taken. It is fifty-two. We tried hard to up it in practice but to no avail. Ted is one of those swimmers who thinks he gets something out of his kick. As a consequence there is a limit to how much blood he sends to his arms. I damn his kick.

By 11:10 A.M. Greta and Abo-Heif have gained a quarter of a mile on Guiscardo. In doing so they have also increased their lead over Dennis and Ted by $3/4$ of a mile. The only consolation is that Ted has caught Dennis. They are now swimming together. It is now a race within a race. Greta and Abo-Heif are keeping the pressure on each other and in doing so are pulling ahead of those behind them. Ted and Dennis in battling each other are now gaining on Guiscardo. I am stirred by conflicting emotion. The gaining is balanced by the losing.

At 11:15 A.M. an interesting thing happens. Abo-Heif yells something in Arabic to his boat. Greta is between him and his boat. A few moments later his handler has a cup nestled in a container at the end of a pole held out over the water. Abo-Heif then crosses right in front of Greta, temporarily breaking her stroke. In five seconds he has eaten his food. The one body length lead Greta had obtained is regained almost at once by Abo-Heif. Two minutes later Greta eats using exactly the same technique that Abo-Heif used on her just minutes before. She maintains her position also. It means they are dead serious on being number one at all times. There are still more than fifty-three miles left in the race but neither will give an inch to the other. Abo-Heif has now stepped his stroke rate up to eighty while Greta maintains sixty-six. Abo-Heif seems to be working much harder than Greta. It's a paradox. Greta must be wondering how he has anything to give after the C. N. E. A lot of other people are wondering that also.

Guiscardo has now slipped to one half mile behind the leaders. In doing so Dennis and Ted are gaining on him. His stroke rate has dropped to fifty-six. It is ten fewer per minute than what he maintained during the first $1\frac{1}{2}$ hours. The fascination of the battle taking place keeps me aboard the *Northland* longer than I should. I decided to stay aboard a little while longer before I return to Ted.

Over the next half hour the variation in Abo-Heif's stroke rate becomes evident. One minute he will be doing seventy-four, the next eighty. He just seems content to stay with Greta. At 11:30 A.M. I see that there is a rower change for Ted. Ray will save himself for the night. Good. At 11:30 A.M. Greta removes her goggles and throws them into her boat. Abo-Heif, knowing what's coming, does the same. Greta goes into a sprint. She is set on breaking Abo-Heif. She pulls three yards ahead but Abo-Heif doggedly pulls even. He will not let her get away. I see now why Abo-Heif has earned the reputation he has. Once you are in the vicinity of him he is like a leech. It seems that he derives extra energy from the company of another swimmer. He "rides" them like a horse.

At noon I decide to leave the *Northland* to take up station aboard our mother boat. One of the official boats has pulled alongside and I get in. We clear the *Northland* and make a great circle to head back. We pass Guiscardo on the way. I estimate he is 3/4 of a mile behind the lead. He is eating. As soon as it's down he resumes stroking. For a half minute I count, it come to thirty-two; double it and sixty-four is entered in my notes. Another quarter of a mile and we are alongside Ted and Dennis. They are swimming together although not as close as the lead swimmers are. It is important that their stroke rates also be taken, for then one can tell when they begin to weaken and slow down. Here is a contrast that is striking to watch. Whereas Greta and Abo-Heif differ by ten to fourteen strokes per minute, Ted and Dennis differ by twenty-three. Ted reaches out longer and recovers longer. Dennis's hands enter the water just a little ahead of his face and come out a little behind his shoulders. Yet they stay together in spite of Ted's fifty-two and Dennis's seventy-five strokes per minute. "Greta and Abo-Heif: 1 mile ahead. Guiscardo 1/4 ahead," is printed on the blackboard and held up for them to see. Ted makes a circle with his thumb and forefinger without breaking stroke and continues, then lifts his head several times to look ahead for Guiscardo.

At 12:15 P.M. Dennis eats, taking his tea and sugar in a paper cup which he immediately discards in the water. It is a good technique used by all experienced marathoners. You don't have to worry about returning a container to a boat; that takes time. Seeing Dennis eat, Ted decides to eat also. A paper cup is filled with Sustagen and handed to him. As he finishes he asks for two pills. Two cortisone pills are put in a cup and he swallows them. It will be interesting to see if our strategy works out. There are now doubts because of the pace Greta and Abo-Heif are setting.

A Piper Cub flies low over us and circles, gently oscillating its wings in recognition. It is John Musial, who we have checking the course. Every four hours or so he will fly the radio beacon between

Chicago and Benton Harbor. By watching the plane we can tell if we are on course. The 1961 experience has made a deep impression on us. As we watch him fly on we are consoled. The course looks good. The swimmers have been pushing now for over four hours. By dead reckoning it means they have covered eight to nine miles. It seems little enough when one thinks of the fifty yet to go. There are many who consider such a thing as we are doing tedious. They have limited resources. There are so many things to be done. There is a man who is completely dependent upon you. You must cater to his every need the moment he makes them known. He may want to know the time. Are we gaining or losing on those ahead? What is the water temperature, weather forecast? You try to anticipate these questions by periodically using the blackboard. You even let him know his stroke rate. If he starts to drop a few strokes he can then pick it up. Thus the reason for the blackboard. A swimmer doesn't want to waste time and energy by stopping to talk. In fact for the duration of the swim, which will encompass a day and a half, Ted's verbalizing will encompass only two paragraphs or so.

The skyline of Chicago begins to disappear at 1 P.M. Our visual contact with land is now gone. There are eight-inch waves hitting the swimmers from behind. The water temperature is up three degrees from the sixty-six at the start. Ore boats plying their trade between Gary and upper Michigan can be seen. Occasionally the squawking of gulls is heard as these aerial masters wheel and turn over the boats. The lake is in a quiet and beautiful mood compared to the efforts of the swimmers.

At 1:30 P.M. Ted takes a feeding of pineapple-flavored sustagen. While he eats I point out Guiscardo just four hundred yards ahead. Ted quietly nods as he quickly returns to business and to regain the twenty feet Dennis has taken while he ate. It is recovered rather quickly. Dennis will never give an inch if he can help it. But now he can't help it. It shows when he hurriedly curses his trainer when he is slow in reacting to a request for tea and sugar. A half hour after eating Ted begins to stroke faster and Dennis has broken. We look on surprised. The winner of last year's race is now only stroking sixty-four. He must be way off today. In another fifteen minutes Dennis has fallen two hundred yards behind. We wait to see if he will recover but we doubt it. Guiscardo is now only three hundred yards ahead. It is 2:15 P.M. and I am so intrigued with what is happening that I lose all concern for where Greta and Abo-Heif are. Now is the time to think in stages. We are losing Dennis and gaining on Guiscardo.

You don't come up on a swimmer as if you were passing in a car. The differences in speed are in tenths of a mile per hour. It is a long process. It takes us an hour to catch him. By 3:10 P.M. we are even. Guiscardo has a stroke rate that is only a couple more than Ted's.

When we reach him there is no swimming together. His eyes look vacantly at us through the goggles. Goggles are like the frame of a picture. They accentuate the eyes within them and the swimmer takes on the appearance of a creature from another planet. Guiscardo makes an effort to stay with Ted but he is helpless. I will be surprised if he lasts much longer. At 3:45 P.M. he eats, two hundred yards astern of us. Fifteen minutes later Ted has a feeding of orange-flavored Sustagen and one cortisone pill. Loretta gets back into the rowboat. I want a few hours on the mother boat to stretch my legs and relax. I will be spending the night in the rowboat.

From the mother boat the binoculars scan the horizon ahead of us. The boats attending Greta and Abo-Heif can be seen. They are about 1½ miles ahead. In eight hours they have maintained about a one tenth mile per hour faster average than Ted. Will they be able to maintain it throughout the evening hours? We will see. At 4:05 P.M. Guiscardo's mother boat comes alongside him. There is a short discussion, then Guiscardo can be seen hauling himself over the gunwale of his rowboat. Guiscardo is out of the race! The word is quickly passed along to Loretta, who tells Ted by means of the blackboard. He gives the recognition sign. We are now in a solid second place, or third if you count the shared lead. Our spirits are lifted. Now our attentions are devoted to the information that we can obtain on Greta and Abo-Heif. We no longer concern ourselves with Dennis. He is gradually slipping farther and farther behind. The second stage of the race has begun.

There are no boats to be seen other than our own. Every few hours one of the official boats from up front comes by. We anxiously ask for information on the lead swimmers. We are told that Greta and Abo-Heif are still swimming together and are about two miles in front of us. Most of the other competitors have given up. The only one we can see behind us is Dennis, about one mile to the rear. We are frustrated in not being able to get information on the lead swimmers quickly. We know that the air waves are constantly active as officials of the race keep in contact, but we do not have a radio of sufficient sensitivity to pick them up. All we have is a standard broadcast portable, which Chuck uses also as a navigation instrument. It has a movable horizontal aerial. It points in the direction in which a Benton Harbor station comes in the best. It checks accurately with the compass.

The distance Ted has traveled is now being determined by his stroke rate. All throughout Ted's training we have carefully tallied his time for the mile. As he went each one-mile lap it was entered in a log. We have found that it is quite accurate. We were amazed that the human body, according to our data, is very similar to a machine—a biological machine. When Ted was putting effort into his stroke he would travel 2.3 miles per hour. To travel at this speed he had to stroke sixty-two per minute. It came out to twenty-seven minute miles. This could be kept up for five miles or so before he slacked off. Sixty strokes per minute gave two miles per hour, or thirty minute miles. Fifty-five strokes per minute and he was doing 1.5 miles per hour and thirty-two minute miles. Except for the first mile or so Ted had settled into fifty-two strokes per minute. I figured that he was maintaining about a 1.7 miles-per-hour average. He would slack off somewhat after the first twenty miles but no more than one-tenth to three-tenths. He has been swimming for eight hours. 1.7 times 8 gives us 13.6 miles covered. Our calculations will prove to be quite accurate. One may find fault with the above but the whole story is not yet told.

We learned that the power delivered by Ted's stroke will diminish over time. We have calculated that also. Ted will vary his stroke rate little. He will always stay within the range of fifty to fifty-six. He will slow down naturally as he tires. We estimate that the first twenty miles he will average thirty-five minute miles—the second twenty, forty minutes, and the third twenty forty-five minutes. Fishermen and ancient Polynesians who made their voyages for decades in familiar waters were extremely accurate with their dead-reckoning. The Polynesians traveled hundreds of miles between islands with stick maps of the ocean currents and observations thereof. We are not foolish enough to move without compass and radio in setting the course, but we do have faith in the human machine swimming alongside us to determine the distance we have traveled. It is a strange contrast to be doing this in a highly instrumental world.

At 6:00 P.M. Ted eats and has a cortisone pill. Fifteen minutes later an official boat comes by. Greta and Abo-Heif are still two miles in front. The official says they are stroking sixty-eight per minute. He doesn't know which one. I could tell him it is Greta but I don't.

7:30 P.M.: another feeding. Then a cortisone pill. Ted then asks for an aspirin tablet. He takes thirty seconds for this attention before resuming.

At 7:45 P.M. a motor launch appears rapidly approaching from the rear. As it gets near it slows down and comes alongside. I see Dennis's coach standing aboard. He must be coming for information on us. No! I think I see Dennis sitting aboard wrapped in blankets. His coach calls out. "Connie, Dennis is out!" I look in disbelief. It could be a confidence game for a sneak around during the coming night. I ask, "Where is he?" He points to the blanket-swathed form. The blanket also covers the head. "Pull down the blanket," I say. Dennis himself removes the corner of the blanket covering his head. It is Dennis. I feel somewhat guilty, but it could be a $15,000 mistake. Dennis's coach yells, "Bring him through, Connie." We give him a thumbs up sign. We tell Ted. He replies, "I don't believe it." We point out Dennis sitting aboard the launch. Ted sees for himself, gives the ok sign and continues. He never even stopped. He just twisted his head up to the opposite side while looking for Dennis. The motor launch pulls away with Dennis. They will probably take him to the central sight-seeing boat. I wonder if Greta or Abo-Heif will be next. Abo-Heif can't continue after his earlier swim just two days before. Would life be so sure?

The sun disappeared on the western horizon a half hour ago. We have only about one hour of good visibility left. I get into the rowboat for the night. Ray comes with me, relieving the other rower. The change is made quickly. I give Ted a thumbs up sign. I know he feels better having me with him during the night. There is a gentle chop to the water. It will not hamper Ted or us. It looks like an idyllic night. Only the throb of the mother boat breaks the silence. At 9:15 P.M. it is dark. There will not be a moon tonight. Ted has moved closer to the rowboat. He swims just two feet outside the oars and just off the rear end of the rowboat. Nighttime brings the urge for close contact out. It's a big, dark expanse. The psychological horrors of the shipwrecked must be one of the ultimate pains to be experienced. Ted stops momentarily and says, "That was my fifth piss, Connie. Make an entry." He is ribbing me for my compulsion to take notes. Only a physiologist can appreciate what wondrous tales are held in that golden liquid. Bill Blair carried Ted's urine collected on his long training swims back to his laboratory as if it were ambrosia. There he made all kinds of analyses that told him in what state Ted was. The catechol-amine level told him if his body was adapting to stress. The nitrogen breakdown told if he was using his body protein or that from the food. Yes, urine is a wonderful substance to those who have the intelligence to understand what it can tell. In the middle ages doctors used to diagnose diabetes by tasting the urine of their patients. A finger dipped in the urine and tasted on the tongue could be used to recognize the sugar there if the patient were a diabetic. Such wondrous things are above, or below, most mortals.

At 9:50 P.M. an official boat comes by. Greta Andersen is out of the race! Fantastic! We ask for details. They say she got seasick from watching the bobbing lights of her boat. Balderdash, I say. Much later when I talked to her rowers I got the story. All throughout the early evening hours Greta or Heif were trying to break each other. Recognizing that night time could separate them, leaving them with an unknown they went desperately for the sole lead. Every fifteen minutes or so one or the other would sprint out ten yards ahead of the other. The other would immediately pull even. It was just before night fall around 8 P.M. that Abo-Heif took a fifteen-yard lead that Greta did not recoup. He held it for awhile and then sprinted another fifteen yards ahead of her. He held this thirty yard lead. Then, as the rowers said, he seemed to go wild, moving his stroke rate up to eighty for the next half hour and continued to pull away from Greta. At the end of an hour and a half Greta saw the inevitable. She was tired. When she thought of sixty miles and the second place $2,000 she decided it wasn't worth it. At 9:35 P.M. she gave up. Before she got in her boat she readjusted the top part of her bathing suit. She had been swimming with it tucked down around her waist. This swim was following the same pattern as the 1961 swim. As far as we knew there were now only two swimmers left in the race: Abo-Heif and Ted. We were all saying to ourselves, "What kind of man was this Egyptian. Was he human?" The night would tell.

It is strange the effect that darkness has on most souls. Unknown and unfamiliar surroundings add to the natural terrors of night. The closing in of night has caused many a marathoner to give up. This will be Ted's fifth through-the-night effort. We wonder if Abo-Heif has had as many.

Whenever it is feasible night offers the comfort of hidden operations, safety, and surprise. War parties, police raids, and assassins have taken advantage of it for thousands of years. So will we. All lights are put out aboard the *Asteria* around 11 P.M. We think that Abo-Heif is now beginning to hurt. Around 10 P.M. an official boat came by asking if we had an extra bathing cap. We said no. We had plenty of them, but it would be idiotic to give them to a competitor. This is not a boy-scout or college meet. The swimmers have spent a great deal of money and time preparing for this swim. Ted has been wearing a rubber cap since the start. Abo-Heif has not. Even though the water temperature has receded from its 3 P.M. high of seventy-two degrees to sixty-seven degrees now it can be quite cool to a swimmer who has been pushing for fifteen hours. The air temperature of sixty-five degrees calls for a light jacket. It was Abo-Heif's need for a rubber cap that caused us to make our decision to "sneak" up on him.

We have seven hours of darkness in which to do it. Ted is informed of the plans. It will necessitate him staying as close to the boats as possible. It is very difficult to maintain the rowboat in the proper position. Ted is always in danger of being hit by the oars. If he stays farther away we find it extremely difficult to see him. We risk losing him in the blackness. We decide to let him work off the *Asteria*. He will swim just off the side of it. This works for about twenty minutes before Ted complains of the exhaust. We cannot move to the other side since we would then be opposite his breathing side. The most satisfactory position turns out to be about ten yards astern of the *Asteria*. Ten yards behind Ted, follows the rowboat. It is now 1 A.M. Ted is stroking fifty-six. He seems to be moving faster than at any other time during the swim. At 2 A.M. he eats and has a cortisone and aspirin tablet. We can now see the lights of Abo-Heif's boat. It is very difficult to estimate distances over water at night. I hesitate to make a judgement. It must certainly be less than a mile. By 3 A.M. definite progress has been made. The lights aboard Abo-Heif's boat are more distinct. The information is relayed to Ted. By 4 A.M. Abo-Heif is a scant two blocks ahead of us when we have to make a critical change of rowers. Ray had been rowing since 8 P.M. He had rowed also the first five hours of the race. He needed a rest. In making the change the rope thrown to us from the *Asteria* missed and sank into the water only to become entangled with the propeller. Thirty minutes of hectic time was lost before it was freed. It was while we were working to free the propeller that an official boat came by and asked who we were. There was no choice but to tell. They informed us that it was against boating and race regulations to run without lights. We were forced to turn them on. We learned that when Abo-Heif was informed that we were only two blocks behind him that he went into a ranting Arabic monologue castigating his wife and trainers for not keeping him informed of an approaching swimmer. As soon as the prop was freed, Ted renewed his efforts to catch Abo-Heif. His stroke was hitting highs of fifty-eight as he slipped through the water. By sunrise (around 5:30 A.M.) we could just glimpse Abo-Heif's boat one mile ahead of us before the haze and fog obliterated him forever. It was a severe blow to have the haze move in at such a time. It was frustrating not to be able to give Ted the information he and we desired so much. We did not know where Abo-Heif was. There was no official boat around. We dare not leave Ted with just a rowboat in the middle of Lake Michigan while we took off in the *Asteria* looking for Abo-Heif.

We learned later that Abo-Heif whittled down his feeding stops considerably after being frightened by Ted's approach. He would only stop every two or three hours throughout the rest of the morning and early afternoon. It was only around 2 P.M. when he was told that he had a four- or five-mile lead did he relax for the remainder of the distance.

By 10:30 A.M. the haze had cleared off enough for visibility to be extended to half a mile. If it had only been twice that there would have been an interesting development. It was our Piper Cub airplane flying over at 10:30 A.M. who saw that Abo-Heif was only ¾ of a mile ahead of us at this point. It did us no good however for the information could not be given us. All we learned from its flight was that we were on the correct route.

The early morning hours were not tedious. Abo-Heif, we knew, was in the vicinity. Approximately forty-three miles had been covered and it was still a race. Lake Michigan that morning was calm and beautiful. Just the *Asteria* with Chuck, Loretta, and three young rowers. Ray and I were in the rowboat attending Ted. It is a constant battle to find a comfortable position in a rowboat. You damn the safety regulations that say never stand up in a rowboat or canoe. No doubt that was written for beginners. Fishermen and naval men do it all the time. There is no other way to relieve the inevitable ache in the small of the back except by standing with feet wide apart. Other positions are tried from time to time. Hands are put behind you as you lean back, pushing your belly forward in order to get the curvature of the spine to go the other way a little. Other times you lower your legs over the rear of the boat letting them drag in the water as you make your hands beat like the legs of a swimmer. The swimmer gets the idea as he starts to kick harder. You clap your hands and nod your head in a pantomime of a mother acknowledging a good deed by her child. The analogy is not too far off for the swimmer is much like a child now. It appears that he is totally dependent on his handlers and does all that they ask. The illusion is there, but can rapidly be destroyed if you ask one thing. Demand more speed when he is on the verge of collapsing or of starting an excruciating cramp in some muscle and he will curse you or give you an obscene gesture. If he or she is too far gone and is in the transition from trance to coma, he or she will just ignore you and go on stroking. For hours I have been using the legs dragging over the back, hand-clapping, and smiling routine. Ted seems to respond very well. I am able to keep his stroke up to fifty-four and fifty-six for ten minutes at a time before he slips down to fifty-two. The routine begins again.

By 11 A.M. I have had it. It's been fifteen hours of riding the lake. Every muscle of my body is sore. I let the *Asteria* know that I would like to take a rest. I crawl into the small bunk within the hold of the *Asteria,* not even bothering to take off the sneakers. The thermometer reads ninety degrees inside the boat. There is no wind whatsoever. The only consolation is that the sun is not beating down on you. But there is something else beating—the motor. Its beating and throbbing, even though at idling speed, is very disconcerting. Lying down on my back I shut my eyes and doze. It is difficult but the responsibilities of the swimmer are too much to let one really sock out, even if conditions were ideal. We are not like the fun-loving, beer-drinking flippants who came along for the swim as if it were a big booze party. Every sporting venture attracts such pariahs. Any excuse will serve to be together. As soon as the conversation lapses, the mind is dulled, and the fly bites are noticed, they want to leave. They do in most cases leave after a few hours, but the boats that have been assigned as mother boats to the swimmers are stuck. Then, on occasion, the tempers flare and arguments begin. We are lucky in that we have found a serious and pleasant captain.

An hour later I awake from a doze feeling more tired than earlier. Then the sudden flittering back and forth of several birds within the cabin of the boat erases all signs of fatigue. They are fall warblers. They are relatively hard to get near when you see them on shore. If you by chance are able to focus on them for fifteen seconds they frustrate you and are off to parts unknown. Now they were using the boat as a resting point. They have been swept out over the wide lake while in search of insect food. Exhausted, they lose their fear of man. One has now landed on my toe. I remain as immobile as possible and study the beautiful creature. Every feather can be seen among its dull greenish-brown plumage. I don't know what kind he is. I wish I had my manual. He flits to my belt and lands. One can become drunk on such a sight. Little as he is, it is a wild creature forced to ignore the possible danger it could be in. Next he flits to the beak of my cap and I can feel the motions it makes. There are now three of them flittering about for the flies in the cabin. It is a pleasant interlude. Then one thinks of what would have happened to them if we were not around. Many of them, no doubt, would have ended up in the water. There they would have drowned. Nothing would have been wasted for they would have been eaten eventually by the fish that inhabit the lake.

The lake is like one huge trap for millions of birds and insects. Many times when I have been swimming, wearing the goggles of course, I have seen flies, gnats, bees, dragon-flies and other insects by the tens of thousands lying on the surface of the lake awaiting their fate. Many of them drown before they are eaten by the fish that come to the surface for them. Others are eaten almost immediately. Yes, tons of insect food must fall daily on the surface of the lakes over the world. You might say it's biology in action.

I remember vividly the first time I swam to the water intake plant two miles off the shores of the south side of Chicago. Pulling myself up the breakwater that surrounds the plant I was greeted by its caretakers and given a tour of the two buildings. The caretakers must have thought I was crazy, for I was impressed by the predators on the buildings. Here upon the isolated building which was two miles out in the lake were spiders' webs by the thousands. There were also several hundred barn swallows nesting on the steel girders of the catwalk that joined the two buildings. It was easy to understand why, when one was clear of the water, for almost immediately flies by the hundreds descend upon you. Offshore breezes carry them out. "Salvation" awaits them if they by chance find themselves in the vicinity of the water intake plant. It is a short-lived salvation for their predators soon find them. It is interesting to find that you will be bothered by flies in the boats until you are about two to five miles from land. Then their numbers drastically decrease.

I watch the warblers for another hour then wearily climb to the deck to see how Ted is doing. During my rest Hal came by in one of the official boats. He relieved Loretta in the rowboat. He is one of the pool supervisors that allowed Ted to have a whole lane to himself when he was training during the winter. He is a talkative, ebullient personality that whips and drives his charges. He is doing that now to Ted. He stands in the rowboat inspiriting Ted with his verbal harassments. He is quite different in personality from myself. I am quiet and try to elicit the most from my swimmer by subtle praise. The contrast is evidently good for Ted since he is maintaining the fifty-six-strokes-per-minute rate. Hal yells that Abo-Heif is only about a mile and a half ahead. I curse him for not coming back in a boat in the early morning hours and telling us. He says the official boat wouldn't allow it. All I can think of is conspiracy. It is easy to feel that way in a fatigued state.

By 1:30 P.M. I am back in the rowboat to attend Ted. All hopes that Abo-Heif may quit are now gone. We have gone about forty-six miles. Abo-Heif has done about forty-eight. Abo-Heif, from the information that Hal has given us, is in good shape and is responding well to the coterie of boats that surround a potential winner. The huge pleasure excursion boat that holds hundreds of people is full of Egyptians who live in Chicago. They are singing and cheering him while waving the Egyptian flag. This is the perfect incentive to a marathoner in the last stages of a swim when he seeks any excuse to give up. Abo-Heif is now racing the sun. He, as well as Ted, does not want to spend a second night in the water. We also learn from Hal that Abo-Heif is taking a "special" concoction from a brown medicine bottle every hour and a half. Hal says that fifteen minutes after taking it his stroke rate picks up to seventy-two or more. We fantasize stimulants, but again we are probably wrong. The nectar of the gods containing all the magical ingredients purporting to give impossible energy and strength cannot replace a good constitution, talent, and sugar. Abo-Heif is good. There is no question about it. All the magical ingredients in the world cannot make a champion out of a mediocrity. We take consolation that it is Ted behind him that keeps Abo-Heif moving. When Hal was observing Abo-Heif throughout the night and early morning of the second day the swimmer would constantly ask where Erikson was. He was not coasting in with no fears of a competitor. He knew that Ted had completed two Lake Michigan swims. Abo-Heif was swimming with fear as well as ability.

All through the afternoon hours we push with hopes of overtaking the Egyptian. There was no question of not completing the race now as in previous years. We know the distance can be done. Every $1\frac{1}{2}$ to $2\frac{1}{2}$ hours Ted would eat. During this phase of the swim Ted preferred hot nutriment with pablum and egg yolks. His stroke rate never fell below fifty-two and indeed the majority of the time held at fifty-four and fifty-six. There was no waiting and breast stroking to let the feedings go down. Ted would immediately pick up the stroke to the original pace. There was fame and $15,000 awaiting the outcome of this race to say nothing of the horrors of a potential second night.

There were fifteen miles of "truth" left. Everyone settled down for the outcome.

It was difficult for Ted. Just how far should he push. At times he would mention that his leg was bothering him. A delicate balance had to be reached. He had to swim hard but not hard enough to cause a swimming cramp. Every ten minutes when he began to falter in his stroke rate I would urge him on with pantomime. Approximations of Abo-Heif's position were given to Ted. At 3 P.M. we found we could receive the Benton Harbor radio station. They gave Abo-Heif's position from the city. They said he was six miles from the finish. Ted was ten. It was a blow. We knew now that only illness or a cramp would stop the Egyptian.

Around 4 P.M. Ted said he'd never catch him. We could say nothing. You don't deceive a scientifically oriented man like Ted. We replied as only we could. Keep swimming. Anything could happen. "Yeah, to me too," replied Ted. That squelched our ersatz enthusiasm. He was right.

Every half hour the news broadcast gave Abo-Heif's position. By 5 P.M. he was in sight of his goal. An estimated arrival time was given of 6 P.M. It came and went. Abo-Heif had still not arrived. Our hopes were raised. Perhaps the newsmen and swim officials were in error. The 6:30 broadcast destroyed our hopes. Abo-Heif saw that he had made it. He was stopping periodically and waving to his Egyptian friends. At one point he took of his rubber cap, waved it around his head and flung it away from him. He then started to swim in a direction back toward Chicago. The crowd thought that he had gone mad as they yelled, "No, No, the other way!" Abo-Heif, always the showman, was delighting the crowd. Here was no dead personality that awaited the plaudits of his admirers. He reversed the stage as all great personalities do. He knew the crowd craved recognition as much as he did. They went wild. He waved constantly to them. He clapped with them. He back-stroked in order to get a better view of his effect upon the crowd.

At 6:43 P.M., after thirty-four hours thirty-eight minutes of not only swimming but racing, Abo-Heif touched the sands of Benton Harbor. He stumbled momentarily forward in the three feet of water as he gained his footing. It takes a little while to regain the sense of balance after being in a horizontal position for so long. When Abo-Heif waded to knee-deep water he started to run out of the water to the surprise of the thousands of spectators who awaited him on the beach. Here was no exhausted hulk of a man but a smiling world's champion ready to enjoy his fame. Almost immediately his wife was at his side with an Egyptian flag in her hand. Moran, almost as happy as Abo-Heif, grasped his wrist and raised it in victory.

Abo-Heif waved off the waiting stretcher that would try to take

They Don't Start Out Slowly 181

him to the nearest hospital. For twenty minutes he walked up and down the beach shaking hands and speaking into the microphones of newsmen. Cameras recorded his arrival for posterity. After all the interviews were over Abo-Heif finally conceded to let himself be tucked into the stretcher, but on one condition. He wanted no part of the hospital. He wanted to be taken back to his hotel room in Chicago.

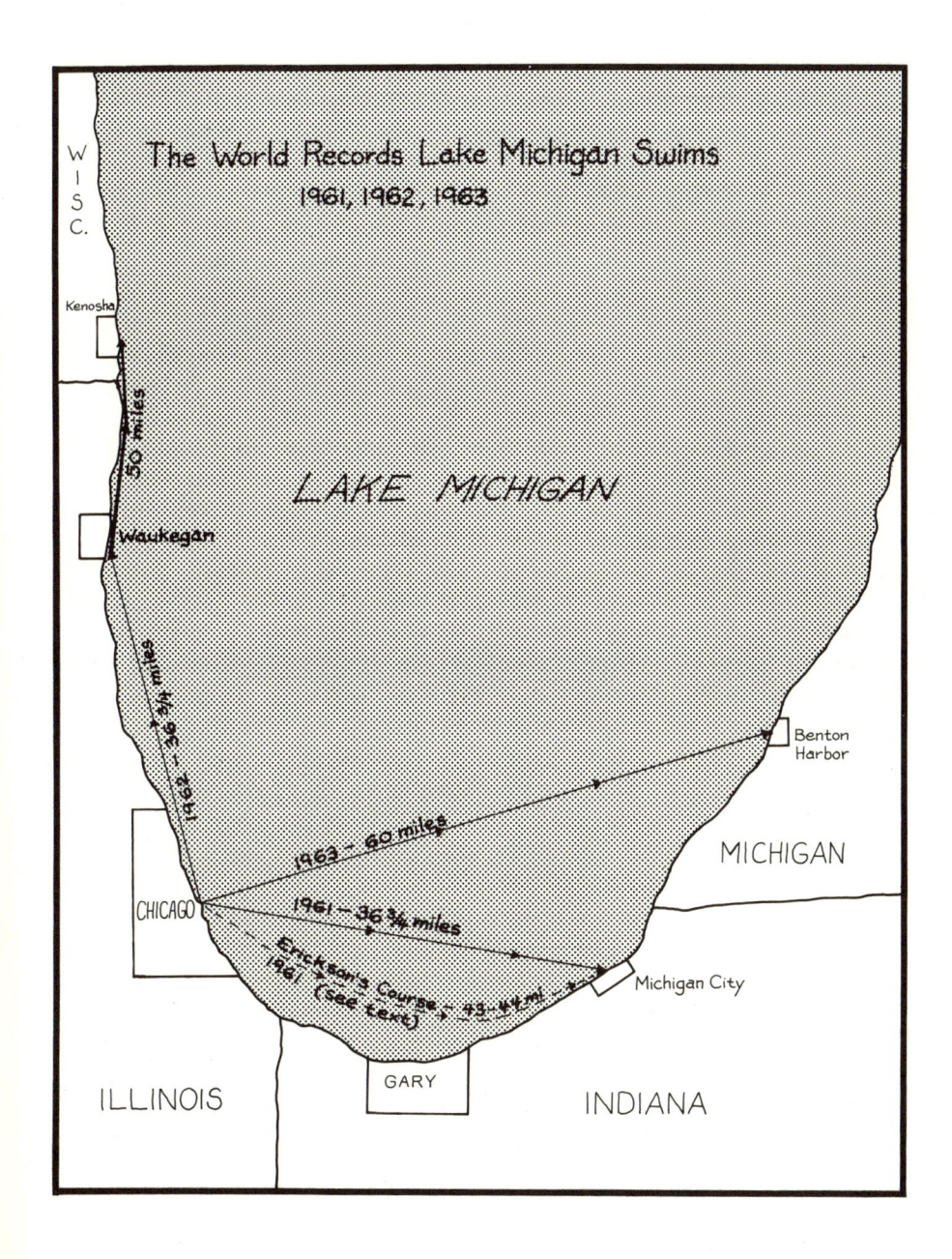

The World Records Lake Michigan Swims
1961, 1962, 1963

None of the whimperings characteristic of hospitals for him. He was driven back to Chicago within a couple of hours of his sixty-mile ordeal. There was a look of pleasant satisfaction on his face. He was the world champion of professional swimming as well as the holder of the longest distance ever swum in open water—a record that stands to this day.

When the newscast told of Abo-Heif's arrival a pall settled over us. We wondered if we should tell Ted. We did. It is a tribute to Ted that he continued. He said, "Well, we might as well swim to finish." At 9:36 P.M. Ted Erikson arrived at Benton Harbor. It took him two hours and fifty-three minutes longer than Abo-Heif, but he did finish. He now shares the record with Abo-Heif for distance at least. That two hours of swimming in the dark was a trauma but Ted stuck with it. Ted then went to the hospital for a good night's sleep. He wanted no part of the two-hour drive back to Chicago. Around 1 A.M. he awoke from muscle spasms and was given muscle relaxant injections and sleeping pills by the doctors. We wondered if Abo-Heif suffered like Ted. A few days later at the prize-giving ceremonies we learned from his wife that he did. He groaned and moaned like a baby, but such was his character that only his wife was permitted to witness it. Such is the character of "iron men." Perhaps it is what makes them champions. Perhaps it is also why women live longer than men. Perhaps . . . But in this day of technological wonders there are men who still push themselves to the limits of their physiological rope.

The sixty-mile Lake Michigan swim was the last of the "cross-the-lake" swims in Chicago. Whether because of lagging public interest, or rising expenses (Moran's outlay for the 1963 swim was over $40,000 exclusive of prize monies) the swims were dropped. In the six years that Moran sponsored the swims he revolutionized the sport. It is always risky to put down one's reasons as to why the swims were successful. The fortuitous circumstances that bring together the sponsor and the great swimmers needed to make the event was money. A wit once said that courtesy separates men from boys. One might say that money does also.

11
The Incredible Abo-Heif

charisma (kar 'iz ma), n. (Gr. charisma—gift) Theol. A special divine or spiritual gift; a special divine endowment conferred upon a believer as an evidence of the experience of divine grace and fitting him for the life, work, or office to which he was called.
Webster's International Dictionary, 2nd Ed.
In the 1960s the word took on special meaning as it was applied to those entertainers who could draw the largest gate receipts. Something more than "personality."

It's been said that he is the living reality of all women's fantasies—a cultured Neanderthal man. The only difference is that, whereas Neanderthal man was facially ugly, Abo-Heif is strikingly handsome. Abo-Heif today presents the picture of a well-fed businessman when dressed in a suit. In a bathing suit his well-muscled five foot ten inch height and broad-shouldered frame is well covered with fat. You can imagine how much fat when you are told that his weight varies between 220 and 240 pounds. It wasn't always so. When Abo-Heif was in his twenties he then weighed a more esthetically appealing 175 pounds. However, with the years and the fat came ever more success in the professional swim circles.

Underlying this hulk of a man is charm personified. Fluent in English, which is not his native tongue, his warmth and camaraderie comes through. His gestures and mannerisms are enthralling. Born in 1929, the son of a retired school teacher and Parliamentary member, Abo-Heif was sent to England from his native Egypt for his secondary education at the age of 17. He was the eighth of fifteen children of which ten are now living. He spent a year's preparation at Eton, and then went to Sandhurst Military Academy from which he graduated. Serving in the Egyptian army he was automatically promoted to major, and then after fifteen years promoted on ability to colonel. Along the way he somehow managed to learn to play the piano, speak six different languages, become the world's professional swimming champion three times, and marry a beautiful Greek opera singer. He also fathered a son. Along with recognition as a world champion professional swimmer has come the recognition and adulation that can only be equated with the religious awe with which Americans hold Babe Ruth. Whenever he drives down the streets of Cairo or Alexandria he is besieged with autograph seekers and handshakers. In fact, whenever Abo-Heif wins a race there are headlines in Egyptian newspapers. While the reverence with which swimmers are held in Egypt slipped momentarily after Nasser took office, they are still accorded the personality cult adulation with which no normal living human being can do without. King Farouk used to give his Channel race winners a home all paid for. All that Abo-Heif got out of Nasser, besides recognition, was a street named after him.

To see Abo-Heif in action, both physically and socially, is to see smoothness. Not only does he have a feeling for the water, but also for people and situations. It may not, however, always have been that way. Those who knew Abo-Heif in his early and late years say that they were two different people. A loud mouth, boisterousness, and publicity seeking were his trademarks. Everyone knew when Abo-Heif was around. You just listened to the mounting noise as he approached. Babbling in his native Arabic it always appeared to the uninformed that he was engaged in a verbal battle royal. While this may have been so in some cases it was entirely the opposite in others. It was just his youthful vigor finding an outlet in self expression.

Abo-Heif won his first race, an amateur one, when he was ten years old. From that time on he combined the sport with his education until at the age of twenty-three he turned professional. A beautifully muscled body and strikingly handsome features made him one of the most popular swimmers with the women. For four years he never did consistently well. He made his break into the pro ranks at a time when there were tried and true Egyptian swimmers who had been at the game for years.

Abo-Heif was twenty-seven years old when he made his first major triumph in professional swimming. The 1955 Billy Butlin English Channel Race was the fourth race to be held since the original race in 1950. Public attention for the annual event was increasing every year. Superb swimmers from all parts of the globe were attracted because of the publicity and the prize money offered. The results of the race were sure to be published on the front pages of most of England's leading newspapers. In fact, one of England's leading experts in physiology, Dr. L. G. C. E. Pugh, was leading a team of researchers in pre- and postrace examinations of the entries. After the prerace examinations were over the researchers favored the American swimmer Tom Park to win because of his very high metabolism, great speed, and strength.

When the swim began the water temperature was approximately fifty-eight degrees. Park, as expected, took the lead early and held it throughout ¾ of the race. For the first four hours he kept up a rate of sixty to sixty-four strokes per minute. Over the next two hours it fell to fifty strokes per minute. From there on Park slowed down from his 2.4-mile-per-hour average to something like one mile per hour. Abo-Heif, who had been swimming a few tenths of a mile per hour slower, did not break, and with but a couple of miles to go caught Park and with a flurry of strokes finished some thirty minutes ahead of him. Some said Abo-Heif was lucky because he had followed a straighter course and Park had gotten sick in the water. All this is true, but belies the fact that from that day on Abo-Heif began to make a name for himself that would culminate in his being called the greatest marathon swimmer in the history of the sport.

One wonders what Abo-Heif was doing the next few years, for the winner's and finishers list of the major professional swims do not even list him. Perhaps he was fulfilling his obligations to the military. Then again love and marriage entered the picture, for somewhere around 1955 Abo-Heif met and married a beautiful Greek opera singer named Menard. Later they had a son. In any case the year 1963 proved to be his year; he came back into the swimming world with the proverbial splash and such outstanding feats that from that day on he assumed, and never relinquished, the title of the superman of the waters.

He took first in the Capri-Naples swim ($1,200), an eighteen-mile swim from the island of Capri to the city of Naples. He took second at the Atlantic City Swim (twenty-five miles) in the United States a few weeks later for another $2,000. A week later followed the nineteen-mile Lake St. John swim in Canada where he again placed second. The flying Dutch schoolteacher, Herman Willemse, took first. Then the gods smiled for the next two races.

The famous fifteen-mile Canadian National Exhibition swim was next. This was the grandaddy and the most prestigious of all professional swims and had been held since 1927, excepting the war years. This was the race that attracted the best because of the prize money offered: $6,000 was the winner's take. This year's race would prove also to be one of the most thrilling in the annals of sports history. What helped to make that true was the fact that this year the water was cold: fifty-five degrees cold. It was also a fairly long race. From the start of the race the expected happened. The slender nemesis of Abo-Heif, the Dutch schoolteacher Herman Willemse, took the lead followed by the top female swimmers Greta Andersen and Marty Sinn. The Canadian champion Cliff Lumsden was doing his best to get rid of Abo-Heif who was swimming right next to him. This is a favorite trick of Abo-Heif, who derives tremendous stimulus from swimming alongside of someone until he nears the finish line, then leaves him in a flurry of strokes. For fourteen miles Willemse led the pack. Somewhere around the tenth mile Willemse began to feel the cold and slowly weakened. Somewhere around the fifth mile Abo-Heif had broken Lumsden and had begun to work his way up the rankings. Greta Andersen was next. When he caught her she dropped out realizing that when you are caught at that stage of the race it means only one thing: you've had it.

The next victim on the party line was the beautiful Marty Sinn who was about a quarter mile ahead at the ten-mile mark. With frenzy Abo-Heif went after her and caught her around the twelfth mile. For two miles they fought a neck-and-neck battle that brought them even with Willemse at the fatal fourteen-mile mark. It was here that Abo-Heif pulled the trademark finish that would characterize him and enshrine him in the memory of those who have seen him do the exact same thing in many another race. He began a sprint that carried him ahead of both the other swimmers and into first place. He finished two minutes fifteen seconds ahead of Miss Sinn and seven minutes ten seconds ahead of third place Willemse. It was a dogged, wearying race of seven hours thirty-seven minutes twenty-six seconds. That one race carried on in such cold water was enough to end the season for the rest of the swimmers. Now comes the incredible part of the story.

The C. N. E. race was held on a Saturday. On the following Tuesday—less than three days later—the famous Lake Michigan swim was being held. This was the swim that would go down as the longest open-water swim in history. It was sixty miles across Lake Michigan from Chicago to Benton Harbor-St. Joseph. When the rest of the swimmers went home Abo-Heif and his wife came to Chicago. With only two days rest from his C. N. E. endeavor Abo-Heif plunged into the water at 8 A.M. Tuesday morning, August 21, 1963 off Chicago's lakefront, and the rest is history. Thirty-five hours later and $15,000 richer, Abo-Heif waded ashore on the beach along the eastern shore of Lake Michigan, the first man to make a sixty-mile open-water swim: a record that still stands to this day.*

Abo-Heif was thirty-four years old when he set that record. But he did not seek the easy chair after this phenomenal accomplishment. He kept on swimming and winning races at an age where most athletes retire. In 1969, at the age of forty-two he won the twenty-three-mile

---

* People have gone farther and longer, but down river. In 1966 Leonore Model supposedly swam sixty-six miles around a six-mile lap course in a lake in Utah, but this swim remains questionable because of possible lap errors. In any case, Abo-Heif's swim remains unquestionable because of the large number of observers with him every moment.

Major Abdel-Latif Abo-Heif and wife at one of the award ceremonies celebrating his sixty-mile Lake Michigan swim. He flashes his renowned smile that has won him thousands of friends all over the world. Courtesy Verne Petro.

The greatest marathon swimmer in history, Major Abdel-Latif Abo-Heif. His fame is as great out of the water as in. He speaks six languages fluently, plays the piano, was a major in the Egyptian army, is married to an opera singer, and is the father of a twelve-year-old boy. Courtesy Gilles Berthiaume.

Chicoutimi race. In 1971, when he was forty-four years old, he placed second in the twenty-six-mile Guaymas, Mexico race, a truly striking showing for a man his age. The reader must remember that the sport calls for a cardiovascular system of a much younger man.

Abo-Heif shows the strain today when he finishes a race. He is a tired man. One wonders what he draws on to be able to finish in the top three. Yes, the fatigue is noticeable today, but only after he gets out of the water. In the water he is the same threat he always was. Only a few know why he only raises his hand from the hip to acknowledge the cheers of the crowd at the award ceremonies. A few years ago the arm was raised above his head in a wave. Age and effort have taken their toll. The younger swimmers will have a long wait if they expect him to quit in the water. While conscious, Abo-Heif doesn't know the meaning of the word.

12
Lake St. John:
The Paul Bunyan Swim

It's a good size lake lying in the middle of the northeastern province of Quebec. The area is inhabited by French-Canadians who have always earned their living as lumberjacks or paper mill hands. A sturdy people, their measurement of a man is determined by how many trees he can cut down in a day, how many miles he can cover in a day on snowshoes, or how far he can swim. Many a local man had dreamed of swimming Lake St. John. He would become a hero the stature of Paul Bunyan if he succeeded. The French-Canadians take their heroes seriously. For years the nineteen-mile wide, twenty-eight-mile long lake defeated the amateurs who periodically made attempts to conquer it. Then, in 1955, came a local swimmer, choosing the shortest points of land on either side. The closest I can come to determining the distance is something like eighteen miles. He accomplished it in some 11½ hours. When Jacques Amyot heaved his weary body onto the docks at the city of Roberval he had reason to be happy. Everyone remembers the man who is first. For the next two years whenever Jacques walked into a restaurant the proprietor would be glad to pick up the check. The local television stations interviewed him *ad nauseam*. His sponsor delighted in the publicity he had gained simply by advancing him $500 for training purposes. Roberval's eight thousand population had something to chew on for months following his accomplishment.

Jacques Amyot's feat released the inevitable flood that follows any first. It was like the scores of runners who came after Roger Bannister and the climbers following Hillary and Tenzing. The following year, 1956, another French-Canadian named Paul Des Ruisseaux, following the same route that Amyot did, was successful with the excellent time

Lake St. John: The Paul Bunyan Swim

of nine hours thirty-one minutes. The ones that follow know there will be no attention doing the same thing in a longer time. Thus they drive themselves for the record. You don't rest on your laurels in any profession. When Des Ruisseaux came back in 1957 and lowered his already existing record by more than an hour the publicity finally sledged home to the local merchants. More than ten thousand spectators had come pouring into Roberval from the small towns in the province to see Des Ruisseaux finish. In the short time they were there they had dropped more money than the merchants would see for the rest of the year.

By 1958 the swim was formalized into a race in which the world's best marathon swimmers were invited. Prize money and expenses for one week before the swim were offered to lure them to such an out-of-the-way locale. It was a huge success, vastly exceeding the most avaricious of men. The radio stations gave almost a minute-by-minute account of the progress of the race. The battle between Greta Andersen and Helge Jensen took on the status of male versus female so that two hours before the expected end of the race spectators had swelled the Roberval Harbor to a screaming, fun-seeking, and expectant crowd of over twenty-five thousand. Crowd control became almost impossible and the local police had to call in the provincial police to aid them. To the surprise and delight of the crowd Greta Andersen won the race. The greatest female marathon swimmer in the history of the sport was at the high point of her career during that and the following year. At the award ceremonies following the race there was hardly a dry eye as the tall, handsome woman walked to the stage amidst the refrains of the "Star Spangled Banner," for she was now a United States citizen. That year marked the beginning of the St. John races.

The promoters were prepared for the following year. Grandstands were set up at the arrival point to accommodate a large portion of the crowd. Needless to say there would be an admission charge to enter the premises. Logs and lines of buoys were set up in the harbor so that each swimmer arriving would have to course up and down five lanes that totaled a mile in length. It would give the spectators a prolonged view of the swimmers. (See diagram.) Later, in 1965, the final mile of the race would be called the sprint lap with additional prizes to the fastest time for this portion. It served to enliven the tired swimmers to do their best and also provide a show for the spectators. It would also tend to eliminate any collusion between swimmers to "water ballet" in together for a "tie." That year they also decided to lengthen the race by starting it a mile up the Peribonka River rather than on the shores of the lake. The wits promoting the race then called it a twenty-five-mile race. However, close measurement on the Canadian Hydrographic Chart # FR 6010 shows the distance to be only nineteen miles. I don't doubt that some of the tail-end swimmers have swum twenty-five miles but they probably had drunken rowers in their boat that took them all over the lake. The Lake St. John rowers are noted for taking a case of beer in the rowboat with them. They promptly procede to consume the whole case within a couple of hours with corresponding results. The professional swimmer and his coach make sure they have sober and good rowers for this swim. They also have a chart of the lake and a large, accurate compass. When the lead course-setting boat is lost in the haze you're on your own. Many a swimmer has ended up off Point Bleu, which is some 3½ miles northwest of Roberval. By the time he comes in, the time limit is over and he's earned nothing for his day of swimming. His gripes and pleas go unheeded. He soon learns to beat his head against the nearest wall or cry buckets of salty tears in his lonely hotel room. No one sympathizes with a "poor loser."

In 1959 Helge Jensen recouped his shame by winning the race he lost to Greta the year before. I find no record of Greta that year at St. John. Either she retired from the race or was off somewhere else in the world making a record.

In 1961, Herman Willemse, the "Flying Dutchman," began a three-year reign. Herman, as the photos show, still had enough left at the

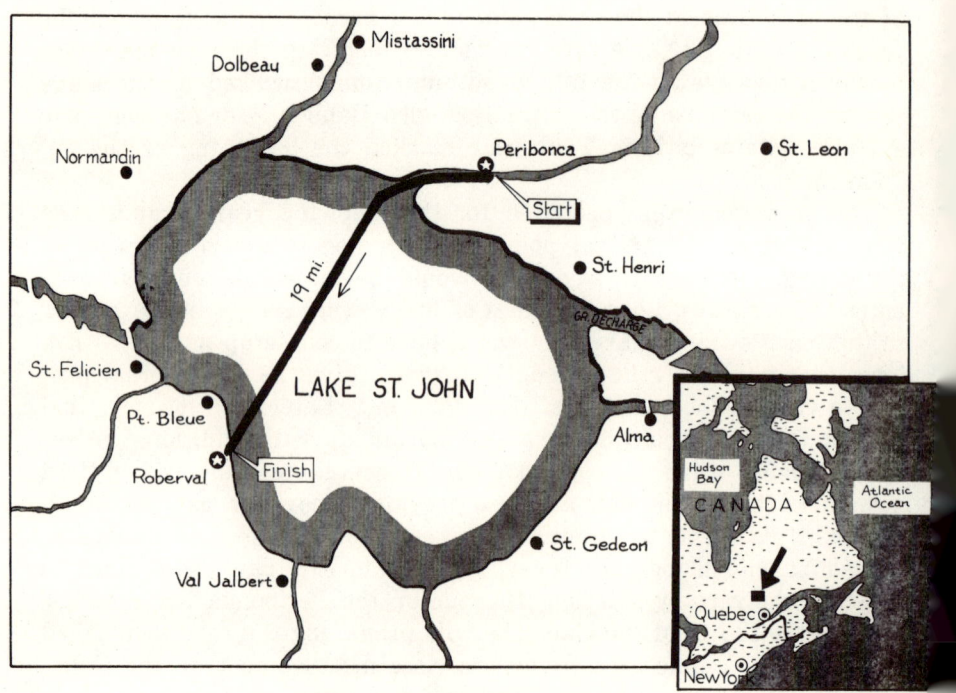

The Lake St. John swim.

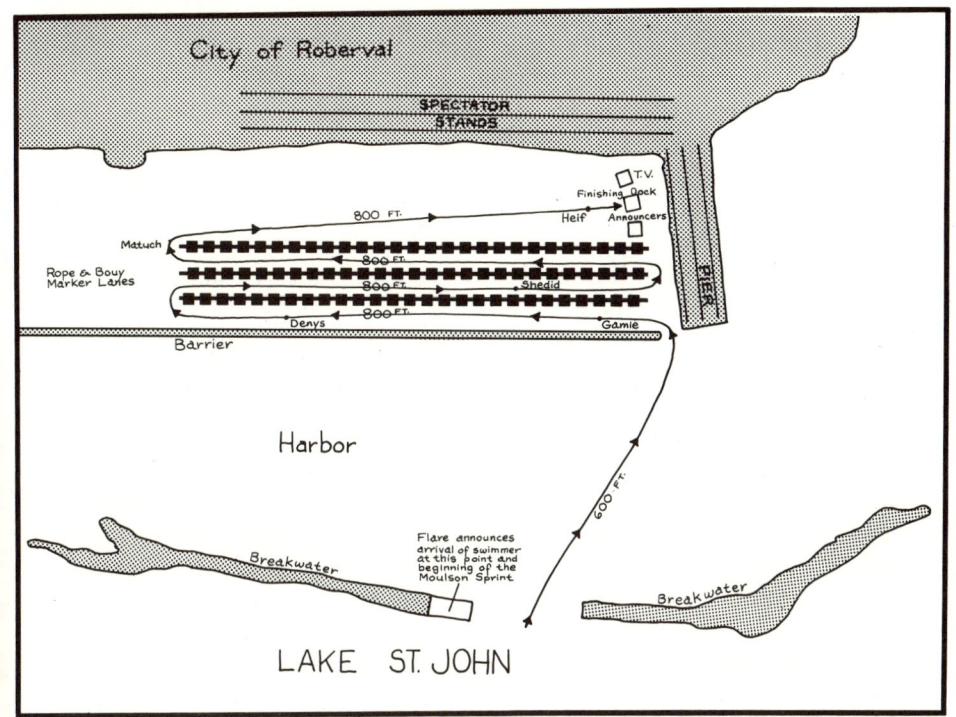

What the swimmer completing the Lake St. John race finds awaiting him at the finish. After eighteen miles of grueling competition, the final mile (approximate) is a sprint. The swimmer having the fastest time earns an extra $500. It serves to prevent collusion between swimmers who tie, and stimulates the swimmers to do their best before the public. Sometimes there will be as many as four swimmers in the lanes at the end of the race, each battling to catch the one ahead of him. Such a situation happened in 1970 (illustrated). The crowd of fifty thousand spectators went wild.

end of the race to wave and smile to the crowd. His three wins are second only to Horatio Iglesias, who in 1971 gained his fourth St. John victory. Judith DeNys followed Greta Andersen in 1966 in being the only other female winner of the race. Needless to say the crowd's pleasure was only exceeded by the male swimmer's chauvinism.

By 1965 the crowds attending the finish of the race had reached a startling fifty thousand individuals. The fame of the Lake St. John race had reached such proportions that in 1969 the prime minister of Canada, Pierre Trudeau, acceded to the wish of the local politicians that he be the official starter. He was also at the finishing dock nine hours thirty-two minutes later to greet the winner, Horatio Iglesias from Argentina. Marathon swimming is a big thing in Canada, especially when the prime minister shows up.

One of the things that makes the St. John swim interesting is the final "mile" sprint, now called the Molson Mile since the $700 offered for the first and second fastest times is paid by Molson Breweries. It is interesting because more often than not the winner of the race does not show the fastest final "mile." At the opening in the breakwater marking the harbor entrance an official stands with a flare gun. As a swimmer passes this point the official fires the flare, which immediately causes the officials at the finish line to start the stopwatches. They are stopped after the swimmer finishes his laps and arrives at the finishing dock. In some cases, like that of Herman Willemse in 1965, the fourth-place swimmer overall will turn in the fastest final mile. He did it again in 1966. It wasn't until 1969 that Horatio Iglesias became the first winner of the race and the sprint. The promoters of the St. John race do their best to make it an exciting finish for the spectators. It is quite a sight to see the crowd of fifty thousand individuals, television cameras, photographers, and announcers describing the finish when four swimmers are battling the last mile in various lanes. I can remember well the 1970 race when Abo-Heif, Matuch, Shedid, Judith DeNys, and Gamie were all visible in various spots in that final mile, each attempting to catch the swimmer ahead of him and at the same time trying to stay ahead of the swimmer behind. The aching bodies pushing themselves to the limit was a sight once witnessed never to be forgotten. Yes, the beautiful girls that strive to meet the Paul Bunyans after the race little know that the swimmers have earned their recognition. The response of the crowd makes their long lonely hours of training now seem worthwhile. Few men can resist the fame that attends the accomplishment. Fewer can resist the financial rewards. None resist the smiling face of a provocative and beautiful young girl. Some say it's the only reward. They might be right.

Greta Andersen fifteen minutes after winning the eighteen-mile Lake St. John swim in eight hours and seventeen minutes (1958). She beat all competitors including the men and became the first woman to swim the lake. She was twenty-eight years old. Courtesy Bilodeau of Roberval, Canada.

The strain of being first shows on the "Flying Dutchman" Herman Willemse as he climbs the arrival dock after winning the 1962 Lake St. John race. The effects of the long immersion can be readily seen in his hand. Courtesy Bilodeau of Roberval, Canada.

Greta Andersen after coming in fourth at Lake St. John in 1962.
Courtesy Bilodeau of Roberval, Canada.

The beautiful Mary Kok of Holland a few minutes before the start of the 1962 Lake St. John race. The strain of her eleven-hour ordeal is shown in the photo taken a few minutes after she finished. Courtesy Bilodeau of Roberval, Canada.

Lake St. John: The Paul Bunyan Swim

The greatest swimmer in the history of marathon swimming shown winning the 1965 Lake St. John race. Atop the platform Abo-Heif waves in triumph. A portion of the fifty thousand spectators can be seen in the background. Courtesy Bilodeau of Roberval, Canada.

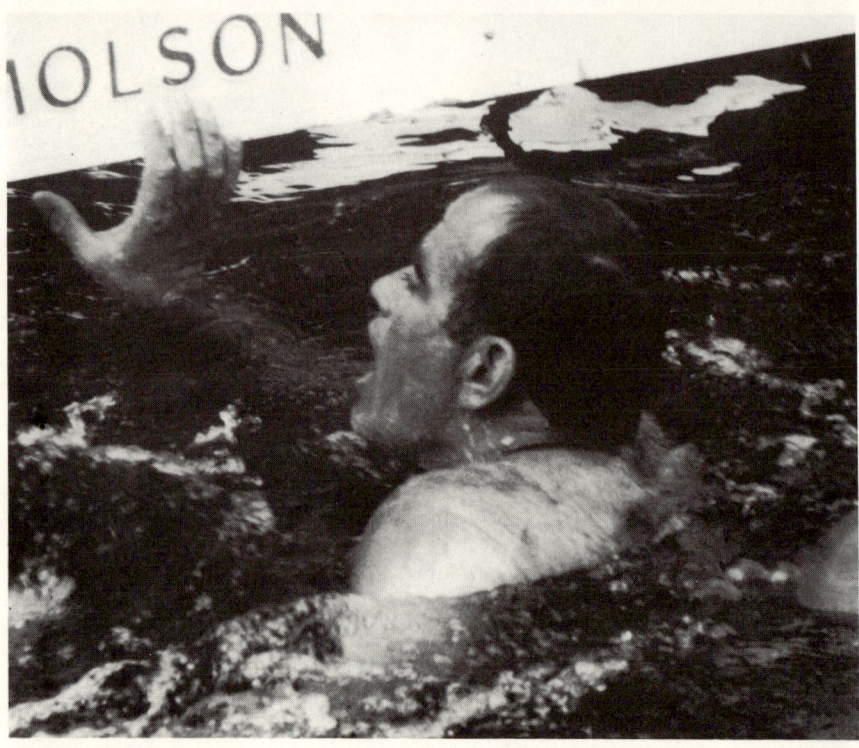

Lake St. John: The Paul Bunyan Swim

The Lake St. John race can provide some thrilling endings. Here the Canadian Rejean LaCoursiere and Egyptian Shazly, after nineteen miles of swimming, are fighting for second place (1965). LaCoursiere won by one tenth of a second. Abo-Heif had finished eleven minutes earlier to take first place. Courtesy Bilodeau of Roberval, Canada.

St. John Records

Year	Date	Swimmer	Distance	Time	Notes
1955	(July 23)	Jacques Amyot	21 miles	11:32:10	
1956	(July 29)	Paul-W. Des Ruisseaux	21 miles	9:31	
1957	(July 28)	Paul-W. Des Ruisseaux	21 miles	11:15	
1958	(August 2)	Greta Andersen	21 miles	8:17	
1959	(August 4)	Helge Jensen	24 miles	8:55:51	
1960	(August 7)	Rejean Lacoursiere	24 miles	9:30:12	in reality
1961	(August 5)	Herman Willemse	24 miles	10:07:06	19 miles
1962	(August 4)	Herman Willemse	24 miles	9:3	
1963	(August 3)	Herman Willemse	24 miles	8:32:50	
1964	(August 8)	Nabil El Shazly	24 miles	10:33:21	
1965	(August 7)	Abdel-Latif Abo-Heif	25 miles	8:34:35	
1966	(August 6)	Judith DeNys	25 miles	8:38:57	
1967	(August 5)	Horacio Iglesias	25 miles	8:55:15	

Molson Sprint (established in 1965)

Year	Date	Swimmer	Distance	Time
1965	(August 7)	Herman Willemse	20 M	95:6/10
1966	(August 6)	Herman Willemse	15 M	18:7/10
1967	(August 5)	Judith DeNys	14 M	54:1/10

Lake St. John: The Paul Bunyan Swim

Past Performances
(21 miles from 1955 to 1958; 24 miles from 1969 on)

1955

Jacques Amyot (Canada)	11:32:10

1956

Paul Des Ruisseaux (Canada) (not official)	9:31

1957

Paul Des Ruisseaux (Canada)	8:17

1958

Greta Andersen (USA)	8:17
Helge Jensen (Denmark)	8:32
Rejean Lacoursiere (Canada)	9:03
Joan Florentin (USA)	9:46
Gerard Caouette (Canada)	13:38

1959

Helge Jensen (Denmark)	8:55:51
Rejean Lacoursiere (Canada)	9:24:52
Joan Florentin (USA)	10:42:02
Jacques Amyot (Canada)	11:34:39
Robert Cossette (Canada)	13:00:52

1960

Rejean Lacoursiere (Canada)	9:30:12
Carlos Larriera (Argentina)	9:53:10
Aloma Keen (Canada)	14:29:45
Robert Cossette (Canada)	14:44:00

1961

Herman Willemse (Holland)	12:07:06
Rejean Lacoursiere (Canada)	10:16:10
Tom Park (USA)	10:33:17
Helge Jensen (Denmark)	10:38:02
Syder Guiscardo (Argentina)	10:48:33
Mary Kok (Holland)	10:59:19
Robert Cossette (Canada)	14:37:17

1962

Herman Willemse (Holland)	9:03:00
Cliff Lumsden (Canada)	9:55:03
Rejean Lacoursiere (Canada)	9:58:11
Greta Andersen (USA)	10:14:02
Tom Park (USA)	10:54:02
Mary Kok (Holland)	11:14:08
Jacques Amyot (Canada)	13:28:00
Pierre Bourdon (Canada)	13:37:18

1963

Herman Willemse (Holland)	8:32:50
Abdel-Latif Abo-Heif (Egypt)	8:53:43
Rejean Lacoursiere (Canada)	8:53:43
Mohamed Aly (Egypt)	8:58:58
Cliff Lumsden (Canada)	9:06:45
Alfredo Camarrero (Argentina)	9:33:41
Syder Guiscardo (Argentina)	9:46:42
Jorge Lopez (Argentina)	10:04:46

1964

Nabil El Shazly (Egypt)	10:33:21
Abdel-Latif Abo-Heif (Egypt)	10:45:10
Rejean Lacoursiere (Canada)	10:47:45
Cliff Lumsden (Canada)	10:49:43
Roberto Horatio Reta (Argentina)	10:54:15
El Gueli (Egypt)	10:58:37
Judith DeNys (Holland)	11:17:00
Dennis Matuch (USA)	X
Ted Erikson (USA)	X
Florencio Romero (Argentina)	X

X—finished after time limit

Official Records
1965

1	Abdel-Latif Abo-Heif (Egypt)	8:34:35
2	Rejean Lacoursiere (Canada)	8:45:35
3	Nabil El Shazly (Egypt)	8:45:35.1
4	Herman Willemse (Holland)	8:53:19
5	Dennis Matuch (USA)	9:52:52
6	Cliff Lumsden (Canada)	9:55:15
7	Kurt Pluntke	10:55:20
8	Jean Couture (Canada)	10:56:55
9	Ken Jensen	11:01:40
10	Armand Cloutier (Canada)	X
11	Robert Cossette (Canada)	X

X—finished after time limit

Molson Sprint

1	Herman Willemse (Holland)	20:05.6
2	Rejean Lacoursiere (Canada)	22:00:00
3	Abdel-Latif Abo-Heif (Egypt)	22:09:01
4	Nabil El Shazly (Egypt)	23:46:02
5	Dennis Matuch (USA)	24:01:00
6	Cliff Lumsden (Canada)	24:46:09
7	Ken Jensen	26:11:02
8	Jean Couture (Canada)	26:48:02
9	Kurt Pluntke	32:11:09

1966

1	Judith DeNys	8:38:57	$3,500
2	Tom Bucy	8:58:50	$2,000
3	Rejean Lacoursiere	8:59:35	$1,500
4	Herman Willemse	9:05:39	$1,000
5	George Park	9:44:16	$ 700
6	Abdel-Latif Abo-Heif	10:30:04	$ 450
7	Cliff Lumsden	10:30:04	$ 450
8	Kurt Pluntke	11:05:15	$ 300
9	Conrad Corbeil	11:42:46	$ 300

After the 12-hour time limit: 1 Mary Lou Whitwill, 12:11:56; 2 Jean Coutre 12:41:28.

Did not complete the race: Albert Hreische, Gilles Potvin, Gerard Caouette, Pedro Galmez, Yvan Daniel, Guilio Travaglio, Roger Piche, François Asselin, Armad Cloutier.

Lake St. John: The Paul Bunyan Swim

Molson Sprint

1	Herman Willemse	15:18:07	$500
2	Judith DeNys	15:23:05	$200
3	Abdel-Latif Abo-Heif	15:39:08	
4	Cliff Lumsden	15:50:08	
5	Tom Bucy	16:49:00	
6	Rejean Lacoursiere	17:02:04	
7	Conrad Corbeil	18:55:02	
8	Mary Lou Whitwill	20:00:09	
9	Georges Park	20:50:00	
10	Kurt Pluntke	21:32:05	

1967

1	Horacio Iglesias	8:55:15:00
2	Rejean Lacoursiere	9:18:15:00
3	Judith DeNys	9:22:28:01

special $500 purse as the first woman to finish

4	Herman Willemse	9:38:21:00
5	Georges Park	9:52:04:03
6	Diki Bohadzi	9:53:41:01
7	Bill Barton	10:10:26:04
8	Klime Savin	10:12:16:00
9	Dennis Matuch	10:39:18:02
10	Ed Forshrey	10:56:59:04
11	Conrad Corbeil	11:19:48:02
12	R. Horacio Reta	11:38:04:04

Those who left the water: Guilio Travaglio, 9:20 a.m.; Hedy Schmidt, 10:35 p.m.; Kurt Pluntke, 11:25 p.m.; Tom Bucy, 1:30 p.m.; Margaret Park; François Asselin; Charles Grover.

Finished after the 12-hour time limit: Ben Bouchard, Pedro Galmez, and Roger Piche.

Molson Sprint

1	Judith DeNys	14:54:01
2	Horacio Iglesias	15:29:00
3	Rejean Lacoursiere	15:56:08
4	Dennis Matuch	18:21:03
5	Kime Savin	18:22:00
6	Georges Park	18:32:06
7	Diki Bojodzi	19:26:00
8	Bill Barton	20:01:03
9	Conrad Corbeil	21:05:00
10	R. Horacio Reta	21:09:00
11	Ed Forshbrey	22:40:06
12	Herman Willemse	23:44:00

1968

				SPRINT	
1	H. Iglesias—Argentina	9:31:11:06	$3,500	13:49:09	
2	Abo-Heif—Egypt	10:14:24:04	$2,000	10:44:08	$500
3	Judith DeNys—Holland	10:40:48:05	$1,500	12:55:08	
4	R. Lacoursiere—Canada	10:47:16:07	$1,000	13:32	
5	Dennis Matuch—USA	10:51:44:05	$ 700	12:49:04	$200
6	George Park—Canada	11:45:40:06	$ 500	13:43:05	

7	G. S. Lake—England	11:54:26:07	$ 400	14:34

Finished after the 12-hour limit: Linda McGill (Australia), 12:02:33:07; R. Reta (Argentina), 12:11:40:09.

Extra prize for first woman: Judith DeNys: $500

Official time of withdrawal

1	Wickens	7:05 A.M.
2	Conrad Corbeil	8:45 A.M.
3	G. Travaglio	9:15 A.M.
4	Thomas Bucy	9:20 A.M.
5	Fausto Ramirez	12:00 P.M.
6	Real Lavoie	12:10 P.M.
7	Pedro Galmes	12:50 P.M.
8	Hassaan	2:40 P.M.
9	Margaret Park	3:17 P.M.
10	Steve Ramsden	5:37 P.M.
11	Sherbini	6:00 P.M.

Withdrawals after the regulation time

Ben Bouchard	7:45 P.M.
Gilles Potvin	9:10 P.M.

Departure was at exactly 6:11 A.M.

Lake St. John Official Times 1969

1.	Iglesias	9:32	11.6 + Sprint	
2.	Schans	10:12	35.9	
3.	Abo-Heif	11:12	05.5	
4.	Matuch	11:17	25.1	All in 4 lane sprint at same time.
5.	LaCousiere	11:20	21.1	
6.	Gamie	11:27	23.3	
7.	Lake	11:59	24	(36 seconds under 12-hour time limit)

1971

1.	Iglesias, Horacio	8.39.43.00	4.	Shedid, Marwan	21.45.01
2.	Scheydel, Jan Van	9.07.05.03	5.	Lake, Stephen	21.50.03
3.	Khamis, Mamoud	9.14.54.06	6.	Khamis, Mamoud	21.52.04
4.	Heif, Abou	10.09.54.08	7.	Gamie, Mohamed	23.49.06
5.	Shedid, Marwan	10.11.41.06	8.	Lacoursière, Régent	25.04.06
6.	Lake, Stephen	10.13.58.06	9.	Matuch, Dennis	28.43.04
7.	Matuch, Dennis	10.26.46.00	10.	Guiscardo, Marcello	31.30.06
8.	Lacoursière, Régent	11.06.02.04	11.	Shedid, Hafez	36.05.04
9.	Montpetit, Yvon	11.13.36.00	12.	Montpetit, Yvon	36.53.06
10.	Gamie, Mohamed	11.15.45.06		Retraits	
11.	Guiscardo, Marcello	11.21.35.00		Diana Nyad	9h.45
12.	Shedid, Hafez	11.58.45.00		Marwan Saleh	9h.56

Sprint Quebecair

			Guillarmo Venturini	10h.06
1.	Schans, Johan	15.59.03	Abou Magid Kigab	10h.10
2.	Iglesias, Horacio	16.05.08	Naste Jonceski	10h.10
2.	Deffaa, Arthur	16.05.08	Gaston Paré	12h.11

Sprint Molson

			Johan Schans	13h.25
1.	Iglesias, Horacio	18.42.03	Arthur Deffaa	14h.33
2.	Scheyndel, Jan Van	20.03.06	Thomas Hetzel	16h.09
3.	Heif, Abou	20.40.04	Mervyn Sharp	16h.58
			Robert Perry Cameron	18h.25

Lake St. John: The Paul Bunyan Swim 207

1972

Only three swimmers completed the swim under the twelve-hour time limit due to inclement weather. There was a thirty-mile-an-hour wind that caused four- to five-foot waves. The wind and waves were against the swimmers. The water temperature was sixty-five degrees. There were twenty-three entries. Among those who dropped out were Horacio Iglesias, Jan Van Scheyndel, and Judith DeNys. A few made it over the time limit.

1.	Jan Van Scheyndel	10:48	$3,500
2.	R. Villagomez	11:37	$2,000
3.	Dennis Matuch	11:44	

Sprint Molson

1.	Jan Van Scheyndel	21:05	$500
2.	R. Villagomez	24:30	$200

Liste Officielle des Arrivees
Traversee Lac St-Jean
1970

1.	Johan Schans	8h.27mi.50sec6dix.
2.	Horacio Iglesias	8h.39mi.36sec4dix.
3.	Jan Van Scheyndel	8h.53mi.36sec5dix.
4.	Abdel-Latif Abo-Heif	9h.14mi.45sec8dix.
5.	Dennis Matuch	9h.19mi. 9dix.
6.	Marawan Fathe Shedid	9h.25mi.11sec
7.	Judith DeNys	9h.32mi.20sec7dix.
8.	Mohamed Gamie	9h.47mi.43sec4dix.
9.	Regent Lacoursière	10h. 8mi.45sec3dix.
10.	Geoffrey Stephen Lake	10h.32mi.15sec2dix.
11.	Junior Erikson	10h.36mi. 1sec5dix.
12.	Gaston Paré	10h.48mi.26sec4dix.
13.	Michael Paesler	10h.49mi.15sec
14.	George Park	10h.56mi.50sec8dix.
15.	Yvon Montpetit	11h.23mi.39sec8dix.
16.	DES. Renfords	11h.44mi. 9sec4dix.

Sprint Molson

1.	Jan Van Scheyndel	19mi.13sec.6dix.
2.	Horacio Iglesias	19mi.19sec.5dix.
3.	Abou Heif	19mi.46sec.6dix.
4.	Johan Schans	21mi.10sec.3dix.
5.	Judith DeNys	21mi.15sec.8dix.
6.	Michael Paesler	22mi.12sec.2dix.
7.	Geoffrey Stephen Lake	22mi.36sec.5dix.
8.	Marawan Fathe Shedid	23mi. 3dix.
9.	Dennys Matuch	23mi.42sec.1dix.
10.	Junior Erikson	24mi.14sec.4dix.
11.	Regent Lacoursiere	25mi.23sec.
12.	Mohamed Gamie	26mi. 5dix.
13.	DES. Renfords	
14.	Yvon Montpetit	36mi.15sec.2dix.
15.	Gaston Paré	39mi. 2sec.3dix.
16.	George Park	39mi.22sec.2dix.

Ont Complete Apres Le Temps Reglementaire
Fausto Ramirez
France Boisvert

Retires

Whittell Martell	8h.20mi.a.m.
Carlos Aguirre	10h.32mi.
Hassan Abdeen	11h.17mi.
Stella Taylor	12h.30mi.
Patricia Thompson	6h.

13
Swim, Man, Swim! This One's for Real: Some Great Life-and-death Swims

Professional marathon swimming races arouse the admiration of those who recognize the talents involved. Swims from sinking vessels and ditched aircraft in which survival is involved earn the admiration of everyone. Hardly a day goes by that some account isn't published of a life-saving swim after an accident in or over water. Some of these swims are of a heroic nature. They are accomplished without benefit of food and navigational aids. Many are done without companionship, thus adding to the despair the swimmer feels. The story of these swims began when man first took to the water in vessels. The inevitable results were shipwrecks. The accounts of most swimming feats by survivors are lost in history. There were many who drowned since the vast majority of sailors were land-lubbers who never had or took the time to learn how to swim. The heyday of shipwrecks was no doubt the eighteenth and nineteenth centuries. The trafficked areas of the world offered many a storm and rocks upon which to meet doom. Cape Horn probably holds the record for foul-weather sinking. In the days of sail many ships spent months waiting for conditions to clear, which it never did totally, so that they could beat their way around the southern tip of South America. In more civilized areas natural traps like Eddystone Reef, fourteen miles off Plymouth in the English Channel, would be a hazard. Eddystone would be hard to beat for fatalities. This reef alone was responsible for thousands of deaths when merchant and military vessels would plough into the large and well-hidden reef in the Channel's turbulent waters. It wasn't until the late 1600s that a lighthouse was finally erected on the reef. It not

209

only saved many lives, but made the fame of the engineers who succeeded in constructing the tower.

While marathon swims, which are conducted under rules, have a drama of their own, it is an artificially created one. A synthetic creation offered for many reasons. If you come in last in a race you've lost time and money. If you don't finish you climb into your boat. On the other hand if you find yourself swimming because of some catastrophe you've got your life to lose. Some of man's greatest swimming accomplishments have been "unauthorized" ones. The accounts of these swims make fascinating reading.

I have been loath to accept many accounts of such swims unless thoroughly documented. Invariably they are exaggerated. One such account was that of an Italian merchant seaman who fell overboard in the Mediterranean sometime in the 1950s. The account stated that he accomplished thirty-six miles in fourteen hours. If he did it would have been a world's record. The time for that distance is held by a professional swimmer, Dennis Matuch, in the 1962 Lake Michigan swim, who accomplished the feat under ideal weather conditions, with excellent navigation and periodic feedings in twenty-one hours. He also had the benefit of being chased the whole time by Greta Andersen. The Italian seaman to have done the distance without navigation and food and wearing clothes places his accomplishment in the realm of mythology. If he is free of duplicity then the "Fairytale Award" should go to the reporter handing in the story.

The accounts that I have accepted as valid stand up with the known facts of professional swimmers. They have also been thoroughly documented by professional scholars who have, for one reason or another, an interest in such accomplishments. Such is George Albert Llano, Ph.D., research and editorial specialist of the Arctic, Desert and Tropic Information Center of the United States Air Force. Llano made a study of sea survival experiences for the United States government. Whenever survivors of sea disasters could be located they were either interviewed or sent forms to fill out. Next, the rescuers were contacted and subsequent information tallied. The files of rescue services the world over were combed, as were records kept by Coast Guards (e.g., English Life Boat Service), and Air-Sea Rescue services. When enough information was collected charts were made and incidents either accepted or rejected. The acceptance or rejection was based on whether the data were sufficient and acceptable. Many of the other accounts that follow were the results of my own research and strict adherence to the facts and plausibility were constantly kept in mind.

For pure indifference it is hard to beat the feat of four Hawaiian fishermen in the Molokai Straits in 1939. The straits, which lie between the islands of Oahu and Molokai, are famous for their treacherous currents and choppy waters. Every sailboat that has ever entered the straits will testify to it. The straits even frustrated the famous swimmer Greta Andersen three times when she tried to be the first person to swim it. The four young fishermen were spending a morning at their trade five miles off Molokai. Suddenly some planks sprung in their small craft and it promptly began to sink. The four young men discussed their situation calmly as the ship went down. Their leader, in fact, continued to smoke his cigarette as the waters rose to his armpits. Treading water, they chatted about the best way to reach shore. For ten minutes they continued to talk while in the water. As all Polynesians they were born to the water and they felt no doubt they would make land. The reason for the discussion was that while they were only four or five miles off Molokai the currents were such that if they attempted to swim to the island the currents along the coast would carry them out to sea. Oahu was twenty miles in the other direction. Knowledge of their environment gave them almost immediate decision. It would be longer, but safer and easier to strike out for Oahu. For fourteen hours they breast stroked and talked continuously, for Hawaiians are of a communicative nature. They hoped their wives wouldn't be too mad about them being late. They wondered what they would have for supper that night. They made plans for a new boat. After fourteen hours they stepped ashore at Oahu and begged the pardon of a fellow Hawaiian for disturbing him, but could he manage to contact their wives and tell them they were all right? The Hawaiian fishermen, as most simple people, were prepared to forget about the incident, but a few tourists were around and made a big to do. Their story was written up and they became a minor sensation for a few days. If they had not come ashore at the beach below Diamond Head their feat would have gone unnoticed. "Why get excited about a little swimming," was the comment of one. "Our ancestors have been doing it for centuries." The swim was accomplished in water temperatures in the mid and upper seventies, which lends credence to the same fisherman's comment. "It was just like a long bath."

To show that the above incident was no freak occurrence, almost the same thing happened in 1964, but with a different cast. On this occasion a power boat struck a log and went down, dumping its four occupants in the water ten miles from Oahu. The first two, Polynesian-Hawaiians, reached Bamboo Ridge after seven hours of swimming. They were followed four hours later by the two American-Hawaiians who were quite a bit more tired from their efforts. Whether they were slower swimmers or took the roundabout way wasn't mentioned, but it seems that the easy going Polynesian personality tends to turn a disaster into a sporting event.

Llano, in his search of naval archives, came up with many incidents during World War II in which airmen from ditched aircraft swam for eight to sixteen hours before making land, or being picked up by rescue craft. Such lengthy swims could only take place in the warmer waters of the Pacific theater. When such incidents took place in the North Atlantic, the English Channel during the winter, or the Baltic Sea survival time was considerably less. Depending on the amount of clothing worn by the swimmer and his body fat, survival time ran from six minutes to no more than an hour.

The accounts of the Pacific Ocean dunkings make spine-chilling reading because on many occasions the swimmer was nudged, nibbled at, and scraped by sharks. One horrendous account has an airman pushing his unconscious buddy, wearing a life jacket, ahead of him while sharks gradually dismembered the body. This airman was extremely fortunate that the sharks took no more than inquisitive nudgings on him.

The last-mentioned incident is perhaps the most unique one because it represents one of the longest active swimming efforts of an untrained person I could find. Although the men involved all had life preservers it took constant swimming by the only survivor to reach the shore. An Ecuadorian flight officer, with two companions, was forced to land their malfunctioning airplane in the Pacific on a flight between Esmereldas and Salinas. All three managed to remove their clothing and don life jackets before entering the water. To make matters worse the accident occurred around five in the afternoon which meant there were only a few more hours of daylight. Hooking their arms underneath the preserver straps they began stroking in the general direction of shore. As the sun set the wind picked up until the waves forced the less competent swimming companions of the flight officer to swallow water. Some five hours after ditching one of the crewmen died. It was then that the flight officer began pushing the corpse ahead of him. An hour or so later sharks made their appearance and began eating the body. In a few minutes the remaining head and shoulders was pulled under and disappeared forever. The captain's sublieutenant weakened to the point where he had to be pulled along by the captain. After another five hours of swimming the sublieutenant died. Again the captain treated the corpse in the same manner as the other crewman, and began pushing it ahead of him. It wasn't long before dark images appeared in the water around him fully illuminated by the moon. A repeat horror took place as the sharks began their second feast. The captain, terrorized by the sharks brushing his body, turned loose the corpse and swam away from the area. Suppressing his fear as much as he could, he continued swimming throughout the night. When daylight appeared he could make out the coast. To his horror he found that the sharks were still with him. Whenever he dropped his legs to rest he could feel their bodies brushing his legs. All that day he kept swimming until by sundown he found himself some five hundred yards from the rocky coast. Like swimmers in similar situations this proved to be the most arduous part of the swim. Armchair readers may wonder why, but need only visit the coastline of any large ocean in the world. On almost every occasion they will find huge breakers pounding the shore. If the shore is rocky, rather than sandy, all the worse. The swimmer at this stage no longer has the energy to battle the heightened waves.

After a superhuman effort the flight captain succeeded in working his way over the waves breaking on the rocky coastline with an effort that made Robinson Crusoe's landing look like child's play. He was more a corpse than a living human when he finally dragged himself the last few inches up the beach. There the captain slumped and awaited discovery, which came hours later when coastal inhabitants discovered him. It is a pity that I could find no record of the captain's subsequent recovery. However one fact emerges from this accident. That flight captain, after thirty-one hours of swimming and seeing his fellow officers eaten by sharks, had served his time in hell. St. Peter should swing wide the gate and have the horns polished to their highest luster. There's no doubt about it. This man should receive a hero's welcome.

A similar incident, with all too little facts, is mentioned by John M. Waters, Jr., a captain in the United States Coast Guard. He tells of Captain Paul R. Shook who ejected from his plane sixty miles off Ft. Myers, Florida. Captain Shook spent thirty-nine hours, with life jacket, in the water before being rescued. The captain was fortunate in not being noticed by sharks in an area that reports six shark attacks a year. While statisticians say that chances of being killed by a shark are less than being killed by lightning, it is of no consolation to those exposed to the threat.

The number of incidents of "man overboard" began to mount into the hundreds, if not thousands, as I scanned the literature. A British seaman swims twenty-four hours in the Mediterranean before staggering ashore. An American swept overboard from his sloop by huge waves off Miami Beach, Florida manages eighteen hours of stroking before being spotted by a fishing boat. These were swims made without benefit of life jackets. The number of incidents reach such levels that many sailing vessels today, when conditions call for it, have their crew attach belts to themselves that are attached to long nylon lines fixed to the boat proper. Many a racing vessel has preserved its lead and possibly a man's life when a man overboard was reeled in.

The longest swimming effort with life jackets was by two Navy pilots. One succumbed after twenty-four hours. The other kicked and stroked, and on the eve of his third night in the water after seventy-three hours of swimming he stumbled over a coral reef and reached the shore. The flier mentioned how fortunate he had been that the life jacket was fitted with neck pieces that held his head clear of the water during his dozing periods.

The longest survival swim without life jacket or any other support is held by a Dutch submariner during World War II. Finding himself in the water from a war-damaged submarine, he removed his clothing and began his life-saving swim. For thirty-five hours he continuously stroked toward the Java coast. When he succeeded in making the sandy shore he established an unofficial record that stands to this day. While he did not go as far as Abo-Heif and Erikson when they established the world's professional swim marathon record of sixty miles, he did spend the same amount of time in the water. He had no benefit of feeding either. I would calculate that the man swam at least thirty miles and possibly more. Such is the stuff of which men are made.

All of the above achievements were made in warm water (above seventy-four degrees) and by swimmers without major injuries. When just idle drifting or major injuries are considered, even more amazing accounts are discovered. Japanese sailors from an aircraft carrier, who found themselves in the waters of the South Pacific after their vessel was sunk during the battle of Midway, established a record for immersion time. Six of them survived $5\frac{1}{2}$ days in the water with life jackets. This immersion time is the longest authenticated one I have come across.

Being dumped into the water far from shore is damaging enough to the psyche even when healthy and uninjured. Being placed in the same situation with serious body maiming becomes truly frightening. A most unusual case comes out of the Caribbean area during World War II. Eight American submariners found themselves in the water after their submarine had hit a drifting German mine. Of the party, two were seriously injured, one to the extent of having had one of his hands blown off. A tourniquet was quickly applied and the party struck out in the general direction of the Florida coast. Within two hours three men had succumbed, one of whom was one of the other seriously injured men. Hour after hour the five remaining men stroked on. After one day and one night three men were left. After one and a half days of swimming two men reached an inhabited shore. They were the only two survivors of the submarine. One of the men who climbed the beach was minus a hand. The tourniquet had remained firmly fixed as well as did the man's indomitable courage.

It seems fitting to end the description of warm water, "man overboard" swims with the story of the young Korean Chung Nam Kim. Kim decided to take a stroll around the Liberian freighter he was on one night in August, 1969. The weather was ideal one hundred miles off the Nicaraguan coast. Whether he took a misstep or simply tried to walk where the ship ended he didn't know, but the next moment Kim found himself in the water. To make matters worse no one witnessed his unplanned immersion. For about twelve hours Kim swam, becoming increasingly depressed with his situation. Around midmorning he spotted what looked like a shark and his despair took a sudden jump for the worse. Upon closer examination he saw that it wasn't a shark at all, but a large sea turtle. Slowing stroking toward it he was amazed to find that it did not swim away. Not being particularly choosy at the moment as to what served as a float he succeeded in climbing onto the back of the creature which to his further surprise did not dive. For the next three hours Kim rode on the back of his new-found friend.

At the end of that time he was spotted by the Swedish ship *Citadel*. The lookout of the *Citadel* had sighted the head of a man in the water. Captain Horst Wedder and crewmen of the *Citadel* were amazed to see Kim and the turtle beneath him. A lifebelt was thrown to Kim and he was hauled out. He immediately collapsed on the deck. Marine biologist, Malcolm Gordon, of the University of California expressed the unlikelihood of the usually very sensitive sea turtle allowing someone to use it as a life raft. However, Mr. Gordon, talk to Kim and the crewmen of the Citadel. It would be hard to find twenty men agreeing on the facts in an attempt to foist a canard on the public.

Survival time in cold water is drastically reduced. The dramatic change testifies to the conducting power of water in drawing heat from the human body. Aquatic mammals have evolved specific adaptations to either minimize or eliminate heat loss. One method is to increase body size. The laws of physics state that while the volume of a body increases to the cube, the surface area increases only to the square. Thus, with more internal cells producing heat, there is a corresponding diminished ratio of exterior, or surface, cells, losing heat. When a surface area of fat cells that are not heavily vascularized is added a further heat conserving mechanism comes into play. Finally there is the external hair, or fur of the animal, which upon closer inspection shows it to be a most marvelous water-repellent coat. In reality the fur coat of these mammals is actually two separate and distinct layers. The coat immediately next to the skin is a dense, tightly woven flufflike layer. Growing out from between these hairs is the much longer and more "fibrous" hair. Both of these layers are coated by oily and waxy secretions from the skin which give them hydrophobic (water-shedding) and air-trapping qualities. Thus, for truly aquatic mammals like the otter and polar bear water rarely, if ever, succeeds in actually reaching the skin of the animals. Not only does this mechanism prevent heat loss but, due to the trapped air, it gives added buoyancy, thus making swimming that much more efficient.

In returning to man we see that the only benefit he may have is fat, and that this is only of very limited value in waters below fifty-three degrees. Studies made by physiologists the world over have shown that you are in serious trouble if you find yourself in water with temperatures in the thirties for any time over five or six minutes. If you are young and fat you may last a half hour at the most. All of the above was learned at first hand by maritime men in the northern climes long before the scientists began making their studies. It became even more evident to the air and sea rescue services in the North Atlantic and Baltic Seas during World War II. They learned fast that they had better get their sailors and pilots out of winter waters quickly. The charts created by physiologists relating water temperature and survival time are quite interesting. While the exceptional individual will exceed their predictions now and then, it does not negate their validity for the great majority of individuals. The well-known aphorism of life-insurance statisticians, "Statistics hold for the mass but not for the individual," applies here. Since their business is based on proper and adequate numbers and their interpretation and they are quite successful, it bodes well to stick with them. With this in mind the reader may peruse the graph. I have plotted some of the great professional and solo swims on the chart when the data was available. Now we shall see how it stacks up with some of the most well-known cold-water immersions.

The waters around the Aleutians average forty-seven to fifty-two degrees during the warmest month, which is August. In March, the coldest, the sea will average between thirty-six and thirty-eight degrees. If there is slush ice, a low of twenty-nine degrees will be reached. (The reader should remember that saltwater turns to ice some four degrees lower than fresh water.) It was in such slush ice that one man of ten from a torpedoed vessel survived a half hour immersion during World War II.

A most remarkable case was that of a twenty-two-year-old pilot who survived two hours of swimming off the coast of Oregon in April (the tail end of winter in North America). Five of his companions succumbed. The doctor who attended the young pilot immediately upon rescue could not feel his pulse. He was revived with whiskey and blood plasma. Although no water temperature was given in the report one can safely say that it was somewhere between forty-five and fifty degrees.

That the fat-padded marathon swimmer has caused many a scientific investigator to raise his brow in amazement is understandable. The Canadian National Exhibition and Juan de Fuca Swims are examples. Three of the C. N. E. races had no finishers because of cold water. Juan de Fuca was attempted eighty times before it was conquered. The reader will learn of these swims in their proper chapter.

Only death can convince some men that they are human. Such a man was Jason Zirganos, a major in the Greek army. Zirganos was one of the first entrants in the first professional English Channel race. In his early forties, he did not do better than seventh. Zirganos kept coming back over the years until in 1954 he placed the best ever for him, fourth. Zirganos attracted the attention of Dr. L. G. C. Pugh and his colleagues and he generously allowed tests to be made on him during some of his swims.

Zirganos was one of those ebullient and charming men who crowd two careers into one lifetime. A professional soldier, he had risen to the rank of major in the Greek army. He always found time to balance his sedentary officer's duties with swimming. By the time he reached his early thirties he had exhausted all the short bay swims that surround his native Greece. With the long leave of absences earned from his army career he began to seek out the famous long-distance swims of other countries. It wasn't long before he heard of the first Channel race to be held in 1951. Packing clothes and taking enough money to last him for the one month he felt necessary for training, Zirganos booked passage to England. As mentioned above, Zirganos did a quite respectable seventh in that race. It becomes even more respectable when we learn he was forty-two years old. His twenty-plus hours in a solo attempt a few years before was bettered by his sixteen-plus hours this time. Zirganos used Lake Windermere as well as the Channel for a training ground. He racked up four successful swims that year of the ten-mile-long lake, which registers about sixty degrees.

It was in 1954 that Zirganos attracted the attention of Pugh and his colleagues. In his easy going manner he quickly agreed to let the investigators make the desired physiologic tests on him during training swims in the lake. As one reads the straightforward scientific report of Pugh, which appeared in the British medical journal *Lancet*, there seeps through an insight into Zirganos's personality that Pugh had no intention of putting there. But it is there all the same. Here was a fat man who took great pride in his endurance of the cold. While he may not look as attractive as his leaner and younger competitors, nor swim as fast, he could exceed them in "taking" cold water. Realizing he was out of the money in competing with the younger swimmers in races, Zirganos began undertaking solo swims to bolster his sagging ego. In 1953 Zirganos showed up in Istanbul, Turkey, announcing, to those interested, that he intended to swim the *length* of the Bosphorus. This would have gone unnoticed except for one fact. Zirganos had arrived in the fall months. Many swimmers had conquered the width; it was only one to two miles, and some had done the fifteen-mile length, but all had been done in the warm summer months when the water temperature was delightful. (In 1931 the daughter of Ambassador Grew, Anita, twenty-two, attended by her illustrious father, swam the link between the Black Sea and the Sea of Marmora in August taking four hours thirty minutes.) The reader need only look at his atlas to see that the Bosphorus lies approximately forty-one degrees north latitude. When he took his plunge the water temperature registered 46.4 degrees. After four hours Zirganos was taken from the water in a semiconscious state and remained that way for three hours. Evidently the major's quest for fame was now taking a suicidal bent. As the years rolled by news of the "crazy" Zirganos would filter through to the other swimmers. Each attempt was characterized by the major drumming up prepublicity attention. By 1958 Zirganos had extended his quest for attention to America. This time he would swim around Manhattan Island. The twenty-six-mile swim had been done many times, but Zirganos, up to his old tricks, showed up in September to make his try. It wasn't until October 5th that he began his swim. The water temperature was in the mid-fities. Leaving from Battery Park at the foot of Manhattan Island he began to swim up the East River. Some twenty-three hours later, in the Hudson River which flows along the West side of Manhattan, Zirganos was blue and incoherent. His attendant hauled him aboard the cabin cruiser where he was swathed in blankets and rushed to the nearest hospital. Zirganos spent two days there recovering. At age forty-five most men learn to adjust to the encroaching limitations of age. Not Zirganos. It would take one more swim to convince him that he was no longer the man he used to be. That last swim would take his life.

It was a year later that Zirganos found himself on the shores of the North Channel of the Irish Sea. The North Channel had defeated more swimmers than any other body of water in the world. Florence Chadwick failed twice. Greta Andersen twice. It wasn't until 1947 that the indomitable Tom Blower, thirty-three years old and in the prime of life and condition (including a weight of 252 pounds), became successful. The low reading of forty-nine degrees and a high of no more than fifty-three degrees speak for themselves. The only other time it has been conquered was in 1970. Kevin Murphy, the third person to make a double crossing of the English Channel, did it. Zirganos began his swim on September 27, 1959. It was a case of a forty-six-year-old man undertaking one of the most difficult swims in the world. The twenty-two-mile North Channel would have its final say. It took 16½ hours for age and water to get to Zirganos. At that time he went unconscious with a horrible gasp. Quickly he was hauled aboard the boat. The dusky blue hue that Zirganos had turned meant serious things to the doctor aboard the attending boat. Quickly he asked for a pen knife and began cutting Zirganos open. When the heart was exposed, the doctor could see the rapid erratic fluttering, described by medical men as ventricular fibrillation. Immediately the doctor began direct heart massage in an attempt to reestablish normal heart rhythm. Five minutes later the doctor realized that Zirganos had swum his last. Quietly he placed a blanket over the now blanching body. Zirganos was only three miles from the Scottish shore when he was hauled from the water.

Any time a swimmer chooses to make a swim in water that is under fifty-five degrees he is running a risk. The extreme stress placed upon the body will bring out any latent weakness. However there are always surprises. Such a surprise was the swim undertaken by the young twenty-six-year-old Estonian, Alexander Lass in 1931.

The Gulf of Finland is an offshoot of the Baltic Sea. It separates Estonia from Finland. Young Lass decided to swim from Reval (now called Tallin) on the Baltic coast to some spot on the Finnish coast. It was a bright, warm, and sunny day in 1931 when Lass left Reval. Whether it was in his plans from the start, or whether it was the forty-seven- to fifty-one-degree water, Lass got out of the water after fifteen miles at Nargo Island. After a good night's sleep he jumped into the water the next day and completed the swim, going from Nargo Island to Porkala Island off the Finnish coast. That second segment was some twenty-five miles and it took him nineteen hours to do it. This forty-mile swim, though in two segments, was accomplished in about a thirty-five hour time span, which is a real accomplishment if water temperatures given in the report are accurate. Mr. Lass's claim to fame rests in a three-paragraph squibb on the front page of the August 19, 1931 edition of the *New York Times*. The Baltic States spawn some tough characters.

Cold-water swimming can have after effects just as serious as those of a boxing knock-out. It is only rather late in the history of the sport that medical men realized the seriousness of being forcefully rendered unconscious. Nowadays all boxers are automatically suspended upon being knocked out until a medical examination proves that the boxer has not suffered or has recovered from brain damage. No such ruling exists for swimmers. Perhaps the future will tell us if any permanent damage has been suffered by a swimmer in cold water. More than one swimmer has been taken unconscious from the water during a swim. The Juan de Fuca Straits (separating the state of Washington from Vancouver, B.C.), the Farallon Island swim, twenty-five miles off the California coast, and the famed C. N. E. have all seen unconscious swimmers—some blue, others white—taken from their waters. It seems unlikely that cooling down to the point of unconsciousness is too detrimental, that is, if the person is removed immediately, and warmed up. Certainly when one looks at hypothermia from the standpoint of it being an adjunct to certain medical treatment, including surgery, it can't be all bad. The heart seizure of Zirganos can be attributed to age and overindulgence. Certainly people die while occupied in any of life's endeavors. To single out one is unfair.

As mentioned in chapter 5 the reasons people make long swims are many. In a few cases the overriding reason is money. This in my opinion is correlated with the basically normal personality. When the reasons are "attention," "personal," or fame I have found neurotics.

A more apt example of psychopathology could not be found than in Britt Sullivan's quest for fame.

Miss Sullivan found herself discharged from the Waves, an American military service, in the early part of 1962. The good-looking, buxom, twenty-eight-year-old brunette from Omaha, Nebraska was at a loss for something to do. With the money saved up from her service she drifted around her home town. It was by chance she came upon a newspaper article announcing the Lake Michigan fifty-mile swim. She sent off her application, which the promoter accepted for its publicity value rather than for Britt's swimming ability. A good-looking and shapely twenty-eight year old added sex appeal to an all too often male muscle show. When Britt showed up a week before the swim she became an immediate hit with the newsmen. Here was a tough-talking, beer-drinking, cigarette smoking "Moll" who energized the conversation. She was a delightful contrast to the all too often muscled brain of the professional athlete talking training and diet. Britt made the rounds of the Chicago night spots with her dates. Her free and easy going sexual innuendoes were enough to gain her immediate and constant attention. During that publicity week she was never observed to go into the water for training. Her comment that she would do the swim on beer and cigarettes assured the more professional competitors that they had nothing to fear from her.

When the gun went off at the start of the race the conventional hell broke loose as competitors fought for position. That is, all except Britt. She turned on her back after a few strokes and asked for a can of beer and a cigarette. Three hours later she was still only a couple of blocks from the starting point, whereas most of the other swimmers were four to six miles on their way. Such was the debut of Britt Sullivan in professional swimming circles.

When Britt sent in her entry for the 1963 Lake Michigan swim she was politely turned down. Not to be daunted she drifted around the country trying to stir up publicity for her swimming. 1963 slipped by with little accomplished. 1964 found her making a spectacular announcement that gained her the publicity she coveted. She was going to "swim the Atlantic Ocean." Newsmen, realizing the "silly-season" was about, cleverly edited any detailed account of just how she was going to accomplish the feat. The accounts would have one believe that it was going to be a nonstop feat. Her real plans were to swim for long periods and then climb aboard her escort boat for rest and food. The announcement was a joke to any thinking person. With all the fanfare characterizing those who are deluded, Miss Sullivan arrived at Coney Island, New York's most popular beach. It was the latter part of June, 1964. The proper press photos were taken and Miss Sullivan, with her ample bosom swaying, flicked her last cigarette on the sands, and strode into the water. Her escort boat, a thirty-five-

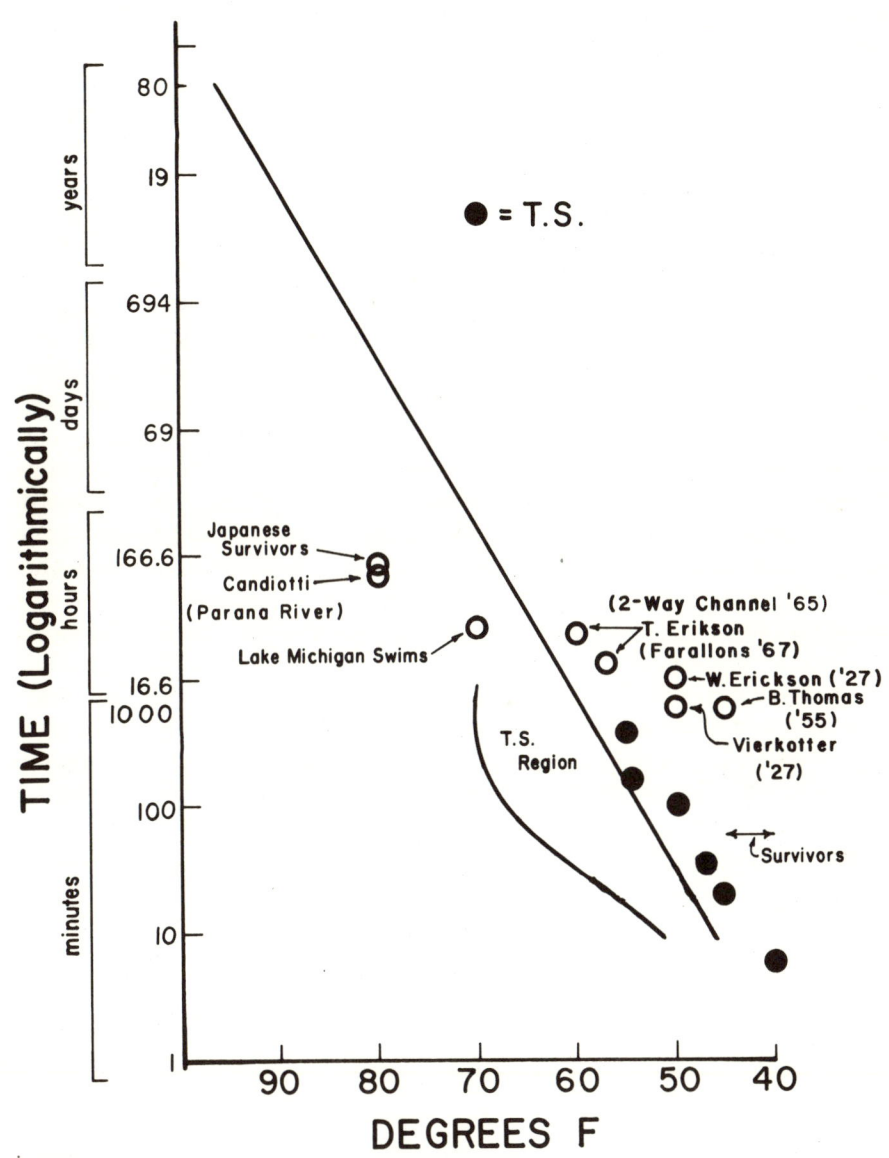

The relationship of water temperature to length of immersion: The ability to stand cold water varies with the individual. Ted Erikson was one of the best cold-water swimmers. The straight line represents Ted's theoretical limits. The circles represent the accomplishments attained by the named swimmers. Theoretically a man could live a lifetime immersed (head above water of course) in water between 95 and 98°F. Maceration of the skin precludes this, however. (TS= training swims.)

foot sea-going launch, had pulled out into the ocean about a quarter mile and waited. This was to be the basic plan throughout the swim. She would swim for the boat which would again pull out a quarter mile on the course after she had reached it.

The first day's swimming was eventful enough when a group of sharks made their appearance. Britt needed no convincing that things would be quite a bit safer aboard the escort temporarily. Instead of swimming for eighteen hours that first day, according to her original plans, Britt was only in the water about six hours. The next day, after sleeping the night away on board the escort, she began the same routine. Intermittently she clambered aboard the escort and back into the water whenever she needed food or rest. Late Sunday evening she failed to rendezvous with her escort off Fire Island, which was about twenty miles from her starting point. Around midnight her boat captain radioed the Coast Guard. An air-sea rescue operation began that lasted two days. Britt Sullivan was never seen again. One can imagine the reaction of the Coast Guard commandant receiving the first word of her being lost. It is common knowledge among Coast Guard personnel that incompetent swimmers and small boat voyagers are the bane of the service. In the last few years a rash of attempts by would-be sailors to sail their fifteen- and twenty-foot boats across the Atlantic Ocean has caused the Coast Guard many hours of effort in searches. When they get into trouble they start a chain of reactions that may end up costing tens of thousands of dollars. The sea was quick to cover any clues as to what may have happened to Miss Sullivan. Britt found the oblivion her actions would lead one to believe she was seeking.

14
Tools of the Trade

You don't have to be Sherlock Holmes to identify the trade of a man. The welder's face mask, the businessman's briefcase, and the carpenter's toolbox tell us their professions. Athletic trappings are more specific. The equipment necessary for the baseball or football player to indulge in his sport is phenomenal—spiked shoes, padding, mitts, bats, helmets, and so on. Swimming is just about the only sport that does away with all the paraphernalia. The only exception is running. But even the runner needs a pair of trunks if he is running in public. The swimmer can even eliminate this basic garment, that is until he gets out of the water. The famous Ethiopian marathon runner Abebe Bikila dispensed with shoes and actually ran barefoot the entire twenty-six miles in the 1958 Rome Olympics. To those who begrudge the necessity of purchasing sports equipment in our modern day society there is always one outlet—swimming. Find yourself a desolate beach and you don't even need trunks. There comes a time when the marathon swimmer discovers that there is one basic piece of equipment that makes distance swimming more pleasurable: goggles. If he is swimming in salt water they become a necessity.

Across the world from the Orient to Europe primitive peoples long ago learned of their importance. They were developed primarily for underwater work such as spear fishing and sponge diving. The reader may wonder how these primitive societies, unversed in glass-making technology, evolved goggles. They used naturally transparent substances like mica and shell. Pieces of these substances were inserted into custom carved wooden frames of an elliptical, concave shape that fit over the outer orbit of the eye. A string of natural fiber was used to tie the goggles in place with a minimum of pressure. A person unfamiliar with such a device may wonder how a water-tight seal could be gotten without the use of rubber. The secret lies in the custom-fitting to the peculiarities of the individual's outer eye and surrounding tissue. The differences between each eye were considered. The two pieces were joined at the nose by another piece of string that could be shortened or lengthened accordingly to match the interocular distances between the eyes. These goggles differed from those with which most of the readers are familiar. They did not sweep around the eyes at a distance of about 1½ to two inches. They fit within the orbit of the eye itself. As a consequence they were much smaller and many swimmers believe they offer less water resistance when swimming. These goggles are still being made by the inhabitants of the South Pacific Ocean today and can be bought for as little as fifty cents. A few swimmers use them today. A tribute to their success is shown by the fact that modern manufacturers have copied the design using plastic. This is especially true in Australia. However, they are not popular with most swimmers because of the hardness of material used and the inability to get a good seal because they are not custom made.

With the advance of the rubber industry one can buy goggles today in just about any shape and size. At a marathon event today you will see as many as five or eight different styles. Each swimmer will swear by the style he is using. The reason for such wide variation in choice is simple. The human face is a tortuous maze of complex curves that varies with each individual. The width, length, and nose variations—to say nothing of the interocular differences (the distance between the eyes)—mean that the individual has to select the style that most effectively seals for him. The matter becomes more limited to the swimmer who chooses to place his prescription lenses in goggles. If this is the case he has to find a pair of goggles that handle the standard fifty millimeter diameter lens and also, and it is of utmost importance, each lens must be held in a plane parallel to the eye. Most goggles curve or slant the glass in front of the eyes. This is minor when plain glass is used, but becomes the focus of distortion when a prescription lens is used.

Anyone who did his swimming before the 1950s can tell you of the barbarous swimming trunks they used—heavy woolen or cotton trunks that held water for hours after leaving the water. It was a godsend by the textile industries when they began to make the light, comfortable, and fast drying nylon trunks. Old-timers who have used both stand in awe of the torture of men and women who went to the beach at the turn of the century with what would amount today to a full dress garment for bathing. A bust of the inventor of nylon to which a swimmer can bow each time he returns from a dip should be in the home of every swimmer. It is one of the few things we really should appreciate.

Marathon swims have been lost because a swimmer did not wear a rubber bathing cap. The cold water cooled down his body to the extent that he had to get out. It is one of the secrets of cold water swimming.

Researchers during World War II found out that survival time for airmen and seamen dumped in the North Atlantic was increased fivefold if the head were kept out of the icy water. Extrapolating this to cold water swimmers, it becomes evident that wearing a rubber cap (and not the inefficient men's cap that leaves the ears exposed as well as the neck, but a women's cap that covers these all-important regions) in cold water cuts down heat loss some twenty percent. It also keeps the base of the brain warmer and as a consequence you can swim much longer in cold water than without a cap. I speak after eight thousand miles of swimming in my life, sometimes for one mile in waters as cold as forty-six degrees. Any swim, especially in cloudy weather, in waters below sixty degrees makes the cap a necessity. Two of my swimmers always use hats in cold water. Erikson even had a specially made skin-diver's hood made for his Farallon Islands swim. He still swears by it to this day.

Greasing the body remains one of the most enigmatic practices that I am still undecided about. All types of grease are used. Captain Webb used porpoise grease. Swimmers today use vaseline, lanolin, and various other heavy machine greases. Lanolin is by far the most used, but not the most popular. Purchased in one-pound jars, its consistency is almost like tar and its application difficult. Applied at normal temperatures it goes on with difficulty painfully pulling on the hairs of the body. The secret of fast, painless application is to place the jar in a pan of gently boiling water for about a half hour. It then melts to a thick, viscous liquid that can be easily and quickly spread over the body with the hands. You don't heat it up much past the melting point, which is far below the boiling point of water. Using this technique the author has applied the lanolin in three to five minutes. In a matter of minutes it has resolidified on the body of the swimmer. Once on it stays. Abo-Heif still had a significant amount clinging to him after his thirty-five-hour Lake Michigan swim. The mechanical friction of the water removes vaseline rather quickly and is not recommended. I always use anhydrous (without water mixed in) rather than hydrous (water mixed in) lanolin. There was one report where an investigator thought that swimmers would inhibit the metabolism of the skin by using grease and was for that reason against its use. He also suggested that the mechanical friction of the water rapidly removed, or significantly diminished, the lanolin or grease, thus removing any insulative layer at first present. However he found with later studies that only two to three millimeters were sufficient to give insulative results. Anhydrous lanolin stayed on in this thickness. In any case I have not seen any heavily greased swimmer suffer any negative effects from its use. Abo-Heif's swim alone should be testament to that fact. Any prolonged swimming in water below sixty degrees means the swimmer better have fat first and then grease. While the question of grease is still unanswered there is still the psychological uplift gained from its use. A full circle thus seems to have been made. Personally I believe most of the swimmers will use the stuff. Aside from its purported insulative value there is one other value of significance. It serves as a lubricant around the friction points of the body. Since the limbs are pivoting, twisting, and turning there are certain points subject to "burn": armpits, groin, shoulder, and chin. In fact any point with hair stubble and contact with another point will eventually "burn" from friction. As the head turns for air the chin comes in contact with the shoulder in some swimmers. The loose skin around the back of the neck is also intermittently pulled tight and slackened. Eventually the hairs rubbing on the skin will "burn."

Many an amateur can be spotted by the indiscriminate application of grease on the face, forearms, and hands. These areas must be kept free. If not, the proper sealing of the goggles will never take place. Once in the water you can't spend time fooling around with malfitting goggles. The hands and forearms should be kept free of grease because the arms and hands must "bite" the water for propulsion. Slippage here means loss of efficiency.

Noseclips are an individual matter. It is surprising how many swimmers get along without them. When one thinks about the perfect timing and coordination necessary in stroking and breathing one can appreciate the fact that water in the nose seldom bothers the efficient swimmer. I think in all my years I've seen only two or three professionals using the rubber noseclip.

Any physician will tell you that an occupational disease of swimming is ear infections. Water is an excellent carrier of all kinds of bacteria and fungus. The ear canal is a perfect incubator. Warm, dark, and moist, it represents Valhalla to bacteria. If by chance the ear drum is punctured, and this is amazingly common among the general population, all the worse, for then an inner ear infection results. Most swimmers eventually use ear plugs, but a few lucky ones don't have to. Some swimmers have swum for decades, hours every day without the slightest ear problem. Even the most inefficient ear plug at least lowers the possibility of infection because it limits the amount of water flowing in and out the ear canal. However, these rubber plugs eventually irritate the skin to the extent of soreness. I highly recommend the use of lamb's wool or unsterilized cotton soaked with a mineral oil-Vaseline mixture (about three quarters oil to one quarter vaseline). The oil repels any water and coats the inner ear, thus preventing it from becoming macerated. Any bacteria are also coated with the oil, which inhibits their metabolism. This is the reason that most of the medicinal ear drops used by doctors are in an oil base. The proper amount of cotton can be selected according to the

Tools of the Trade

various ear canal sizes of the swimmers. They are much more comfortable also.

All in all the expense involved is a pittance compared to the hundreds of dollars that can be spent by the practitioners of such sports as golf, baseball, and fishing. At its very basic, swimming costs absolutely nothing. You can even go swimming with an old pair of pants cut into shorts. At the most a pair of nylon trunks and goggles can be purchased for under ten dollars. One of the most memorable swims ever to take place—the thirty-six-mile Lake Michigan swim in 1962—was won by a man who spent twenty-one hours swimming with only trunks. He had no goggles, ear plugs, or noseclips. All he had to accompany his muscles was a pair of three-dollar nylon trunks. The $4,000 he won was a nice return on such an investment. Of course his training time is not considered. In any case I have seen champion swimmers in the heat of close competition rip off goggles and hat and toss them into the boat. Either the goggles were leaking or the hat slipping. This caused them to free themselves of the offending paraphernalia. After all, one should not confuse the accoutrements with the act.

15

The Twenty-four-hour Swim: La Tuque

The impact of Abo-Heif's and Erikson's sixty-mile swim across Lake Michigan in 1963 was felt far and wide. News of their accomplishment served to cause many promoters to reevaluate the swimmer's potential. Throughout the world those interested in swimming were impressed. Among those impressed was a group of businessmen in the small town of La Tuque in the Quebec province of Canada. It was a small town of only fifteen thousand people, many of whom worked at the paper pulp manufacturing plant on the outskirts. For years this plant, one of the world's largest, had been supplying a good percentage of the paper pulp used in Canada and the United States. It was a prosperous town within the limits of its population. However, its businessmen were always open to further opportunities of increasing revenue. Many of them had traveled the hundred or so miles to Lake St. John to watch the marathon swim held there every year. Impressed as they were with the feats of the swimmers they were even more impressed with the ringing cash registers of the local merchants as they supplied the needs of the thousands of tourists who flooded the town for the festivities of the swim. It wasn't long before the La Tuque merchants were talking of holding some annual extravaganza in their town. The only trouble was what kind?

La Tuque is in the middle of a mountainous, tree-filled province. The nearest large lake was St. John some hundred miles to the north. The St. Maurice River, flowing alongside the town, was jammed throughout the year with logs being sent to various mills downstream. Irked by the prosperity Roberval enjoyed due to the St. John swim, the concession supervisor of the small public park centered in the midst of La Tuque looked at the tiny block-long, spring-fed lake in his park and bewailed his fate. It would be a two-block swim to cross the lake and back. Fat chance of attracting a crowd to see someone swim Lake Louie. Almost any six year old could do it. Why three times around the lake and you had swum a mile. Six times, two miles; nine times . . . and then the idea took hold. Abo-Heif had gone thirty five hours in Lake Michigan. What if a line of buoys were set up around the edge of the lake and a few swimmers raced each other around. After, say, eight hours, the swimmer with the most number of laps could be declared a winner. But eight hours is too short. If the swimmers raced each other around the lake for twenty-four hours it would be a spectacle for the crowd that would surely come to watch. In the majority of marathon swims the competitors came to the spectators. They awaited the swimmers at the finish. The fifty thousand individuals at the end of the St. John swim had neither the facilities nor the money to go out and watch the swim while it was taking place in the lake. However, here at Lake Louie there was a sidewalk running around the lake and ample sloping grass that gave an excellent view at all times of the water area. In a sense, Lake Louie and the surrounding park allowed the participants to be brought to the crowd.

The concession manager brought his idea to a few members of the chamber of commerce. A few liked the idea well enough to back it. Others said it couldn't be done. When Abo-Heif's thirty-five-hour swim was mentioned they changed their outlook. One of the listeners said that the proposed event could be enlivened even more if, instead of making it an individual race, you made it a team race. If swimmers paired off into teams they could come in to rest while their partner took over. Periodic changing of partners would add to the interest, for there would always be a fresh swimmer serving to draw the attention of the crowd. It soon became evident that the idea was unique. There was something different to offer those interested in the sport. Here was an opportunity to offer a close-up of world champion swimmers in action never before possible in the history of the sport.

The winter of 1964–65 saw the chamber of commerce soliciting the local merchants for donations to sponsor the swim. The committee in charge of the swim incorporated and soon the news of the "twenty-four-hour La Tuque Swim" was reaching the world's marathon swimmers. The first La Tuque swim would be held on July 24–25, 1965. It would start at 3 P.M. on Saturday and finish at 3 P.M. Sunday. It would be the most opportune time in that it would allow the tourists to arrive for the weekend. They would bring money and every merchant would be open to fulfill their wants. The merchants now only had to wait to see if their investment of $20,000 could be recouped.

Many of the swimmers arriving at La Tuque in 1965 were surprised at the small lake. It seemed little more than a large outdoor swimming pool. Buoys had been set up around the lake in a more or less circular fashion. Plunging into the lake for practice swims they were delighted

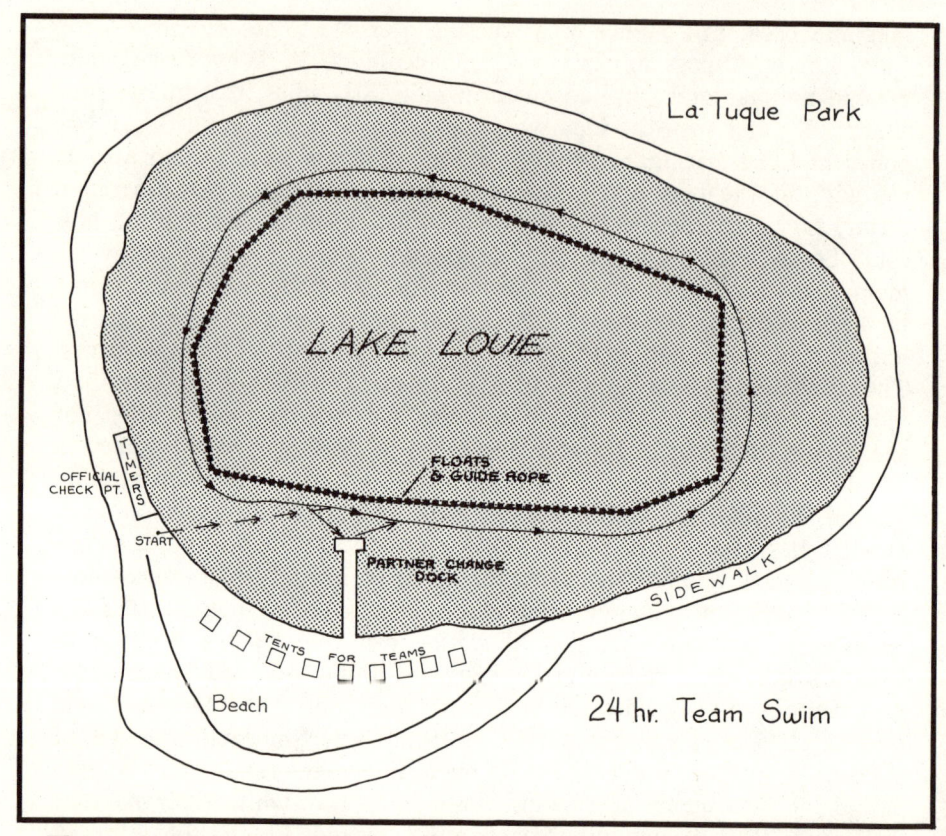

The swimmers at LaTuque swim around the outside of a series of floats in a counterclockwise direction. One full circle is one third of a mile. A team member may swim as many laps as he chooses so long as at least one lap is completed. Team members may change only at the change dock.

to find it an agreeable seventy-two degrees. Little did they suspect that even seventy-two degrees could take on a chilling aspect in the middle of the night when bodies were fatigued. Rules and regulations were discussed. The most important was that a swimmer had to swim at least one lap before being relieved by his partner. The change of partners could only take place at one location, the change dock. Each team would be numbered with indelible ink on the right shoulder and back. As he passed the official timer's dock he would be given credit for the lap swum. A swimmer could make as many laps as he chose before being relieved by his partner.

Immediately the teams began to discuss among themselves how they should swim the race. Should each member go one lap or more? Should they do so it would mean jumping into the water every seven, eight, or nine minutes, which was hardly enough time to recuperate? It didn't take long to swim a third of a mile. It was a decision that to this day still causes controversy among the swimmers. The winning teams have usually done one or two laps for several hours before going to three. Throughout the night there will be a few times when they go as many as six, but only to allow a partner to have a little extra time to digest his food.

Tourists began to drift into town Saturday morning and by noon, three hours before the start of the race, several thousand were in the park surrounding Lake Louie. Traffic was tying up the streets to the extent that the local police had to cordon off the area around the lake to prevent any more cars from coming into the area. An hour before the race autograph seekers were besieging the famous athletes who would soon be showing their merits. The townspeople and tourists were trying to pick the winner of the race. It was a tough decision to make, for all the teams were renowned. There was the team of Egyptians composed of Abo-Heif and Shazly. Abo-Heif had swum sixty miles and had won numerous other swims including an English Channel race. Shazly had won the Capri-Naples and a Suez Canal race. The team of Erikson and Matuch seemed unbeatable. Erikson had crossed Lake Michigan three times. Matuch had won the thirty-six mile Lake Michigan race in 1962. The twenty-four-hour La Tuque swim seemed made for these hardy men who had both swum further than any of the competitors except Abo-Heif. Even Herman Willemse, teamed with Rejean LaCoursiere, had never swum over seventeen hours. It would certainly be a most interesting swim. Every swimmer would not only be trying to do better than the other teams but also better than his own partner. The psychological ploy used by the sponsors was well planned. It could hardly be anything else than a tour de force.

As always the start of a race is fascinating. The twenty-four hour proved no different than any other. There was no saving of energy. The teams went right for the lead from the start. Willemse and La Coursiere went one lap apiece for the first couple of hours and were able to gain a slim two thirds of a mile lead on the Egyptians. Strangely enough the team of Erikson and Matuch seemed to be holding back as if to say, "It's twenty-four hours and a lot can happen." Spectators were sure that this famous pair would make their move later on in the race. Willemse and LaCoursiere extended their lead little by little over the Egyptians, who seemed to be in a frenzy as they wildly flailed the water in an attempt to "hold" Willemse and La Coursiere.

And so it went, hour after hour. Like clockwork each member of a team would take his short rest and then begin the twenty yard walk to the changing dock to relieve his partner. It was a high-pressure race in which your competitors were always in sight. An open-water swim allowed the leaders and trailers to be lost, but not here. You knew only too well what the situation was when you were passed by a faster swimmer. It was a frustrating experience to be swimming with every ounce of your being and have a faster swimmer inexorably creep up, come alongside, and then pass you. The meaning of the word *impotency* was learned by many swimmers during that twenty-four hours. There were times when the swimmers despaired of continuing, but being committed to the lure of $3,500 first prize, they continued to the body-wracked finish. When the gun announced the end of the twenty-four-hour race at 3 P.M. Sunday the team of Willemse/LaCoursiere was holding a comfortable lead over the Egyptians of ten laps. After twenty-four hours of the most tortuous swimming they had managed to cover fifty-five miles while the second place Egyptians had covered a little less than fifty-two miles. The favored team of Erikson and Matuch had learned again the lesson that it doesn't pay to pace. They had covered only forty-five miles in their twenty-four hours. There were only two other teams that finished the race but they were far back. Two other teams had dropped out. The first twenty-four-hour La Tuque race was a huge success and the merchants were more than happy to regain their initial expense plus a huge profit. From that year on there was no question of holding another race at La Tuque. The race had caught the fancy of thousands of Canadians.

A definite pattern became evident the second year the twenty-four-hour race was held. Swimmers would team up with each other according to how well they did in the previous races held the year before and the current year. Since the La Tuque swim usually was the second or third swim of the season, the swimmers would select a partner nearest to his own capacity. In 1966 Willemse and La Coursiere naturally teamed up again. Matuch and Erikson were back together as well as many new teams. The famed Judith DeNys and Cliff Lumsden were a top team as well as Tom Bucy and George Park. That year Willemse and LaCoursiere had a little more difficulty in winning the twenty-four-hour grind. They finished the race a scant three laps (one mile) ahead of the second place team of Bucy and Park. The third place finishers, DeNys and Lumsden, were the like distance behind Bucy and Park. As the contenders became familiar with the race it became more and more difficult to maintain a position. That year two teams dropped out of the race after about twelve hours of swimming, which always stimulated the other teams to continue, hoping that other teams, especially those ahead, would do likewise.

The 1967 race saw an "easy" win by the team of Iglesias and La Coursiere. At the end of twenty-four hours they had a comfortable lead of thirteen laps ($4\frac{1}{3}$ miles) over the second-place team. The highlight of that year's race was the dropping out of two teams while they were in second and third positions after eighteen and twelve hours respectively. Willemse, teamed with Judith DeNys, and Hancox, teamed with Margaret Macrae, both from Australia, both had to quit because of stomach problems.

One need only look at the tabulations of the 1968 race to see what a battle it was. The first four teams were in "reach" of each other throughout the race. The real story of that race was Abo-Heif. This fantastic swimmer swam almost twice as many laps as his partner, Matuch. Matuch, never much of a sprinter, was unable to hold up his end of the team. Abo-Heif was averaging a full minute faster per lap than Matuch so that as a consequence they could never make any significant gain on the leaders until the last few hours of the race. Abo-Heif made a superb effort to catch the team of Barton and Wickens in the last hours of the race as they began to weaken. It was a heartbreaking scene to see Abo-Heif in the final minutes of the race coming to within fifty yards of catching and passing Barton but only to have the gun, signaling the end of the race, go off. Abo-Heif, at the age of forty-one, teamed up with Iglesias the following year and they won the twenty-four-hour LaTuque.

By perusing the data of the LaTuque swims the reader will get a good impression of the magnitude of the battles that are held there each year. Add to the tables the human element of swimmers forcing themselves into the water in the middle of the night to relieve their partners when the urge to grab a few extra minutes within the tent resting is overwhelming, and one will understand the importance of dependability and teamwork. At some time or another a swimmer is unable to come out and his partner is forced to swim extra laps until it is determined whether the incapacity is temporary or permanent. The remarkable Abo-Heif swam twenty-nine hours of a thirty-hour team swim in 1966 in Montreal (it was only held one year) when his partner Travaglio was unable to handle the "cold" (to him) sixty-eight-degree water. It was an exhibition of endurance by Abo-Heif that amazed all who witnessed and heard of the swim, for Abo-Heif still managed to put his "team" in first place at the end of the race. The twenty-four-hour La Tuque race offers a unique exhibition of high-powered swimming at close-up vantage points. Anyone with the slightest interest in swimming has a unique opportunity to see the many different styles of stroking as practiced by the world's best. Don't fail to see at least one twenty-four-hour race. It is a chance to place your own small endeavors, no matter what they may be, in the proper perspective.

As in any other race, the start of the twenty-four-hour LaTuque race starts with a bang as teams attempt to get the lead as soon as possible. This is the start of the 1966 race. Courtesy Gilles Berthiaume.

Herman Willemse of Holland (left) and Rejean LaCoursiere (right) smile as they contemplate the forthcoming $3,500 check for first place. Between them they completed 170 laps or 55.5 miles in twenty-four hours in the 1966 race. Courtesy Gilles Berthiaume.

After eighteen hours of swimming in the 1968 race, the American Tom Bucy has trouble with his stomach. There was serious doubt at the time as to whether he would be able to continue. He recovered to finish along with his teammate Rejean LaCoursiere to finish second in the race, a scant three laps behind the winning team of Horatio Iglesias and Judith DeNys. Courtesy Gilles Berthiaume.

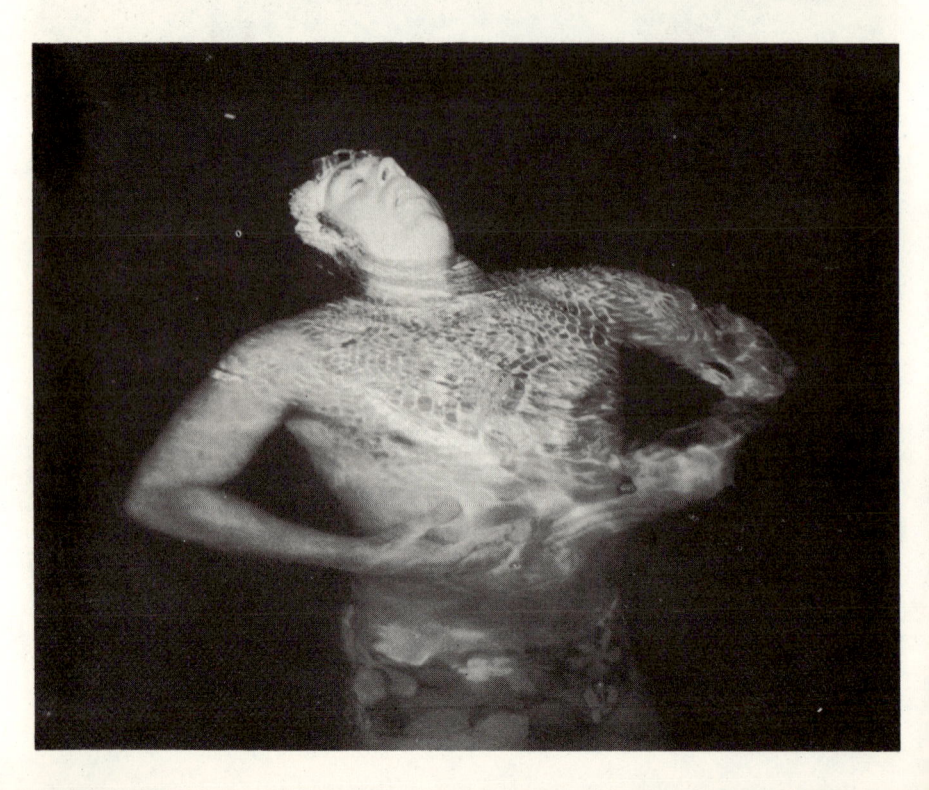

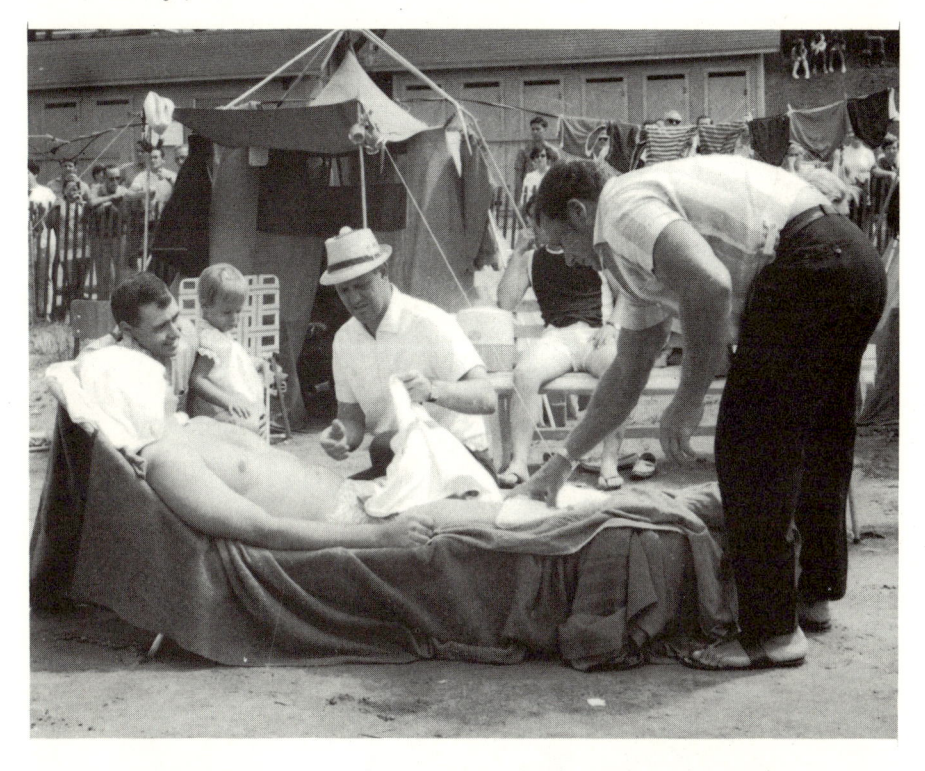

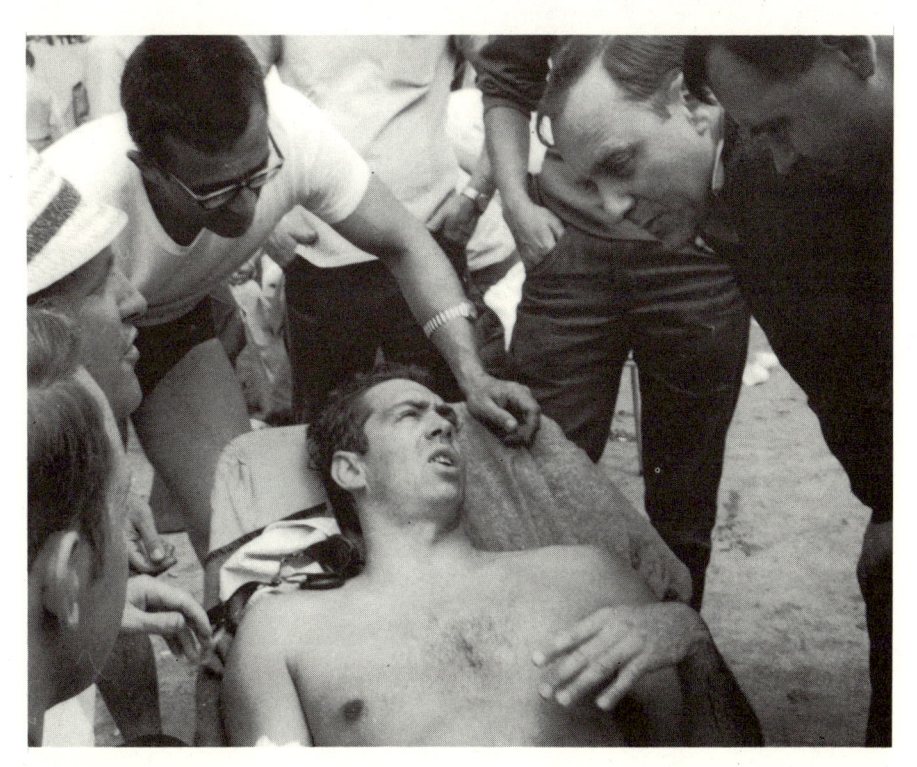

The Twenty-four-hour Swim: La Tuque

The fourth-place finishers in the 1968 race, Abo-Heif and Matuch. Abo-Heif swam twice as many laps as his faltering partner in this race and was within fifty yards of catching the third-place team when the gun announcing the end of the race sounded. Courtesy Gilles Berthiaume.

Abo-Heif at various stages of the 1969 race when he and Iglesias were on their way to victory. Courtesy Gilles Berthiaume.

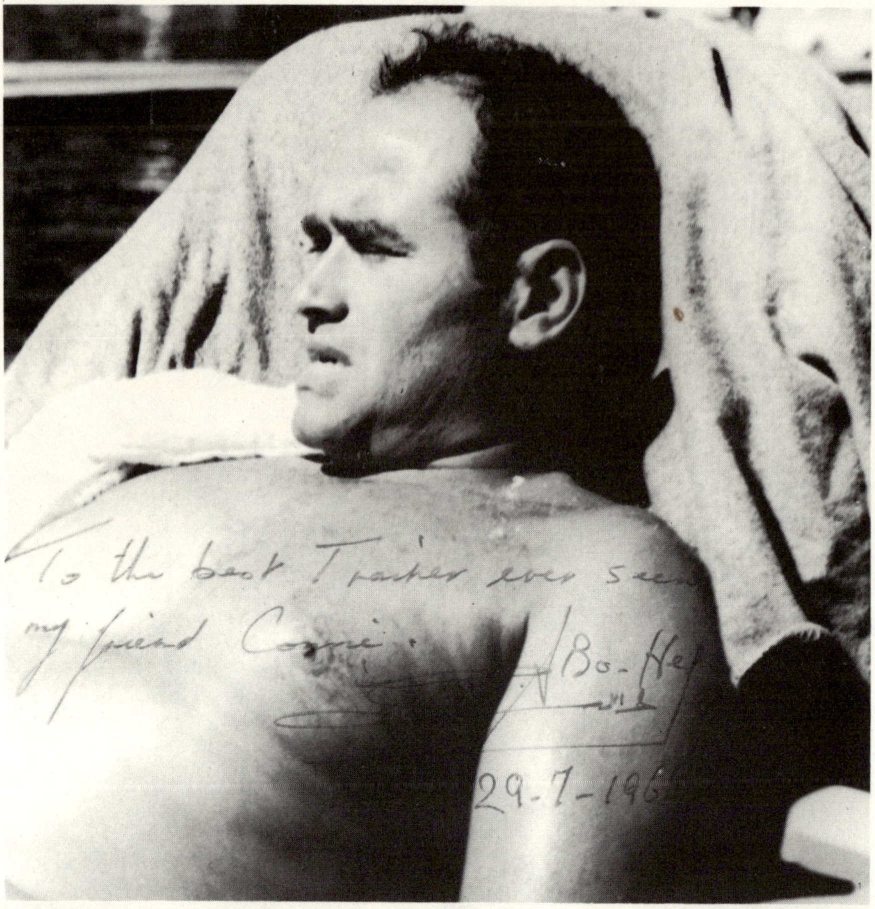
To the best Trainer ever seen
my friend Cossie

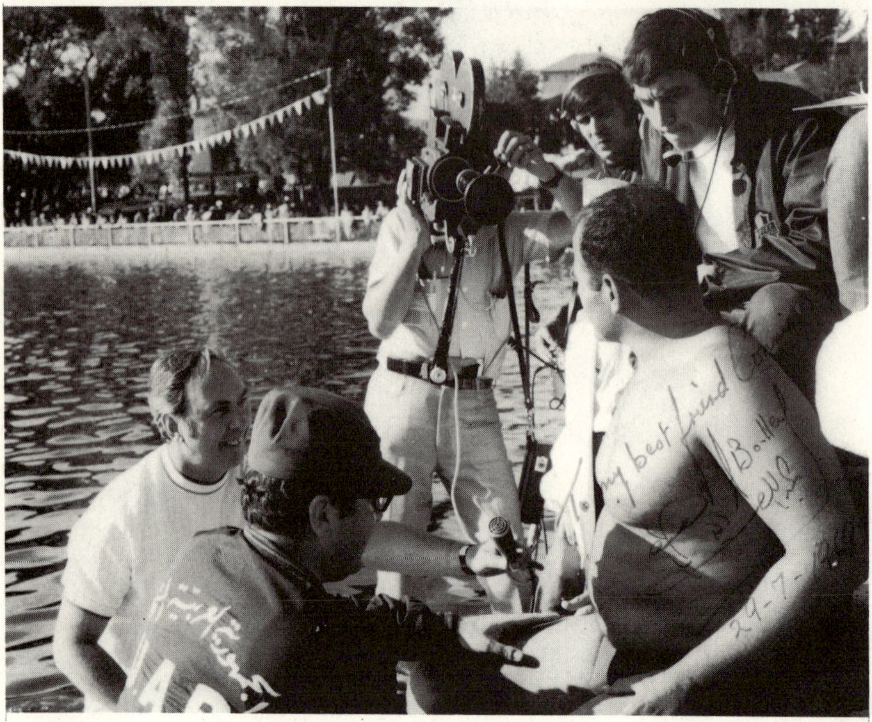

The Twenty-four-hour Swim: La Tuque 241

Third-place finishers in the 1969 LaTuque race. Roberto Reta of Argentina on the left, and Dennis Matuch of the United States. The well-padded bodies make them excellent cold-water swimmers. In warm water they do not do well. Courtesy Gilles Berthiaume.

Dennis Matuch of the United States about to relieve his partner in the middle of the night. Courtesy Gilles Berthiaume.

Horacio Iglesias of Argentina tags his partner Abo-Heif in the 1969 race. Courtesy Gilles Berthiaume.

In 1970 Abo-Heif's partner Aguire could not stand the cold water, and as a result Abo-Heif swam most of the race. Here the weariness and pain are evident on his face. The pair finished fourth. Courtesy Gilles Berthiaume.

In the 1970 race Rejean LaCoursiere of Canada shows his weariness with seven more hours left in the race. His powerful physique is evident. He and his partner Jan Van Scheijndel of Holland finished second. Courtesy Gilles Berthiaume.

The 1970 team of Mohammed Gamie (Egypt) anl Dennis Matuch (United States) finished fourth. Gamie is one of the few Negroes in marathon swimming. Courtesy Gilles Berthiaume.

In 1970 the team of Horacio Iglesias (left) and Johaan Schans (right) set a new record when they completed 179 laps or 58.4 miles in twenty-four hours. Courtesy Gilles Berthiaume.

Resultats Finals 1965

Equipes	Tours Completes	Moyenne Par Tour Min.	Sec.	Temps.	Rang
Herman Willemse Rejean Lacoursiere	171	8	25	24.00	1
Abdel-Latif Abo-Heif Nabil El Shazly	161	8	57	"	2
Dennis Matuch Ted Erikson	142	10	8	"	3
François Asselin Gilles Potvin	117	12	18	"	4
G. G. Jensen Maurice Fortier	112	12	51	"	5
Bob Weir x John Lumgair	108	10	28	18:49:54	

Retires pares: x   18:54:10

Gagnants des Sprints

Noms	No.	Temps Min.	Sec.
G. Travaglio	1	7	8
G. Travaglio	2	7	20
B. Barton	3	8	25
H. Wellemse	4	8	37
J. Couture	5	11	54
D. Matuch	6	8	54
B. Barton	7	9	8
B. Barton	8	9	12
D. Matuch	9	11	36
T. Erikson	10	10	22
H. Willemse	11	8	7

Tours Plus Rapides

No. Tours	Noms	Temps
3	H. Willemse	6.54
7	B. Barton	7.04

The Twenty-four-hour Swim: La Tuque

Resultats Final 1966

Equipes	Tours Completes	Moyenne Par Tour		Milles	Rang.
		Min.	Sec.		
Rejean Lacoursiere Herman Willemse	170	8	28	55.44	1
Thomas Bucy George Park	167	8	37	54.46	2
Judith DeNys Cliff Lumsden	164	8	47	53.49	3
Pedro Galmes Billy Barton	144	10	00	49.96	4
Conrad Corbeil Jean Couture	139	10	22	45.33	5
Dennis Matuch Ted Erikson	134	10	45	43.70	6
Gilles Potvin Roger Piche	117	12	18	38.16	7
Yvan Daniel Pierre Bourdon	112	12	51	36.53	8
Ed Forsbey Kurt Pluntke (retire apres 13.15.44)	82	9	42	26.74	—
Alberto Hreische Giulio Travaglio (retire apres 4.32.24)	29	9	24	9.46	—

CHAMPIONAT MONDIAL DE NAGE PAR EQUIPE

RAPPORT DES CHRONOMETREURS

LA TUQUE, QUE.   DATE JUILLET 1967

RANG FINAL	NOMS DES NAGEURS DE CETTE EQUIPE	TOURS CHAQUE	TEMPS ACC. PAR NAGEUR HR.	MIN.	SEC.	MOYENNE /TOURS MIN.	SEC.	MILES CHAQUE	TEMPS /MILE MIN.	SEC.	NO. TOURS EQUIPE	MOYENNE /TOURS MIN.	SEC.	MILES EQUIPE	TEMPS/M. EQUIPE MIN.	SEC.
1	Horatio Iglesias	86	11	48	57	8	9	28.05	25	16						
1	Regent Lacoursiere	83	12	11	3	8	48	27.07	27	0	169	8	22	55.12	25	41
2	Billy Barton	85	13	27	1	8	51	27.72	29	6						
2	Harry Wickens	71	10	32	59	8	55	23.16	27	19	156	8	43	50.88	26	43
3	Conrad Corbeil	72	11	42	9	9	40	23.48	29	53						
3	Klim Savin	81	12	17	51	9	6	26.42	27	55	153	9	15	49.90	28	22
4	Georges Park	80	12	1	53	9	1	26.09	27	39						
4	Real Lavoie	72	11	58	7	9	52	23.48	30	34	152	9	18	49.57	28	31
5	Ted Erickson	68	11	25	32	10	7	22.18	30	54						
5	Denis Matuch	78	12	34	28	9	41	25.44	29	39	146	9	45	47.62	29	54
6	Pedro Galmez	64	10	41	58	10	1	20.87	30	44						
6	Roberto Reta	79	13	18	2	10	6	25.76	30	58	143	9	55	46.64	30	26
7	Margeret Park	76	13	3	57	10	13	24.79	31	37						
7	Whittle Martell	61	10	56	3	10	45	19.89	32	58	137	10	18	44.68	31	36
8	Gilles Potvin	62	12	37	0	12	12	20.22	37	25						
8	Ben Bouchard	61	11	23	0	11	11	19.89	34	19	123	11	30	40.11	35	17
9	Pierre Bourdon	59	12	58	28	13	14	19.24	40	26						
9	Ben Demontreuil	51	11	1	32	12	53	16.63	39	45	110	12	50	35.88	39	22

* NOTE, LES TEMPS DU PREMIER ET DU DERNIER TOUR DU MARATHON NE SONT PAS INCLUS DANS LA MOYENNE INDIVIDUELLE

// JOB   X   X   X
// XEQ CHRON   FX1

The Twenty-four-hour Swim: La Tuque

CHAMPIONAT MONDIAL DE NAGE PAR EQUIPE

LA TUQUE, QUE.   DATE JUILLET 1968

RAPPORT DES CHRONOMETREURS

RANG FINAL	NOMS DES NAGEURS DE CETTE EQUIPE	TOURS CHAQUE	TEMPS ACC. PAR NAGEUR HR.	MIN.	SEC.	MOYENNE /TOURS MIN.	SEC.	MILES CHAQUE	TEMPS /MILE MIN.	SEC.	NO. TOURS EQUIPE	MOYENNE /TOURS MIN.	SEC.	MILES EQUIPE	TEMPS/M. EQUIPE MIN.	SEC.
1	Horacio Iglesias	86	11	55	27	8	17	28.05	25	30	166	8	24	54.14	25	47
1	Judith DeNys	80	12	4	33	8	51	26.09	27	45						
2	Regent Lacoursiere	88	13	25	34	9	4	28.70	28	3	163	8	41	53.16	26	38
2	Tom Bucy	75	10	34	36	8	28	24.46	25	56						
3	Billy Barton	79	12	1	29	9	7	25.76	27	59	161	8	50	52.51	27	6
3	Harry Wickens	82	11	58	31	8	46	26.74	26	51						
4	A. Abou Heif	102	15	28	12	9	6	33.27	27	53	161	8	53	52.51	27	17
4	Dennis Matuch	59	8	31	48	8	41	19.24	26	35						
5	George Park	78	12	19	45	9	18	25.44	29	4	149	9	26	48.59	28	57
5	Real Lavoie	71	11	40	15	9	51	23.16	30	14						
6	Pedro Galmez	63	10	51	35	10	20	20.55	31	42	138	10	8	45.01	31	5
6	Roberta Reta	75	13	8	25	10	14	24.46	32	13						
7	A. Nomen Sherbini	86	15	15	26	10	35	28.05	32	37	132	10	42	43.05	32	50
7	M. A. Salam Hassaan	46	8	44	34	11	24	15.00	34	57						
8	Gilles Potvin	68	12	28	22	11	0	22.18	33	44	131	10	50	42.72	33	14
8	Ben Bouchard	63	11	31	38	11	0	20.55	33	39						
9	Benson Huggard	58	11	49	58	12	11	18.92	37	31	124	11	23	40.44	34	56
9	Stephen Ramsden	66	12	10	2	11	3	21.53	33	54						
10	Tom Hetzell	52	11	55	50	13	50	16.96	42	11	101	13	54	32.94	42	39
10	Hasan Abdeen	49	12	4	10	14	34	15.98	45	18						

* NOTE. LES TEMPS DU PREMIER ET DU DERNIER TOUR DU MARATHON NE SONT PAS INCLUS DANS LA MOYENNE INDIVIDUELLE
// JOB   X   X   X
// XEQ CHRON   FX1

CHAMPIONAT MONDIAL DE NAGE PAR EQUIPE

LA TUQUE, QUE.   DATE JUILLET 1969

RANG FINAL	NOMS DES NAGEURS DE CETTE EQUIPE	TOURS CHAQUE	RAPPORT DES CHRONOMETREURS							MOYENNE EQUIPE /TOURS		MILES EQUIPE	TEMPS/M. EQUIPE	
			TEMPS ACC. PAR NAGEUR			MOYENNE /TOURS		TEMPS /MILE		MILES CHAQUE	NO. TOURS EQUIPE				
			HR.	MIN.	SEC.	MIN.	SEC.	MIN.	SEC.			MIN.	SEC.		MIN.	SEC.
1	Horacio Iglesias	88	11	52	29	8	6	24	49	28.70	165	8	37	53.81	26	27
1	Abou Heif	77	12	7	31	9	26	28	57	25.11						
2	Mohamed Gamie	79	12	37	54	9	37	29	24	25.76	162	8	47	52.83	26	56
2	Johan Schans	83	11	22	6	8	12	25	11	27.07						
3	Roberto Reta	73	12	29	59	10	5	31	29	23.81	145	9	42	47.29	29	47
3	Denis Matuch	72	11	30	1	9	36	29	22	23.48						
4	Steve Ramsden	64	11	36	18	10	52	33	21	20.87	140	10	6	45.66	31	0
4	Jorge Lopez	76	12	23	42	9	43	29	59	24.79						
5	Conrad Corbeil	61	10	32	15	10	29	31	46	19.89	135	10	34	44.03	32	24
5	Yvon Montpetit	74	13	27	45	10	54	33	27	24.13						
6	Pedro Galmez	64	11	27	8	10	49	32	54	20.87	133	10	42	43.38	32	50
6	Fausto Ramirez	69	12	32	52	10	54	33	26	22.50						
7	Harry Martinen	76	13	44	24	10	56	33	15	24.79	133	10	44	43.38	32	56
7	Fred Bowler	57	10	15	36	10	51	33	6	18.59						
8	Farouk Sulliman	62	11	52	17	11	29	35	13	20.22	123	11	42	40.11	35	53
8	Risto Bimbilovski	61	12	7	43	11	55	36	34	19.89						
9	Thomas Hetzell	43	10	0	23	13	57	42	47	14.02	111	12	50	36.20	39	21
9	Hassan Abdeen	68	13	59	37	12	18	37	51	22.18						
10	Michel Poirier	54	11	19	51	12	47	38	35	17.61	105	13	33	34.24	41	33
10	Stela Taylor	51	12	40	9	14	54	45	41	16.63						
0	Ron. K. Nail	36	5	25	43	9	2	27	43	11.74						
0	R. W. Haroutnian	32	6	20	6	11	59	36	24	10.44	68	10	4	22.18	30	53
0	Thomas Bucy	34	5	12	28	9	11	28	9	11.09						
0	Regent Lacoursiere	27	3	57	36	8	52	26	58	8.81	61	8	54	19.89	27	17
0	Benson Huggard	27	5	18	20	11	32	36	7	8.81						
0	Peter Schwenker	28	4	39	33	9	59	30	35	9.13	55	10	32	17.94	32	18
0	Ben Bouchard	30	5	52	8	11	30	35	58	9.78						
0	Gilles Potvin	25	4	24	55	10	41	32	28	8.15	55	10	43	17.94	32	53

* NOTE. LES TEMPS DU PREMIER ET DU DERNIER TOUR DU MARATHON NE SONT PAS INCLUS DANS LA MOYENNE INDIVIDUELLE

The Twenty-four-hour Swim: La Tuque

LA TUQUE, QUE. DATE JUILLET 1970

RAPPORT DES CHRONOMETREURS

RANG FINAL	NOMS DES NAGEURS DE CETTE EQUIPE	TOURS CHAQUE	TEMPS ACC. PAR NAGEUR HR. MIN. SEC.	MOYENNE /TOURS MIN. SEC.	MILES CHAQUE	TEMPS /MILE MIN. SEC.	NO. TOURS EQUIPE	MOYENNE /TOURS MIN. SEC.	MILES EQUIPE	TEMPS/M. EQUIPE MIN. SEC.
1	Horacio Iglesias	91	12 14 50	8 0	29.68	24 0	179	8 2	58.38	24 39
1	Johan Schans	88	11 45 10	8 1	28.70	24 33				
2	Regent Lacoursiere	83	12 36 7	9 8	27.07	27 38	165	8 43	53.81	26 45
2	Jan Van Scheijndel	82	11 23 53	8 14	26.74	24 57				
3	Abou El Enien	86	13 0 10	9 1	28.05	27 17	160	9 0	52.18	27 35
3	Marawan F. Shidid	74	10 59 50	8 55	24.13	27 20				
4	Denis Matuch	76	12 0 29	9 29	24.79	29 3	157	9 10	51.20	28 7
4	Mohamed H. Gamie	81	11 59 31	8 48	26.42	26 39				
5	Michael A. Praesler	77	11 57 0	9 19	25.11	28 32	156	9 13	50.88	28 18
5	Jon Erickson	79	12 3 0	9 4	25.76	27 26				
6	Geoffrey Lake	78	11 40 14	8 59	25.44	27 31	151	9 32	49.25	29 14
6	Yvon Montpetit	73	12 19 46	10 4	23.81	30 26				
7	Billy Barton	64	10 25 47	9 47	20.87	29 58				
7	Bob Duenkel	80	13 34 13	10 10	26.09	30 23	144	10 0	46.96	30 39
8	Abou Heif	101	18 46 18	11 6	32.94	33 40				
8	Carlos Aguire	36	5 13 42	8 45	11.74	26 5	137	10 30	44.68	32 13
9	William Lafferty	62	11 48 20	11 20	20.22	34 10				
9	Des Renford	65	12 11 40	11 15	21.20	34 30	127	11 20	41.42	34 45
10	Farouk Suliman	58	11 21 20	11 45	18.92	36 0				
10	Hassen Abdeen	62	12 38 40	12 2	20.22	35 41	120	12 0	39.14	36 47
11	Stella Taylor	58	12 40 18	12 52	18.92	38 46				
11	Michel Poirier	56	11 19 42	12 8	18.26	37 12	114	12 37	37.18	38 43
12	Benson Huggard	53	12 39 10	14 19	17.29	43 54				
12	Thomas Hetzel	48	11 20 50	14 3	15.65	42 9	101	14 15	32.94	43 42
Ret	France Boisvert	48	7 44 49	9 41	15.65	29 40				
Ret	Gaston Pare	49	7 45 7	9 32	15.98	28 38	97	9 35	31.64	29 23
Ret	Jorge Lopez	37	5 40 15	9 12	12.07	28 11				
Ret	Guillero Venturini	34	5 26 47	9 40	11.09	28 45	71	9 23	23.16	28 48
Ret	Gilles Potvin	40	7 24 18	11 11	13.05	33 24				
Ret	Raymond Cusson	31	7 7 9	13 47	10.11	42 13	71	12 16	23.16	37 37
Ret	Henry Martinen	39	6 20 26	9 45	12.72	29 53				
Ret	Fred Bowler	27	4 14 42	9 30	8.81	28 2	66	9 37	21.53	29 29

* NOTE, LES TEMPS DU PREMIER ET DU DERNIER TOUR DU MARATHON NE SONT PAS INCLUS DANS LA MOYENNE INDIVIDUELLE

// JOB   X   X   X
// XEQ CHRON   FX1

CHAMPIONAT MONDIAL DE NAGE PAR EQUIPE

LA TUQUE, QUE.   DATE JUILLET 1971

RAPPORT DES CHRONOMETREURS

RANG FINAL	NOMS DES NAGEURS DE CETTE EQUIPE	TOURS CHAQUE	TEMPS ACC. PAR NAGEUR HR. MIN. SEC.	MOYENNE /TOURS MIN. SEC.	MILES CHAQUE	TEMPS /MILE MIN. SEC.	NO. TOURS EQUIPE	MOYENNE /TOURS MIN. SEC.	MILES EQUIPE	TEMPS/M. EQUIPE MIN. SEC.
01	Horacio Iglesias	91	12 26 19	8 8	29.68	24 22	176	8 10	57.40	25 5
01	Joan Schans	85	11 33 41	8 10	27.72	25 1				
02	Abou Heif	91	13 5 56	8 38	29.68	26 28	168	8 34	54.79	26 16
02	Marawan Saleh	77	10 54 4	8 26	25.11	25 10				
03	Diana Nyad	85	11 49 7	8 21	27.72	25 34	167	8 37	54.46	26 26
03	Gaston Pare	82	12 10 53	8 55	26.74	26 39				
04	Carlos Aguirre	81	11 48 6	8 46	26.42	26 31	166	8 40	54.14	26 35
04	Paul Villagamez	85	12 11 54	8 37	27.72	26 5				
05	Richard Hart	83	12 0 16	8 39	27.07	25 53	164	8 46	53.49	26 55
05	Denis Matuch	81	11 59 44	8 53	26.42	27 14				
06	John Erickson	82	12 12 46	8 56	26.74	26 42	163	8 53	53.16	27 16
06	Geffrey Lake	81	11 57 14	8 51	26.42	27 8				
07	Arthur Deffaa	84	11 40 53	8 22	27.40	25 19	161	8 56	52.51	27 25
07	Salim Rawdah	77	12 19 7	9 37	25.11	29 6				
08	Hafiz Shedid	80	12 59 1	9 38	26.09	29 10	154	9 21	50.23	28 40
08	Marawan Shedid	74	11 0 59	8 58	24.13	27 5				
09	Georges Bourque	54	8 33 50	9 31	17.61	29 10	139	10 21	45.33	31 45
09	Yvon Montpetit	85	15 26 10	10 42	27.72	32 1				
10	Mervyn Sharp	66	12 43 40	11 37	21.53	35 5	132	10 54	43.05	33 26
10	David Gollop	66	11 16 20	10 14	21.53	30 55				
11	Daniel Boyle	59	12 24 4	12 40	19.24	38 10	116	12 24	37.83	38 3
11	Michel Poirier	57	11 35 56	12 10	18.59	36 37				
12	Thomas Hetzel	62	12 41 0	12 20	20.22	37 11	115	12 31	37.51	38 23
12	Benson Huggard	53	11 19 0	12 40	17.29	38 6				
13	Reg Hufstetler	51	11 46 43	13 42	16.63	41 11	103	13 58	33.59	42 51
13	James Doty	52	12 13 17	14 9	16.96	42 32				
Ret	Rejean Lacoursiere	53	8 19 18	9 28	17.29	28 29	105	9 5	34.24	27 52
Ret	Jan Van Scheindel	52	7 35 39	8 46	16.96	26 51				
Ret	Edouard Dubord	19	4 18 6	13 41	6.20	39 43	38	13 16	12.39	40 41
Ret	Ben Demontreuil	19	4 6 25	12 58	6.20	39 44				

* NOTE. LES TEMPS DU PREMIER ET DU DERNIER TOUR DU MARATHON NE SONT PAS INCLUS DANS LA MOYENNE INDIVIDUELLE
// JOB X X X

The Twenty-four-hour Swim: La Tuque 253

CHAMPIONAT MONDIAL DE NAGE PAR EQUIPE
RAPPORT DES CHRONOMETREURS
LA TUQUE, QUE. DATE JUILLET 1972

RANG FINAL	NOMS DES NAGEURS DE CETTE EQUIPE	TOURS CHAQUE	TEMPS ACC. PAR NAGEUR HR.	MIN.	SEC.	MOYENNE /TOURS MIN.	SEC.	MILES CHAQUE	TEMPS /MILE MIN.	SEC.	NO. TOURS EQUIPE	MOYENNE /TOURS MIN.	SEC.	MILES EQUIPE	TEMPS/M. EQUIPE MIN.	SEC.
01	Horacio Iglesias	89	11	50	16	7	58	29.03	24	26						
01	Johan Schans	90	12	9	44	8	6	29.35	24	51	179	8	2	58.38	24	39
02	John Erickson	90	12	30	11	8	19	29.35	25	28						
02	Raul Villagomez	82	11	22	49	8	20	26.74	25	31	172	8	19	56.10	25	32
03	Marawan Sheedid	86	12	20	59	8	37	28.05	26	24						
03	Jan Van Scheindel	84	11	39	1	8	19	27.40	25	30	170	8	28	55.44	25	58
04	Dennis Matuch	83	12	28	0	9	1	27.07	27	37						
04	Dyana Nyad Miss.	83	11	32	0	8	20	27.07	25	33	166	8	40	54.14	26	35
05	Carlos Aguirre	82	11	55	7	8	43	26.74	26	44						
05	Marcello Guiscardo	81	12	4	53	8	57	26.42	27	26	163	8	50	53.16	27	5
06	Yves Lavoie	77	12	1	51	9	22	25.11	28	44						
06	Yvon Montpetit	82	11	58	9	8	40	26.74	26	32	159	9	3	51.86	27	46
07	Mohamed Gamie	78	12	13	17	9	24	25.44	28	49						
07	Taby El Enen	77	11	46	43	9	7	25.11	27	58	155	9	17	50.55	28	28
08	Said Masri	69	12	25	49	10	49	22.50	33	8						
08	Mahmoud Khamis	82	11	34	11	8	25	26.74	25	48	151	9	32	49.25	29	14
09	Phillip Ballop	72	11	10	6	9	18	23.48	28	31						
09	Angel Bernatene	75	12	49	54	10	10	24.46	31	8	147	9	47	47.94	30	1
10	Sultan Kigab	72	12	7	39	10	0	23.48	30	38						
10	Naste Jonkeski	66	11	52	21	10	48	21.53	33	5	138	10	26	45.01	31	59
11	Hassan Abdeen	60	11	26	12	11	22	19.57	34	50						
11	Edward Bennett	76	12	33	48	9	55	24.79	30	24	136	10	35	44.35	32	27
12	Samia Mandour	68	12	31	39	11	3	22.18	33	53						
12	Fausto Ramirez	63	11	28	21	10	48	20.55	33	4	131	10	59	42.72	33	42
13	Mervin Sharp	71	13	20	25	11	16	23.16	34	33						
13	Thomas Hetzel	56	10	39	25	11	25	18.26	35	0	127	11	20	41.42	34	45
14	Daniel Boyle	59	11	47	38	12	4	19.24	37	0						
14	Michel Poirier	66	12	12	22	11	6	21.53	34	0	125	11	31	40.77	35	19

* NOTE, LES TEMPS DU PREMIER ET DU DERNIER TOUR DU MARATHON NE SONT PAS INCLUS DANS LA MOYENNE INDIVIDUELLE
// JOB X X X
// XEQ CHRON FX1

16
"La Belle Extraordinaire": Greta Andersen

She is a big woman, five feet ten inches tall. Her weight varied from 145 to 168 pounds during her professional career. Her shoulders are broad but so are her hips—thank God. It adds so much to her physical appeal. So many excellent female swimmers taper at the hips. They look masculine. Another point in her favor is that she is generously endowed breastwise. She has more muscle than the average woman. She's done a lot of swimming. The muscles are covered evenly and perfectly with the proper amount of fat that characterizes women. Her complexion is flawless, and her flesh like marble. She is a handsome woman, reminiscent of the Nordic shield-maidens who fought side by side with the Vikings. She is also a "superwoman," for she probably holds more swimming records and titles than any other person in the world—man or woman. She has beaten every man she has ever swum against in a professional race at least once. And best of all she is feminine.

I first met Greta Andersen in 1962 when she came to Chicago for the fifty-mile Lake Michigan Swim. She was then thirty-two years old and approaching the end of her professional career. She was talkative. She was nervous. I could understand why many had said she was dominant. It took a strong personality to overcome her ebulliency. She had that person in her husband-trainer. She became a baby in the water under his curses and advice. When I saw her swimming during the first fifteen minutes of that race she had developed a "hitch" in her left arm when she stroked. It only reached out a little more than halfway as much as the right arm did. I didn't think she'd last the race. But Greta did. She won the fifty-mile segment of that race. It was a world's record in two senses. She swam farther than any other person had ever done before in open water—man or woman. I should have remembered that Greta was full of surprises. A look at her record would have told me that. In fact Greta pulled her first surprise when she was born. She was delivered at twelve pounds. It could have been an omen. She was to be big on endurance also.

Greta was born in Copenhagen, Denmark in 1930. Among those who were impressed with her twelve-pound weight was her father. He must have passed on some excellent genes to his new daughter for he was the Danish gymnastic champion just three years earlier. To solidify such a statement Mr. Andersen's son and Greta's older brother was to become a bicycle champion for five years. Greta showed so much energy from her first day that only constant attention by her mother would placate her. Her mother soon learned that breast feeding helped to quiet the baby. As a consequence she was breast fed for three years.

As soon as Greta was old enough to walk she was into things. Nothing escaped her attention. She was unusually strong and healthy for her age. In the early years only the rough and tumble activities of the boys satisfied her. In fact she became the neighborhood sensation by beating up the older boys, a habit she retained, although in a different sense, in later years when she swam against them. Greta showed no inclination for sports in her early years. By the time she reached fifteen this presented a serious problem, or so her athletically oriented father thought. He soon remedied this by enrolling Greta in a swim school taught by Elsa Jacobson, who held eleven world records at the time. There were seventy-five other students in Greta's class so naturally she did not get any particular attention. In fact, she didn't get any attention at all. As a result she soon found herself swimming seventy-five yards in the pool without lifting her head for breath. No one had taught her how. Soon the instructor caught this and corrected the defect. From this point on, a graph of Greta's accomplishments would show a rising line. In six months Greta was the second-fastest swimmer in Denmark. It was soon evident that if the girl paid attention to her training she would be able to make the Olympic team in 1948. For the next two years Greta broke every girls' Danish swim record and some international ones also. When the time trials for the Olympics were held she qualified easily.

The 1948 Olympics were held in London. The Danish team did all the things that young athletes do when away from home the first time. Old tourists envy the enthusiasm the young show for every nook and cranny of a new country. Greta was only seventeen and no one exceeded her enthusiasm. It wasn't restricted to swimming alone. She was always in demand by her fellow companions.

When the Olympics were over Greta had in her possession the gold medal for the hundred-meter freestyle event. She swam the fastest time of any girl and clocked 1:06.2. Nestled alongside that acme award was also a silver medal. The relay team, of which she was a member, won second place in the four-hundred-meter event. It was a joyous seventeen year old who proudly placed the medals in her father's hands when the Olympics were over. Fulfilled expectations—is there any more happy state?

What does an ex-Olympic swimmer do after the games are over? Most go back to school. Some go on to college. Greta went back and finished high school and continued swimming. She had, at most, only another year or so of swimming before the law of economics made her earn a living. She made a good year of the time left. She continued to enter Danish and international meets. Among them was a world's record for the hundred yards that lasted seven years. She swam that race in 58.2 seconds. When the demands for earning a living made her temporarily give up swimming, she had accumulated the following amateur accomplishments: thirty-five Copenhagen championships, twenty-four Danish championships, 4 European championships in addition to her two world's records mentioned above.

Greta was now twenty years old. The few part-time jobs she tried did not offer her satisfaction. There had to be something connected with swimming that would offer her a chance to make a living. It was 1950 when she decided to visit the United States. She was immensely impressed with its beauty and its people. When she arrived in San Francisco, she knew that California would be her home someday. Her friends found her a position with the Crystal Plunge, an ornate and expensive pool catering to wealthy Californians. For six months she did exhibition swimming. Greta was never one to ignore conditioning. As a result when she received an invitation to represent her native Denmark in the European championship at Vienna she was in top form. She won the four-hundred-meter event with a time that lasted for three years.

The couple of years she spent back in Denmark were not satisfying. Visions and memories of the great West Coast would return. In 1953 she pulled a muscle in her knee, which required an operation. It was while recuperating that she made her final decision. Her future home would be the United States.

In 1953 Greta returned to the United States and settled in Glendale. Her friends found her a job as a swimming instructor. Again, it was only a short time before the frustrations returned. While she had met a lot of interesting people, among them her future husband to be, there was still something lacking. For two years she had worked as a swimming instructor and found that at the age of twenty-five there must be something that offered more of a challenge. The answer tentatively came one evening when Greta and her fiancé came out of the water from an evening swim in the ocean at Long Beach. There were several other swimmers on the beach who, impressed with Greta's form and speed, came over to talk. They happened to be members of an all-year swim club. A couple of them had swum the Catalina Channel. Greta, unaware that such a thing as marathon swimming existed, listened with a rising pulse as they talked of the longer swims. Before the conversation was over three hours had gone by. To Greta it seemed like minutes. In the course of the conversation they mentioned the Salton Sea marathon swim meet to be held about three months hence. Greta went to sleep that night planning her next day's workout. She planned to see if marathon swimming would take her out of her nervousness and doldrums. The next day, while Greta swam, her fiancé sent off a leter to the promotors of the Salton Sea swim asking for an entry blank.

The Salton Sea lies in the middle of nowhere. In the middle of lower California, surrounded by desert, it runs about thirty miles long and $10\frac{1}{2}$ miles wide. Its temperature is a salubrious seventy-eight degrees. When the date of the swim arrived, April 29, 1956, Greta was there. Throughout her four months of preparation she had been swimming six or eight miles a day. Most of her work was done in pools under the watchful eye of a timer with stop watch in hand. From time to time she would go down to the ocean, especially on weekends, to enjoy the company of other long-distance swimmers during her four-hour workout. Little did Greta know that her experience and training under the eyes of professional coaches in Denmark as an amateur would hold her in good stead. Hard, laborious, and tedious training combined with dedication were traits instilled in her while young.

In that first professional race she ever entered Greta was beaten by several men. She was, however, the first woman to finish and set a record (for women) for the $10\frac{1}{2}$ mile course of four hours twenty-five minutes. She left the water with a satisfaction that only physical exhaustion can bring. The congratulations and greetings by spectators and competitors were deeply felt. Greta felt that professional marathon swimming was something that fulfilled the lack she had been experiencing in her life until then. Two days later the Atlantic City swim officials received a letter from Greta. "Would they be so kind as to send her an entry blank?" They did, and the climb to the title of "The greatest female swimmer in history" began.

When that race was over Greta was the first woman to finish. She got fourth place, but she was only twenty-six minutes behind Cliff Lumsden, the winner. It would only be a matter of time before she would move up. In fact it would only be about a year when the swimming world would be shaken up like it had never been before. All that was needed was a little experience. A swimmer needs the help of good navigation and the proper foods to eat while in the water. Greta learned fast. Her mind became a sponge as she learned how valuable this precious information could be. She was now twenty-six. When she was twenty-seven her fame was established in marathon swimming circles.

Her first race in 1957 was on May 5th. It was a fifteen-mile one from Huntington Beach to Long Beach, California. She was the first woman to finish. She took six hours fourteen minutes. The money she earned was deeply satisfying. It would have taken her two months working as an instructor in the pool to earn the equivalent amount. The next swim would be the longest one she had yet undertaken, twenty-six miles. It was in a resort area around Guaymas, Mexico. It would begin some miles North of the city of Guaymas at another hotel along the western coast of the Gulf of California. The course would be along the erratic shoreline and finally end after sweeping around a broad peninsula in the harbor at Guaymas. It has been said the swim was made for marine biologists, for it offered innumerable chances to study fish, sharks, porpoises, manta rays, and whales to say nothing of seaweed. When that swim was over Greta was second. The famous Tom Park had beaten her in. She clocked twelve hours for the twenty-six-mile course. Her second-place finish, however, was salved by the fact that she became friends with Tom Park, who taught her some of the tricks of the trade.

July 25 found her back at Atlantic City. She moved up to third place in that race, again finishing behind her new-found friend and nemesis Tom Park. The promoters made it a tougher swim that year by having the swim start against the tide. The winner, Alfredo Camarero of Argentina, finished in twelve hours seventeen minutes, Tom Park in 12:25, and greta in 12:36. Pressure was becoming a way of life.

On August 3, 1957 Greta set a record for women at the fifteen-mile Owen Sound marathon in Canada. Her time of six hours fifteen minutes broke the men's record set in 1933 of seven hours thirty-three minutes. Alas for Greta, "the woman's record" was beginning to daunt her. She knew that the men could be had. She had had enough of coming in after them.

The money won from the four swims allowed Greta to purchase a plane ticket to London. She had crossed the Channel several times before on a ferry as a teenager. This time she would be swimming across as a contestant in the Butlin Race. At five in the morning of August 21, twenty-four contestants from around the world ran through the surf at Point Griz-Nez. There would be only two finishers in that race. One was a woman and she astounded the world. When Greta Andersen stepped ashore at Dover some thirteen hours fifty-three minutes later she was something more than the first woman to finish. She was the first swimmer to finish. She was the first woman in the English Channel race to beat the men. The only other swimmer to finish the race landed at Dover over two hours later. It was rough water all the way with some of the waves cresting at 3½ feet. The attending worldwide publicity made Greta an international personality. The three thousand dollars she earned felt good to the twenty-seven year old who at last felt that she was doing something that satisfied her. Earning money and fame while doing something you like puts you in a good frame of mind. Greta completed her circle of happiness when she returned to the United States and married the man who had been willing to not only spend time with her out of the water, but while she was in it. The man who held the stopwatch along side the pool and on the beach was now her husband. What more could a girl ask for?

1957 was a warm-up for 1958. It was this year that Greta made outstanding swim after outstanding swim. The first professional swim of the year was the Guaymas, Mexico swim. She made sure that every detail learned in 1957 was remembered and applied. Her husband-coach and she made every effort to get there early and line up dependable boats, which was not hard considering the number of wealthy Americans living there. When the international field showed up she knew that she would need all the planning. Throughout the winter months she had stepped up her training schedule to forty miles per week. She knew that any race she now entered would demand top speed throughout the duration of the race. Among the field of twenty-seven international swimmers that showed up was Tom Park. He would become one of America's top swimmers that year. Only Greta would surpass him.

It took Greta six hours before she broke away from Park after a grueling battle. For the next four hours he hung doggedly within sight before she finally lost him. She knew she now led the field, and the excellent navigation and handling she received gave her the satisfaction that she needed at that time. When she came into the harbor at Guaymas, she was the only swimmer to be seen. She was the winner of the race. Only eighteen other swimmers of the twenty-seven who started finished. She had beaten the men in the cold water of the English Channel. She now had beaten them in the warm, seventy-five-degree water of the Gulf of California. Greta Andersen was turning the topsy-turvy world of professional marathon swimming over. With that swim, proving her Channel victory no fluke, every interested person in the swimming world awaited the result of any race that she entered.

The next race, Atlantic City, on July 14 saw Tom Park regain his ego with a win. Greta came in third behind Cliff Lumsden. The next race at Lake St. John on August 2nd would be interesting. The nineteen-mile race (not twenty-one as the promoters say) was won by Greta in record time of eight hours seventeen minutes. She had again, for the third time, beaten the men in a professional race. She was also the first woman to swim the lake since races were inaugurated in 1955.

When Greta showed up for the 1958 English Channel race the eyes of the world were on her. It was well they were, for she became the only swimmer ever to win that race twice, and in consecutive years. Her time of ten hours fifty-nine minutes was only nine minutes slower than that of the Egyptian el-Rheim, who won the race in 1950. Greta was establishing a professional record that would only be equalled—not exceeded—by two other swimmers, and both were men.

The Channel race ended the professional circuit. When Greta returned home she wanted to get only one swim out of the way. While the Catalina Channel offered no prize money she realized that money could be made in a publicity swim. She would undertake a Catalina Channel swim under one stipulation. It would be a double crossing. She had become tired of hearing about George Young, Florence Chadwick, and Tom Park. She would put her best efforts into this swim and quiet the gremlin that periodically made an appearance. Besides, a double crossing had never been done before. Critics said it couldn't be done. Critics had said the same thing about many things before. If the doers listened to them little progress would have been made from engineering to marriages.

A few swimmers had made the swim since George Young's feat in 1927. Byron Summers did it in a respectable time before he set his record in swimming around Manhattan Island in 1927. Florence Chadwick and Tom Park had swum from the island to the mainland in 1952. A few weeks later they, at different times, swam the reverse route. Greta would attempt to break both records at the same time.

On October 5, 1958 she began her double crossing, leaving from Emerald Bay on Catalina Island. The straight-line plot to Point Vincente would be about nineteen miles, and not the twenty-one miles erroneously published by the newspapers. Conditions were ideal, for the water was flat and warm: seventy-two degrees. Navigation presented no diffiiulties as she maintained a strong and steady stroke throughout the first few hours. Three hours after she started visibility changed drastically. A fog had rolled in and her navigators had to rely on dead reckoning for the rest of the journey. Luckily no wind sprang up at this time to hamper her speed. As a result Greta reached Point Vincente, the exact point where George Young had landed some thirty-one years before, in the fantastically short time of ten hours forty-nine minutes. She had broken the record held by Tom Park. It was no elated Greta, in spite of a world's record, that sat in ankle deep water on the rocky beach of Point Vincente. She had overextended herself and dreaded her commitment to undertake a swim back to the island. For seventeen short minutes her husband and boat handlers tried to talk her out of making a return trip. She had the record, why punish herself? Shrugging off her friends she raised herself from the sitting position she had so tiredly assumed and walked back into the water. If she had known what she was in for she would never have gone on—or would she?

It took her two hours before her aching muscles no longer bothered her on the return journey. Things went "so-so" for the next couple of hours and then the weariness and pain became ever-increasing. Soon she was swimming mechanically and with vacant eyes. Hour after hour she stroked, now a bundle of excruciating pain-racked nerves. It was evident to all aboard the escort vessel that she would never even approach the record for a mainland-to-island crossing. Tom Park's time of nine hours ten minutes in 1956 was inviolate. It would be lucky if Greta completed her swim at all. Greta did, however, complete that leg of the round-trip crossing, but it took her fifteen hours and thirty-eight minutes. Instead of three records she did have two: the fastest time ever recorded for an island-to-mainland crossing, and the only double crossing of the straits, a record that stands to this day. Her time for this notable achievement was twenty-six hours fifty-three minutes. Not bad for a thirty-eight-mile swim. Even the most hardened of cynics would have to admit that. Greta came back a year later to make a try for Park's record. In 1959 she made the mainland-to-island crossing in eleven hours seven minutes. It was almost two hours slower than Park's record, but she now held the woman's record that had been previously held by Florence Chadwick. Except for 1962, this was Greta's star year. She would continue to make headlines in the swimming world, but except for 1962, there would always be a man ahead of her. She would have to learn that "women's winner" would have to be enough.

1959 was a frustrating year for Greta. She had trained just as hard as in the previous years, but the men swam with a diabolic fierceness in horror of being beaten by her. The first professional swim of the circuit was an ominous sign. It was at the Atlantic City swim on July 17 that she learned of the heartbreaking experience of being right up with the leaders until the last two miles, and then, poof, they began to pull out on her. It is enough to look at the times of the first three finishers. The minutes that separate them tell the story: first, Cliff Lumsden, 10:54:05; second, Tom Park, 11:00:15; third, Greta Andersen, 11:07:25. Being the woman's winner was no palliative. It was the same story at Capri-Naples, and the English Channel— "Women's Winner." No matter the designation, being number one overall was the thing.

In 1960 I could find no record of Greta swimming in any of the races. Maybe she did enter a few and withdrew after not finding herself up in the pack. Maybe she decided to retire. She was now thirty years old.

What really had happened was that Greta had gone to Hawaii with her husband. The year before she had tried to swim the unconquered Molokai Channel, which runs between the island of Molokai and Oahu. She was defeated by the tricky currents. Now, in 1960, with the backing of television stations and others, she was back to try again. The money she had earned from the professional races was hard money. Granted, there was some gratification from the fame, but it was hardly worth the effort of the race and the long months of training. Now she was being offered a chance to capitalize on a solo publicity swim that would allow her movie rights for lecture and sale. Several retired professional men had offered to work out the tides and currents for her swim. If successful, the twenty-six mile Molokai Channel swim would allow her a chance to convert the publicity into money and earn perhaps five times what would have been earned in a professional race.

Greta made a valiant attempt to swim the channel, but it was a sad story. Her navigator didn't read about the Hawaiian fishermen who made four fifths of the swim in 1939 without the benefit of navigation and feeding (see chapter 13). He rigidly stuck to the charts, which pitted Greta obliquely, and then directly against the current. After some eighteen hours of swimming Greta could see that she was being swept out and away from Oahu. She knew she was defeated and disconsolately gave up. All the marvels of modern civilization and science had failed to take into consideration the variables that were evident to the fishermen in the area. Even Dr. Paskowitz who prepared the scientific formula for Greta could not supply the "extra" that was needed for a successful swim. A year later, in 1961, a local swimmer and AAU champion named Keo Nakama dove into the channel off the southwestern tip of Molokai. Nakama's course took him across the current during a period of neap tide. Nakama, combining excellent navigation with superb swimming skill, was successful in conquering the Molokai.

In any case in 1961 there are records of her. She began a pattern that year of dropping out of any race when she was not in the money. That meant being in the first three. Greta knew better than to suffer extra agonizing hours in the water for a pittance. She was a professional and professionals expected to make money. Only amateurs expected no remuneration. Besides, she found her newly open swim school in a Los Angeles suburb gradually increasing in members and demanding more and more of her time. The only swim she completed in 1961 was the C. N. E. The third-place money was enough to pay expenses and leave a little left over.

In 1962 she followed the same pattern. It was a tough race at Lake St. John for she was beaten out of third place by LaCoursiere by six minutes. When that race was over, Greta and her husband snuck

"La Belle Extraordinaire": Greta Andersen

out of the race area as quietly as possible, but not for reason of shame. Somehow most of the swimmers had not heard of the race in Chicago. It was a two-part race combined into one. There was a thirty-six-mile choice and/or a fifty-mile choice. How this unusual race originated is told in detail in chapter 2. It was a wise choice for Greta for it allowed her to hold the World's Long Distance Open Water Swimming Championship, although for one short year. It was a long and tough race in which throughout the first thirty-six miles she was within feet of the winner, nineteen-year-old Dennis Matuch of Chicago. It was a frustrating thing to lose a thirty-six-mile race by several hundred yards. She had no choice when the lifeguard got out of the water at that point but to go on for the $10,000 prize awaiting the swimmer completing fifty miles. The $10,000 she collected for winning that race did much to raise Greta's spirits. She was now a world's champion again.

1963* was Greta's last year as a competitor in professional swimming. She was now thirty-three years old and the up and coming younger set prevented any "middle-aged" athlete from collecting, Abo-Heif being the only exception. Greta finished fifth at Atlantic City, only seventeen minutes ahead of the beautiful college coed, Marty Sinn. A few weeks later at the C. N. E. the twenty-year-old passed Greta at around the three-mile mark in the cold fifty-five-degree water. It was then that Greta left the water full well knowing that time and youth had taken its toll. She would enter one more swim and then call it quits.

On August 21, 1963 Greta showed up for the sixty-mile Lake Michigan swim. Abo-Heif and Ted Erikson also showed up. Greta lasted twelve hours before Abo-Heif finally broke away. Realizing that forty-five miles remained to be swum she signaled her boat and all was over. Few realized that as Greta Andersen pulled herself into the rowboat they were witnessing the retirement of the greatest female swimmer in the world. Greta never again entered a professional race.

Today she is happily married to a doctor in Los Angeles, her first marriage having ended in divorce. She is still the handsome woman she always was and loves her job as housewife to a respected member of the community. They balance well—the academic and athletic, that is when she isn't attending her now fabulously successful swim school, signing endorsements for wristwatches, health foods, swimming pools, and outboard motors. And best of all she enjoys the conversations with both professional and amateur swimmers when they talk of the "big swims."

Greta entered the 1964 Lake Ontario swim but did not finish. She

---

* The 1964 Lake Ontario swim temporarily lured her back. She left the water like all the rest, without finishing.

was also lured back to the English Channel in 1964 and 1965 in an attempt to make a double crossing. On the three occasions she tried, the first crossing was always made, but somewhere into the second leg weather, fatigue, and age (she was now thirty-four to thirty-five) got the better of her. The game was up. Erikson was successful a few weeks after her last try in 1965 and set a record while becoming the second person in history to do it. Greta went home knowing that age had in the end conquered. After all, she had been swimming now for twenty years.

17
The Solos

While the professional races offer the excitement of matching man against man the solo swims pit man against his environment. This is not to say that the elements do not affect competitors in a race. They certainly do, but each and every swimmer has the stimulus of a competitor in the vicinity. Long before the advent of the professional race, individuals were giving longing looks over bodies of water that dared to be swum. A few of their attempts were successful, more were failures. Thus the scene was set for monomania. Given the time and leisure the idea of making that swim would grow. The mere idea would suddenly shift to preparations and plans. Manhattan Island was such a lure to an eighteen-year-old lad in 1915.

Then, as today, Manhattan Island was the hub of New York City. The island runs twelve miles in length, but the great difference in width at either end, as well as its irregular eastern coastline, adds up to twenty-eight miles if one were to swim or walk its coast. Concentrated on this island is the greatest density of people and buildings in the United States. The two rivers and bay that surround the greater portion of the island play host to the greatest mercantile marine traffic in the world. Wharfs and docks by the hundreds almost completely surround the island, excepting only a few scattered park areas and the narrow Harlem River, which is used only for navigational purposes. Manhattan contains all the famous and infamous ingredients that go into the making of a metropolis. Millions lived and sweated for a living like in any other gigantic city. It was all there from the classiest hotels and apartments on Riverside Drive to the slums of the Bowery, from the fancy shops on Fifth Avenue to the sleazy pawn shops on West 23rd Street. The working class had little interest in any sporting endeavor when they dragged themselves home after a sixteen-hour day. The rich members of the city's more exclusive athletic clubs were among the few who enjoyed life. Their sons and daughters could swim in the club's pools and these private clubs were in their turn proud of their pools and clientele. In summertime the offspring of the financially well off would take the family car, which was a real luxury in those days, and drive out to the pleasant private beaches on the ocean at Rockaway. Such was the son of Robert E. Dowling, President of the City Investment Company and an official of the Amateur Athletic Union.

Robert W. was only fourteen years old when his father put him under the tutorship of a plush New York athletic club. The boy responded well and soon made excellent showings in the short amateur races held in the pools. When only seventeen he entered the longest race he had ever swum in, the two-mile "marathon" from the Battery, at the foot of Manhattan Island, to Sandy Hook. He placed sixth in that 1914 race. When the winter of 1914–15 was over, young Robert was tired of the pools and expectantly looked for the opening of the beaches that surround New York. When summer finally arrived his days were spent in the ocean. The deep tan he acquired while swimming made Robert the envy of his pals. It was after one of his long training swims while he was talking with one of his buddies that the subject of swimming around Manhattan Island came up. When they got home they pulled out the atlas and marked off the mileage. The minimum they could get was twenty-eight miles. The idea was soon put to Robert's father who, being a sympathetic man, agreed with his son's proposal. After all, the boy could be doing less wholesome things like visiting the dives that existed in the city. When his dad learned that no one had ever made the swim before and that "experts" said the tide and cold water made the swim impossible it was too late to back out. His son had entered into preparations that included his father as coach. When a son puts faith in his father how could the man resist?

When August 15, 1915 rolled around Robert and his dad found themselves waiting atop the sea wall at the Battery. A short while later a motor launch containing T. J. Howland, a professional swimming instructor, and John J. Walsh of the Amateur Athletic Union showed up. Almost two hours were spent in deciding which way to go before the Hudson River route was agreed upon. At 8:55 A.M. young Dowling dove from the sea wall and began his swim. True to the era it was the trudgeon crawl that carried him out into the Hudson River.

Robert made excellent time and by noon, after three hours of swimming, he had reached the southern end of Central Park, which lies approximately in the center of Manhattan Island. He was making well over two miles per hour, which put to rest fears of the current. At least the fears were temporarily laid to rest, for Robert was riding the flood tide of the Atlantic Ocean, which effectively neutralized the basically downward flow of the Hudson River. By two in the afternoon he had arrived at Spuyten Duyvil, which marks the northern bank of the Harlem River where it enters the Hudson River. In five hours he had been able to cover the twelve miles that marked the length of the island along its western shore. Now all that was needed was to enter the narrow river and swim in an easterly direction for about a mile before swinging southerly for the contemplated "easy" ride down the Harlem and then the East rivers. However, Robert arrived at Spuyten Duyvil when the full force of the changing tide was seeping past the entrance to the Harlem River at Spuyten Duyvil. The ebb had now begun and the mighty Hudson was flowing at three miles per hour into the Harlem River. If Robert had arrived just an hour sooner he could have easily been around the corner and would have enjoyed the current sweeping him along down the river. There was absolutely no chance of making the entrance to the Harlem. In fact, he was gradually losing ground. Making the best of an unlucky situation, the boy's father and coaches had him turn around and head back for the Battery. If he made it back it at least could be said that he swam the equivalent distance, if not around the island. Robert swam well for the next three hours and then, whether due to weakening or disheartening, he was taken from the water at 5:30 P.M. just off of 79th Street, tired, but not exhausted. He had managed to cover about six miles on his return trip. After eight hours thirty-five minutes of swimming the boy had managed to cover $18\frac{1}{2}$ miles. No one needed to say that a second try was well worth the effort. In fact, on the boat ride back to the docks a September attempt was already being planned. Only this time the defeating point would be the starting point. They would get the charts and tide tables out and make maximum use of their brains as well as the boy's swimming ability.

It was Sunday, September 5, 1915 when the early morning hours found Robert and his crew at the railroad bridge marking the western end of the Harlem River. Only one and a half short blocks away lay the Hudson River. The boat moored to one of the pilings near the shore while Robert, in his bathing suit, climbed to the bridge fifteen feet above. At 8:30 A.M., with a sign from his father, he dove into the water. Surfacing a few moments later, he stroked strongly for the Hudson with his trudgeon crawl and was soon headed south toward the Battery. There was no question there was a current behind him as he rapidly clipped off the miles. By 1 P.M. Robert had reached the end of Manhattan and was rounding the Battery. Throughout the morning he had been busily dodging the heavy motorboat traffic but it was not enough to hamper his three-plus-mile-per-hour average. He had covered the twelve-mile segment in just $4\frac{1}{2}$ hours, which shows the discerning historian that he had the help of a one-plus-mile-per-hour current.

Whether it was currents or taking too long to eat his beef broth and chocolate, it took Robert one hour to make the one mile up the East River to the famed Brooklyn Bridge. In any case we know that there was little or no current in the East River for the next four hours contrary to reports of such. By 6:15 P.M. he had reached the entrance to the Harlem River, some 8¼ miles from the Brooklyn Bridge. This was a respectable 8¼ miles in four hours. When one learns that he was doing the breast stroke quite a bit during these hours one can only conclude that he was actually riding a tide up.

Swinging into the Harlem River he began the last leg of his trip. He had covered some twenty-two miles of his journey and needed to go only six more miles before success was his. The three miles up the Harlem River to the Washington Bridge proved to be the nemesis. It took the rapidly tiring Robert 3½ hours to make the tortuous ascent. It was 9:45 P.M., the sun had set 2½ hours before, and now all was dark. Only the lights aboard his escort vessel and along the shores of the narrow 1½-block-wide channel gave illumination. Robert had only one more mile to go. His starting point, which was the railroad bridge, would not be visible until he made the last turn. When he did there it was just a half mile away. By this time there were fifteen other boats that came on the site. They began to blow their horns to cheer the lad on. At 10:15 P.M., amid the cheers and horns, the boy arrived underneath the bridge he had left at 8:30 A.M. that morning. Robert W. Dowling had become the first person to swim Manhattan Island.

All the pundits who said the currents made such a swim impossible were red-faced. His time of thirteen hours forty-five minutes for the twenty-eight mile trip was quite respectable considering the stroke he used. Whatever became of Robert is not recorded, but there is one thing he proved. Manhattan Island could be swum, and that was all swimmers needed to know. While it hasn't been done recently, because of pollution and boat traffic, there still crops up from time to time a swimmer who makes the swim. Today's honed and polished swimmers do it faster, but the newspaper articles always include the name of the first person to do it: Robert W. Dowling on September 5, 1915.

As usual, record setters are rarely allowed to enjoy their accomplishments for long. While his record for being the first to swim around Manhattan Island could never be taken away from him, Dowling's time could. It was almost one year later to the day that a swimmer swam around the island in eleven hours thirty-five minutes, two hours and ten minutes faster. Was the swimmer a college-bred whiz with the muscle and form to match? No, but a diminutive miss, by the name of Ida Elionsky. Miss Elionsky was practicing women's liberation some fifty-five years before the current movement. To add chagrin to embarrassment it wasn't until eleven years later that a man was capable of breaking her record. During the interim, how-

The Solos

ever, there were a couple of other women who were not waiting for the men's assault on Miss Elionsky's record. Miss Charlotte (Lotte) Schoemell and Mille Garde were doing quite well in their chosen vocation.

First there was Miss Mille Garde, using her maiden name to the frustration of her husband who was rowing the boat, who at no time stopped to chat or whimper, but only to feed. She swam around the island in fifteen hours fifty-seven minutes to become the second woman to do it. That was on June 26, 1921. A few years later she also became the second woman to swim the English Channel. Miss Garde left the water after circling the island with a few cuss words because she came nowhere near Miss Elionsky's record. Much to her credit she never again tried the swim, somehow knowing that a person's whole life could be spent in chasing after elusive records. She knew that time and place play a big part in such things.

On September 19, 1926 another of the "weaker sex" swam around the island. What the men were doing is a question that deserves asking, but the answer escapes me. Perhaps it was Gertrude Ederle's conquest of the Channel that stimulated Miss Charlotte Schoemmel into swimming around Manhattan on September 19, 1926 in fourteen hours twenty-one minutes. But in any case she kept right on going that year. On October 17, 1926 she swam 165 miles down the Hudson River from Albany, New York to New York City. As in the Manhattan Island swim she used every stroke in the book: crawl, breast, trudgeon, and side stroke. I didn't bother looking this swim up, because like so many river swims the newspaper accounts are "foggy." They always neglect to mention when and if the swimmer gets out of the water for a night's sleep in a nearby hotel and in the morning picks up where he left off the previous night. There's also the "current" question, which can be anything from two miles per hour to twelve miles per hour. In any case Miss Schoemmell's "165-mile-swim" earned her undying fame for the sensation seekers, and notoriety among the serious. Among those "records" of Miss Schoemmel's that I've seen (and I must confess they are few) there is one that I accept. That is August 18, 1966—the date Miss Schoemmel died. She was seventy-one years old. County death recorders and attending physicians usually are pretty sure when they sign death certificates.

1927 saw the record for Manhattan Island set. A California college whiz by the name of Byron Summers made a detour of over a thousand miles while on his way to the first Wrigley Swim in Toronto. He put his college training to good use by picking up nautical charts and tide tables during the first twenty-four hours he was in the city. He then made a trip to the 89th Street Volunteer Life Saving Station and explained how important it was to have knowledgeable rowers and navigators. They quickly agreed to give Byron all the help he needed.

One of the important decisions made was to accomplish that part of the swim that always gave swimmers the most difficulty. This was the section around Hell's Gate, which is where the East River makes contact with the Harlem River. It was this area, and the Harlem River, where the swimmers always slowed down. Byron planned to leave from the 89th Street Station and head north swimming as hard as he could. He estimated that in three hours he would be through the Harlem River and at Sputyn Duyvil. In doing so the toughest 7½ miles of the circuit would be over, and if things continued to go well he could ride the tide down the Hudson and be at the Battery in four or five hours. Planning would then allow him to take full advantage of any slack or flood tide and he could complete the rest of his journey full blast knowing the hard part was over. And there you have it. That's exactly what happened, for when Byron came out of the water after making his circumnavigation of Manhattan he had the record: a phenomenal eight hours fifty-six minutes. He averaged, with the help of tides, a spectacular three miles per hour. I like to think of Byron Summer's swim as one of the pivot points in the history of marathon swimming that made it a thinking man's sport. Generations of swimmers were to attempt the Manhattan Island and other tidal swims, but alas, many were not readers. They were doomed from the start, if not from completing their swims, at least to hours of extra effort.

Byron showed up a month later for the Wrigley swim in Toronto. As history reports only three men completed that swim. That was a swim in which all the brains in the world were worth less than twenty pounds of fat. Byron didn't have the fat.

In 1927, Bill Sadlow, Jr., and in 1928, Hershel Martin tried Summers's approach, both leaving from the 89th Street Station. They came close, which is a testament to the coming state of the art, but not close enough. Sadlow made his circuit in nine hours eight minutes, Martin in nine hours forty minutes.

Throughout the next thirty years there were sporadic swims around the island, but by this time the public had lost interest and the city officials took interest. They took interest, however, of a different sort. Every time a swimmer took to the course they caused many a curse among the seagoing and docking vessels that plied their trade in this world's busiest harbor. Soon their vitriolic comments reached city hall and the city fathers clamped down saying that hereafter any swimmers were forbidden to swim in the shipping lanes without permission from them. Naturally, permission, except on rare occasions, was never given. Bread and butter were more important to New Yorkers than athletic contests in the rivers surrounding the city.

By 1959 it took a bill in the city council, or political pull, to swim the island. In 1959, luckily, it took a little less effort for that was the year the area was celebrating the 350th anniversary of the Dutch exploration of the Hudson River. F. & M. Schaeffer Brewing Company contracted a twenty-five-year-old mother of three to swim the island for publicity. A year before, on August 23, 1958, Diane Struble had proved her abilities, when she swam the then unconquered Lake George lying northwest of New York City. The powerful Mrs. Struble swam the thirty-two-mile-long lake in thirty-five hours. The five-foot three-inch blond who weighed 138 pounds had inclement weather for that swim but the seventy-two-degree water allowed her to put in the time necessary to complete the swim. Manhattan Island waters can be anything from sixty-five to seventy-eight degrees. Major Zirganos tried it in October when it was fifty-five degrees and had to be taken to the hospital for three days recovery. Needless to say he didn't make it. Her thirty-five hours in the water, however, was a record of sorts for immersion. Abo-Heif was in the water for the same length of time in 1963 when he swam Lake Michigan, only he made sixty miles.

Now, on August 15, 1959, with the blessing of the F. & M. Schaeffer Brewing Company, and City Council's okay, Mrs. Diane Struble took to the waters from the Battery and headed up the East River. Her course exhibited shades of historical ignorance. This was the era of mass communication and advertising. Would Schaeffer & Co. have it any other way? There were newsmen, television cameras, and interviewers. Television men were thinking of Florence Chadwick and the millions of viewers who watched her in her early 1950s crossing of "Catalina Straits." There were millions of viewers on the East coast also.

Diane stayed within one hundred yards of the shoreline throughout her swim. When she finished, a tedious eleven hours twenty-one minutes later, a crowd of five hundred greeted her. She made an effort to circle the island an unheard of second time, but city officials put a quick end to it when two burly lifeguards hauled her out. Enough wrath of sea-going captains had been earned already. Newsmen, always ready to believe any claim to a current victory, said it was a new woman's record. Schaeffer & Co. would have liked to pass it off as such, but the ghost of Lotte Schoemmel showed up in the form of her son who waved a clipping of his mother's accomplishment in 1926. He also mentioned that fact that Diane was only the fourth woman to make the swim, since Ida Elionsky and Mille Garde, as well as his mother, had done it also. Mr. Schoemmel was politely hustled away from the television cameras by policemen while Mrs. Struble accepted her plaudits. It is a credit to the *New York Times* that when they published the account of Diane's swim the next day they also included the previous women's accomplishments. Mrs. Struble showed up a couple of years later for the Lake Michigan swims, but after swimming a few hours she got out of the water and slipped into limbo.

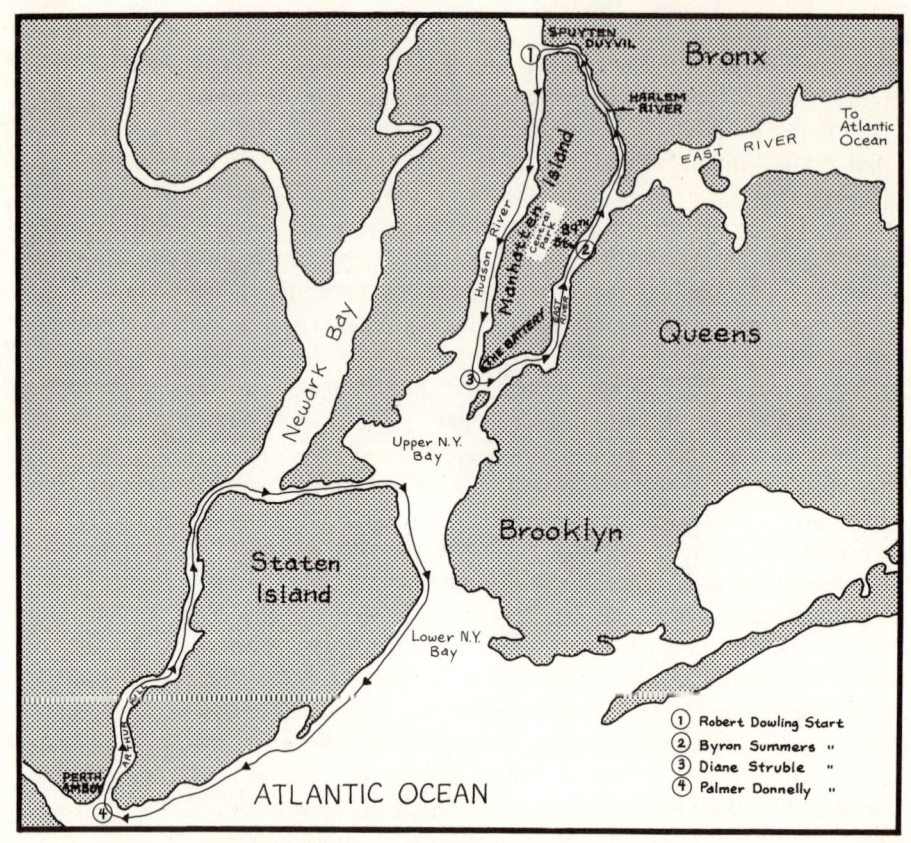

The Manhattan and Staten Island swims.

She was never quite up to the professional class.

By the 1960s traffic and pollution were so great in the rivers around Manhattan Island that even if a swimmer desired to make the swim he was soon disenchanted when he got near enough to smell the water. The Manhattan Island swim died a pollution death. Perhaps it will be reborn if the rhetoric of ecological improvement is transmitted into action.

In 1961 the sister island of Manhattan, Staten Island, was swum for the first time in history. A husky twenty-one-year-old lifeguard, deciding that looking at the sensuous bathing beauties on his beach could get him in marital difficulties with his new wife, took to the water at Perth Amboy. Starting at 5:47 P.M. he went up the Arthur Kill Straits, a real industrial sewer, and swam throughout the night with the solace of his two sisters, his mother, and his wife in the accompanying boat. In the early afternoon of the next day he ran into difficulties with the tide (as most amateurs claim when they get tired) and paddled around for an hour waiting for it to change. Recuperated by his rest, rather than from his "tactical" decision, Palmer Donnelly settled down to swimming again. By the time he reached his starting point he could hardly move his arms. He weakly dragged himself aboard a floating raft where he was allowed to rest for an hour before being floated ashore in a rowboat to a waiting ambulance, which took him home to recuperate. Finishing at 6:57 P.M., Donnelly had made the thirty-five mile circuit in twenty-five hours for a respectable 1.4-mile-per-hour average. It would be interesting to see what a pro could do. Well, on second thought, Donnelly was now a pro. He earned $2,000 for the swim. It was put up by civic leaders and a local newspaper. To some it was a tough way to earn college tuition and family expenses. You would never convince a swimmer of that fact, however. They love to swim.

To give a little comic relief to the recitation of these by no means small efforts of serious swimmers I should mention a few of the endeavors of those people addicted to swimming pools. While the present day marathoner realizes that a certain amount of pool training can effectively knock down his times, he still shuns them in favor of invigorating outdoor water. Pool water is invariably kept around eighty degrees, which in ten minutes has the well-padded marathoner panting. However, there is a class of swimmer that likes the sepulchrelike calm of the water and the dead air that are characteristics of the pool environment. They will spend their lifetime swimming in such, to the outdoor lover, mausoleums. One of the most remarkably boring records of all time must certainly have taken place on July 27, 1930 when Corrine Rossberg and Mrs. Myrtle Huddleston climbed out of the Rockaway Beach Pool in New York City after floating around for eighty-five hours fifteen minutes. An observer on the scene made the comment that it was difficult to tell who was yawning the hardest, the performers or the spectators. One is reminded that before the advent of the tranquilizing drugs in the late fifties, doctors used to calm down manic patients by putting them in hot baths. You would think that normal people would react by going crazy under like situations. Perhaps the two ladies were.

Wherever there is water man will eventually get into it. As a consequence he finds himself swimming in the most unlikely places. Many of the swims made by a local swimmer to a local landmark—like the fourteen-mile swim from Boston Harbor to the Boston lighthouse—became an annual affair. Readers of the back pages of their newspapers accept these swims as the natural holiday events of the area. If there is no water around, the town may become famous by holding other races, like the Kansas one that became famous for their annual ladies' pancake foot race. However, once in a while a unique swimming event takes place that is blurbed around the world when it is completed. Such was Captain Alfred Baron's swim in August, 1914.

Captain Baron thought a unique event to mark the opening of the Panama Canal would be to swim it. The newspaper account says he was successful in covering the forty-eight mile length, but his time and other pertinent information are sadly lacking. Of the four accounts that I've come across, and there were many others who claimed the feat, I've been forced to place three in the "maybe" column. In 1929 the notorious publicity seeker Richard Haliburton, who also wrote several bestsellers, told of his "dramatic, adventurous, thrilling, and spectacular" swim of the Canal from Colon to Panama City. He says the route was fifty miles. He swam a mathematical 49¾ miles before discretion forced him to leave the water because of sharks. This account reads like a sensational publicity stunt calculated to stir the blood of the thousands of women who read about it in the *Ladies Home Journal* for June, 1929. Throughout the five-page article one gets the feeling that Haliburton made the swim in stages. That is, each segment was swum after a good night's sleep. Haliburton hedges too much for me.

A Dr. Robert R. Legge tried to make the swim in October, 1958. He had plotted a 28½-mile course and planned to do it in less than twenty-four hours. I guess the earth shrank from 1929 to 1958 because of Dr. Legge's calculations. If the Panama Canal did go from fifty miles to 28½ miles in twenty-nine years, it looks like swimmers will be doing the Atlantic Ocean in another couple of hundred years. I never could find out if he made the swim, but one thing is sure: fifty-three-year-old Dr. Legge should follow the advice he no doubt gave to many patients. He should get a wheelchair. On a note of levity it should be mentioned that Dr. Legge had to plunk down seventy-two cents in toll charges before he made the attempt: the minimum for a one-ton vessel in ballast.

In order to protect myself from the reader for treating the above claims to glory so flippantly I will end with a legitimate swimmer and a legitimate swim of the Panama Canal in October, 1966. The swimmer was one of recognized accomplishments and known to the coterie the world over. He was Mihir Sen of Calcutta. 1966 was a big year for Sen for among his accomplishments were: Palk Strait from India to Ceylon, a geographic thirty-five miles, in twenty-five hours thirty-six minutes (he broke the record of his countryman Mr. Navaratnaswamy who made the swim in twenty-seven hours in 1954.); the Straits of Gibraltar, in eight hours one minute; the Dardanelles, in thirteen hours fifty-five minutes, and the English Channel in fourteen hours and forty-five minutes.

In the latter part of October, 1966 Mihir showed up at the Panama Canal. On October 29 he started his swim from the Atlantic Ocean end. For fifteen hours Mihir clipped along at the pro rate. Then disaster struck in the form of leg cramps. Mihir got out of the water and massaged his legs for an hour and thirty minutes. He then felt able to continue his swim, even though defeated in his nonstop attempt. Seventeen hours and forty-five minutes later Mihir reached the Pacific Ocean. Mihir Sen had made the fifty miles in thirty-two hours forty-five minutes swimming time and, counting his one and a half hours out of the water, thirty-four hours fifteen minutes elapsed time. Needless to say it was only in piecing together several different accounts of the swim that I was able to arrive at the truth. No account gave the complete story, thus many will continue to believe that Mihir's swim was a nonstop one. Let the buyer beware.

Let us for a moment reverse our tracks and mention a pool accomplishment that deserves a note. After we left Myrtle Huddleston in her New York pool in 1930 after eighty-five hours fifteen minutes of floating I commented on the ennui of her endeavor. Well, it wasn't enough for Myrtle to rest on her laurels, for she came back a year later to extend her "fame" by two hours. In 1931 she spent eighty-seven hours twenty-seven minutes in the same pool. This time she quieted her critics by swimming a few lengths every once in a while. It would be nice to know just how many lengths she did do. This leads us into the names of a few people who did put some effort into pool swimming. Such was John Van Wormer who became bored with some of the basket cases that wheeled themselves down to the Illinois Athletic Club pool in 1963. The club's fame had slowly declined ever since the era of Johnny Weismuller and Van Wormer decided to recapture a portion of it. So Van Wormer swam twenty-five miles in the pool, which was a record for that pool. Relishing in the glory of fellow members' handshakes and the plaque awarded him, Van Wormer sat back to enjoy what he felt would be a lifetime record engraved in the archives of the club. He had a short reign, for several months later two renowned professional swimmers showed up at the club and made Van Wormer's "record" look like a Girl Scout patty-cake championship. Ted Erikson and Dennis Matuch, both of Chicago, jumped into the I.A.C. pool on April 4, 1963. Matuch would attempt to break Van Wormer's twenty-five-mile record for time, and Erikson would try to establish a world's record for all pools. Twelve hours fifty minutes later Matuch left the water after swimming twenty-six miles. He knocked a couple of hours off Van Wormer's now defunct record. Erikson, methodically swimming, also broke Van Wormer's record, but kept on going. At the end of twenty-two hours seventeen minutes Erikson was chased out of the pool by the manager because ladies day was approaching and the paying members of the club would be mad if their wives missed their swim. In that time however Erikson had raked up forty miles (3,520 lengths), which became a world's record that was to last for a couple of years. It was then that a young Milwaukee swimmer did forty-five miles in a pool. The lad mentioned seeing "cotton balls" floating on the water during the last hours of his swim. I think I would have seen a lot more. Erikson saw red, not because of his record being superseded, but because of the pool manager chasing him out of the water after forty miles a couple of years earlier. He felt that he could have easily gone fifty miles. I guess we should admire such accomplishments, but being a lover of the outdoors, I have to dig deep to find the remnants of his admiration. Pool swims smack too much like marathon dancing and flagpole sitting. Perhaps it's heresy, but. . . .

To prevent the reader from being jaded by these miscellaneous swims mentioned I'll drop the subject now. However, I will pick them up intermittently throughout the rest of the book. Perhaps, however, I should throw a bone to the serious readers, who may also include those not interested in sports. There is an island in Polynesia called Nina Fo'ou where in the twenties and thirties the water was so rough and the reefs so treacherous, that no boat dare come closer than half a mile to the island. Only an excellent swimmer, with a long pole to ride like a surf-board and superb timing, can make headway with any degree of safety through the surf. The swimmer will loop two forty-pound cannisters loaded with mail over each shoulder, enter the water and make his way through it with corresponding planing and diving. Thus it can be seen that swimming can serve a useful and productive trade.

18
How to Swim Six Miles or More an Hour: The River Swims

The river swims are enigmas. They lend themselves to distortion and therefore gigantic claims of enormous distances swum. The experienced swimmer and trainer cannot be fooled by these claims. They know the top average speed of a good pro is around two miles per hour. After twenty-four hours this speed drops off by three to five tenths of a mile per hour. After a day and a half in the water it's anybody's guess as to when the swimmer will fall asleep. It was only after giving the subject some thought that I decided to include some of the river swims and only because there are a few professional races held therein. The point should be made, however, that all those huge distances claimed to be swum were by individual swimmers. For some reason they seem to shy away from participating in a group race. They are too slow and seek fame with the solo attempts. But more of that later.

A river is just a body of water that moves. How fast it moves is characteristic of time and situation. Some are slow, almost oozing bodies, while others are wild and turbulent racetracks. Primitive man chasing game, fleeing enemies, or swimming from an overturned canoe or raft soon learned all he needed to learn about rivers, especially the wide ones. He learned to respect them, and being utilitarian minded, to use them. Ancient man being also a conserver of energy rarely ventured into their depths bodily. There were too many predators awaiting him, from the tiny candiru, a needlelike fish, with a one-way barb that swims up the urethra, in some South American rivers, to crocodiles and man-eating fish like the piranha. He stuck to surface vessels.

Exploration of new lands by the original natives or Europeans demanded the crossing of rivers. In most cases they sought to ford the river, that is, wade across at some point where it was shallow enough. If such an area could not be found after many miles of wandering along the bank they finally built rafts on which to load their livestock and supplies. Accidents did occur and when they did the pioneer drowned. People in those days rarely knew how to swim. It wasn't until several generations later when the towns had reached a sizable proportion that the sporting element of river swimming came to the fore. Before this the challenge was swimming across the river. This could be any distance from a few yards to five or six miles in some of the larger rivers like the Missouri and Mississippi. It didn't take long before a swimmer realized it was much more fun and delightfully pleasant to be carried along with the current once he overcame his initial fear. It was an effortless feat and highly exhilarating to watch the banks of the river go sliding by. A swimmer soon learned that by getting "into the mainstream" he moved ahead effortlessly. The term was actually adopted from riverboat operators. The advantages of such an act, whether literal or figurative, are readily seen. Well, it remains more or less without effort, unless it becomes a race. Then the idyllic endeavor is forgotten and the situation becomes much like that of the *Alice in Wonderland* character who said, "It takes all the running you can do to stay in the same place. If you want to get any where you've got to run twice as fast."

The earliest American records that I could find, and I must confess to not looking too hard, are the Mississippi and Missouri river swims. It seems these swims got their start around the turn of the century when the Missouri Athletic Club became the sponsor of a ten-mile swim down the Mississippi River at St. Louis. The Kansas City Athletic Club soon followed suit with their own ten-mile Missouri River swim. It soon became a rivalry and it wasn't long before they were holding their races on the same day. These ten mile swims, if they were ten miles, were accomplished in times like one hour twenty-eight minutes and one hour fifty minutes. It can be seen that the swimmers were aided by a five- to six-mile-per-hour current. I guess criticism of these swims should not be made since man will swim wherever there is water, and since the river was the only large body available they naturally swam and competed there. The Great Lakes and Atlantic and Pacific Oceans are pretty far away from St. Louis and Kansas City.

With the success of the first two Wrigley swims, Catalina Island in 1927, and the first Toronto marathon in 1928, everyone got into the act. In 1928 there was a professional marathon river swim from Montreal to Sorel, a distance of thirty miles. The winner of that race was none other than the "winner" of the second Wrigley marathon at Toronto, Georges Michel. He was the only finisher and covered the distance in the St. Lawrence River in eleven hours ten minutes. The

The River Swims

$500 he pocketed was enough to live on for a couple of years then.

The nineteen twenties was the era of crazy stunts. In the United States there were all sorts of attention-getting acts from flagpole sitters to marathon dancers and cyclists. After the stock market crash in 1929 there was a sudden sobering up. There were also many who had lots of time on their hands. One individual who found something to do to wile away the time was an Argentinian named Pedro Candiotti. He lived in one of those back-river towns that isn't even large enough to earn a place on the map of Argentina. However, within

Parana River and Rio de La Plata Swims

Candiotti's lifetime goal was to swim from Santa Fe to Buenos Aires, a distance of some three hundred miles. He never made it. Abertondo, the first man to make a double crossing of the English Channel, once did fifty miles in the La Plata.

walking distance was the famous Parana River that flows for hundreds of miles in Northeastern Argentina before it joins with the Uruguay River in emptying into the River de la Plata. Like so many addictions Candiotti's early swims began with just "little ones" of twenty or thirty miles downstream. By the end of the year Pedro was hooked. He was making twenty-four-hour swims from the town of Santa Fe to other towns seventy-five miles downstream. By 1931 Pedro was ready for his claim to fame. At the age of thirty-eight he realized that he had only a few years in which to make good. And what he wanted to make good at was a swim from Santa Fe to Buenos Aires, a distance of three hundred miles. The water temperatures would give no difficulty for it would be in the upper eighties. While much is to be said for Candiotti's endurance, not much is to be said for his planning. No matter how you slice it the last forty miles of the swim would be subject to the tidal effect of the Atlantic Ocean. Any swimmer after reaching the Rio de la Plata would have to face at least one flood tide *after* having spent some two to three days swimming and floating.

The urges of the psyche and the body's urge to release its energy overcame any latent fears of possible failure and thus, Pedro Candiotti began his three-hundred-mile swim on March 13, 1931. Three days later seventy one hours fifty-five minutes to be exact—Pedro was taken from the water some 4½ miles below Baradaro. He had covered some 211 miles. How many miles he actually swam is anybody's guess. After thirty to forty hours of swimming it is a wonder if any progress is made. We can be sure the current did a lot for Pedro. That swim marked the first of what would be about twenty different attempts by him to satisfy his life-long ambition. His last attempt was sometime in 1943 when he left from Rosario. He was in the water some 74½ hours before the tide turned against him. After some fifteen years it was made clear to him that the tide would always defeat a swimmer in that last forty miles. He hadn't even been able to make the swim when it had been whittled down to 205 miles. All in all, when Candiotti looked back on his attempts even he was surprised at his best effort. That was in 1935 when he had "swum" from Santa Fe to Zarate, a distance of 281 miles. It had taken some eighty-four hours. Candiotti spent more time in the water on long swims than any other swimmer. He also started a whole series of long swims in the United States. Before long there were claims by the hundreds of swims down any river of suitable length.

In 1938 Charles Zimmy was said to have swum 147 miles down the Hudson River from Albany to New York City. He was legless. Clarence Giles then spent from June 30 to July 3, 1939 in the Yellowstone River when he "swam" the 288 miles from Blendive to Billings in seventy-seven hours. Everybody was amazed at his 3.7 miles per hour average when credit should be given to the Yellowstone River. Also,

The River Swims

claims like that come out of back-woods areas where the "folk" like to put on their city brethren. When I put my compass to my National Geographic Atlas and Rand McNally Road Atlas I could get no more than 220 miles between the two cities. Sixty-eight miles is a considerable amount of error than can be taken care of by the bends and turns in the river. Such are the canards foisted upon the gullible.

In July, 1940 John V. Sigmund was supposed to have swum nonstop from St. Louis, Missouri down the Missouri River for 297 miles. He was in the water eighty-nine hours forty-nine minutes. It was claimed to be a swim that was officially recorded and checked. In the sources I've seen there is no arrival point given. While it is entirely possible that these distances have been done it must be remembered that the river does most of the work. When we begin to compare the professional races in rivers, especially those held in South America, we see that after fifteen hours or so the swimmers have ceased to put much effort into it. In June, 1970 the great Abo-Heif attempted to accomplish what Candiotti had failed to do. He went sixty hours in the water and was said to have been within fifteen miles of Buenos Aires before falling asleep in the water. All I know is that when I

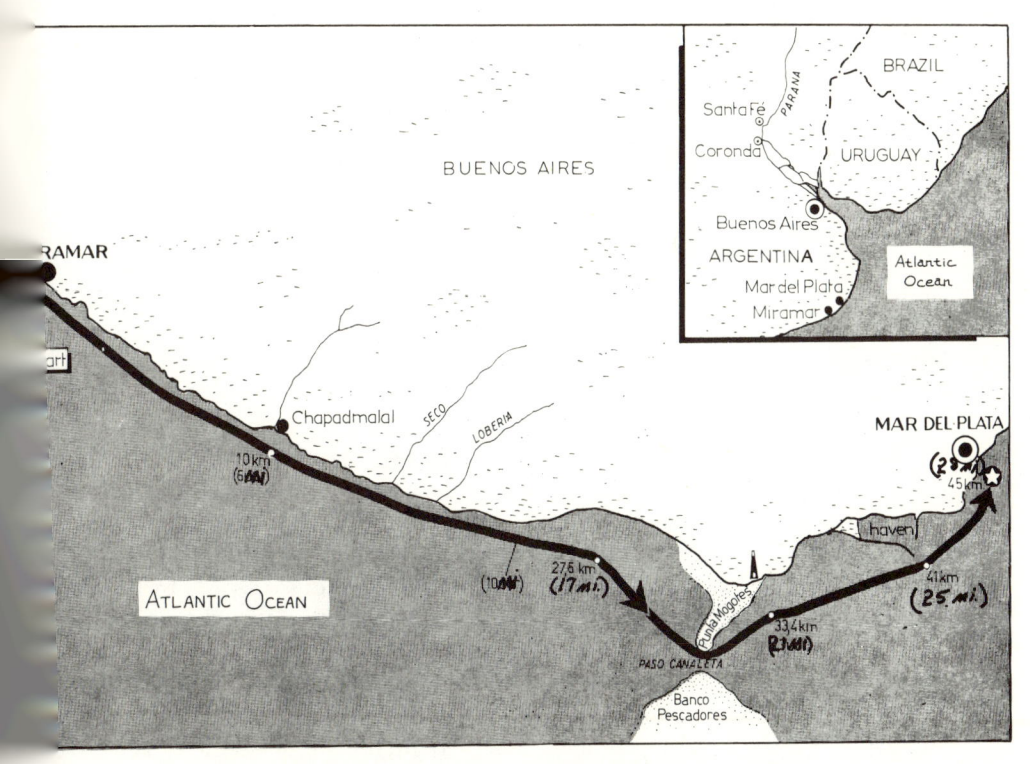

The Argentine Miramar to Mar Del Plata swim.

saw Abo-Heif a month later he was some forty to fifty pounds lighter than normal. The swim and consequent diarrhea had taken its toll.

In any case the 1950s saw the arrival of professional swimming in South America. The resort areas catering to the wealthy tourist did their best to stir up interest in the area around Buenos Aires. There was never any steady year-to-year swim. It was a spontaneous thing in which a group of hotel owners would get together a couple of months before such and such a date and announce a swim. The swim would be held that year, only to be dropped for several years, and then be picked up in some other locale. By the mid-1950s there were a few established swims in South America. There was the Parana River Marathon, which ran from Corondo to Santa Fe, Argentina. In 1970 the promoters made this a twenty-four-hour team race in one of the small lakes around Santa Fe. Swimmers suffered in the eighty-degree water. Then the coastal cities of Miramar and Mar Del Plata decided to hold a swim in the Atlantic Ocean between their two cities. It was a distance of twenty-seven miles. Among the entrants in these swims was Antonio Abertondo. He learned he was out of his class in these professional swims so he began his long swims in an attempt to surpass the famous Candiotti. Among Abertondo's long swims was one in which he crossed the fifty-mile-wide River de la Plata where it separated Uruguay from Argentina. He accomplished the distance in something like thirty hours. He went on to historical fame when he became the first man to make a double cross of the English Channel.

By the late 1950s professional swimming had reached such popularity in Argentina that as many as 300,000 would watch a race from the bridges and banks of the Parana. The amount of publicity gained by the promoters was tremendous when one considers the total purse of only $4,000 to $5,000 offered for these twenty-five- to thirty-five-mile swims. In fact one year there was a tremendous "fight" between the promoters and swimmers when the swimmers found out that the checks they received for the race were no good. Somebody had made off with the money. From this day on many foreign swimmers will not enter a South American race unless the prize money is held in escrow.

There are a few river swims in Europe, mainly in Yugoslavia. Whether the Suez Canal can be considered a "river" swim is debatable. I hesitate to accept the accounts I read about river swims unless I'm there myself to judge conditions. There is no doubt that they can be the most challenging and exciting of swims. With due respect to Candiotti I think the champion current swimmer remains the human sperm. The tiny creature swims *against* the current in the uterus, which flows downward and outward, and then through most of the uterine tube. The battle these microscopic creatures make is a story in itself. At its fastest it moves about 1/18,000 mile an hour. It's a fatal race for millions. Only the one that reaches the egg first survives, that is if twinning is not involved. The rest are doomed. Human marathon swimmers never had it so good.

19
Two of the Toughest Swims in the World: Juan de Fuca and the Farallons

It has to go down as one of the toughest swims in the world. The double-crossing of the English Channel is tough; the Irish Sea is tough; Lake Ontario can be tough depending on the water temperature. The Strait of Juan de Fuca is always tough, for the water temperature never goes above fifty-three degrees. In most cases it hangs around forty-eight degrees. The strait separates the state of Washington from the Canadian island of Vancouver. At its narrowest point the strait is only eleven miles wide, and each shore is a sparsely populated area. The Canadian side is also dangerous in virtue of a group of rocks known as Race Rocks, around which the ebb and flood tides "race." A swimmer in the wrong place at the wrong time cannot avoid being swept into rocks.

For this reason the *Victoria Times* offered $1,000 to the first person crossing the strait between the city of Victoria on the Canadian side, and the city of Port Angeles on the American side. The distance was twenty miles. The newspaper made the offer in April, 1955 and early July saw four men and three women having tried and failed in their attempts to collect the thousand dollars. If they had paid attention to their school geography lessons they would have remembered that Juan de Fuca lies at a forty-eight degrees north latitude. An attempt in late July or the month of August would have given the water time to warm up a little. As it was they plunged in too early in the season. The water was registering in the low or mid-forties. Perhaps the fear of someone else being successful spurred them on and greed overcame discretion. But then marathon swimmers are not noted for discretion. Among those who were attempting to collect the "easy" buck was a Tacoma logger named Bert Thomas. After four unsuccessful tries

Thomas went home to his wife saying that the only thing that would beat the straits was fat. Over the winter Bert, with the help of his loving wife, who was also an excellent cook, had managed to add forty pounds to his already huge six-foot two-inch frame. On his last attempt he had weighed 230 pounds. In just a little over ten days before his latest attempt Bert, putting Diamond Jim Brady to shame, added a further ten pounds by consuming gallons of milk and pounds of steak, potatoes, bread, and desserts. The 270 pound, barrel-chested American then had himself driven to Port Angeles on the American side. To hell with leaving from Victoria; he had done that four times and each time had met with failure. It was mid-July, and the water had "warmed up" to forty-eight degrees. He and his crew climbed into the launch and began their run out to the breakwater protecting the city. The harbor was a dirty, oil-streaked industrial harbor that included sewer run-offs from the city. The ebbing and flooding tides took tons of sewage daily from the cities on the straits. The twenty-nine-year-old behemoth stepped out onto the breakwater from the launch along with a few of his handlers. He greased down and wisely put on a rubber bathing cap. It was not one of those useless men's caps that doesn't cover the ears and rides high on the head, but a snug and efficient women's cap that covers the ears and reaches down low on the neck. Bert must have thought he was going to be in the water a long time for he was starting his swim at 6:50 P.M. He would have only a couple of hours of light before the night would cast its blanket over the scene. Then again there was a gentle ebb tide at that time. Bert, after his four previous failures, was now listening to the men whose business was to sail the straits.

In two hours Bert had put almost four miles between him and Port Angeles. The wind remained calm for once, and a gentle swell replaced the usual chop. There were three boats accompanying Bert: a cruiser, a schooner, and a rowboat. The schooner would ply ahead seeking favorable currents while the cruiser and rowboat stayed with Bert. By midnight Bert was half way across and riding a flood tide away from Race Rocks. The gentle ebb had pulled him to within three miles of the rocks, but now he was being gently pulled to the east again. It was a case similar to the English Channel. Maintain a fixed bearing—as long as the tide direction is from the side—and let it take you with it. You don't swim any farther even though it may look like it on the map. The straight-line distance remains the same. The seventy pounds of insulative fat kept Bert in a remarkably good humor. Around 1 A.M. he asked, "How am I doin? I want the truth." One of his handlers said, and it was not the truth, "You've gone 1½ miles in the last twenty minutes." Bert then called out, "You fellas got nothing to worry about. Sit back and relax." Bert saw the city of Victoria from a distance of about eight miles. There was no difficulty in picking out his goal.

If it were any other night there may have been some difficulty, but tonight, no. Sixty percent of the inhabitants had turned on their lights so the city appeared as a sparkling jewel. With a goal like that Bert needed no other incentive. He picked up the pace and, surprisingly enough, when dawn broke he was close enough to the Victoria shoreline to see the crowds gathering. Bert landed at 6:07 A.M., having made the swim in eleven hours seventeen minutes. His wife's arms, the crowd's cheers and the municipal ambulance prepared to whisk him downtown for a hot shower and the $1,000 check, all of which felt good to a man who was the first to conquer a strait tougher than the English Channel. It was also good to collect an additional $2,000 in bonuses.

The swim got such publicity that the next year two of the biggest names in professional swimming showed up to see if they could wring some money out of the area. They were doomed to failure. It was a local, onetime swim they were informed. The pros decided that they shouldn't waste time, however, and jumped in anyway. It would make a good training swim. In August, 1956, the famous Marilyn Bell of Lake Ontario fame, left Victoria and headed for Port Angeles. It was the reverse direction of that Thomas had swum. The tides pushed Marilyn several miles to the east of her intended route so that as a consequence she changed her goal to Green Point, some five miles east of Port Angeles. The cold water got to Marilyn and she went unconscious $5\frac{1}{2}$ miles from her goal. Her friends, including Cliff Lumsden, jumped into the water to prevent her drowning. She was put aboard the boat and sped to shore where she came around in the local hospital.

Cliff Lumsden waited around for a week while Marilyn recovered from the shock of her first immersion. He then took the same course as Marilyn originally intended and became the second person to swim the strait when he arrived at Port Angeles. He took eleven hours thirty-five minutes. He went an extra mile when at the last moment he switched to Green Point. Whether it was a planned change is a question.

Marilyn Bell was still recovering from her first immersion and beginning to plan a second try when a Long Beach, California housewife by the name of Mrs. Amy Hiland became the third person, and the first woman, to swim the straits. Her course took her from the breakwater at Port Angeles to William Head. Whether it was the original course planned, or a last-minutes alternative because of weakening or tidal drift, I don't know. In any case hers was a fifteen-mile course and it took her ten hours fifty-one minutes. That was on August 18th. Inflamed Marilyn Bell, her thunder stolen, dove into the water from the Port Angeles breakwater and headed toward Victoria with fire in her eyes. She needed it, for the water was as cold as ever. In any case (she started at 11:30 A.M.) she made Victoria in ten hours

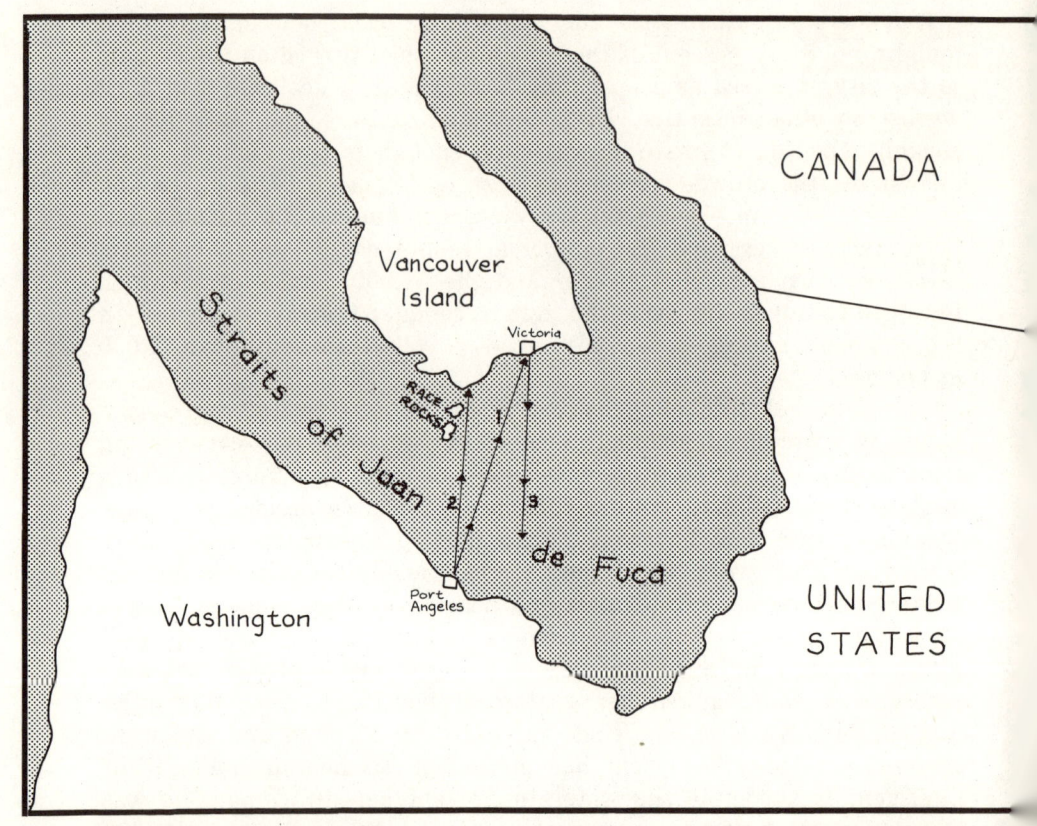

The Strait of Juan de Fuca separates the state of Washington (United States) from the island of Vancouver (Canada). The water temperatures vary from the mid-forties to no warmer than fifty. This makes it one of the toughest swims in the world.

1. Bert Thomas's successful first (July, 1955).
2. Mrs. Amy Hiland's route (August 18, 1956); she was the first woman to succeed.
3. Marilyn Bell's unsuccessful first attempt (August, 1956). She later followed Bert Thomas's route and set the record.

thirty-nine minutes for a new record. When she arrived at the Victoria beach at 10:09 P.M. there were only a handful of people gathered there. She was now the fourth person to do the straits, and the second woman. But people had lost interest. There were no crowds running into the tens of thousands waiting for her like Lake Ontario a couple of years before. She was now eighteen years old and running to fat. She was no longer the demure 120-pound girl she was when she made that swim. She was now 150 pounds and it didn't look good on her five foot two inch frame. Marilyn made that swim her final effort and within the year she was married. Three children were soon to follow.

The short history of one of the world's toughest swims came to an end as quickly as it started. Today only a few of the old-timers remember that Straits of Juan de Fuca. They remember Bert Thomas also; the rest, maybe. The new swimmers ask, "Juan de Fuca, where's that?" Go back to your geography books kids. That swim, done in forty-eight-degree water, is one of the toughest in the world. What is the other? Stay with your map of the west coast of Canada and the United States.

Run your finger from the Straits of Juan de Fuca southward about six inches. You'll then come to San Francisco and one of the seven engineering wonders of the world: the Golden Gate Bridge. Forget about Alcatraz. It's only a mile from downtown San Francisco and has been done countless times by freelancers and members of swimming clubs. In fact one magician did it with handcuffs. No trick to it, he just let the tide take him to shore. The tide ripping into or out of the harbor entrance is just like a river stream. Just hope it's going in the right direction. No, direct your finger directly west from the city of San Francisco out into the Pacific Ocean. If your map is good you'll find some printing somewhere about thirty miles out. It will say Farallon Islands. If you run your finger to Bolinas Point, some ten miles north of San Francisco, to the Farallons the distance will be twenty-one miles. A point to remember in the story to follow: the largest of the group—Southeast Farallon—is an irregularly shaped rocky island with a maximum length in any direction of only five hundred yards. The only inhabitants are some lighthouse tenders and the birds. The light is one of the most powerful on the coast of California, standing 358 feet above the water, and it protects the heavy steamer traffic from coming to grief on the rocky shores of the Farallons. The lighthouse keepers don't mind it and the birds appreciate the sanctuary. A few fishing boats ply their trade out there. In 1963 swimmers began arriving from boats to momentarily step ashore before diving into the water and heading for the Golden Gate, and the "golden" fame and fortune that awaited the first person to make the swim. They would be startled if they were told that it was the 1960s, not the 1920s. Only a few die-hards would be interested in such feats today.

By 1964 fifteen top swimmers had failed to make the swim. Most of them had heard of the Lake Michigan swims, which gave a stimulus to all kinds of long-distance endeavors. A few of the top men from Southern California came up to look at the scene. They bought the Coast and Geodetic map #5072 and got out their rulers. Measuring from the largest southeast island to the Golden Gate Bridge they came up with 30½ miles. This was the only acceptable goal. Over the years

San Franciscans, whenever they discussed the swim, talked about the tentative landing being somewhere on the shores bordering the city. Ideally, the best landing would be within the bay itself. Fisherman's Wharf was one select spot. The rulers were also run to other points along the coast. Ten miles could be knocked off the swim if you landed at Bolinas Point, some ten miles North of San Francisco. Another possible landing point was Point Reyes, a further ten miles up the coast. To either of these two points the swim would be about twenty-one miles. The only greetings that a successful swimmer would receive at these points would be from some seals. The cliffs and rocky beaches prevented any accumulation of people. It was therefore with covetous eyes that the would-be hero looked at the Golden Gate Bridge area. Water temperatures for the swim could be anywhere from the mid-fifties to the low sixties. However this was only half the story.* San Francisco Bay is one of the largest bays in the world. The opening leading to the bay, which the Golden Gate Bridge spans, is actually less than a mile wide. Tremendous amounts of water enter and leave through this narrow passage during flood and ebb tide. Beneath the bridge at maximum ebb tide the velocity of the water moving out can reach ten miles per hour; at maximum flood tide, six miles per hour. Ergo, if a swimmer is in the right place at the right time he gets a free ride beginning about five miles directly west of the bridge. For four hours he will receive the benefits of a tidal current sweeping into the narrow inlet. It starts at about one-plus mile per hour and ends up at about six miles per hour under the bridge. If he is anywhere in the vicinity before and at ebb tide he might as well get out of the water and go home. There isn't a swimmer yet who can make headway against a four- to ten-mile-per-hour current. After learning the above facts, the swimmer usually learned from his boat captain the final one. They had better stay clear of the main shipping channel. The two-thousand-foot-wide channel marked by lighted buoys shows the best route for oceangoing vessels. They cannot stop on a dime. Besides, any vessel lolling around in the area better have a good excuse ready for the Coast Guard. If not satisfactory, a fine sharpens the infringing captain's awareness of where he should and should not be. All points considered, the fact offering the greatest obstacle to the completion of this swim was, and remains, the water temperature. Using all your skills you could outwit the tides, but in the final analy-

---

* In 1963 there were several shark attacks on scuba-divers in the waters around the Farallons. Leroy French, while spear fishing, was attacked twice by the notorious white shark. It took five hundred stitches to sew up the wounds on his buttock, calf, hands, and foot. It was four months before he left the hospital. He returned to diving. Just about the time French was leaving the hospital Jack Rochette, another diver, was attacked by a shark in the same spot. He also survived.

sis, the body had to be immersed in the heat-draining water. By the time Ted Erikson arrived in San Francisco in 1966, the number of failures had increased to seventeen. When he arrived in San Francisco, Ted made his way as soon as possible to the Dolphin Club, whose members are veteran swimmers. Ted learned of some of the big names that had tried the swim and failed. Greta Andersen was one, Leonore Modell was another. Leonore held the record for being the youngest swimmer to ever cross the English Channel. She was only thirteen when she did it. Leonore was taken from the water exhausted a scant three or four miles from the Golden Gate on September 4, 1965. She was back for another try this year.

Veteran swimmer Ike Papke was also back for another try. Ike was a friendly 240-pound Hawaiian grandfather who worked for the Matson Steamship Company, whose navigation department was even now plotting the course for this year's attempt. He and Ted hit it off well in the clubhouse of the Dolphin Club. One of the interesting points discussed was the club's annual swim across the bay. It was just one of the swims the club planned to help enliven the membership. In fact one year they got too much publicity when one of the tugs coursing through the bay cut through a pack of six of the swimmers accidentally. Two of the swimmers were severely injured—one losing a hand, the other a foot. The tug kept on going unaware of the damage it had done. Another interesting swim discussed by Papke and Ted was the Alcatraz Island swim. Alcatraz has gained fame throughout the world because of its movie-subject material. It is supposed to be an impossible swim that none could survive once dropped in the water from the island. As far as the Dolphin Club members were concerned it was pure hog-wash. Alcatraz lies only one scant mile from the north boundary of San Francisco. At slack tide a poor swimmer could almost float ashore. Members of the club had done it many times. In fact a few years back a magician had his hands tied behind his back and actually let the current drift him to a landing spot on shore. A competent swimmer could actually swim, paying attention to tidal conditions of course, to almost any spot in the bay from Alcatraz.

And so it went for hours. Yet with all the accomplishments discussed, the Farallons remained unconquered. The Dolphin Club was even getting annoyed with its own members and was now offering to pay boat expenses to any competent swimmer willing to make the try. Ted contacted the president and let it be known that he would devote the month of August to attempts on the Farallons. Now that he was here he took a great interest in the facts being recounted to him by Papke. The next day Papke drove him out to Baker's Beach where they spent a couple of hours in the fifty-five-degree water, keeping an eye out for sharks at all times. Papke, in passing, mentioned that it was only ten years ago that the fiancee of a man was attacked by a shark. He dove into the water to rescue her, only to be killed himself. These were not pleasant thoughts and not a bit consoling to a marathon swimmer. Ted would keep it in mind however. How could anyone not?

Ted spent a week testing out the waters around the harbor and by mid-August he was ready for his try. Knowing that tidal conditions would only be significant three or four miles from the bridge, it would not be important to pick a particular date. However, the time of departure from the islands was all important since it governed the arrival time in the vicinity of the Golden Gate. If you could be within three or four miles of the Gate at the beginning of flood tide you had a free ride the rest of the way. If not, forget it.

On August 15, 1966 at 6:15 A.M. Ted and his crew were idling a hundred yards off the Southeast Farallons in their motor launch. Quickly he greased up, putting on a rubber cap and goggles, and was rowed ashore in a dinghy. Ted took the water temperature. When he read the dial, he shook his head and flipped it to a crew member. It registered fifty-two degrees. At 7:40 A.M. Ted began his swim. By noon the water had moved up to fifty-five degrees and Ted had covered almost eight miles. By mid-afternoon the water temperature had increased by only one more degree. It was then that shark fins began to appear around Ted. The captain of the launch brought out his high-powered rifle and fired a few shots at the creatures. They disappeared from the vicinity but reappeared several hours later. It was a weary Ted Erikson that was still stroking as the sun went down that day. It was now 8:30 P.M. and the bridge was only four miles away. But the water temperature had taken its toll. Ted had slowed down to less than one mile an hour, far below his norm. By midnight it was evident that he had reached the end of his endurance. They were only a scant two miles from the bridge. In another hour the ebb tide would begin. For another forty minutes Ted ignored the pleas of his crew and seemed little more than wearily flailing the water while his vacant eyes, on the verge of unconsciousness, stared out from beneath the rubber goggles. At 12:40 A.M. it was all over. He was out cold as if he had been hammered unconscious by a pugilistic opponent. Quickly, crew members dove into the water to prevent him from drowning. He was quickly hauled aboard with ropes. Blankets were wrapped around the spasmodically shaking form. The boat captain radioed ahead to the yacht harbor to have an ambulance waiting. It was only a ten minute run before the boat reached the yacht club in the inner harbor; too soon for the ambulance to have arrived yet. Crew members massaged Ted in hopes of reviving him. They were scared, for he appeared on the verge of imminent death. His body felt like ice and appeared blanched white. The ambulance finally arrived and Ted was on his way to the hospital. He had regained enough of his senses to call for a hot water immersion in a bathtub. Just before he went in the nurse got his temperature at ninety-degrees. Two hours later, while still in the tub it was ninety-three degrees. Ted spent the night in the hospital and left the following morning. It would be two weeks before he felt ready for another try. Seventeen hours in water varying from fifty-two to fifty-six degrees can take a lot out of a man.

Two weeks later, on September 1, 1966, Ted made his second attempt. The water temperature was about the same as on the first try, but after ten hours Ted became nauseous and had to quit. He was surprised to find that the nausea disappeared a couple of hours later with the return of his appetite. He revised his earlier diagnosis of bad food to sea-sickness from watching the bobbing boat from the water while he was swimming. Ted never mentioned it but perhaps he never did recover from that first swim, which was every bit as tough as the 1964 Lake Ontario and even tougher than Juan de Fuca. Any way you cut it, swimming in waters that registered in the low and middle fifties for the periods of time that Ted did, places him in a very select category in which only a few other swimmers are capable of earning a place.

Ike Papke waited until everyone had gone home before he made his attempt. It was rather late in the year, October 17 to be exact, but the water temperature was still in the mid-fifties. Ike set his goal for Stinson Beach some ten miles North of the Golden Gate. It would only be a twenty-two-mile swim to this point. In any case a swimmer would have made the mainland. After the great Ted Erikson, the conqueror of the round-trip channel, had failed, any swimmer making the mainland would have earned the right to call himself the conqueror of the Farallons. Starting at 2 A.M. and following the course laid out by his employers, Ike Papke made excellent progress. However, with only $1\frac{1}{8}$ miles to go he was taken from the water in almost the same condition as Ted. The cold and the kidney pain had finally gotten to him. The forty-year-old grandfather said that he would never again try to swim the Farallons. And to this day he hasn't.

Ike Papke need not feel bad over his $1\frac{1}{8}$-mile loss. Twice in the twenty-three-mile Saguenay River swim swimmers have given up with far less to go. In 1968 Pedro Gomez of Argentina collapsed just thirty yards from the finish line. After swimming twenty-two-plus miles, he was defeated by the last thirty yards. The same thing happened to young Jon Erikson in the 1971 race. That year due to tidal conditions the race was about sixteen miles, and the seventeen-year-old swimming son of Ted collapsed just fifty yards from the finish.

Ike Papke's attempt was the last one in 1966. The fall season now setting in put an end to any more Farallon Island attempts. But there were two men who were settling down to a winter's hobby of studying the nautical charts, tide tables, and water temperature maps of the area. Needless to say one was Ted Erikson. The other, and nobody had ever heard of him, was a forty-one-year-old Army Signal Corps officer by the name of Colonel Stewart A. Evans. Col. Evans throughout that winter would make a meticulous study of the available navigational material. He was also sure not to miss his daily swim in the army pool when he finished working each day. Col. Evans was taking his middle-age paunch seriously and he meant to do something about it. Being also a practical man he was goal oriented. Mindless laps in a pool were not very satisfying to the body or the soul. So each night, when he got home, he took out his nautical chart and scanned the line running from the Southeast Farallons to—not the Golden Gate Bridge—but Bolinas Point. The Colonel knew all too well that he was forty-one years old. If the great Ted Erikson, with all his accomplishments, failed making the Golden Gate, what chance had he? He would take the short route. Twenty-one miles was enough for a forty-one-year-old man. Ted could have the thirty-one-mile route. That was for the younger men.

Everyone looks for spring. Winter, and its enforced limitations, produce an ennui in swimmers no less than in others. They look forward to the return to outdoor immersion in the lakes, streams, and oceans. Ted Erikson began his training in Lake Michigan in April when the water registered in the upper forties. Col. Evans began his outdoor training half a continent away in the Pacific Ocean at about the same time in water that was the same temperature. Little did they know that unusual climatic conditions were already influencing the waters of the Pacific Ocean around San Francisco. It would affect them both. The law of chance, dressed as a jester, was preparing his hand with a smile.

The first serious attempt in 1967 was supposed to be made by young Miss Modell. She never did show up. For one reason or another her coach was off on other affairs. The weeks wore on as a few unknown swimmers made their feeble attempts. Success did not crown their efforts. As the weeks rolled by Erikson stayed in Chicago. He was planning to wait until the last of the summer. He figured that the water would be its warmest sometime in September. His reasoning would turn out to be true except for one fact. It would also be at its warmest the last two weeks in August. When Erikson picked up his Chicago newspaper for August 28, 1967 he kicked himself for his cautiousness. Colonel Stu Evans had become the first man to swim from the Farallons to the coast.

The forty-one-year-old army officer had left the Farallons at 10:15 P.M. on Sunday, August 27th. He was surprised to find the water temperature fifty-eight degrees. He and his handlers would be even more surprised to find it warming up to a welcome sixty-one degrees during the daylight hours. Col. Evans was feeling quite happy over the water temperature and kept up a strong stroke rate of fifty-eight per minute. He had learned well during his study and conversations with marathon swimmers of the terrible psychological effect of darkness. He thus chose to make sure that he would not be caught in a situation where he would be forced to swim at night during the latter hours of his swim. He would get at least the first half of his swim over with at night while he was strong. When dawn broke he would have the whole day, twelve hours, to accomplish the latter half—an elementary deduction, but one that all too many swimmers never think about.

All went well for the Colonel. He did slacken his pace somewhat, but his stroke rate never fell below forty-four per minute. The tidal stream drew him south, and then north of the straight line between the islands and Bolinas Point. His boat captain kept a constant compass heading, however, and the Colonel was never forced to swim a foot farther than a crow's flight distance. By dawn his situation looked good as he steadily stroked toward his mainland goal. Around 9 A.M. he was complaining of pain in his left shoulder. It had been bothering him for the last several hours but he had not mentioned it to the crew. He had consumed all the lemon jello he had. He had to be satisfied with carbonated drinks for the rest of the swim. Now came other trouble along with the shoulder pain. Shark fins began to appear around the boat and swimmer. Shots were fired in the water and boats began to run down the sharks. It was over an hour before they left the vicinity. By 10 A.M. the Colonel was in agony. He could hardly clear the water with his left arm. Bolinas Point was now drifting away from him to the north as the tidal current carried him south. If he didn't land at Duxbury Point he would have to swim an extra mile to the indented mainland. Stirred on by this unenviable situation he renewed his efforts. Relays of his swimming companions from the Dolphin Club jumped into the water to urge him on. Four hundred yards from shore he winced in agony and stopped. When the pain subsided he started again. There were five hundred persons gathered on the beach at Duxbury Point cheering the Colonel as he sounded in five feet of water. He stood up and slowly began to wade ashore. Ten yards from the dry sand he toppled forward and fell. "Crawl, Stu, crawl," yelled the crowd. He did, right up to the beach. The sand caked to his form and it was a grotesque looking, but all too human, Colonel that planted a kiss on his waiting wife's lips. He had landed at 12:03 P.M. The Farallons had been conquered in thirteen hours and forty-six minutes. Granted it was the shorter twenty-one-mile route, but all the same it was done. Miss Modell and Mr. Erikson had both been in the same waters and had gone farther in their attempts for the Golden Gate. Colonel Evans was the sensible one when he took the shorter route. After all the English Channel swimmers pick the

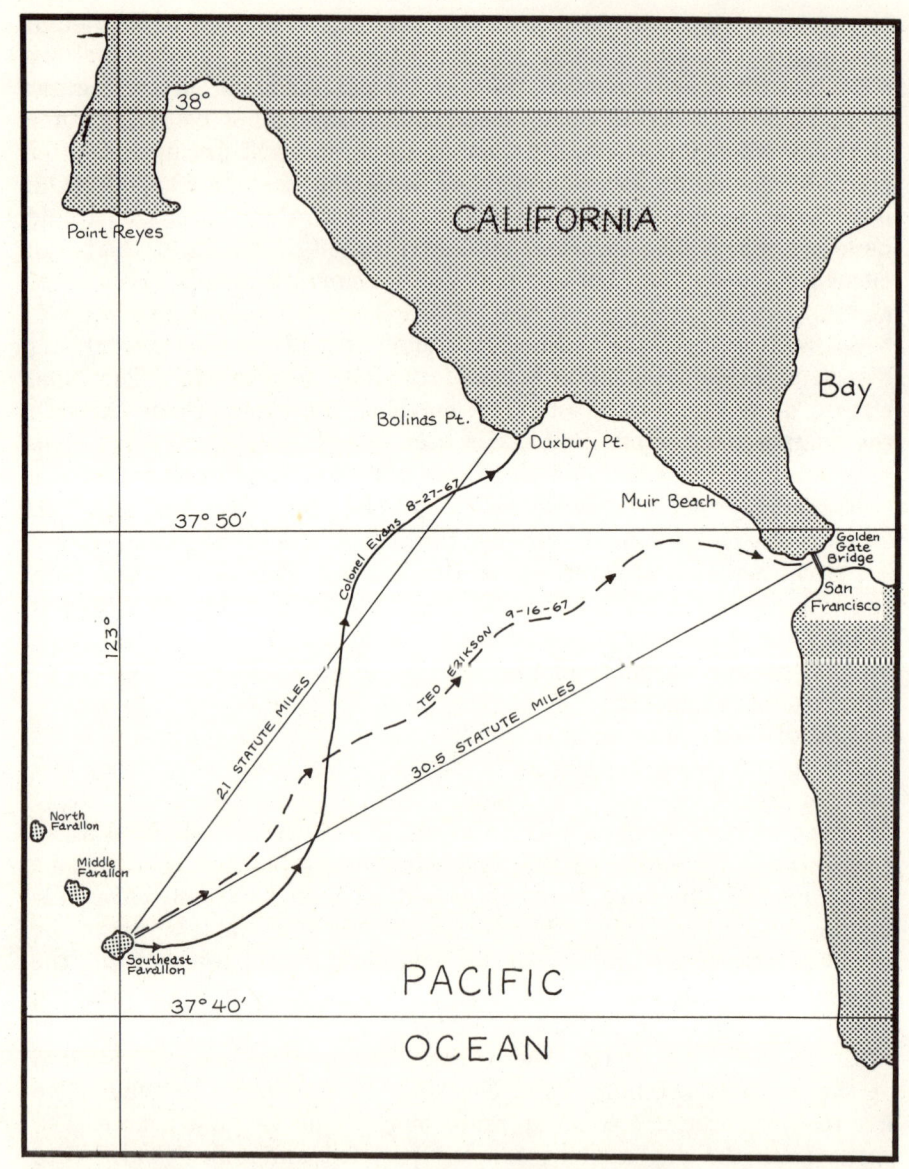

After decades of failures, the Gulf of the Farallons was conquered twice within a three-week period in 1967. The first person to make the mainland was Colonel Stewart Evans, who picked the shortest route: Southeast Farallon to Duxbury Point, a distance of twenty-one miles. Three weeks later Ted Erikson took the thirty-one mile route to the Golden Gate Bridge. It is a swim that is tougher than the English Channel because the water is colder and the distance longer. Tidal streams can hit ten miles per hour underneath the bridge at maximum ebb tide, and six miles per hour at maximum flood. You get a free ride to the bridge and beyond if you are at the right place at the right time. If not, get out of the water.

narrowest distance to swim between England and France. It's tough enough that way. Should the Farallons be any different? Ted Erikson thought differently; or did he? On his second attempt the year before he had set his goal as Muir Beach some four or five miles north of the Golden Gate. This year, with the success of Colonel Evans, there was only one alternative left: the Golden Gate and San Francisco. He had trained hard for six months. Over eight hundred miles of swimming were invested in the final swim of his career. Yes, the Farallons would be his last swim. This year he would retire after making some of the most extraordinary swims in the annals of marathon swimming. The story of Ted's swim is descriptively told in the observations of Paul W. Girard, who was the official observer on behalf of the Dolphin Club. The notes of the official navigator of the swim, Doug Lathrop, make interesting reading from the standpoint of navigation.

LOG

Swimmer: Ted Erikson
Date: September 16, 1967
Boat: Evie-K, Berkeley
Pilot: Captain David Kinley
Destination: Farallon Islands—Golden Gate Bridge
Start Time: 7:22 a.m. PDT
Finish: 10:00 p.m. PDT dead center, Golden Gate Bridge

OBSERVATIONS OF:
Paul W. Girard
1431 Michigan Street
Fairfield, California 94533

3:10 a.m. I board the Evie-K at the Berkeley Yacht Harbor with the Captain David Kinley and his son, David. The engines are started and the Captain tells me that the rectifier for the alternators is out of order, but that sufficient electrical power is being maintained by the battery system. Radio communications from the boat during the swim will be limited.

3:18 a.m. The Evie-K clears the Berkeley Harbor light enroute to the Dolphin Club where Ted Erikson and his party will board. It is a perfectly clear, dark morning, balmy almost to the tropical point. I estimate the outside temperature at 68°. Visibility is 5 miles or better. No wind.

3:43 a.m. Crossing close astern a tug and barge. Alcatraz Island is off the starboard bow. The fog is beginning to set in.

4:02 a.m. Entering Aquatic Park toward Dolphin Club. We receive signal from wharf and visual and audio to go the Standard Oil Wharf to pick up swimming team. Water is too low for boat to enter safely.

4:25 a.m. Swimmer and team aboard. We take KSFO's boat and newsman in tow. Enroute to the Islands all is uneventful. 5 miles west of the Farallons we encounter large amounts of red plankton in the water. It looks like a red tide. It is very pretty. The plankton is a good sign of warm water.

6:50 a.m. Ted comes up from bunk after taking a nap. Frank Drum and I add two packs of shark repellant to the Cheveron FM-2 grease he is to use. It is a mess. The grease is a blue-grey now and somewhat lumpy as though it had rocks in it. I spend about 5 minutes picking out the larger stones and throwing them overboard. The grease looks good.

7:18 a.m. Ted is fully greased now. Silicone on the upper shoulder and part way down the arm. Vasoline under arms and in genital area. FM-2 grease over the remainder of the body except forearm, calf and feet. He boards the Boston Whaler piloted by Jerry Thompson of KSFO and heads for the beach about 75 yards south of the arch rock. The island is very clear. I watch from the Evie-K with binoculars. Ted climbs from the boat at 7:22 a.m. and walks ashore. He stoops down and raises his right arm and opens his fist then plunges back into the water. He is swimming at 7:22 a.m. Jerry Thompson is staying close to Ted's left side and heads him toward the Evie-K about 50 yards to Ted's right. Water temperature is 60°!!

7:44 a.m. I count 60 strokes per minute. The sea is calm and he is making good time. Frank Drum is now aboard the KSFO boat and watching closely. The rest of the team is lined against the railing. All eyes are on the swimmer. There is some slight wear of the grease over the shoulder area, but nothing to be alarmed about.

8:30 a.m. Water temperature is still 60°. I have never seen it so warm and David Kinley is slightly amazed noting that he has been on the sea for over 20 years and that this temperature is very rare. It is albacore temperatures, Kinley notes. Ted looks strong. Some haze beginning to set in between the swimming party and the Islands. Young Dave, Ted Moffett, the photographer and I are watching from the rubber life raft on the port side of the Evie-K. Ted has covered an estimated 1 mile. The sea continues to look like a lake. There is not a boat in sight. We are monitoring 2182 kc. Jerry Thompson has completed at least one direct broadcast to KSFO. We used the radio station time as being official.

8:37 a.m. Ted's stroke drops to 58 per minute and I now detect a very fine mist that appears to be rain.

8:55 a.m. The rain is getting heavier, but it doesn't bother anyone. Islands are no longer visible. The fog horn is now sounding. We put two fishing lines over the side to check set. One at 50 and one at 60 feet. We are heading 65°.

9:20 a.m. We are heading ENE. The fishing boat Anna V passes our starboard heading west.

9:30 a.m. Water temperature 60°. Stroke 55. Seagulls are swimming 10 feet away from Ted. We continue our ENE heading.

10:15 a.m. Farallones bear 240°. Pt. Bonita bears 236° to Farallones. Slight northern set detected. Wind is 3 knots from the south. Lightship bears 78°. These headings put us near the Lightship, but we know we are not near it. Ted has completed about 6 miles now and his stroke is 56 per minute based on a 1 minute timing. 165 strokes in 3 minutes timed by Doug Lathrop.

10:30 a.m. Water temperature 62°. I have some doubts about the accuracy of the thermometer.

10:45 a.m. Fog to our stern is lifting and the islands are again visible. It is warming up considerably. Hank Schram on the Salmon Queen just gave a fishing and weather report to KSFO. He is not in sight.

10:50 a.m. David Kinley advises me that at 10:40 a.m. the wind shifted to westerly at about 5 knots. We are now at the period of maximum current for the Gulf of the Farallon. Turbid currents and slight wavelets. Dead ahead are overcast and fog. Kinley is very optimistic. Pacer John Parent has just entered the water and is swimming to Ted's right.

11:00 a.m. Jerry Thompson is broadcasting to KSFO and we are monitoring.

11:07 a.m. Frank Drum is put back aboard the Evie-K and I send in two rolls of 35 mm film to Associated Press by way of Thompson who is heading back to Sausalito for a nap.

11:10 a.m. We are dead NE of the Islands now and have covered about 7 miles. RDF exact position is difficult to determine because of Farallons strong radio signal drowning out the Lightship.

11:30 a.m. Ted calls for his first feeding of peaches and dextrose. He wants it *cold*, this is the first time in my three swims with him that he has taken anything cold. This is a good sign to me that the water is warm. The sun is warm on our backs. Ted is maintaining stroke of 54 per minute. The Pilot Boat Golden Gate calls on 2182 regarding our estimated time of arrival (ETA). We are 25° ADF from Duxbury per the Annabelle.

11:45 a.m. Pacer John Parent comes out of the water and complains of leg cramps. KNEW radio transmitter is at 62°. Captain Kinley asks Pilot Boat Golden Gate for radar fix, but is advised, "Our main radar set is out of order and the other set is not working."

12:10 p.m. Islands are no longer visible. Fog is setting in. It is partly clear to our starboard side. I am heating peach feeding for Ted's second feeding at 12:30 p.m. Slight swells now. Sun is at 10 o'clock.

12:17 p.m. Fog is closing in fast. Visibility is less than one quarter of a mile.

12:20 p.m. I take water temperature so it will be ready for Ted at 12:30 p.m. feeding. It is 61° and holding. Fantastic!!

12:30 p.m. Second feeding of peaches and dextrose slightly warm. Ted is in good spirits. We start to hit fairly rough water and the cup bounces around as I try to feed from the raft using a 10 foot pole I rigged the night before. We have passed the five hour mark. Ted is very alert. He knew exactly what time it was when I passed him the feeding. He wants tea mixture in one hour. The feeding takes about 20 seconds and he is off and running again.

12:45 p.m. Compass heading is 60°.

1:15 p.m. I heard two horn blasts. They sound like they are coming from the port beam. I can't see any vessel, but the horn is fairly loud. Ted is still looking strong. The captain made a sign that says, "Girls A Go Go." and flashed it over the side. Ted looks up and smiles.

1:25 p.m. Tea and heavy dextrose mixture heating for 1:30 p.m. feeding. Five to six knot breeze blowing from the port side. Stroke is 56 per minute. Water temperature is 60°. Four sea lions are playing off the starboard side. At first I thought they were porpoises.

1:30 p.m. Ted takes tea feeding from young Dave and I. There is a lot of good natured hollering from the deck. There is some slop, but not much. It is still overcast. I take the thermometer into the raft. The water is 61°—fabulous. Ted and crew are in good spirits. We continue to conserve electricity and have not made any calls to shore. Still no fish on the lines we have out. I write my notes in the raft. It is bouncing all over the place.

1:54 p.m. The water is flattening out, just as predicted by the captain earlier. The Salmon Queen is on 2182 kc talking to Dave. Hank says he will be out about 4:15 p.m. Our position is about 4 miles WSW of the Lightship. We are making very fast time and may have to go in the North Channel. Our heading is 55°.

2:00 p.m. Ted slows so he can try to take a leak. He has not thus far.

2:03 p.m. KEWB is at 53°. I hear a plane motor directly overhead, but can't see anything.

2:05 p.m. Ted wants to talk, but we all know that if we get him started that he may not stop. He is all smiles. It really looks good. The sun is trying hard to break through the overcast.

2:10 p.m. I throw a dye marker overboard to check our progress. It disappears fast. Ted is really making tracks now. The lightship is at 111° RDF, KEWB at 54°, and the Evie-K is heading 55°. Lathrop is cursing a blue streak. By these figures and Doug's plotting Ted has covered 17.6 miles (nautical) or 20.2 statute miles.

2:20 p.m. The captain figures we are 5 miles WSW of the Lightship. Water temperature is 61°. We have yet to hit any water in the 50s. This is really fantastic. The plankton has disappeared now.

2:30 p.m. Tea and dextrose feeding. We egg Ted on a bit. He chides, "I still can't take a piss." He is really full of beans and all smiles, but he continues to work though he has not come closer than about 8 feet to the raft off the port side. During the feeding the team shouted to Ted, "Dinner at Alioto's on Fisherman's Wharf." Ted gets a kick out of this and grins as he has done so many times during this arduous trip. Ted's stroke is 56 and the water temperature remains at 61°. Dave Kinley spots oil on the water and says this is an indication that we are west of the Lightship.

2:45 p.m. A B-52 crosses the bow on the port tack at about 10,000 feet. It is clear above in spots, but the fog is still thick ahead and astern. I go to the bow to try to listen for the Lightship horn, but I can't hear it. The blue sky is the first we have seen for several hours.

2:49 p.m. A radar picket jet crosses the bow headed toward what I believe is the north—or our port.

2:53 p.m. A jet transport crosses our stern at about 10,000 feet to the starboard in an arc.

2:55 p.m. LAND to the port side!! It is Pt. Reyes. We can see the Farallones to our stern. What a sight!

2:57 p.m. A fishing vessel crosses the starboard bow at about 1 o'clock, 12 o'clock being dead ahead. The boat is about 2 miles away.

3:02 p.m. Ted has been swimming behind and away from the raft. We slow down for him to catch up and he says, "I know it's difficult, but I'd like to see people's faces alongside." This is a repeat of the first and second swims. He has a dreaded fear of being left out in this beautiful ocean. We tell him land is visible but he won't look. "All I want to see is the bridge," he says. This is a good sign. The bridge it will be . . . The fog is heavy ahead. We can't see the bridge, but it is clear to the starboard and astern. The water temperature is 62°—getting warmer!!

3:10 p.m. Lightship off the starboard beam about 3 miles, at 2 o'clock. Slide Ranch is off the port side at 9 o'clock. We are definitely ahead of schedule. Lathrop plots the course and figures we are North 1.7 miles of projected position at this time and about 1 hour ahead of schedule. This could mean some trouble. Ebb is south. We should hit Bouy 1 soon. Wind is from WNW. The lightship is pointing WNW.

3:27 p.m. Heading due east. A small cruiser (outboard) with about five Negro occupants closes 200 yards to the starboard and slows down but does not stop.

3:30 p.m. More tea and dextrose. He looks good but gulps the tea and takes off.

4:45 p.m. Point Bonita is at 1 o'clock. Two ships are passing toward the west off our starboard about 5 miles. The lightship is at 3 o'clock off the starboard. Dave and I feel our spirits are higher than on any other swim and that Ted is in better spirits than we have ever seen him, in or out of the water. Just after last feeding Ted says he has had first urination of the entire trip. This is a good sign according to the doctor.

4:47 p.m. South Tower of the Golden Gate Bridge is visible from the top at about 12 o'clock. At least we know we are heading the right way.

4:50 p.m. Stroke 52. John Parent is ready to go into the water to set the pace. Ted has slowed, but Parent will perk it up. Ted just wants a little competition!

4:53 p.m. The Golden Gate is now fully visible.

At 4:46 p.m. The Salmon Queen tells Dave by radio it will be alongside in one hour and Point Bonita is 70°. Kinley relays 4:35 p.m. readings to me:

                    62°—Point Bonita
                    170°—Lightship
                    90°—Golden Gate Park
                    65°—South Tower of Golden Gate Bridge
                    62°—North Tower of Golden Gate Bridge

Ted still looks good. Stroke 56. Water Temperature 61°.

4:55 p.m.   More peaches. Still smiling. I am getting weary.

5:05 p.m.   Pilot tug off the port side at 7 o'clock. Point Bonita bearing 66° per visual. John Parent in bunk and resting.

6:00 p.m.   Salmon Queen alongside. Duncan McLeod pacing in wet suit and red cap. It still looks good, but tides have us north of the bridge.

5:45 p.m.   We are eight miles from the bridge, per Salmon Queen and heading 62°.

6:10 p.m.   Wind is blowing 8–10 knots WNW. Two ships passing to the starboard at 3 o'clock. I can't make out the names by binocular. I try to feed Ted coffee with wheat germ and he rejects it violently as being too rough. I substitute peaches.

6:45 p.m.   I have been in the raft and am now soaked to the skin. It is a son-of-a-bitch. The water is too damn cold for me, but Ted doesn't seem to mind.

7:10 p.m.   Hank Schram suggests to Dave that we change course. Some words are shouted back and forth and Dave comes on deck and tells Hank, "I'll let you know after we finish if I should have changed. Then you and I will talk about it." The Salmon Queen is too close to the starboard side.

7:30 p.m.   Offered peaches, dextrose, wheat germ. Refused. He wants tea.

8:00 p.m.   Bearing 80° from South Tower. Muir Beach is magnetic.

8:15 p.m.   The thermometer has been lost over the stern by Ted Moffett, the photographer. I can't figure out why he had it.

8:45 p.m.   Quite a bit of hollering. We make a flag from a blue and white striped beach towel and a rubber life ring belonging to "Ted Erikson" and string it up on the bridge. It is quite a laugh. Ted is stroking 51.

9:00 p.m.   Red and green lights in line. Point Diablo and Lime Point.

9:10 p.m.   Fed nectar and dextrose. He gulps it down and continues.

9:14 p.m.   We are between Mile Rock and Point Bonita about ½ mile off shore from Point Bonita. There is no doubt about it now. We are going to make it. Lt. Col. Stewart Evans has gone into the water from the Salmon Queen. He and Duncan McLeod are pacing, Evans on the right.

9:30 p.m.   Dave cautions Coast Guard that we will set off flares when we are under the bridge. What a sight it is. A sight seeing boat is pulling under the bridge to our starboard. People are lined up against the railing of the bridge and I see a flashlight or two. I break out the flares and instruct the team on their use. What a glorious moment it will be. This calls for some brandy. I also get

	out the champagne, but wonder if Ted will use any.
9:45 p.m.	He is still strong, but not strong enough to head for Aquatic Park. We will bring him aboard after we cross under the bridge at the green lights or dead center. The TV lights are on now and I see a flare on the bridge. The tempo is running high. The confusion among the team and the Salmon Queen makes it hard to understand what anyone is really saying. It is obvious we have a winner in this one.
9:50 p.m.	I fire a flare. Perhaps prematurely, but I have to get into the raft with young Dave. Our work will be cut out for us.
10:00 p.m.	We made it. Ted shakes the hand of Col. Evans and Evans and McLeod herd him to the raft. We haul him aboard the raft with a white towel around his middle. He is coherent and I plant a kiss right on him. Dave and I decide he is to stay in the raft until he has enough strength to safely mount the ladder. Captain Dave waits for the photos to be taken and then begins toward Aquatic Park. Flares still going off and now the orange smoke starts to billow up from the daytime flares.

We ride about 3/4 mile inside the Gate in the raft and then help Ted up the ladder and onto a bed made from a sleeping bag. He is piled high with blankets. Les Thompson of MGM is aboard now and shooting 35 mm movies.

10:40 p.m.	We arrive at Aquatic Park. I must be gassed. The Dolphin Club pier is a mass of humanity.
10:42 p.m.	We back the Evie-K into the dock and Ted is helped over the rail to be greeted by the press with mikes, notebooks and TV cameras. What a glorious day.

He is helped directly to the showers. I'm a mess and can hardly walk, but I make it up the back stairs, strip immediately and into the shower to help get the grease off the hero of the hour. The press is clamoring for pictures but we have to get him into the sauna before he catches cold. Time out for pictures and interviews. KRON-TV is asked to leave the room.
Ted is in the sauna with the rest of the crew. He looks good, but is now starting to talk a little thick tongued. Frank Drum and George Farnsworth warn about him staying in the bath too long. More pictures in the sauna! Finally I had to grab him by the arm and help him out of the hot room and back to the shower.
He looks and feels good now. Joe Minutitoli is here. What a welcome sight.
More interviews and finally we make it outside. Ted, Joe, Nancy and I head for Fisherman's Wharf No. 9 and dinner of all things. Ted has a bowl of clam chowder and a bottle of German beer. He has told the television and press crews all kinds of stories. Like: Heck I'm really 62. Why did you pick Sunday, "That was the

only time we could get a boat," and he didn't swim further because he didn't want to show favoritism between anyplace in San Francisco. What a character! We leave Fisherman's Wharf about 12:30 a.m. and head for Oakland and a bed. What a day, I'm bushed and wish I had Ted's energy.

CERTIFICATION

The foregoing transcript is a copy of original notes taken by Paul W. Girard, 1431 Michigan Street, Fairfield, California on Sept. 16, 1967 aboard the vessel Evie-K out of Berkeley, California while accompanying Ted Erikson of Chicago on a distance swim between the Farallon Islands and the Golden Gate Bridge.

1 NAUTICAL MILE = 1:15 STATUTE MILES

Assume 30 min. miles for 1st 5 hours (2 stat. miles/hr.)
              35 min. miles for 2nd 5 hours (1.7 stat. miles/hr.)
              40 min. miles for remainder (1.5 stat. miles/hr.)
              1.7 knots 1st 5 hours
              1.4 knots 2nd 5 hours
              1.2 knots remainder

0724 Into water. Water temp. 60° F
62°M Calm seas. Overcast. ¾ mi. visibility overcast
No sea anchor
Jump off spot   37° 41′ 50″
                  122° 59′ 52″

0830 Position eyeballed from Farallon Islands
62°M 2 mi. bearing 55°M
Water temp. 60°. Air temp 63°.

0930 Position estimated. Farallon Islands fogged in.
62°M Can't pick up Pt. Reyes. Farallon Islands and Lightship on same bearing.
Guess traveled 2 mi. on same bearing as 0830. Water 60°F.

1030 Position unknown. Radio direction finder not accurate.
62°M Best reading 55°M from North Tower estimate 1.7 mil.
56 strokes/min. 62°F water.

1200 Radio bearings unreliable (indicating 5 miles traveled since 1020)
62°M Location plotted. Just a guess. Water 60°F

1300 Bearing from radio station over top of North Tower 55°M.
60° Assume speed 1.7 kt. Fog, some chop, water 60°F.

1400 Bearing from radio station 53°M. Assume speed 1.4
60° Fog, chop, water 60°F

1500 Radio bearing from Light 119°M, Farallon Islands 230°M
Clearing up. Cannot see lightship yet because of fog.
Don't think very reliable. Water temp. 62°F

1515 Visual bearing from lightship 135°, West peak of Tam 22°M

1630 Visual bearings Mount Tam 27°M Pt. Bonita 62°
Muir Beach 32°, Bolinas Pt. 330°M Lightship 170°
South Tower 65°, Water temperature 62° stroking 56.

1700 6 miles from Pt. Bonita (Hank Schrams radar) Bearing 66°
Water 60°F

1745 8n miles from bridge (Hank Schram) Bearing 62°M (Evie-K)
Water 60°F

1830 9s mi. from Bridge (Hank Schram) Bearing 62°M to North Tower

1920	3½ n miles from Muir Beach (Hank Schram) visual bearing Point Bonita 62° (Evie-K) Water 61° Chop and swells. Wind WNW 15–20. Sundown
1930	Offered peaches, dextrose, wheat germ. Turned it down in favor of tea.
1950	Offered tea, dextrose and wheat germ. He took.
2000	Bearing from South Tower of Golden Gate 80°M Bearing from Muir Beach 208°M
2015	Ted stroking 47 per minute
2017	Ted stroking 51 per minute
2045	Tried to feed Ted tea and dextrose. Refused. Visual bearing Pt. Bonita 68°M Mile Rock 100°
2100	Red and Green lights in line. Pt. Diablo and Lime Pt. Almost in line.
2105	Fed Ted nectar and dextrose.
2114	Between Mile Rock and Pt. Bonita. ½ mile from Pt. Bonita.
2202	Under center of Bridge
2204	In raft. Good shape. Coherent. Happy staying in raft. Steaming for Dolphin Club.
2213	In Evie-K. Wrapped in blankets. Making knots.

20

The Saguenay River Swim and Ralph Willard

It's a trick swim; all river swims are trick swims, but the Saguenay River especially. But it is a most interesting swim because of the play of currents and tides. The river lies in Eastern Quebec and flows from Lake St. Jean (John) to the great St. Lawrence River. The race is always started from the city of Chicoutimi, which lies in the vicinity of the upper third of the river. For sixteen miles the swimmers ride the current downstream; that is if the promoters choose to start the race under favorable tide conditions. Then they round a cape leading into Ha Ha Bay. After seven more miles of swimming, if they are lucky, they arrive at the finish, which is the city of Bagotville. The tidal effects of the St. Lawrence River as fed by the great Atlantic Ocean affects the Saguenay. The narrowing rivers offer the ideal conditions that tax boats as well as swimmers. It is for these reasons that the Saguenay River swim offers more surprises than any other. A swimmer can be holding a comfortable one-half mile lead at one point and fifteen minutes later lose it to a swimmer who was in fourth place. A favorable current has put him in first place by one-half mile. It was the Saguenay that made the fame of Ralph Willard. He has finished the swim three times. Other swimmers have finished more often, but they were young men in their twenties and thirties. Ralph was in his middle fifties when he did it. Wily Ralph knew how to use the currents.

The Saguenay River swim became known when a local swimmer named Robert Cossette completed it. Cossette had been left crippled in one leg as a result of polio in his youth. The normal pursuits of youth were out of his reach—that is, all but swimming. As a result, he spent hours in the water and became quite proficient. When he was approaching middle age the Lake St. John swims were inaugurated.

He entered a few of those races and was successful in finishing. Living in the town of Chicoutimi, he was forced to use the Saguenay River as training grounds. It was only natural that he eventually dreamed of making the swim to Bagotville. His successful solo swim stirred so much public interest that the chamber of commerce decided to hold a professional race in 1963. It has been held every year since.

As mentioned earlier the swim can be made "easy" or difficult depending on when it is started. If the starting time is chosen when the St. Lawrence is ebbing there will be a current in the Saguenay that varies from one to five miles per hour. However, as the river widens near the Bay de Ha Ha the current diminishes appreciably. If the swimmer and his trainer are smart they will begin to hug the southern shore of the Saguenay at this point. What usually happens is that the lead swimmers make the turn into Ha Ha Bay while the tide is still going out. As a consequence what had been a favorable current with them in the Saguenay now becomes an outgoing tide, or current, in Ha Ha Bay. They are slowed down considerably, if not actually stopped in the water at this point. The swimmers who have been trailing the leaders may find, to their surprise, that when they make the turn into Ha Ha Bay the lead swimmers are just two blocks or so ahead of them. The one or two mile lead they had enjoyed has been entirely eliminated. The race now takes on a different aspect.

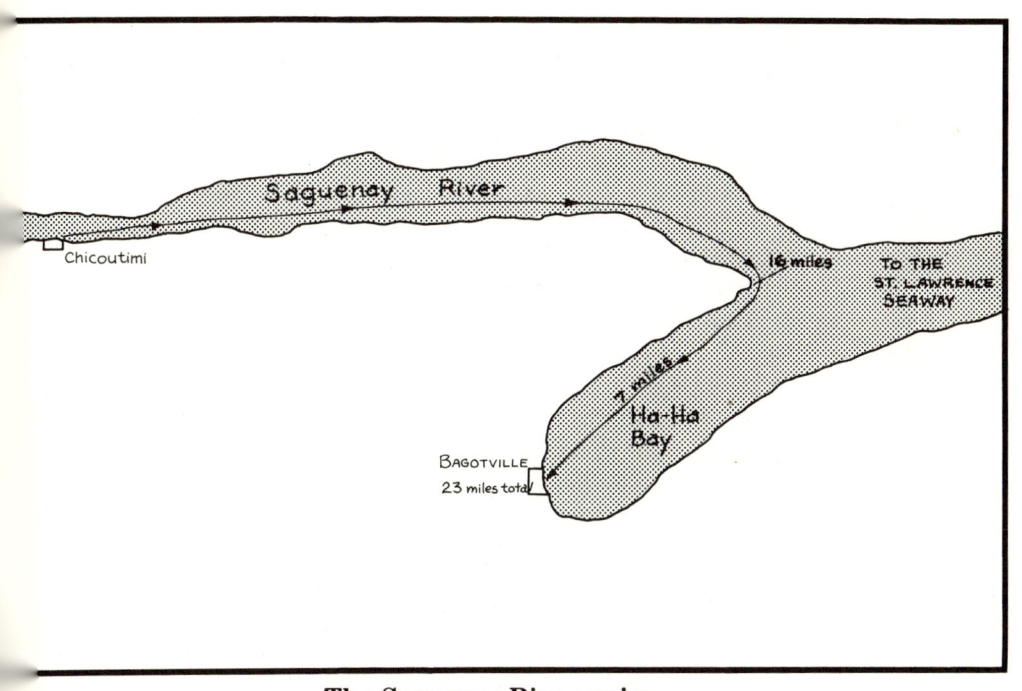

The Saguenay River swim.

What looked like a walkaway race for one or two swimmers now becomes a thrilling six- or seven-man race with each swimmer fighting to reach the finish, which still lies six miles away. The lead swimmers have been bucking the tide for an hour or longer while the slower swimmers have still been riding it down the Saguenay. On the other hand with an earlier or later start the swim can be calculated so that there is a favorable tide for the swimmers throughout the race. If that is the case the race can be over in 6½ hours. If the race is calculated so that the swimmers will always be bucking an unfavorable tide there will be no finishers. The 1969 race was just such a race. Unfavorable tides, inclement weather in the form of three-foot waves and a cold water temperature of fifty-seven degrees prevented any swimmer from finishing within the ten-hour time limit set by the promoters. Abo-Heif went the farthest and he was still five miles from the finish. Matuch was second in that race and was taken from the water a mile behind Abo-Heif. These are the variables that make the Saguenay a most fascinating swim.

The reader may judge from the above that the Saguenay is never swum the same way from year to year. To the uninitiated it is a trick swim. To the experienced it is a scientific challenge. The experienced trainer will be watching every swimmer in view every moment of the race. He will watch the lead swimmers who exchange the lead due to the variability of the currents which, while they remain basically the same in the river, may shift laterally from time to time for a short distance. The fastest current is usually down the center of the river. This "lane" may be one hundred yards wide or only ten depending on circumstances of geography. At the start of the race you will see the knowledgeable swimmer immediately swim a long diagonal course, which carries him to the center of the river in order to catch the maximum current. As he slips into the mainstream he is suddenly whipped ahead of his followers. The trainers of the following swimmers, if they are alert, will watch for that point in which the lead swimmer picks up the current. He then works his swimmer to that point. As the race progresses the swimmers will not be in a tandem alignment. They will be separated laterally. It is now that the trainer must be prepared to shift "lanes" for the rest of the race since the maximum current will shift from the center of the river to areas closer to shore. By watching swimmers who are suddenly approaching from behind at a speed that is beyond their capacities the trainer will know they have caught a current. He will then move his swimmer over to that "lane." It is a challenging race that has been won by slower swimmers following the "rules," either by chance or design.

Now that the reader is familiar with the vagaries of this particular swim he will be able to follow the action of the 1967 Saguenay River swim. This swim is usually the first swim of the season on the North

American continent and is looked forward to by swimmers and spectators alike. It marks the first meeting after a year of separation. Festivities, band marches, and parties are thrown in the cities of Chicoutimi and Bagotville. Quarter-mile sprints for prizes are held for the competitors. It was at one of these sprints that the famous spur of the moment statement by Abo-Heif was made. Out-classed by the younger and leaner swimmers over the quarter-mile course, Abo-Heif and Matuch waded the last ten yards several hundred yards behind the winners. Abo-Heif turned to Matuch, gave his famous grin, and said, "We'll see if they can sprint twenty-three miles Saturday." In the big race Abo-Heif finished first, Matuch second.

Along with the festivities the conversations would run rampant. Invariably the name of Ralph Willard came up and everyone would say, "Watch out for Willard. He's one of the toughest. He's entered some of the toughest races on record and completed them." This would go on for hours and days, but none saw Ralph Willard because he never showed up until the eve of any swim. He was always the last to make his appearance. Whether it was because he had to wheedle permission from his wife or tend to his job one never knew. When Ralph finally did show up he sort of snuck into the town so that few knew of his arrival.

His beat-up fifteen-year-old car would groan to a stop outside of swim headquarters looking as if it were on its last mile. In it were boxes containing food and also blankets. Ralph was too frugal to spend ten dollars just to sleep in a motel. He made the thousand mile journey from Peekskill, New York living in his car. Having been assigned a bed in the school dormitory where the swimmers were bunked, Ralph would then sneak down to Ha Ha Bay for a one-mile swim. He said it settled him after a day's driving. He would then inconspicuously appear at the local restaurant for dinner. The swimmers who recognized him would hail Ralph. Surprise would mark the faces of those who had never seen him. They would then begin to think that they had been had. Ralph didn't look like a swimmer. He was only five feet seven inches, weighed 180 pounds, and was fifty-five years old. When he smiled his decayed teeth showed. The man was old enough to be their father. They felt this little gnome of a man was a disgrace to the sport. Some one said, because of his snow-white hair, that he looked seventy. A look of relief would come over the faces of the new arrivals to the sport. They jokingly disregarded Ralph. The great "terror" was nothing more than a joke played on them by the pros.

When Ralph had strolled down to Ha Ha Bay for his swim earlier, a few of the swimmers were there looking over the sights. As Ralph peeled off his clothes they looked on with mild curiosity. His body was quite different from the normal man of his age. While he was well-padded with fat it was fat of extreme hardness. A fat person is not a fat person and close obvervation of human overweights make it evident. One may be flabby and repugnant. The other is not because the fat is almost like muscle.

There was another paradox in Ralph's appearance. His skin was flawless and in direct contrast to his weatherbeaten face. His face was that of a man fifteen years older and his body that of a man fifteen years younger. When Ralph began stroking out into the bay it was a peculiar sight. If it weren't for his high position in the water he looked like a man struggling to move. His arms barely cleared the water as he brought them forward. His right arm was especially low and appeared at times to actually push against the water before it went beneath the surface. However, if one had the patience to wait until the end of Ralph's workout, he would learn that Ralph had covered a surprising distance. He moved at a speed of from one to one and a half miles per hour, certainly not as fast as the champs, but fast enough to bring the fifty-five-year-old grandfather in ahead of a few of the younger swimmers. Those who saw Ralph in his workout walked away satisfied that there was at least one competitor they could beat.

In the first Saguenay race Ralph had come in fifth, finishing an hour and twenty minutes after the winner. That was in 1963. The next year he also finished fifth, but was some four hours behind the winner. In both those races there were swimmers that finished after him. In 1965 Ha Ha Bay defeated Ralph. He was in the bay and had only a few miles to go but the outgoing tide was too much for him. He had to give up. Those three years of competition had endeared him to the local townspeople so that when he showed up for the 1966 race he was given a welcome as if he were a long-lost native son. It is quite an honor for an American to be accepted in such a manner by the French-speaking members of the province.

There were about twenty thousand spectators awaiting the start of the 1967 race at Chicoutimi. The promoters had chosen the starting time of 9:00 A.M. This year's race would take place in a swift current since it was planned to start several hours after the beginning of ebb tide. At least the first segment would be easy. What happened after the swimmers reached Ha Ha Bay remained to be seen.

As always, the atmosphere was electric. The crowd awaited with anticipation the end of the preliminary announcements by the master of ceremonies. In order to make a more exciting race, the promoters were offering two sets of prizes. The field was divided into groups: competitors who had never won a professional race and those who had. The winners of any professional race would start one hour after the others. Each race would technically be a different one, but psychologically it would make for a great race. The swimmers who started earlier would be fighting to stay ahead of the "master" swimmers, and the "masters" would be fighting not only each other, but those ahead of them. The "masters" race included two greats: Herman Willemse and Rejean LaCoursiere. As each swimmer's name was announced there was thunderous applause as they strode to their starting position on the dock. When Ralph Willard's name was announced along with his age there was a deafening response. As he walked along the dock he held up his hands in acknowledgment. His face was creased with his friendly smile. After the eighteen entrants were announced a hush fell as all awaited the gun.

It was very interesting to watch the start. The better swimmers, who make it a business to learn the best route beforehand immediately made a long diagonal from the bank side dock to the center of the river, which is about a half mile wide at that point. A few sheep followed while the lost continued to swim along the bank. Ralph made practically a right angle turn from his dive to make what amounted to a perpendicular course to the center of the river. When I saw this I must confess that I was somewhat befuddled. One half hour later my befuddlement was replaced by amazement.

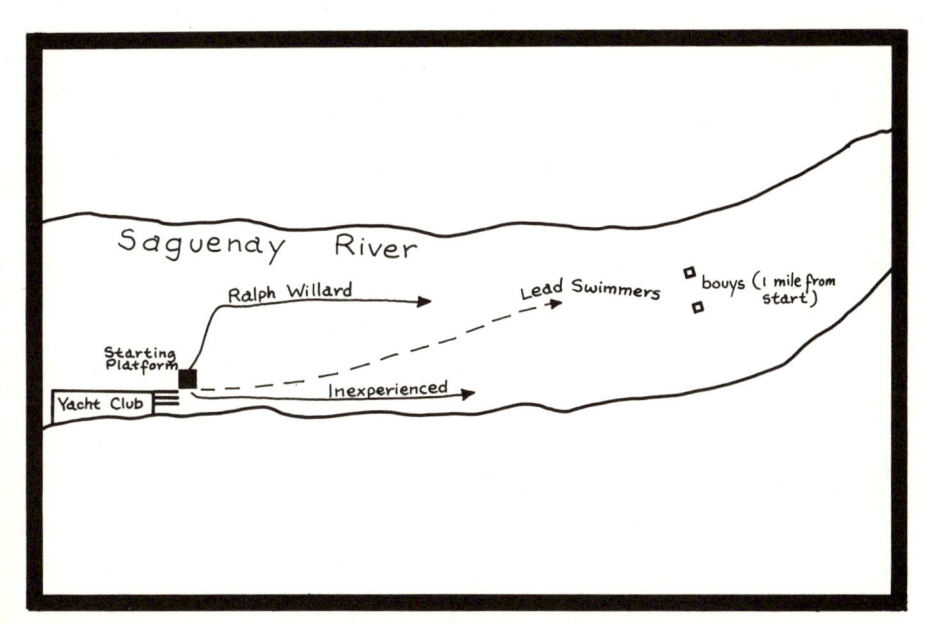

How fifty-five-year-old Ralph Willard starts the Saguenay River swim. He wastes no time getting into the fast current in the middle of the river. The wily grandfather's technique had him in fifth place after the first mile. He naturally lost ground to the younger swimmers as the race progressed, but his ability to seek out the currents throughout the race has allowed him to beat swimmers in their twenties and thirties at the end of the twenty-three-mile race.

By the time the lead swimmers had reached the first navigation buoy one mile from the start, they had only a two-hundred-yard lead on the next four swimmers, who were by no means slow. And who was in fifth place? None other than fifty-five-year-old Ralph Willard. By getting into the mainstream as soon as possible the wily old man was keeping in a competitive position. However, as the race progressed Ralph would fall behind as his younger competitors took advantage of the currents also. But Ralph was always on the lookout for the fastest currents and seemed to have an instinct for finding them before anyone else did. He fell farther and farther behind the lead as time went on but he also pulled out farther and farther ahead of the less experienced swimmers. His shrewd use of the currents would make some of the youngsters hang their heads in shame later when they had to be taken from the water exhausted.

Meanwhile the race progressed with the famed Texas swimmer Tom Bucy clinging to his lead over George Park. By the time Bucy began his turn into Ha Ha Bay he had a comfortable one-and-one-half-mile lead over Park. He then got the scare of his life for, as the promoters planned, he found the tide going out—against him. While he struggled to make progress against the tide, Park was still in the river and before long he found himself within two hundred yards of Bucy. This was enough to stir Bucy to greater efforts as he again began to establish a more comfortable lead even though battling against the tide. Bucy and Park battled for over an hour making very little progress. The stage was now set for a thrilling ending, for the swimmers who were trailing Bucy and Park were now rounding the entrance to the bay. It was Ed Foresby, winner of the 1965 race, Cliff Lumsden, and Dennis Matuch, all pushing each other, who came around the last cliff that blocked a clear view of the bay. It was a startling surprise to the coaches of these men to see the leaders fighting to get in just two blocks ahead of them. Instead of being a one- or two-man race, it was now suddenly a five-man race—and soon a seven-man one because the "masters" Willemse and LaCoursiere were a short distance behind the other three. It was touch and go between Matuch, Foresby, and Lumsden. Each time one would stop to feed, the other two would go ahead to enjoy the temporary lead. The last four miles of the race was a thrilling sight for coaches and spectators, many of whom watched with binoculars and telescopes. The reader can judge what kind of race it was by looking at the official times. The planning of the officials had made a thrilling spectacle out of what might have been a humdrum finish in which swimmers came in hours apart. But the story is not over, for Ralph Willard is still to finish.

It was about three hours after my swimmer (Matuch) had finished when I walked back down to the beach for a swim. Having taken my swim and chatted with a few of the people around, I looked out over the waters of the bay. Barely visible on the horizon was a small speck. It was a rowboat. Looking through the binoculars I tried to identify it. The white sides identified it as a swimmer's boat. After nine hours Ralph was still swimming. Hoping to give him a psychological boost, I began swimming out to meet the boat and swimmer. When I reached the boat I climbed in and joined his rowers in giving Ralph verbal encouragement. Ralph, I'm sure, did not need the verbal aid but he did show his appreciation by periodically waving to us. That's the kind of man he is, always ready to share whatever recognition comes his way. In the hour or so that it took Ralph to reach the finish line, there were moments of doubt. Ralph would constantly stop to adjust his leaking goggles. He did not let the rowboat set his course, for his gaze remained steadily fixed on the church steeple that stood behind the finishing point on the beach. The last two hundred yards saw Ralph "sprint" to the finish in fine fettle. As for all the swimmers, the ambulance had been alerted and was standing by when he walked out of the water. Ralph was assisted onto the stretcher and bundled up. He said, "Don't forget my crackers and juices in the boat." Ralph wasn't one to waste money. He asked for his American flag and waved it to the few spectators still remaining on the beach. Later that night at the award ceremonies things would be different.

Since Ralph finished at 6:25 P.M. he had only 2½ hours to recuperate from his swim. When the organizers learned that he had finished they delayed the award ceremonies until 9:30 P.M. Personally I never expected Ralph to show up. It was evident that the swim had taken a lot out of him. The award ceremonies found twenty thousand persons in attendance at the outdoor pavilion. The applause that accompanied the award to each swimmer was standard. It was nothing compared to the ovation that came with the announcement of Ralph Willard's name for the fifteenth place finish. My surprise was doubled when onto the podium walked Ralph neatly dressed and looking only a wee bit tired. It must have been fifteen minutes before the crowd quieted. The fifty-dollar prize was insignificant compared to the clasp Ralph gave the special plaque awarded to him by the Chamber of Commerce for his spirit and friendly contribution to the feelings of all concerned. Later, when I got Ralph aside, I asked him how he got to the award ceremony. He told me he had walked the mile from the dormitory so as to "loosen up." There was a look of triumphant, pixyish glee in Ralph's eyes as he carried his plaque from the ceremony. There must have been more flashbulbs lighting up his countenance that night than the total expended on all the other swimmers. When a fifty-five-year-old, white-haired, grandfather finishes a swim that men young enough to be his sons can't, other emotions are stirred. The greatest cheers and applause do not always go to the winner. At

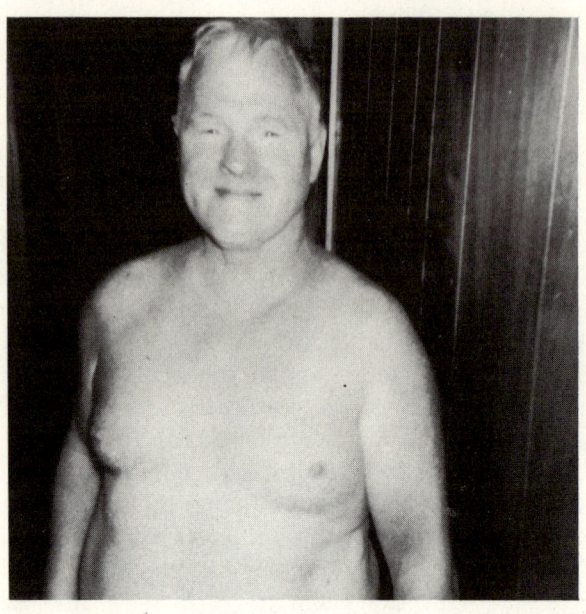

Fifty-four-year-old Ralph Willard the night before the 1966 Saguenay River swim.

Ralph Willard at the award ceremony after finishing the 1967 Saguenay River swim. The fifty-five-year-old grandfather has just completed a one-mile walk from the dormitory.

The Saguenay River Swim and Ralph Willard

least not that July night in a small town of Quebec.

The following listing of the Saguenay River results with the author's comments will give the reader an idea of just how important water temperature and tidal conditions can be. There is one sad comment to be made about this swim and that is its organization. It seems to be the worst run of them all (with due respect to some of the Egyptian swims I've heard about). In the 1968 race the finishing dock was not kept clear of spectator boats with the result that swimmers had to weave their way around them while trying to get to the finish line. Those finishing second through sixth were not properly identified by officials. A big hassle was the result that did not even end at the award ceremony some three hours later.

In the 1969 race the rowboats assigned to swimmers did not arrive at the starting dock until fifteen minutes before the start of the race. The scramble then began to find oars, rowers, and food. It was a mess then and later, for as always the rowers hired for the boats were inexperienced farm boys who tired in an hour and couldn't keep a straight course. If you don't speak French you have a hard time trying to tell a rower what to do. The sad thing is that every year seems to get worse instead of better. I've spent more time changing boats on the Saguenay swim than any other. On one swim I had to utilize five different boats, mostly spectator boats. After a few hours they would get tired and want to leave whereupon I would be forced to hail another. What could be one of the greatest swims for thrills is sadly handicapped by poor organization. It also offers the lowest prize money of any of the swims: $1,100 for first. Anyhow here are the Saguenay River swim results. The first three I missed. The 1970 also was missed.

1963

1	Louis Chiasson, Toronto	7:29:35
2	Pierre Bourdon, Montreal	7:43:20
3	Dr. Edouard Dubord, Victoriaville	8:21:24
4	François Asselin, Arvida	8:23:15
5	Ralph Willard, New York	8:40:40
6	Robert Bouchard, Quebec	9:25:02

The first year was really a competition between local amateurs. The next year the pros heard about it and haven't stayed away since.

1964

1	George Park, Ontario	9:18
2	Armand Cloutier, Quebec	11:18
3	Russel Chaffee, USA	12:39
4	Carole Lavoie, Quebec	12:41
5	Ralph Willard, USA	13:10
6	François Asselin, Quebec	13:12

Ralph Willard was fifty-two when he beat out François Asselin by two minutes. Asselin was in his twenties.

1965

1	Edward Forsby, Ontario	6:29
2	George Park, Ontario	7:17
3	Cliff Lumsden, Ontario	7:22
4	Armand Cloutier, Montreal	8:08
5	Russel Chaffee, USA	no time available
6	Gerard Caouette, Quebec	8:31
7	François Asselin, Quebec	11:20

The winner of this race, Ed Forsby, hit the currents just right. He was not the calibre of swimmer of the three who came in behind him.

1966

This year's race was a two in one: a master's division and a regular. Anyone who had ever won a professional race before was automatically in the master's division. There were two sets of prizes. The masters left one hour later.

Masters

1	Herman Willemse, Holland	6:15
2	Rejean LaCoursiere, Quebec	6:29

Regular

1	Tom Bucy, USA	6:38
2	George Park, Ontario	6:39
3	Ed Forsby, Ontario	6:39:30
4	Cliff Lumsden, Ontario	6:39:30 tie
5	Dennis Matuch, USA	6:40
6	Kurt Plunke, Ontario	6:41
7	Jean Couture, Quebec	7:14
8	Conrad Corbeil, Canada	7:14:02
9	Mary Lou Whitwell, Canada	7:17
10	Pedro Gomez, Argentina	7:25
11	Albert Hreische, Lybia	7:26
12	François Asselin, Quebec	7:38
13	Armand Cloutier, Quebec	8:11
14	Roger Piche, Canada	8:14
15	Ralph Willard, USA	8:25

There were six dropouts in this race but fifty-four year old Ralph Willard finished. The times given by the officials in this particular race should be taken with a grain of salt. I was right in the pack when they finished sitting in the rowboat watching. Third and fourth position were more like five minutes behind Park. Matuch was more like fifteen minutes behind Lumsden and Forsby. The promoters like to give out such close times because it makes for good newspaper and television publicity. They'll do anything for an exciting race. It's a good thing the promoters of all swims aren't like these.

1967

Again a master's and a regular division.

Masters

1	Horacio Iglesias, Argentina	6:03:30
2	Herman Willemse, Holland	6:15:55
3	Rejean La Coursiere, Quebec	6:36

Regular

1	Tom Bucy, USA	6:15:56
2	Klim Savin, Yugoslavia	6:38:36
3	George Park, Ontario	6:53:36

4	Dennis Matuch, USA	6:54:09
5	Bill Barton	7:09:36
6	Conrad Corbiel, Ontario	7:15:36
7	Roger Piche, Canada	7:20:16
8	Real Lavoie, Canada	7:30:26
9	Ben Bouchard, Canada	7:49:36
10	Gilles Potvin, Canada	7:49:36 tie
11	Ralph Willard, USA	8:24:09
12	François Asselin, Quebec	8:24:09 tie
13	Edouard Dubord, Canada	8:44:30
14	Ben de Montreuil, Canada	9:00:06

1968

This year marked the return of the famous Abo-Heif from the Egyptian-Israel war the year before. The forty-one-year-old Egyptian got off to a good start by catching and passing Iglesias in the last mile of the race to capture first place. Matuch and Abo-Heif stayed together until Ha Ha Bay where Abo-Heif decided to follow Iglesias along the bank while Matuch and Park went down the middle. It was a fascinating race in spite of the spectator boats fouling up the finish. This was the snafu finish in which the officials got everybody mixed up. I didn't because I knew the swimmers. This year the master's division was eliminated and all were in one class. The water temperature of 63° in the river and 58° in the bay no doubt contributed to Iglesias's downfall. It also affected Bucy who withdrew from the race as Matuch passed him going into Ha Ha Bay. Abo-Heif went on to win the world's championship this year for the fourth time.

1	Abo-Heif, Egypt	9:10.
2	Judith DeNys, Holland	9:20
3	George Park, Canada	9:20:30
4	Dennis Matuch, USA	9:21
5	Horacio Iglesias, Argentina	9:22:30
6	Rejean LaCoursiere, Quebec	9:26
7	Steve Ramsden, Ontario	
8	Roberto Reta, Argentina	

It was a thrilling race as the first four swimmers whittled down Iglesias's at one time two-mile lead.

1969

One of the roughest marathon races ever held in which only six swimmers out of twenty lasted the ten-hour time limit. The water temperature in the river was 59° and in the bay 57°. The famed Iglesias was passed by Abo-Heif and Matuch just before the bay. Schans was taken out of the water after five hours. Abo-Heif got to within four miles and Matuch within five of finishing. The organizers called a halt and prizes awarded according to position in the water after ten hours. The waves on this one were three feet high and the tides slowed progress to about ¼ MPH.

1	Abo-Heif, Egypt	19 miles
2	Dennis Matuch, USA	18 miles
3	La Coursiere, Canada	14 miles

1970

As usual the organization of the race was a disgrace. The race was scheduled to start at 6:30 A.M. but half the rowboats were lost the night before in a storm. By the time they had been gathered and some semblance of a start organized it was 8:30 A.M. Half the swimmers started the race without boats. Diana Nyad swam the first four hours before her coach found a boat and got to her some eight miles down the river. Horacio Iglesias who depended on a 6:30 A.M. start because of tidal conditions was now two hours off his schedule. When a boat finally arrived for him its motor soon ceased to work and his coach was forced to row a boat in which there were no oar locks. After 9 hours Iglesias was in first place and two miles ahead of Diana who was in second place. The tide that he had hoped to beat now changed against him. The nearest Egyptian was five miles behind him and three miles behind Diana. Diana then was taken from the water cursing her coach. She has a fatal habit of not eating much in her races which is perhaps her reason for weakening. Iglesias was taken from the water with only one mile to go. At that point his stroke rate had dropped to forty-eight which is some ten to twenty fewer than his normal rate. The water temperature was no doubt a contributing factor to the leader's demise also for it was 60° in the river and 56° in the bay. The stalwart Egyptians, no doubt stirred by the need for air fare home doggedly stuck with it. As a result, it was an all Egyptian finish in which they took the first five places. Only three of them qualified for full purse money because of finishing within the twelve hour time limit. The other finishers had to be content with half the prize money. La Coursiere received $87.50 and was not happy. Such are the tribulations endured by lovers of marathon swims.

1 Hafez Fatah Shedid, Egypt   11:49:12
2 Mohamed Gamie, Egypt   11:54:48
3 Maraham Fatah Shedid, Egypt   11:59:45
   Arrived after the twelve hour time limit:
4 Abo-Heif, Egypt   12:02 Abo-Heif fought for full purse money
5 El Enein, Egypt   afterwards. He was unsuccessful.
6 Jorge Lopez, Argentina
7 Rejean LaCoursiere, Canada
   George Park was also a dropout.

21
The Drugs

Can'st thou not minister to a mind fatigued,
Pluck from the memory a hidden loss
Raze out the written troubles of the brain
And with some sweet oblivious drug
Cleanse the heavy muscles of their accumulated lactic acid
Which weighs heavy upon completion of desire?

(With due respect to Shakespeare and *Macbeth*)

If it's anything man has its an inferiority complex. This would be a perfect place to moralize if it weren't for the fact that the moralizers have not been caught. The history of drugs is as old as man and his food. Ever since the first grape fermented, man was there to take advantage of its tranquilizing properties. If there were no grapes around his knowledge extended to other plants that grew in the area. Depending on his geography it is amazing what man came up with: coca leaves (cocaine) in the Andes, cactus buttons (mescaline) in the American Southwest, mushrooms (LSD) in Russia, and arsenic in Turkey, to say nothing of opium. The list is almost endless but the search for drugs to cut pain and/or to stimulate a fatigued body is also endless.

It is understandable that primitive man should seek out pain killers and to a lesser extent stimulants. With lack of medical care his environment was in many cases a living hell. The understanding of the modern-day athlete's drug taking is a little more complex, but understandable all the same. To be a "winner" means recognition and fame. Today, with the communication network, the results of any major sporting event are immediately known in the local area and sometimes flashed worldwide. While the easy-going personality may wonder at the drive of accomplishment, the "driver" does not. He knows it first hand. An attempt to explain the motivations of individuals would be an attempt to explain life. Inheritance, society, health and disease, money and a multitude of other variables are to be considered.

Alcohol was no doubt the first drug used by man. It was cheap and easy to produce. It has a deadening effect on awareness and was the first narcotic. Its use in athletic endeavors, however, is restricted. Overuse and there is deterioration of performance. However, the same can be said for any drug. We have a tendency to look upon the athletic contest as a specially performed set of exercises before an audience. Long before this, ordinary men were in many cases doing the same "set" of exercises to earn their daily bread. Since we may begin just about anywhere in man's history we might as well select the earliest athletic-approaching endeavor. Peruvian Indian runners and pack-carriers are an example. For at least four hundred years they have chewed the coca leaf. They carried the leaves in a pouch alongside another containing pulverized quicklime or ashes, which brought out the full flavor and strength, and placed a quid in the mouth where it was chewed. It took away the sense of hunger and relieved the muscular fatigue of exercise. The Indians were said to have traveled forty miles per day eating only a little roasted maize, but chewing coca leaves. The wonders claimed for the drug contained therein—cocaine—were not subject to strict scientific control. Forty miles a day, even at altitudes of ten and fifteen thousand feet, are not beyond the accomplishments of nondrug users. The chapter dealing with some of the great walking races in England during the nineteenth century have men in their fifties, sixties, and seventies going two and three times as far. Granted, altitude does throw an extra strain on the body, but scientific study does not show a superior performance level of drug users. But let us carry on with some other examples.

Olympic officials today would blanch at what went on during the first few Olympic Games. In the third Olympic Games in St. Louis in 1904, only fourteen of the twenty-seven starters in the marathon race finished. The temperature reached ninety degrees in the shade and the humidity was high. A young postman named Luis Carvajal had established such a lead at eighteen miles that he stopped to talk with spectators. From one he took several peaches and apples. If they had been canned it probably would have been all right, but they were fresh. He consequently suffered cramps further along. T. J. Hicks, an American, was so enthralled when he passed Carvajal that he failed to slow down for the finish. Instead he kept pushing and as a result faltered and was on the verge of collapse several times. His handlers calmly walked over with a hypodermic needle and gave Hicks an injection of strychnine sulfate. He was then given a preparation of eggs to swallow along with brandy. This treatment was repeated several times until he crossed the finish line. Four physicians had to work over him after the race. His exhaustion may be attributed more to the heat and humidity than anything else.

The Drugs

The marathon run at the 1908 games in London produced an even more dramatic finish than that of 1904. Dorando Pietri, a twenty-three-year-old Italian, like Carvajal, held a tremendous lead over his second-place rival. When he began to falter because of the heat his handlers gave him strychnine sulfate also. When Pietri arrived at the gates of the stadium where one hundred thousand people waited he made the wrong turn and collapsed. He was aided to his feet by officials who then actually, with their arms under his, half-carried him across the finish line. They later disqualified him and declared the second-place man the winner. In any case medical examinations were required of all marathon runners when a runner in the 1912 games in Stockholm collapsed at the nineteen-mile mark. He died the next day in the hospital.

Strychnine sulfate was used by doctors as a heart and nervous system stimulant. Claims of mental alertness accompanied its use. Modern pharmacology says that it prevents inhibitory synaptic action in the spinal cord but leaves the excitatory action unaltered. An extreme response is seen when it was used in large doses as a poison in predator control. Anyone who has seen wolves and coyotes in the spasmodic thrashing of approaching death will never forget the horrendous sight. In the minute doses that it was given medically, and to athletes, around the turn of the century, it did "stimulate." Whether it did improve performance is a question that remains unanswered to this day. The effect seems to be more subjective than objective.

As man's knowledge of drugs increased over the years, there were more and more sophisticated approaches as to what and how much should be used. It is not only the athlete that becomes seduced by the would-be goal of superior performance and endurance, but also the academic and entertainment professions. The famous surgeon Sir William Halstead himself became addicted to cocaine. After a few experimental uses he thought he had found the nectar of the gods, a panacea that would allow him to do more research and perform more operations than he had heretofore been able. After a year's use he was sadly disillusioned when he began to fall apart. Only by extreme will power and the sacrifice of several of his scientific colleagues was he able to break his addiction. Before we continue with this fascinating tale of man attempting to surpass himself it would be of interest to examine the kind of personality that is attracted to drugs. Is the drug user a person who perhaps feels inferior and is attempting to overcome his inferiority? In some cases this may be true, but in others it certainly is not. Some are driven by the goal of profit. They have many mouths to feed. How do the promoters of sports events feel about it? A case history of a professional swim I witnessed in 1967 should illustrate the complexity of the problem—if it is a problem.

". . . And furthermore I demand that the sponsors of this swim give a blood test to all competitors after the race. There are too many swimmers who make it a habit to use drugs and I for one, will not stand for it." The speaker went on for the next fifteen or twenty minutes berating those who use drugs in an attempt to increase their performance. His "extemporaneous" speech was at the briefing that was being held the day before one of the major swims in Canada. Invariably the topic of drugs is brought up. Usually it is brought up by those who are amateurs on their first swim who think that all the pros have some hidden weapon to fall back upon. The real pros know there is no secret outside of training. Sometimes it is brought up by those who are genuinely concerned with the health and welfare of the swimmers and the sport. What was unusual about this particular incident, and speaker, was that he turned out later to be one of the worst drug abusers. In the course of his diatribe against drug users he would mention the names of other swimmers who had failed previous swims because of overdosage. To me the speaker was overstating the case. I remembered two previous occasions where he had ended up in a hospital due to his own drug overdose. It was a case of "Methinks the lady doth protest too much."

When the subject is brought up at these briefings there is an interesting response shown by the promoters. They cringe. And well they might, for if there is anything that will put them in a frightened mood it is this. It has all the potential for bad publicity. Since the purpose of the swim is publicity—publicity for the town, the merchants, the beer companies, or breakfast food purveyors—it must be favorable publicity. The use of stimulants by the athlete is not favorable publicity. It reeks of addicts and addiction. Thus if the subject comes up they try to quiet it. It is always a fascinating thing to watch the chill come over the promoters as they try to parry the questions and what they will do about drugs. Lip service is usually paid to the effect that they say there will be a physical examination by doctors of swimmers who complete the swim. This serves to satisfy the swimmers and get the promoters off the hook. They know full well they will not give physical examinations, for if they proved positive it would be unfavorable publicity. In reality the sponsors could not be less concerned if the winner were on drugs. They want a spectacle. The use of stimulants *sub rosa* would not in any way affect the spectacle. Consequently they wish that the subject would never come up. They would be quite happy to let those who choose to use drugs use them, and those who don't, not.

Perhaps the next oldest stimulant known to man after cocaine and strychnine is caffeine. Many of the ten-to-twenty-cups-a-day coffee drinkers would be surprised to learn that they are considered caffeine addicts by physiologists. Caffeine overdosage has caused hyperactivity, nervousness, heart palpitation and muscle twitching in millions.

The Drugs

The most famous and sought after stimulant however has been cocaine. I only covered a little of its history in the opening paragraphs and I should perhaps elaborate on this famous stimulant. Historically cocaine was first introduced to Europe in the sixteenth century by the Spaniard Nicolas Monardes. Its popularization took place in the middle of the last century. It was the Italian physician Paolo Mantegazza who brought back the coca leaf and preached its benefits with an enthusiasm rarely matched in the annals of medicine. A Viennese biochemist isolated the active principal, cocaine, from the leaves in 1859. Gradually as investigators began to experiment with the substance its pychotropic properties began to be appreciated. Freud began his experimental laboratory research with cocaine and did some fine work that stands valid today as a model of its kind. The exhilarating and euphoric effects were rapidly appreciated by the workers of that era. However, since that time it is amazing how little work has been done. Only present-day research into the psychotropic effect of all drugs reawakened an interest in cocaine. In over seventy years of experimental pharmacology there are only twenty or thirty reports on the substance, most of which have been done by the French. Its merits, if any, seem to be dependent upon the state of the individual taking it at that moment. This can be said, however, about any drug. The *International Journal of Psychiatry* (Vol. 119) gives a very vivid description of its effects. "Cocaine has been found to potentiate enormously the action of neuro-hormones epinephrine and norepinephrine. This potentiation of norepinephrine gives rise to a central adrenergic similar to that provoked by LSD."

When the observation of the effects of cocaine are tabulated alongside that of amphetamine they are seen to be similar. "As used by athletes it is taken as a syrup in alcohol." Which leads us into the discussion of the most popular stimulant taken by man in a civilized society—amphetamine.

Gene Smith of the Harvard Medical School in 1960 ran a series of tests on college swimmers using secobarbital (a depressant), amphetamine, and a placebo (a phony pill). Secobarbital significantly impaired performance and amphetamine significantly improved performance. The percentage of improvement averaged about two percent. It must be remembered that these were short-term athletic endeavors. Long-term marathon events show that the competitor burns up all his energy before the end of the race.

To discuss each and every drug for which a claim is made would take a pharmacologist. We will just survey the field. The list of drugs banned by the United States Olympic Committee includes: alcohols, amphetamines, purine bases, camphor, and pharmacologically similar substances including analeptics, cocaine, hormones, lobelline, nitrates, peripheral vasodialators (nicotinyl alcohol), narcotics, strychnine, tranquilizers. The reader may be surprised to see narcotics and tranquilizers listed. Of what benefit will sedatives be in increasing performance? The answer lies in the complexity of the human body. Its physiology operates around the "basic steady state" (the *equilibrium internal* of the famous French physiologist Claude Bernard). At its simplest, the following happens. When the body is low in all the chemicals that give rise to the activities that characterize life and movement the animal rests. During this period there is a build-up and storage of these products. When a particular level is reached the urge to move and take action makes itself felt. The body is much like a wet-cell battery that is capable of recharging itself. When the recharging reaches a particular level discharge is called for. Discharge characterizes the activities of which man and his animal cousins indulge when awake. It continues for the length of time necessary before recharging (rest, sleep) is needed. This is a characteristic cycle that each species and individual follows according to its inheritance. The body itself produces substances that in themselves are powerful "stimulants." Thyroid and adrenal hormones are but two. In the normal body these substances are secreted in the proper amounts as called for. The delicate feedback mechanisms inherent make sure that there is no oversecretion that would upset the total physiology. In other words, the normal checks and balances assure a proper functioning. Some of the stimulants discussed will stimulate various organs of the body to secrete more of the substance they produce. If the organ, due to fatigue, is no longer capable of production, the body is in the dangerous situation of going into shock. However if these natural substances are replaced as they are used no such result may be seen. They are in some cases called metabolic enhancers. Thyroxine, epinephrine, pituitrin, and insulin are examples.

One of the more recent developments in sports physiology, but from a different angle, is the use of synthetic male sex hormones or steroids. They are anabolic or "growth increasing." They have the property of promoting cell growth. They have been taken by those athletes in which strength is of primary importance. Weight lifting, shotputting, and wrestling are examples of the sports where muscle is important. When steroids are taken and the athlete indulges in a heavy work load there is a huge increase in muscle tissue growth above and beyond what would normally take place. The catch is that it works for those who do not have normal amounts already present. For those endowed with high levels to begin with they need nothing to increase their muscles outside of work. All too late the athlete seeking to be Apollo learns that nature and her methods of working never operate in a straight-line relationship. The athlete may find himself with more muscle than is needed for success in his endeavor. He is forever excluded from the endurance sports. The more muscle one has the greater is the need for these muscles to be supplied with more food, oxygen, and replacement substances to maintain them. Thus there is a greater work load or energy demand from the body to supply these elements. Muscle above and beyond the minimum to propel the body becomes a liability. This is one of the reasons why marathon swimmers and runners, while well built, are not exceptionally muscular. All the successful competitors are basically slender men. They have just enough muscle to propel their bodies. Those with an excess will throw an extra strain on the organs of the body to feed the muscles.

In reading several hundred technical reports on the many drugs claimed to be stimulants, I have come to the conclusion that their effects are objectively a myth in the normal body. They do have their use under medical supervision and the diseased body, but no objective effect on the endeavors of the marathon athlete. The subtle feedback mechanisms, physiology, and heredity preclude the breaking of the laws of physics. In the opening chapter there was a survey of endurance over the centuries. In all cases these great feats of endurance were accomplished without drugs. Today, with many people of lesser endowment competing, there are "incapable" competitors attempting to keep pace with those with greater endowment. The search for the magic ingredient that will make them a god is the pitfall in which these individuals fall.

The rationale of stimulants in reality has no scientific basis in the sporting world. If you use amphetamine, which is a cortical stimulant that increases the pituitary output, that in turn stimulates the thyroid and adrenal glands, you better add thyroid and adrenal hormones to handle the call for extras. With the step-up in metabolism caused by these hormones you better make sure that there is plenty of sugar and adenosine triphosphate available to handle the increased pick up, or racing, of the body. In other words, the would-be champion would do well to have an armamentarium of physiologists and drugs to add to the original stimulant. If not there can be a severe breakdown because one link cannot keep pace with the others. And finally, if all the organs are stimulated to production above and beyond their normal rate there is the final limitation of oxygen intake. The vital capacity (the amount of air that can be taken in with a deep breath) is fixed by the heredity of the individual. Those with large lung capacity have an advantage over those with smaller lung capacity. There is no use in stimulating everything else if an intake of oxygen cannot also be increased. Only trouble can ensue when man attempts to supersede his normal inheritance and the natural cycle to which every living creature is subject.

To understand one only has to mention the "good days" and the "bad days" that everyone is subject to. The good days represent the "all systems go" days. All organs and systems are completely rested and at optimum storage levels. What follows is the easy performance in which all accomplishments are done with minimum effort. The bad days represent an under par organ(s) or system(s), any one of which will be the weak link in the chain. I'm afraid that stimulants will have to fall by the wayside as myth unsubstantiated by science along with food faddism and hypnosis. The scientific laws that rule the body are as rigorous as those that rule the planets in their journey around the sun.

22
Discovery

Researching the literature for information on marathon swimming presents obstacles that are unknown to the academic scholar. The data is usually widespread in certain areas of the world and is usually not well catalogued. As a consequence anyone who would attempt to collect his information would find it necessary to travel to those cities and begin digging among the promoters and newspaper files. All too often the information that is recorded is erroneous. Talking with a swimmer who has attended these swims is perhaps better, but the memory is fallible. One would be fortunate in finding a Herman Willemse to talk with, for his memory and honesty are unassailable. All too often the information that I obtained came in bits and pieces. The swims where information has been incomplete I shall do no more than mention. Marathon swims are by no means localized in the western hemisphere. As mentioned in the opening chapters, wherever there is water man will take to it.

Professional swims of twenty-five miles or longer have been held in Yugoslavia, South America, Australia, Mexico, and Egypt. Ten- and fifteen-mile swims have been held in Holland, England, and even Hong Kong. Lack of a professional swim has not hampered the ardent amateur from swimming Loch Ness and many other Scottish and English lakes. One of the more famous professional swims, held since 1954, has been the Capri-Naples swim. This swim is held every year and runs from the island of Capri to the city of Naples in Italy. It is ballyhooed as a twenty-five mile swim, but is really sixteen to seventeen miles. The Suez Canal swim, starting in Lake Bitter and ending in the canal, is a twenty-seven-mile swim of the most grueling kind. The reader has probably gathered from the description of the famous cold-water swims that warm water swimming is a lark. When the water temperature reaches ninety-eight degrees, as it did in the 1966 Suez Canal Swim, stresses of another kind take place. The swimmer runs the serious risk of suffering from heat stroke, which can be just as dangerous as hypothermia. Herman Willemse gave me a personal description of this race in which only three competitors finished. All three finishers took over fourteen hours to complete the course. Herman could not leave his air-conditioned hotel room for ten days following the swim. The excruciating headaches and dizziness prevented any but the necessary movements to and from the toilet. Herman had suffered a heat stroke following the swim. Somewhat the same conditions were experienced by the swimmers who swam around Miami Beach.

Herman goes on to mention, and other swimmers including Greta Andersen agree, that the Egyptians are given to cheating. Herman has seen Egyptian swimmers clinging to their boats as the boat swept past him. Greta tells of one year when an Egyptian swimmer rapidly came from behind, passed and then went ahead of her while calmly munching on a banana; he was holding onto a rope. She was swimming all out. Such are the peculiarities of the lesser Egyptian swimmers. The reader will do well to keep in mind the limits of human capability when reading of marathon swims in the popular media. For any swim in water over sixty-six and fifteen miles an average of 1.5 to 1.9 miles per hour is acceptable. Any speed over 1.9 is subject to serious question. If the water is in the low sixties and fifties the average speed is cut considerably. Of course this holds for "dead" water in which currents and large waves are not evident. I was loath, for another reason, to accept Miss Lenore Modell's "world's record sixty-six-mile swim" made in August 1966. Miss Modell swam around a five-mile course in Lake Natoma, California. After thirty-six hours of swimming in the sixty-six-degree water, she or her coach claimed a new world's record exceeding that of sixty miles by Abo-Heif and Erikson in Lake Michigan. It is very easy to add a lap or two under such circumstances. There is no question that Abo-Heif and Erikson swam the distance since they had to swim a straight-line course over open water with many observers and officials present. I find it hard to believe that other than "interested" parties would keep track of the number of laps Miss Modell covered in her search for fame. If by any chance I have cast doubt on Miss Modell's "record" I apologize. I take the side of the judge when he says "not proved." Unless unassailable documentation comes forth I place her accomplishment in limbo. One would do well to remember that serious scholars have questioned the claims of Peary and Cook that they reached the North Pole in 1908 and 1909. If the claims of Peary are questioned what of us lesser mortals?

In covering the history of the "toughest sport in the world" I hope the reader has gained an understanding of the grasp such feats of endurance have on both its practitioners and audience. Man has al-

Discovery 327

ways sought the limits of his mental and physical capacity. For each and every individual the goal may be forever unobtainable. For a few it will be reached. The next time you stand on the beach and watch some youngster who shows an ability far and above the rest, push ahead your vision into the future and say either: "I hope he never hears about marathon swimming. The rewards are a pittance compared to the agony that must be undergone," or "He's got it. He only needs to experience a few wins, for only those who have won can ever know what it means."

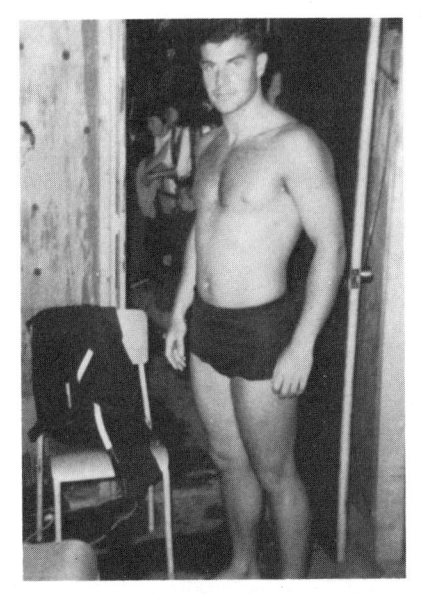

Champion warm-water swimmers. Horacio Iglesias of Argentina on the left and Guglio Travaglio on the right.

Champion cold-water swimmers Dennis Matuch of the United States and George Park of Canada. You may laugh at their beef and fat, but they'll finish in the first three when the water is in the low fifties. Those facial expressions are deceiving. Beneath those exteriors are two of the most considerate gentlemanly personalities in the sporting world.

Appendix I

The World Professional Marathon Swimming Federation was formed in 1963 in order to promote professional swimming. It sanctioned races and awarded points in each race. Methods of awarding points varied from year to year as kinks were worked out. Points were awarded according to: 1. Place; 2. Distance of swim. Extra points were awarded if a new time record was set in a sanctioned race. It soon became apparent that it was to a swimmer's advantage to enter and complete as many races he could in one year. Thus, by accumulating, say, one first, two seconds, and three thirds, he would come out ahead of a swimmer that got two first places and entered no other swims. The swimmers listed below are the cream of the crop if they make the top eight. Solo swims are nonsanctioned swims and are thus not included.

1964
1. WORLD'S CHAMPION: Abo-Heif (U.A.R.), 3,125
2. Herman Willemse (Holland), 2,530
3. Roberto Reta (Argentina), 1,695
4. Jorge Mezzadra (Argentina), 1,655
5. Rejean Lacoursiere (Canada), 1,600
6. Nabil el Shazli (U.A.R.), 1,570
7. Mohamed Zeitoon (U.A.R.), 1,355
8. Carlos Larriera (Argentina), 1,145
9. Dicki Bojadzi (Yugoslavia), 1,040
10. TIE: Cliff Lumsden (Canada)
    George Park (Canada), 800

WOMEN
1. Judith DeNys (Holland), 1,490
2. Mary Martha Sinn (U.S.A.), 860
3. Hedy Schmidt (Canada), 610
4. Mary Lou Whitwell (Canada), 600

1965
1. WORLD'S CHAMPION: Abo-Heif (UAR), 3,451
2. Herman Willemse (Holland), 1,988
3. Travaglio (Italy), 1,489
4. Mohammad (U.A.R.), 1,450

5. Shazly (U.A.R.), 1,425
6. Iglesias (Argentina), 1,397
7. LaCoursiere (Canada), 1,313
8. Reta (Argentina), 931
9. Zidan (Syria), 818
10. Larriera (Argentina), 693.5

WOMEN
1. Judith DeNys (Holland), 1,718
2. Hedy Schmidt (Canada), 955

1966
1. WORLD'S CHAMPION: Travaglio (Italy), 5,645
2. Willemse (Holland), 3,854.5
3. Bucy (U.S.A.), 2,473.5
4. Abo-Heif (U.A.R.), 2,399.5
5. LaCoursiere (Canada), 2,205
6. Iglesias (Argentina), 1,744
7. George Park (Canada), 1,696.5
8. Galmez (Argentina), 1,206.5
9. Barton (U.S.A.), 1,127
10. Saleh (Syria), 891

WOMEN
1. Judith DeNys (Holland), 3,443.5   WOMAN'S WORLD CHAMPION
2. Whitwell (Canada), 1,870
3. Margaret Park (Canada), 791

1967
1. WORLD'S CHAMPION: Iglesias (Argentina), 2,667
2. LaCoursiere (Canada), 2,285
3. Bucy (U.S.A.), 2,119
4. George Park (Canada), 1,797.5
5. Willemse (Holland), 1,529.5
6. Bodjazi (Yugoslavia), 1,000
7. Corbeil (Canada), 893
8. Matuch (U.S.A.), 847
9. Barton (U.S.A.), 794.5
10. Savin (Yugoslavia), 787

1968
1. WORLD'S CHAMPION: Abo-Heif (U.A.R.), 3,563.5
2. Iglesias (Argentina), 3,447.5
3. LaCoursiere (Canada), 2,210
4. Travaglio (Italy), 1,252.5
5. Matuch (U.S.A.), 1,247
6. G. Park (Canada), 1,160
7. Reta (Argentina), 1,064.5
8. Bucy (U.S.A.), 960
9. Corbeil (Canada), 561
10. Lake (England), 528

WOMEN
1. Judith DeNys (Holland), 3,192.5   WOMAN'S WORLD CHAMPION
2. Margaret Park (Canada), 1,196
3. Linda McGill (Australia), 950

1969
1. WORLD'S CHAMPION: Iglesias (Argentina), 3,209
2. Schans (Holland), 3,045

Appendix I 331

3. Dennis Matuch (U.S.A.), 1,502
4. Gamie (U.A.R.), 1,279
5. Hart (U.S.A.), 690.5
6. Pollonini (Italy), 669
7. Reta (Argentina), 546
8. Lake (England), 539.5
9. Wickens (U.S.A.), 391
10. Travaglio (Italy), 389

WOMEN

1. Patti Thompson (Canada), 2,389.5   WOMAN'S WORLD CHAMPION
2. Judith DeNys (Holland), 379

1970

1. Schans (Holland), 2,883.5   WORLD'S CHAMPION
2. Iglesias (Argentina), 2,714
3. Gamie (U.A.R.), 1,563
4. Travaglio (Italy), 1,557.5
5. M. Shedid (U.A.R.), 1,450.5
6. Abo-Heif (U.A.R.), 1,361
7. H. Shedid (U.A.R.), 1,300
8. Van Scheyndel (Holland), 1,227
9. Matuch (U.S.A.), 1,057
10. El Enen (U.A.R.), 1,016.5

WOMEN

1. Judith DeNys (Holland), 2,675.5
2. Taylor (U.S.A.), 1,408
3. Diana Nyad (U.S.A.), 750

1971

1. Iglesias (Argentina), 3,203½   WORLD'S CHAMPION
2. Abo-Heif (Egypt), 2,576½
3. M. Shedid (Egypt), 1,931½
4. Matuch (U.S.A.), 1,885
5. Khamis (Syria), 1,824
6. Echeverria (Mexico), 1,663
7. Lake (England), 1,612
8. Gamie (Egypt), 1,518
9. Van Scheyndel (Holland), 1,339
10. Hemmat (Egypt), 1,273

WOMEN

1. Judith DeNys (Holland)
2. Magdour (Egypt)

1972

1. Iglesias (Argentina), 2,153   WORLD'S CHAMPION
2. Van Scheyndel (Holland), 1,883
3. Villagomez (Mexico), 1,619
4. Schans (Holland), 1,430
5. M. Shedid (Egypt), 1,383
6. Matuch (U.S.A.), 1,266
7. Saleh (Syria), 1,139
8. Jon Erikson (U.S.A.), 918
9. Veljko (Yugoslavia), 890
10. Khamis (Syria), 854

WOMEN

1. Magdour (Egypt)   2. D. Nyad (U.S.A.)

The Top Money Winners

George Young (Canada): $25,000 (1 race; 1927)
Ernst Vierkotter (Germany): $30,000 (1927 CNE Race)
                                2,000 (1928 CNE Race)
                              15,000 (1929 CNE Race)
                              $47,000
Marilyn Bell (Canada): $20,000 (Lake Ontario Swim; 1953)
                            10,000 (prizes)
                            $30,000
Marvin Nelson (U.S.A.): $16,000 (total of four races in 1933, 34)
Cliff Lumsden (Canada): $150,000 plus (Cliff was a consistent winner of many professional races throughout his career: 1949–1967
Herman Willemse (Holland): $50,000 (Herman's career extended from 1960 to 1968)
Abdel-Latif Abo-Heif (Egypt): $50,000 plus
Greta Andersen (Denmark-U.S.A.): $40,000
Tom Park (Canada): $28,000

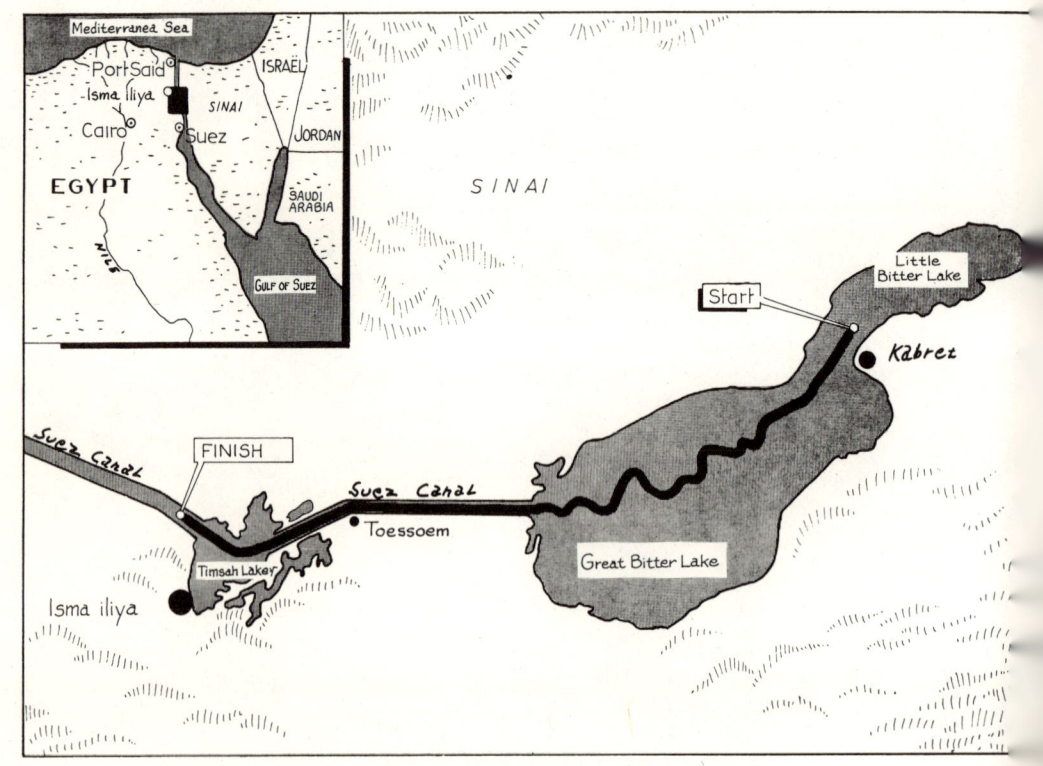

The twenty-seven-mile Suez Canal swim.

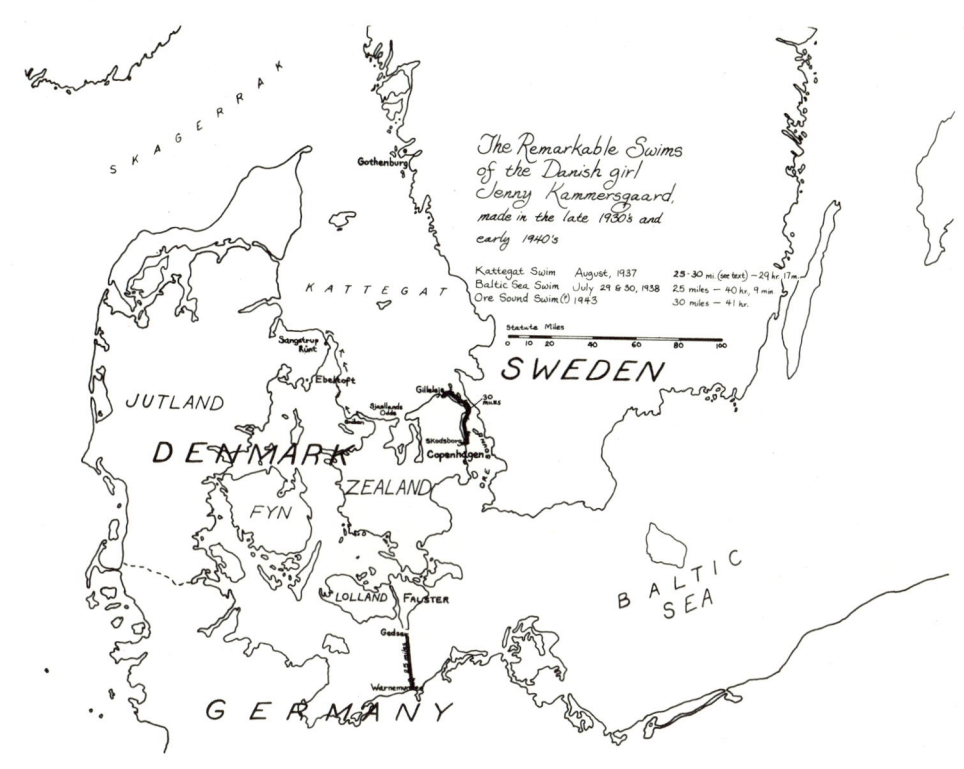

Appendix I

The Remarkable Swims of the Danish girl Jenny Kammersgaard, made in the late 1930's and early 1940's

Swim	Date	Distance	Time
Kattegat Swim	August, 1937	25-30 mi. (see text)	29 hr. 17 m.
Baltic Sea Swim	July 29 & 30, 1938	25 miles	40 hr. 9 min.
Ore Sound Swim (?)	1943	30 miles	41 hr.

Appendix II

The swims made by the Danish schoolgirl Jenny Kammersgaard in the late 1930s and early 1940s presented a problem to document. Hours spent searching the indexes turned up only two English language sources on this most remarkable girl. It was only after writing to Mr. Juhl Bentzen, president of the Copenhagen Swimming Union, that some degree of clarity resulted. He kindly sent me information that allowed me to include her impressive swims.

On August 7–8, 1937 Jenny, then only nineteen years old, swam from Zealand across the Kattegat to Jutland. Zealand is Denmark's largest island and Jutland the main land mass. Jutland is actually a peninsula joined to Germany. She left from Gniben, Zealand and arrived at Sangstrup Klint, Jutland. The straight-line distance between these two points is twenty-five to thirty miles. Due to tides she got a free lateral ride (like the swimmers in the English Channel). When the newspapers reported her swim they did not distinguish between miles swum and miles drifted. She was thus credited with a heroic fifty-five miles. Since Jenny was strictly a breast stroker (at times using a flutter kick in high waves) her time of twenty-nine hours and thirty-seven minutes precludes such a distance. Mr. Bentzen's assurance of water temperatures around Denmark as being in the fifty- to fifty-nine-degree range adds further doubt that she swam more than thirty miles on her successful swim.

On July 28–29, 1938 Jenny caused quite a stir in European newspapers when she swam the international ferry route across the western Baltic Sea from Gedser, South Denmark to Nienhagen, Germany. The twenty-five-mile crossing took her forty hours nine minutes. That is an average of 0.7 miles per hour. Jenny's swim caused such an uproar that she was feted by the mayors of the surrounding towns. Even the arrival of the Netherlands royal couple Princess Juliana and Prince Bernhard at Gedser was overshadowed by the excitement of Jenny's accomplishment. Such was the ado that King Christian and Chancellor Adolf Hitler sent her congratulatory telegrams.

In 1943, when Jenny was twenty-five years old, she made another

Appendix II 335

remarkable swim in Ore Sound (the body of water separating Zealand from Sweden)—remarkable, that is, if you accept unofficial swims. She claimed she swam, unattended mind you, from Skodsborg (which is north of Copenhagen) to Gilleleje. This thirty-mile swim supposedly took her forty-three hours. That is a lot of swimming when you are by yourself. Let us put a question mark after it.

Jenny went on to swim the English Channel in 1950 and 1951, registering over fifteen and sixteen hours on those swims. Her Kattegat and Baltic Sea swims earned her recognition in the records of marathon swimming.

Sources

What to include and what to leave out so as not to weary the reader was ever a challenge. The reader may well ask where such favorites as Johnny Weissmuller, Duke Kahanamoku, and the current Mark Spitz are in this volume? The answer is simple. They never entered the events that are considered marathon. The longest race the famed Weissmuller ever entered was the Chicago River Race and that was only two miles. These three famous swimmers have no doubt swum longer distances but only while in training, or unofficially. Thus they do not concern us. There have been other famous personalities that were accomplished swimmers. Ben Franklin was one. He even invented wooden hand-paddles to aid him. President John Quincy Adams was another. President Adams paddled around in the Potomac River for an hour every morning before going to his duties in the White House. Lord Byron was almost as famed for his swimming abilities as he was for his poetry. He not only swam the Hellespont (of Leander and Hero) but once joined a friend and swam the whole length of the Grand Canal at Venice. The trip (he actually left from Lido Island) took him four hours and twenty minutes. And so it goes. Anywhere in the world where there is water the persons who can swim will be in it. If it so happens that you do not find a name you think should be here it is because he or she did not qualify or the distance was not long enough. The reader may rest assured that the swims in this book are the longest *authenticated* ones in the record.

As far as books on marathon swimming there are only five. Two of them are about women. Jenny Kammersgaard wrote about her Kattegat swim in *Svommeturen* (Gyldendalske Boghandel: Nordisk Forlag, 1937). Unfortunately it was written before some of her later long swims.

After Marilyn Bell made her famous Lake Ontario swim a newspaper man named Ron McAllister wrote about it in *Swim to Glory* (McClelland and Stewart Limited, 1954). It is short on facts and long on conversation.

Gerald Forsberg wrote on the subject in *Modern Long Distance*

Swimming (London: Routledge and Kegan Paul, 1963). His book is quite informative but is limited to marathon events in the British Isles. Also, many records have been set since its issue.

Mr. Sam Rockett wrote about the first four English Channel races in *It's Cold in the Channel* (Hutchinson, 1956). There were four more to come.

When Herman Willemse retired from competition he joined up with Herman Kuiphof and published *Marathonzwemmen* (Leiden: N. V. Uitgeverij Meander, 1970). It was limited to those events he had entered and thus lacks the cosmopolitan approach.

For the connoisseur the most satisfying material will be found in the monographs by scientists. Their demands for documentation leave little to doubt. For accuracy it is hard to surpass George Albert Llano's (Research and Editorial Specialist Arctic, Desert, Tropic Information Center) *Airmen Against the Sea* (Arctic, Desert, Tropic Information Center, Research Studies Institute, Maxwell Air Force Base, Alabama, no date). His research on "life and death" swims was superb. After reading his work I knew what to look for when sifting other accounts.

For those who disagree with me and believe that psychology is more important than genetics I can only suggest the following excellent works: *Biochemical Individuality* (Wiley, 1956) by Roger John Williams; *Physical Fitness of Champion Athletes* (University of Illinois Press, 1961) by Thomas Cureton; *Physiology of Channel Swimmers* (*Lancet*, October 8, 1953), *Temperature Regulation in Swimmers* (National Academy of Sciences, National Research Council, Pub. 1341, 1965), *A Physiological Study of Channel Swimming* (*Clinical Science*, 1960, vol. 19, p. 257) all by L. G. C. Pugh and his co-workers. Some of Dr. Pugh's work was actually done before and after one of the English Channel races. The last monograph also contains some very enlightening information on navigation for the Channel swimmer. Dr. Pugh also points out the value of fat as an insulator in the marathon swimmer. The importance of fat is also discussed by Suk Ki Hong and Hermann Rahn in *The Diving Women of Korea and Japan* (*Scientific American*, May, 1967).

On the subject of drugs the medical journals of America and England were most informative. Perhaps the *Journal of Sports Medicine and Physical Fitness* (Edizoini Minerva Medica, Corso Bramante, Turin, Italy) was the most complete in coverage on this aspect of sports.

The above readings are by no means a complete coverage of the field but they should at least point the interested reader in the right direction.

Finally, the many thousands of hours spent with, and talking to, some of the world champions in this book has acted as a most accurate reference point when reading the literature.

Index

Abertondo, Antonio, 63–66, 279, 282
Absecon Island. *See* Atlantic City
Adams, John Q., 336
Adenosine triphosphate, 323
Adrenal hormone, 23, 322–23
Alcatraz, 287, 289
Amyot, Jacques, 190
Andersen, Greta, 32, 37–39, 63, 80, 91, 95, 114, 117–20, 122, 141, 155, 162–64, 166–74, 185, 191–93, 195, 197, 210–11, 218, 254–64, 289, 326
Arabs, 24, 28
Arctic, Desert and Tropic Information Center, 210
Arctic tern, 22
Argentine professional races, 282
Atlantic City Marathon, 104–5, 134–44, 185, 257–59, 261, 263
Atlantic Ocean, 266, 282, 304; rowed, 27
Australia, 325

Bagotville, 305, 307
Baker's Beach, 289
Baldy, 26
Baltic Sea, 333–35
Baron, Capt. Alfred, 273–74
Bats, 17
Bears, 17, 19
Bell, Marilyn, 13, 103–4, 106–11, 138, 285–87
Benton Harbor, 162
Bentzen, Juhl, 334
Bernard, Claude, 322
Bernhard, Prince, 334
Bikila, Abebe, 223
Bitter Lake, 325
Blower, Tom, 218
Blue geese, 23
Bojadzi, D., 114, 116
Bolinas Point, 287–88, 292–93
Bosphorus, 217
Boston Light(house) swim, 273
Boyton, Capt. Paul, 46
Bross, Chuck, 165, 176

Buckland, Frank, 49
Bucy, Tom, 232, 236–37, 310
Buenos Aires, 279–81
Buoyancy test, 29–32
Burgess, Thomas, 58–59
Butlin, Billy, 63, 74, 184, 258
Byron, Lord, 336

Calais, 56–57, 69–70
Camarero, Alfredo, 258
Canadian National Exhibition Marathon, 60, 94, 96–129, 163, 185, 216, 262, 269–70, 278
Candiotti, Pedro, 63, 279–82
Candiru, parasite, 277
Cap, swimming, 224
Cape Griz-Nez, 46, 50, 55–56, 59, 64
Capri-Naples Marathon, 185, 231, 261, 325
Caretto, Patty, 35
Caribou, 21
Carvajal, Luis, 318–19
Catalina Island Marathon, 60, 83–98, 135, 257, 260, 271, 278
Chadwick, Florence, 91–95, 106–9, 218, 260–61, 271
Channel. *See* English Channel
Channel Swimming Association, 58, 61, 65–66, 68, 77
Chicago River Race, 336
Chicago Swim. *See* Michigan, Lake
Chicago Tribune, 13, 59, 152
Chicoutimi, 304–5, 307–8
Chicoutimi Marathon. *See* Saguenay River
Chipmunk, 21
Christian, King, 334
Coast Guard, 210, 222, 288, 300
Copenhagen Swimming Union, 334
Coppleson, Dr. Verne, 81
Corondo, 282
Corson, Mille Carde, 60
Cossette, Robert, 304
Counsilman, James, 35

Crocodiles, 277
Cureton, Thomas, 337

Dalhousie, Port, 115–16, 119
Dardanelles, 274
Deaths, swimming, 74, 218–19
Dedan, Kimathi, 25
Delara, Luis Rodriguez, 74
Denmark, 334
DeNys, Judith, 114, 116–23, 125, 194, 232–33
Des Ruisseaux, 190
Dickens, Charles, 24
Diet, 130–33
Dolphin Club, 289, 293, 295
Donnelly, Palmer, 272–73
Dover, 46, 48, 51–52, 68–70
Dowling, Robert W., 266–68
Drugs: alcohol, 317, 321; amphetamine, 321, 323; analeptics, 321; arsenic, 317; caffeine, 320; camphor, 321; cocaine, 317, 320–21; lobelline, 321; LSD, 321; mescaline, 317; narcotics, 321–22; nicotinyl alcohol, 321; nitrates, 321; opium, 317; purine bases, 321; secobarbital, 321; steroid, 322; strychnine sulfate, 318–21; tranquilizers, 321–22
Duthie, George, 110, 114
Duxbury Point, 293

Ear-plugs, 226
East River, 267–68, 270–71
Ederle, Gertrude, 57–60, 83–84, 86, 269
Egypt, 325
Elephant, 20
Elionsky, Ida, 268–69, 271
El-Rheim, 62, 97, 260
Endurance, concept, 22
English Channel, 45–77, 97, 216–17, 231, 258, 260, 264, 269, 274, 282–85, 289, 293, 334–35
English Lifeboat Service, 210
Epinephrine, 322
Erickson, William, 99
Erikson, Jon, 71–73, 291
Erikson, Ted, 13, 29, 35–36, 39, 45, 64, 66–71, 81, 148–82, 214, 225, 228, 231–32, 263–64, 275–76, 289–303, 326
Evans, Col. Stewart A., 292–95

Farallon Islands, 219, 225, 287–303
Farouk, King, 62, 184
Finland, Gulf of, 219
Fisher, Brenda, 111
Foresby, Ed, 310
Forsberg, Gerald, 336
Franklin, Ben, 336
Freud, S., 321

Gamie, M., 194, 244
Garde, Mille, 269, 271
Gedser, 334
George, Lake, 97, 271
Gibraltar, Straits, 274
Giles, Clarence, 280
Glass, Hugh, 27
Goggles, 223–24
Golden Gate Bridge, 287–92, 295
Golden Plover, 23
Gollop, Philip, 71
Gomez, Pedro, 291
Gonzalez, 163
Grand Portage, 27
Grease, 225
Grebe, 18
Grew, Anita, 217
Griffith, Joe, 146–47
Grizzly bear, 17
Grogan, E. S., 26
Grover, Charles, 117, 119–21
Grzimek, Dr. Bernhard, 17
Guaymas, 188, 258–59
Guiscardo, Syder, 163, 166ff.

Hagg, Gunder, 44
Ha Ha Bay, 305–8, 310
Haliburton, Richard, 274
Halstead, Sir William, 319
Hamad, 62
Hamid, Sr., George, 137
Harlem River, 265, 267–68, 270
Hayward, Wally H., 28
Hellespont, 336
Hernandez, 163
Hicks, T. J., 318
Hiland, Amy, 285
Hippopotamus, 20
Hitler, Adolf 334
Hong Kong, 325
Hoskins, 46
Howland, T. J., 266
Huddleston, Myrtle, 273, 275
Hudson River, 266–67, 269–71, 280
Human packers, 26
Huntington Beach Swim, 258

Iglesias, Horatio, 131, 193–94, 232–33, 242, 245, 327
Illinois Athletic Club, 86, 103, 146, 275
Illinois Institute of Technology, 66, 148
Infection, 82, 226
Insulin, 322
Irish Sea, 218, 283
Isacescue, Madame, 59

Jacobson, Elsa, 255
Japanese sailors, 214
Jaremy, John, 112
Java, 214

Index

Jellyfish, 81
Jensen, Helge, 191–92
John, June, 17
Johnson, J. B., 46
Juan de Fuca Strait, 216, 219, 283–87, 291
Juliana, Princess, 334
Jutland, 334

Kahanamoku, Duke, 336
Kammersgaard, Jenny, 333–35
Kansas City Athletic Club, 278
Kattegat, 334–35
Keating, Edward, 97, 99
Kellerman, Miss, 59
Kelp beds, 93
Kok, Mary, 198–99
Korbai, Elmer, 149–50

LaCoursiere, Rejean (John), 114, 116ff., 202, 231–32, 235, 244, 262, 309–10
Lakeshore Swim Club, 103, 110
Lamprey eels, 107
Land and Water, 49, 51–52, 54
Lass, Alexander, 219
LaTuque 24-Hour Marathon, 105, 131–32, 228–53
Legge, Dr. Robert R., 274
Leg kick, inefficiency of, 34–35
Leslie, Robert, 19
Leuszler, Winnie Roach, 107, 110
Lido Island, 336
Llano, George Albert, 210–11, 337
Lloyds of London, 45
Loch Ness, 325
Lockley, R. M., 18
London Daily Mail, 61–63
Long Beach, Calif., 256
Longest immersion, 214
Lumsden, Cliff, 103–7, 109–11, 114, 117ff., 138–40, 185–86, 232, 257, 261, 285, 310, 332

McGill, Linda, 80
McPherson, Claudia, 118
Male hormone, 322
Manhattan Island, 85, 92, 218, 260, 265–72
Mantegazza, Paolo, 321
Marathon runners, 28, 318–19
Mar del Plata Marathon, 281–82
Martin, Hershel, 270
Matuch, Dennis, 35–40, 82, 133, 141, 148, 156–57, 162–74, 194, 210, 227, 231–33, 238, 241, 242, 263, 275, 306–7, 310, 328
Mau Mau uprising, 25
May, Ted, 74
Melderis, Ray, 165, 167, 174, 176
Mexican runners (100 miles), 9

Mexico, 325
Miami Beach, 326
Michel, George, 97, 99, 101, 278
Michigan, Lake, 13–14, 35, 112, 145–82, 186, 210, 220, 227, 254, 263, 271, 287, 292
Mills, Enos A., 17
Mississippi River Marathon, 100, 278
Missouri Athletic Club, 278
Missouri River, 278, 281
Modell, Leonore, 71, 186, 289, 292–93, 326
Molokai Straits, 210–11, 262
Molson Mile, 194
Monardes, Nicolas, 321
Monkey, 20
Montreal 30 Hour Marathon, 233
Montreal to Sorel Marathon, 278
Moran, Jim, 145–47, 180, 182
Morvan, 62
Murphy, Kevin, 71, 218

Nakama, Keo, 80, 262
Nasser, 184
Natoma, Lake, 326
Navaratnaswamy, Mr., 274
New York Bay, 59
New York Times, 219
Nienhagen, 334
Nina Fo'ou Island, 276
Noseclips, 226
Nurmi, Paavo, 44

Oahu, 210–11
Oil slick, 82, 92
O'Leary, 28
Olympic Committee, 321
Olympics, 58, 318–19
Ontario, Lake, 93, 97, 102, 104, 112ff., 263, 283, 291
Ore Sound, 335
Otter, 21, 215
Owen Sound, 258
Oxygen intake, 323

Palk Strait, 274
Panama Canal, 274
Papke, Ike, 289, 291
Parana River, 63–64, 279, 282
Park, George, 119, 121, 132–33, 232, 310, 328
Park, Tom, 95, 105, 138–40, 184, 258–61
Penguin, 18
Peruvian Indians, 318
Philosophy, 78–82
Physiology, 43–44, 78ff., 215–16, 224
Pietri, Dorando, 319
Piranha, 277
Pituitary, 323
Pituitrin, 322

Plata River, 63, 279–80, 282
Plate River, 63
Point Reyes, 288
Polar bear, 18–19, 215
Pool swims, 273, 275–76
Porpoise, 18, 31, 81
Portuguese Man of War, 81
Potomac River, 336
Psychology, 78ff.
Pugh, L.G.C.E., 184, 217, 337

Race Rocks, 283
Rat, 21
Reta, Roberto, 114, 117–18, 241
Rockaway Beach Pool, 273
Rockett, Sam, 64–65
Ross, Norman, 86, 91–93, 97–98, 100–103
Rossberg, Corrine, 273
Royal Humane Society, 48
Ryder, Gus, 103–4, 106–7, 110

Sadlo, Bill, 112, 119, 270
Saguenay River, 82, 188, 291, 304–16
Saint John(Jean), Lake, marathon, 114, 135, 190–208, 228–29, 259, 262, 304
Saint Lawrence River, 278, 304–5
Salmon, 23
Salton Sea Marathon, 257
Sandy Hook Marathon, 266
San Francisco, 287, 289, 292
San Francisco Bay, 288
San Pedro Channel, 84, 86, 94–95
Santa Fe, 279–80, 282
Saunders, J., 28
Schans, Johan, 245
Schoemmel, Charlotte, 85, 92, 97, 99, 269, 271
Schoonmaker, W. J., 17
Scotland, 325
Sea Lions, 298
Seals, 18, 82
Sen, Mihir, 274–75
Sharks, 80–81, 212–13, 222, 274, 288–90, 293
Shazly, 202, 231
Shedid, 194
Sherpas, 26
Shook, Capt. Paul R., 213
Sigmund, John V., 281
Simecek, Cynthia, 149–50, 163–68
Simecek, Kathryn, 149
Sinn, Marty, 112, 185–86, 263
Skunk, 21
Smith, Gene, 321
Solitaire, Ed, 135
Sooty tern, 23
South America, 325

Spitz, Mark, 336
Sports promotion, 9
Spuyten Duyvil, 267, 270
Staten Island, 272
Stetser, Ed, 135
Stimulants. *See* Drugs
Stroke rate, relation to speed, 172–73
Stroke style, 35–38
Struble, Diane, 271
Suez Canal, 282, 325, 332
Suit, swimming, 223–24
Sullivan, Britt, 220, 222
Sullivan, Henry, 58, 85
Summers, Byron, 97, 260, 269
Survival swims: Aleutian Islands, 216; Baltic Sea, 216; Caribbean, 214; Chung Nam Kim, 214; cold water, 215–16; Ecuadorian flight officer, 212–13; Hawaiian Americans, 211; Hawaiian fishermen, 210–11; importance of fat, 216; Lass, Alexander, 219; longest immersion, 214; longest with lifejacket, 213; longest without lifejacket, 214; North Atlantic Ocean, 212, 216; Pacific Ocean, 212; sharks, 212; Shook, Capt. Paul R., 213; water temperature, relationship to survival, 216–22; World War II airmen, 211, 214; Zirganos, 216–18

Tahoe, Lake, 71
Tarahumara Indians, 24
Thames River, 48
Thyroid hormone, 322–23
Tide table, 72
Tiger, 19
Tiraboshi, Enrico, 58
Testing of swimmers, 29–35
Thomas, Bert, 283–84
Thyroxine, 322
Toomey, Jim, 135, 138, 141
Toronto Daily Star, 170
Toth, Charles, 58, 85
Trans Continental Foot Race, 28–29
Travaglio, G., 233, 327
Trudeau, Prime Minister Pierre, 193
Turtle, 18

Uruguay River, 279–80

Van Wormer, John, 275
Venice, Grand Canal, 336
Victoria Times, 283
Vierkoetter, Ernst, 60, 97, 99, 101–2
Voyagers, 26–27

Walkers, marathon, 24
Walsh, John J., 266

Index

Waters, Capt. John M., Jr., 213
Water temperature, cause of variation, 97ff.
Watson, Barry, 72
Webb, Capt. Matthew, 47–57, 225
Weissmuller, John, 86, 275, 336
Whales, 18
Whitwell, Mary Lou, 120
Wight, Isle of, 71
Willard, Ralph, 304, 307–13
Willemse, Herman, 102, 112, 114–19, 131, 140–41, 185–86, 192, 194, 196, 231–33, 235, 309–10, 325–26, 337
Windermere, Lake, 217
Women's Swimming Association, 59
Woods, Jim, 112, 114, 163

World Professional Marathon Swimming Federation ratings, 1964–72, 329–31
Worth, C. Brooke, 23
Wozniak, Steve, 139
Wrigley, William Jr., 60, 83ff., 96

Yellowlegs, 23
Yellowstone River, 280
Young, George, 87–98, 101, 110, 260
Yugoslavia, 282, 325

Zarate, 280
Zealand, 334
Zimmy, Charles, 280
Zirganos, Jason, 216–19, 271